C000021623

The Conservative Party and the extreme right 1945–75

Manchester University Press

The Conservative Party and the extreme right 1945–75

Mark Pitchford

Manchester University Press

Manchester and New York

distributed in the United States exclusively
by Palgrave Macmillan

Copyright © Mark Pitchford 2011

The right of Mark Pitchford to be identified as the author of this work has been asserted by him in accordance with the Copyright, Designs and Patents Act 1988.

Published by Manchester University Press
Oxford Road, Manchester M13 9NR, UK
and Room 400, 175 Fifth Avenue, New York, NY 10010, USA
www.manchesteruniversitypress.co.uk

Distributed in the United States exclusively by
Palgrave Macmillan, 175 Fifth Avenue, New York,
NY 10010, USA

Distributed in Canada exclusively by
UBC Press, University of British Columbia, 2029 West Mall,
Vancouver, BC, Canada V6T 1Z2

British Library Cataloguing-in-Publication Data
A catalogue record for this book is available from the British Library

Library of Congress Cataloging-in-Publication Data applied for

ISBN 978 0 7190 8363 1 hardback

First published 2011

The publisher has no responsibility for the persistence or accuracy of URLs for any external or third-party internet websites referred to in this book, and does not guarantee that any content on such websites is, or will remain, accurate or appropriate.

Typeset
by Frances Hackeson Freelance Publishing Services, Brinscall, Lancs
Printed in Great Britain
by CPI Antony Rowe, Chippenham, Wiltshire

Contents

Abbreviations

ACG	Anti-Communist Guardian
AIMS	Aims of Industry
BCAEC	British Council against European Commitments
BDL	British Defence League
BHL	British Housewives' League
BNP	British National Party
BPP	British People's Party
BUF	British Union of Fascists
CCO	Conservative Central Office
CPA	Conservative Party Archive
CPC	Conservative Political Centre
FCS	Federation of Conservative Students
FFF	Fighting Fund for Freedom
HINC	Halt Immigration Now Campaign
LEL	League of Empire Loyalists
MCU	Middle Class Union
NDP	National Democratic Party
NFU	National Farmers Union
NFWI	National Federation of Women's Institutes
NRP	New Reform Party
PEST	Pressure for Economic and Social Toryism
PLDF	People's League for the Defence of Freedom
RPS	Racial Preservation Society
SIF	Society for Individual Freedom
TGGN	The Guild of Good Neighbours
TGWU	Transport and General Workers' Union
TNC	The New Crusade
UDI	Unilateral Declaration of Independence
UIA	United Industrialists Association
WF	Workers' Forum

Preface

This book's purpose is to discover what role the Conservative Party played in the extreme-right's failure after the Second World War. Readers will make moral judgements about individuals and groups mentioned, but I do not. This is partly because views that society now rejects were once commonplace and accepted. Moreover, individuals who once held these views may now repudiate them, and I see no point in criticising them now. The historian's task is to explain. Judgement is a matter for society.

Many institutions have helped me. Cardiff University was very accommodating in allowing me to study for a Ph.D., particularly so long after graduating. I found a very warm welcome at Cardiff University and am saddened that my active association with it seems to be ending. The Arts and Humanities Research Council (AHRC) provided a full doctoral award. This was a life-changing event, without which I doubt that I would have completed my research. The AHRC also granted a scholarship for a substantial period of study at the John W. Kluge Centre in the Library of Congress, Washington DC. I am grateful for the financial and cultural opportunities afforded by the AHRC's generosity. Other institutions also contributed financially. An Institute of Historical Research bursary allowed me to rummage thoroughly through archives in London. The Royal Historical Society and Cardiff University provided funds so that I could attend overseas conferences.

I am indebted to many individuals, and apologise if I have omitted someone from my thanks. The archival staff at the universities of Hull, Sheffield, Birmingham, and at the LSE were very helpful. So, too, were the employees of the British Library in London, and the staff at the Working Class Movement Library in Salford. The people at the Colindale newspaper library were remarkable in meeting my requests. I am especially grateful to Colin Harris, Jeremy McIlwhaine, and their colleagues at the Bodleian Library, who provided exemplary service and a warm welcome. I also want to thank Mary Lou Reker at the Kluge Center for her kindness, and the staff at the Library of Congress for their help and perseverance. Former members of the Monday Club were also generous in giving their time and thoughts, and in allowing me to include their comments. I also wish to thank all at MUP, particularly Tony Mason, and my copy-editor Frances Hackeson, for getting this book into print.

I am grateful to the medical profession for their care over more than two decades, particularly Dr J. S. Broxton, Mr Geoffrey Ingram, Professor Sir Miles Irving, Mr Iain Anderson and Dr H. Sutherland. My friends Peter Hully, John Kerr and Mark Rathburn have kept me sane over many years, mainly by being as rubbish on the golf course as I am. Peter also frequently offered financial assistance, which I will never forget. Thanks, too, to Sarah Lloyd for her encouragement and friendship. Dr Garthine Walker was incredibly tolerant in accommodating me when necessary, which I appreciate very much. All research students are indebted to their supervisors: I am particularly so. Dr Keir Waddington acted as my second supervisor and provided cogent comments that assisted in focusing my efforts. My connection with Dr Kevin Passmore goes back to the early 1990s when I was one of his undergraduates. He was exemplary then, and as a Ph.D. supervisor, and I consider him a friend. His only flaw is a deluded belief that Cardiff Blues will win the Heineken Cup some day.

I wish to end with comments about my family. I appreciate the encouragement of my parents-in-law, John and Mary Rabbitt, whose help and assistance, and care for their grandchildren, has been excellent. John was my year master at De La Salle Grammar, and I am sure that he is as amused by how events have transpired as me. During the course of writing this book, my brother, Michael Pitchford, confirmed what I have long thought about him. On a number of occasions, he made substantial journeys to bring me home when I was having problems. He is the best of brothers. As for our parents, Neville and Mary Pitchford, I will never be able to repay their love and kindness. Without their practical assistance and moral support, I would not have completed this book. They are excellent role models, both as parents and grandparents. As in so much of my life, however, four people have made what I do worthwhile, my wife Joanne, and our children Christopher, Edward and Amy. They have lived with the consequences of my medical condition with love and without complaint. It is to them that I dedicate this work.

Introduction

The Conservative Party is a political phenomenon. A 'Tory' party has existed for over three hundred years, surviving changes that resulted from industrialisation, adapting to the Great Reform Act of 1832, and subsequently introducing its own progressive electoral reforms under Disraeli. A party of landowners, property, and privilege, the Conservative Party not only weathered the century when full democracy emerged but dominated it. It won nineteen of the twenty-six general elections between 1900 and 1997, eleven outright, and gained over 40% of the vote in those it lost. Perhaps most startling is the Conservative Party's domination of politics in the 'hungry thirties', albeit within a National Government, when other western democracies were threatened by, and some succumbed to, authoritarian and extremist alternatives. Of the party's leaders only Austen Chamberlain failed to become prime minister, until William Hague in 1997. The Conservative Party's story is one of consistent success largely explained by its ability to adapt to new circumstances such as an increased franchise, imperialism, and nationalism. Its fierce opposition to change frequently became muted acceptance and party policy, in the course of which the Conservative Party co-opted, and then absorbed, Peelites, Liberal Unionists, Coalition Liberals, and National Liberals. The result is a broad-based electoral monolith. Therefore, it is easy to attribute the extreme right's conspicuous and longstanding electoral failure to the Conservative Party's ability to attract many voters.

Yet the extreme right was a persistent feature of twentieth-century Britain. Prior to the First World War, the Tariff Reform League propounded mass populism, autarky and Anglo-Saxon alliance. The National Maritime League, The Navy League, and The National Service League believed that a liberal consensus antithetical to the demands of empire was dominating British politics, and emphasised defence in reaction. Xenophobia and anti-Semitism existed in the

British Brothers' League, National League for Clean Government, Parliamentary Alien Immigration Committee, the London League, and the Immigration Reform Association. Victory in 1918 arguably deprived the extreme right of fertile soil, but fear of Communism and Socialism helped the National Party to win two seats in the 1918 General Election. Thereafter, fear of the left, Jews and aliens resulted in the formation of movements such as the British Empire Union, National Citizens Union, and Middle Class Union. A welter of mimetic indigenous movements appeared in Britain after Mussolini formed the first fascist government in Italy in 1922. Nazi groups emerged after Hitler came to power in 1933. The Second World War associated these extreme-right groups in the public mind with racism, authoritarianism, and extermination. However, it did not eradicate them. Over two hundred embryonic extreme-right movements materialised in the period 1945–87.

The Conservative Party did not deny its connection with the extreme right prior to 1939. Some Conservatives openly flaunted it. Future Conservative MP Patrick Hannon sat on the British Fascisti's Grand Council. Pugh described Conservative membership of the British Fascisti as a calculated attempt to alter the party's 'limp-wristed attitude towards the left'.[1] The British Fascisti's relations with the Conservative Party were deliberate and open. Its members acted as stewards at Conservative Party meetings, and rented rooms from Conservative local associations. Conservative MPs made no secret of their sympathies for extreme-right regimes, while others betrayed their views by supporting restrictive measures on 'aliens' seeking sanctuary from them. Support for extreme-right views appeared in Conservative publications such as the *English Review*, *Saturday Review*, the *National Review*, and *Truth*. The Conservative Party was associated with *Truth* via its connection with Neville Chamberlain, but so were Oswald Mosley, and former BUF member and subsequent founder of the National Front, A. K. Chesterton, whom it employed. The *English Review* attempted to influence Conservative Party policy in a campaign orchestrated by its editor, the BUF sympathiser Douglas Jerrold, and Lord Lloyd, a Conservative MP until 1925. The proprietor of the supposedly Conservative-supporting *Saturday Review* sided with Mosley against the Conservative Party. Many Conservatives were also members of the January Club, a front organisation of the British Union of Fascists. The mainstream Conservative newspaper, the *Daily Mail*, supported Mosley. One Conservative MP even stated that there were no fundamental differences of outlook between Blackshirts and Conservatives. Individual Conservatives funded Mosley. Some, such as the Duke of Northumberland, financed extreme-right publications that attracted contributions from Conservative MPs and fascists. Other Conservatives formed their own extremist movements. Edward Doran, Conservative MP for Tottenham North, announced in 1933 that he had formed a private Nazi army, 'The Liberators'. Lord Lymington, Conservative MP for Basingstoke (1929–34), founded English Array, a group that harked back to England's rural golden age. and consorted with known fascists who were attempting to form the extreme right into a viable movement. R. Dorman-Smith, Unionist MP for Petersfield

(1935–41), Minister of Agriculture (1939–40) and Governor of Burma (1941–46), joined Lymington's English Array.

Conservatives and extreme-right figures joined organisations such as the National Citizens Union. Their presence in the proliferation of pro-Nazi, pro-peace groups in the 1930s was especially noteworthy given the possibility of conflict. The Anglo-German Fellowship contained peers, Conservative MPs, ministers of the Crown, and extreme-right individuals including the subsequently interned Barry Domvile. The Link was a populist pro-Nazi organisation that sought to attract all classes. It included Conservative MP Sir Lambert Ward and the Duke of Westminster, amongst others. Westminster joined The Link on the advice of Henry Newnham, editor of *Truth*, and headed moves to secure peace with Nazi Germany during the war. Westminster presented a paper written by Henry Drummond Wolff, the Conservative MP who was secretly funding Mosley's BUF, to a meeting of pro-peace activists at his home. Most intriguing was the secretive Right Club. It was a combination of extremists and Conservatives, and included the only MP interned during the war, Captain Archibald Maule Ramsay, Conservative MP for Peebles and South Midlothian. MI5 monitored meetings of these groups and Cabinet members were aware of them. Conservative MPs spoke up for extreme-right individuals interned by the government as potential traitors during the Second World War. Meanwhile, fascist sympathisers sought respectability within the Conservative Party. Sir Charles Petrie, the Literary Editor of the *New English Review*, was a fellow traveller who subsequently argued that if Mosley had identified the BUF more closely with the Conservative Party he would not have attracted as much opprobrium. These examples supported Stanley Baldwin's comment that fascism was simply ultramontane Conservatism. One fascist put it more prosaically when he described the whole of the extreme right as Conservatism with knobs on. However, the Second World War was the extreme-right's watershed. It brought images of genocide that were indelibly associated with right-wing extremism, especially Nazism. Henceforth, no British extreme-right movement used the epithet 'fascist', and it was not until 1962 that an extreme-right party called itself 'National Socialist'.

The Conservative Party's main objective after the Second World War remained the same as before it: to achieve and maintain power. However, Labour's victory at the 1945 General Election presented the Conservative Party with the new paradigm of a Labour government able to implement its radical socialist programme. This programme meant increased state interventionism, governmental planning and controls, a corporate response to industrial relations, the construction of the Welfare State, and nationalisation. Conservatives had opposed a greater role for the state, and the philosophy that shaped it, but Labour's large majority meant that there was little the Conservative Party could do to stop them. The size of the majority also showed that the electorate wanted Labour's policies, especially as they had emphatically ditched Britain's wartime leader. Therefore, the Conservative Party adapted, just as it had in the nineteenth century, accepting much of Labour's programme in opposition and in government. The Conservative Opposition of 1945–51 formulated a position similar to that of the Labour Government. Therefore, the Conservative Party had adapted to changed circumstances and acquiesced in its opponents' political agenda. By the time that the Conservative Party regained office in 1951, most of its membership had accepted the substance of Labour's social revolution. The Conservative Party maintained this consensual approach from 1945 to 1975, with the period between 1967–72, when the Conservative Party under Heath appeared to turn rightwards and formulate a more right-wing programme, little more than a cosmetic reaction whose orientation is often misunderstood. This is not to say that historians have unquestionably accepted this view. However, none deny that areas of agreement existed, while many agreed that a broad framework of consensus existed. Nor have any historians challenged the view that the Conservative Party did react to Britain's new paradigm after 1945.

These investigations identified similarities and differences between the two main political parties. In doing so, they helped highlight differences between the Conservative Party and those groups and individuals that operated at its extreme-right edge. However, no matter what these investigations concluded, the real issue at stake here is not whether a consensus existed, but what the extreme right perceived the situation to be. This perception was unambiguous. After 1945, the extreme right thought that the Conservative Party aped the Labour Party both in opposition and in government, and consistently criticised it for failing to implement 'true Conservative' policies. The right in general attacked the Conservative Opposition of 1945–51 for appeasing the Labour Government and meekly accepting its policies, and persistently assailed Conservative governments from 1951. When the Conservative Party returned to opposition in 1964, it faced an increased internal extreme-right challenge from the Monday Club, and an external extreme-right threat that coalesced in 1967 into the National Front. This threat did not disappear with the unexpected victory in the 1970 General Election. The extreme right viewed the policy U-turns by the Conservative Government of 1970–74 as surrender to the left's militant forces, which provided it with added impetus. This impetus made the Monday Club appear capable of dominating the Conservative Party, or forming its own party. By the mid-1970s, it had helped the National Front to become Britain's fourth political party, with hopes of overtaking the Liberals. Magnifying the threat caused by this impetus were connections between the National Front and Monday Club. Yet, the threat from the Monday Club and National Front was over by the mid-1970s. The Conservative Party bureaucracy forced the Monday Club leadership to purge the club of its extremists and cease connections with the National Front. Thereafter, Margaret Thatcher, Conservative Party leader from 1975, made an obvious appeal to potential National Front voters that contributed to its vote crumbling in the 1979 General Election and subsequent fragmentation. The Conservative Party, on the other hand, governed for the next eighteen years.

The extreme-right organisations listed here were but a few that the Conservative Party faced in the post-war period. Conservative Central Office kept a careful watch on many individuals that they considered extremist both outside and inside the party. The Conservative Party's success in gaining power, and the extreme-right's failure to attain it, was the most obvious manifestation of its role as a barrier to the extreme right in Britain. Yet this relationship remains unexplored, in contrast to the extensive work on many aspects of the Conservative Party and the extreme right.

However, examination of this relationship presents two distinct problems. The first problem concerns definition. Primarily, what exactly was the 'extreme right'? This is a difficult question. Accusations of being 'extreme', 'right-wing', and 'fascist' have been so overused as to result in confusion rather than clarity. Webber understood this and opted to refer to dissident Conservatives and Fascists collectively as the 'British Right' rather than identify its different strands.[2] In a similar vein, Blinkhorn argued that 'the definitions, typologies and taxonomies beloved of social scientists tend to fit uncomfortably the intractable realities which are the raw material of the historian'.[3] Blinkhorn was introducing a study of inter-war Fascists and Conservatives, a period when the extreme right was more prominent and recognisable. His comments are, therefore, particularly apposite for a study of the extreme right after 1945 when many people associated 'extreme right' with the horrors of the Second World War and the extreme right was, consequently, more circumspect and defensive about its antecedents. Additionally, those described as extreme right by historians and social and political scientists do not accept this description. Instead, they see themselves as holding reasonable, even centrist positions. The term 'extreme' is also a subjective one that reflects the views of those that use it to describe groups they passionately disagree with. Yet, an understanding of what constitutes the extreme right is necessary if we are to understand its failure generally and the Conservative Party's reaction to it in particular.

In one sense, the answer to this question is simple: the extreme right was that which was vehemently against the left, to the extent that it demanded either of the Conservative Party, or itself, strong and concerted action against it beyond accepted democratic norms. Even simpler is the view that the 'extreme right' was that which stood further to the right of the Conservative Party. Though simplistic, this approach allows for recognition of groups, and investigation of any ideological shifts by the Conservative Party, along a traditionally accepted linear spectrum. It also avoids the anachronistic error of assuming that today's extreme right corresponds exactly with that of previous years. This, however, is insufficient as it fails to recognise that a number of distinct strands ran within the extreme right. For example, a 'Conservative' strand was authoritarian, supported the institutions of Church, monarchy and parliament, but was extreme in that it desired the dictatorship of social elites. A 'Radical' strand likewise sought an authoritarian dictatorship, but a populist one drawn from the people, which it delineated, while criticising existing elites and their institutions. More difficult to determine were groups that can be termed the 'Freedom Right', difficulty resting on their sub-divisions into those that espoused economic liberty and those that advocated institutional liberty. In a sense, they were 'liberal', but they were also on the extreme right in the sense that in our period implementation of their programme required hard measures against the unions and Welfare State. Finally, there was the 'fascist' and 'neo-Nazi' extreme right that encompassed elements of both the Conservative and radical extremes, though not necessarily the 'Freedom Right'. Crucially, this element of the extreme right expressed its views and objectives violently and often had paramilitary organisations. It was prepared to use violence, be it physical or verbal, unlike the other strands whose violence was implicit. These differentiating characteristics, together with shared views on nationalism and a weak Conservative leadership that failed to reverse a deteriorating and decadent society caused by advancing socialism, formed the parameters that determined inclusion within the 'extreme right' in this book. These parameters avoid the narrowness associated with attempts to identify a 'fascist minimum', which are theoretical concepts that, if used proscriptively and exclusively, would deny revealing comparisons of the Conservative Party's attitude towards different extreme-right groups. They also allowed for the identification of extreme-right individuals within the Conservative Party itself, a crucial element in assessing the Conservative Party's refractory role towards the extreme right.

These parameters are useful in identifying different extreme-right groups, and therefore the Conservative Party's reaction to them. However, in one significant respect argument about extreme-right taxonomy in this period is redundant. For, it is important when examining the Conservative Party's relationship with the extreme right in this period not to focus on what we consider extreme, but on what the Conservative Party thought was extreme. It is only by acting thus that we can begin to understand the varying attitudes that the Conservative Party displayed to different groups, and minimise our own understandably subjective opinions. Put another way, this book examines the relationship between the Conservative Party and those that it believed were right-wing extremists, and not those that we think were right-wing extremists. It is for this reason that the book frequently refers to Conservative Central Office's identification of groups or individuals as 'extreme' or 'extreme-right'. Occasionally, the book does refer to groups that Central Office did not consider extreme right. These are included as points of comparison, the two most obvious examples being the One Nation Group and the Bow Group. However, the overriding criterion for inclusion is Conservative Central Office's belief that a group or individual was extreme-right wing.

Using the parameters outlined within a chronological framework allows exploration of similarities and differences in the Conservative Party's attitude towards the extreme right based on being either in opposition or in government. They also allowed investigation of the political space occupied by the Conservative Party and the extreme right, via examination of policy statements and objectives, political pronouncements and activities, ideological discourse, electoral fortunes, social connections, and language employed therein, at national, regional, and local level. Membership of various extreme organisations by specific individuals became apparent using these parameters. Moreover,

they facilitated answers to questions fundamental to an analysis that attempted to prove a negative – the Conservative Party's role in the extreme-right's
success, an eventuality that did not happen. These parameters helped to place
in context, and evaluate, the evidence of the Conservative Party's role, whether
policies, objectives, personnel, literature or electoral performance. They allowed
an assessment of the extent and impact of the nexus between Conservatism
and the extreme right and its continuity after the Second World War, and revealed the Conservative Party's dual blocking role: firstly, how disillusion with
the Conservative Party forced extreme-right individuals into actions that were
outside the confines and support of this successful, mainstream political levia-
than, spawning a number of extreme-right wing groups and parties. Secondly,
the existence and function of Central Office's reporting mechanism, monitoring activity throughout this period and allowing it to block the extreme right
effectively.

The second problem in an examination of the Conservative Party's relationship with the extreme right concerns the choice of sources. Many sources exist,
but they often contain weaknesses that, while understandable, make judgements on the relationship between the Conservative Party and the extreme right
difficult. In contrast, the Conservative Party Archive at the Bodleian Library
contains extensive material, some of it focused directly on concerns about the
extreme right. It provided numerous sources for this book. To avoid the distrac-
tion of too many note references, some quotations are not acknowledged and in
all instances these derive from the Conservative Party Archive. The scope of the
archive provided wide-ranging investigation of Party manifestos, by-election
campaigns, constituency affairs, and the views of Conservative Party members
and supporters. These documents allowed assessment of individual cases and
consideration of specific themes. Central Office's files within the archive proved
the most valuable source. This is because Central Office reflected the party
leadership's wishes, and was the pinnacle of the party organisation.[4] The party
leader nominated Central office's head, the Party Chairman. A number of Vice-
Chairmen acted in an executive capacity, often overseeing specific aspects of the
party's work, which varied. They were often retired senior and respected Central
Office staff. Responsibility for the daily management of Central Office attracted
a number of titles. In the period 1945–75, the General Director occupied this
role of 'chief of staff', until 1966 when the position was devolved. Central Office
acted as a conduit between the party leader and membership via its various departments and its regional network. It contained many and varied departments,
including the national offices of organisations that represented various sections
of the party, such as the Young Conservatives. Some of these departments disappeared while others emerged to meet changed demands. However, some departments existed throughout the period and provided the main framework
for the book. This included the files that revealed investigations based on the
work of Central Office's regional network, a network that was extensive and
pervasive throughout the wider Conservative Party. Central Office maintained
Regional, or Area Offices. The party leadership greatly increased their size after

1945. Central Office employed Area Agents within these regional offices. These Area Agents exercised considerable influence on the supposedly autonomous local associations and their MPs, and formed part of the bureaucratic machinery of decision-making within their regions. Amongst Area Agents' functions was the gathering of intelligence on other organisations and the forwarding of information and material on them to Central Office. The files generated by Area Agents' correspondence revealed the Conservative Party's attitudes towards various extreme-right groups and individuals, and often the reasons for them. Admittedly, the files of one political party can produce an unbalanced picture that reveals only what that particular party wants to convey. In this instance, a number of considerations argued against this. Central Office's agents regularly forwarded the critical comments of the Conservative Party's right-wing opponents as well their literature containing the views and objectives that differentiated them from it. These files were usually internal correspondence and often confidential, which meant that those involved revealed views that they would not necessarily state openly. Most importantly, these files reveal which groups or individuals Central Office thought were extreme-right, and thus warrant inclusion in this study. Today's Central Office restricts access to some of these files, which do not always show the Conservative Party in a positive light. Central Office's eventual decision to grant permission to view them supported the impression reached from investigating those that have no such restrictions. Consequently, Central Office's files were a comprehensive resource that answered many questions posed by this research. These questions included, why did the Conservative Party view a particular group as extreme-right, what action did it take against these groups, what determined these actions, did the Conservative Party differentiate between extreme-right groups, did the Conservative Party's attitude change over time, and what evidence was there of a consistent approach?

The answers to these questions commence in Chapter 1 with a description of a Conservative Party shocked by Labour's landslide election victory in 1945, thereafter adapting to the new paradigm thus created. It investigates the Conservative Party's varied reaction to those right-wing groups that emerged in opposition to this new paradigm from 1945–51, and reveals how the Conservative Party explicitly charged one of the departments within Central Office to investigate these outside organisations. How the Conservative Party dealt with the extreme right after Churchill regained office in 1951 is the theme of Chapter 2. It confirms that Central Office based its different actions on its perception of the nature of a group or individual's extremism, and the usefulness of such a group to the Conservative Party. Chapter 3 discusses the impact of Conservative governments' domestic and imperial policies on an increasingly vociferous extreme right. It shows how the Conservative Party both alienated and attracted the extreme right while maintaining opposition to any groups or individuals that possessed fascist antecedents or characteristics. Chapter 4 examines the Conservative Party's relationship with the extreme right after it returned to opposition in 1964. It describes how the Conservative

Party responded to the challenge presented when the external extreme right coalesced for the first time since 1945 into a viable political party. It also reveals how the extreme right within the Conservative Party posed an even greater threat, and the action taken against it. Chapter 5 investigates the climacteric in the Conservative Party's relationship with the extreme right after 1945, showing how Central Office dealt with the possible incursion of the external extreme right into the Conservative Party.

These chapters show that the Conservative Party leadership and bureaucracy did limit the extreme right's chances of success. Sometimes, this process included the absorption of some of the extreme right's themes. It regularly included attempts to deter Party members from joining extreme-right groups, which was difficult as some parts of the Conservative Party were sympathetic to these groups' views. This study also shows that the extent of the Conservative Party's opposition to extreme-right groups and individuals varied. The party leadership and bureaucracy consistently blocked those whose extremism involved connections with fascism or Nazism. In contrast, they often used those whose extremism amounted to little more than political inexpediency, or went beyond the consensual image that the Conservative Party wished to portray. When the Conservative Party's stance moved towards these groups after 1964, their 'extremism' diminished and was eventually absorbed during Margaret Thatcher's leadership. Overall, however, this book depicts a Conservative Party that after 1945 constantly investigated extreme-right groups and individuals, and took action against them. Its reveals a Conservative Party that kept all of the extreme right at arm's length until events reduced the extremism of some of them, while consistently limiting the chances of that part of the extreme right that the Second World War had condemned to pariah status.

Notes

1   M. Pugh, 'Hurrah for the Blackshirts!' Fascists and Fascism in Britain Between the Wars, Pimlico, London (2006), 61.

2   G. C. Webber, The Ideology of the British Right, Croom Helm, London (1986), 2–4.

3   M. Blinkhorn (ed.), Fascists and Conservatives: The Radical Right and the Establishment in Twentieth-century Europe, Unwin Hyman, London (1990), 2.

4   The following is based on S. Ball, 'The National and Regional Party Structure', in A. Seldon and S. Ball (eds), Conservative Century: The Conservative Party since 1900, Oxford University Press, Oxford (1994), 169–220.

1

The shock of opposition, 1945–51

A right response to defeat?

The Conservative Party entered the 1945 General Election suspicious of its leaders and split over social policy. The direction of Party policy was uncertain, with the Tory Reform Group, Progress Trust, Imperial Group, and numerous smaller bodies fighting for predominance in a party with a moribund and bankrupt machine. The progressive Tory Reform Committee had already welcomed publication of the Beveridge Report advocating extensive social reform, but right-wing Conservatives had attacked it, noticeably in publications connected with the extreme right such as the *National Review* and *Truth*. The right of the party relished the opportunity to end the wartime coalition with Labour. At the party conference in March 1945, Sir Herbert Williams MP spoke of being free of the coalition's chains. Churchill's conference address, on the other hand, suggested a desire to maintain the coalition, and even including in it MPs who had defeated Conservative candidates. Despite Churchill's desire, there was a genuine expectation of an outright Conservative victory. Conservative MP Christopher Hollis, writing in the *New English Review*, wrote that, 'nobody seriously thinks that the Labour Party have any chance of gaining a clear majority at the election'.[1] Hollis had precedent on his side. Victorious wartime Prime Ministers had won in 1900 and 1918. On polling day, the Conservative-supporting *Daily Express* announced, 'we are winning', and some regional Conservative-inclined newspapers stated belief in a three-figure majority. However, the Labour Party won such a majority. The Conservative Party was profoundly shocked not only over the electorate's rejection of it, but at the scale of defeat and the size of Britain's first majority Labour administration. Some Conservatives even feared permanent loss of office, a feeling strengthened by their Party's inability to win a single seat in by-elections during the period 1945–50, despite fuel and sterling crises, and continuing rationing.

There were a number of reasons for Labour's stunning victory. After the First World War, the government had promised a land 'fit for heroes'. This promise remained unfulfilled due to the Depression of the later 1920s and 1930s. The Labour Party offered a coherent programme to implement this promise in 1945, and the electorate voted for it. The Labour leadership had made a significant contribution to the war effort, especially in domestic affairs where they implemented state controls to ensure that the economy endured and funded the massive demands of the war effort. Their actions meant that the Labour Party's opponents could not portray them as an inexperienced, unpatriotic party that was unfit for government, which Churchill discovered to his cost during the General Election when his comparison of the Labour Party to the Gestapo brought widespread condemnation. Instead, the electorate saw in the Labour Party the possibility of a better future.

In contrast, the electorate in 1945 viewed the Conservative Party's actions before the Second World War negatively. Economic depression had blighted the inter-war period and led to the formation of a coalition National Government. High unemployment had affected many voters and their families. The Conservative Party leadership's alleged doctrinaire adherence to the prevailing policy of laissez-faire exacerbated the hardship many electors had suffered. Laissez-faire ruled out state intervention in favour of free trade, but also meant the acceptance of high unemployment until market forces readjusted the economy. Associating this policy with the Conservative Party alone was arguably unfair because, although there was a strand within Conservatism that advocated laissez-faire, the most prominent exponent of it during Ramsay MacDonald's National Government was in fact the Labour Chancellor Phillip Snowden. However, three factors ensured that the electorate associated their economic hardship with the Conservative Party. First, the Conservative Party governed for much of the inter-war period, either in administrations that were wholly Conservative or in coalitions that they dominated. Secondly, the Conservative Neville Chamberlain replaced Snowden as Chancellor in 1931, and although he moved away from strict laissez-faire, his equally doctrinaire adherence to balanced budgets meant the continuing acceptance of existing high levels of unemployment rather than the adoption of deficit financing to reduce it. Thirdly, Chamberlain introduced the 'Means Test' in 1931, a policy that was more understandable to the electorate than debates over economic policies. The Means Test disproportionately harmed the poorest. It resulted in the electorate viewing the Conservatives as the hard-faced men of the inter-war slump, callously disregarding their hardship and prepared to see individuals face the iniquity of National Assistance interviews rather than provide adequate social security. Similarly affecting the electorate's image of the Conservative Party in 1945 was the pre-war policy of appeasement. In 1938, Chamberlain had signed the Munich Agreement that abandoned Czechoslovakia in return for a promise of peace between Britain and Hitler's Germany. Leading Conservatives had fully supported Chamberlain. Dissidents like Churchill were very much in the minority within the Conservative Party. Although people joyfully welcomed Chamberlain's announcement that the Munich Agreement meant 'peace in our time', the Second World War altered their view. By 1945, people viewed Chamberlain as Hitler's dupe, and possibly even someone who was prepared to pander to fascism.

In the 1945 General Election, the electorate rejected a Conservative Party tainted by indifference to economic hardship and appeasement of the country's enemies. The former was a charge of callousness, which meant that it would be difficult for the Conservative Party leadership to advocate policies that could lead to high unemployment, no matter how many Conservatives favoured it. The latter was a charge that bordered on treachery, which was particularly difficult for the Conservative Party in 1945. In Europe, the right was associated with fascism. The Conservative Party was Britain's right-wing party, and it had clear connections with the extreme right and even fascism before the Second World War. Connections with any group or individual deemed 'extreme right' were no longer tolerable, and no Conservative leader could take Baldwin's sanguine attitude to them.[2] Consequently, the Conservative leadership did what it usually did when confronted by a new paradigm, and adapted. There is evidence that the Conservative leadership understood the need to adapt and counter the party's inter-war image even before the Second World War ended. It set up the Post-War Problems Central Committee (PWPCC) in 1941. It was to the PWPCC that the Tory Reform Committee and Tory Reform Group advocated state interventionism. In addition, Central Office tasked one of its existing bodies with investigating outside organisations.[3] After the war, the Conservative leadership openly implemented a policy review that moved significantly away from its inter-war stance and accepted much of the Labour programme. Behind the scenes, the leadership strengthened the party bureaucracy. This bureaucracy put the job of investigating those extreme-right groups and individuals that could damage the leadership's objectives on a more formal basis. In the period 1945–51, it monitored the extreme right and took whatever action it saw fit. Those whose extremism Central Office considered merely inexpedient attracted minimal action, but those it associated in any way with fascism received harsher attention.

Conservative reaction to Attlee's first government and re-emerging Fascism

The Conservative Party's public response to the 1945 General Election defeat was a thorough policy review that culminated in the *Industrial Charter* and Maxwell-Fyfe Report. The *Industrial Charter* emphasised traditional Conservative themes, but also accepted some nationalisation and an increased role for the state. Many Conservatives welcomed the charter, but the Conservative right thought that it was too much of a step towards Socialism. Right-wing Conservative publications ran articles with headlines such as 'Under Which Flag', 'Has Anyone Heard of Capitalism?' and 'The Milk-and-Water Charter', with journals such as *Truth* and *National Review* prominent in this criticism. The left claimed that the charter would result in the Tory Party's worse split for half a century, and the right agreed. The grounds on which right-wing Conservative MPs attacked the charter on its presentation at the 1947 Party Conference is instructive why it caused a problem. Sir Waldron Smithers informed conference that the charter was a threat not only to the Conservative Party, but also to Great Britain, as it represented an inordinate concession to Socialism at a time when Communism in the Soviet Union appeared the more vigorous ideology. The language he employed was unambiguous and emotive: 'There can be no compromise with Socialism or Communism. You must not let the Conservative Party become infected with the Socialist bug. The Conservative Party must stick to its principles or perish.'[4] Sir Waldron Smithers told delegates to have no fear of Central Office or the party platform, and to save the Conservative Party and England by rejecting the Charter. Smithers wished the Conservative Party to maintain its pre-war laissez faire stance. One commentator thought that at least half the conference supported these views.[5] The Party's right wing, however, suffered an overwhelming defeat at conference. Hoffman described this as the 'rout of the right', explaining that this was because virtually nobody at conference wished to be linked with a doctrine that was associated with the pre-war period and that was now 'out of keeping with the spirit of the times'.[6]

Nor was the Conservative Party's conversion limited to domestic issues. Virtually nobody in Whitehall saw the imminent collapse of the Empire in 1945. For many, there was little suggesting anything other than imperial continuance. The British Empire had proved its ability to endure. It had stood alone in 1940 and remained intact while Nazism and Fascism collapsed. The number of civil servants that departed annually for the colonies trebled after the Second World War. Only Keynes foresaw the possible consequences for the Empire of Britain's severe economic problems. Nobody actually wanted the end of Empire, other than the anti-colonial left. Instead, there were expectations of a new, reinvigorated empire. Indian independence may have been a foregone conclusion, but many, including Labour Foreign Secretary Ernest Bevin, sought a viable replacement. Expectations focused on creating a revitalised oil and mineral-rich imperial dispensation stretching from Cape Town to Iraq, with Africa identified as the new jewel in the Crown. Academics described it as a fourth empire arising out of the debris of the third. This was collective political delusion. Britain was unable to withstand the wave of post-war nationalism because it was economically overstretched. Thus, the impact was great when Transjordan (1946), Burma (1948), Ceylon (1948), and Palestine (1948) accompanied Indian Independence, and revealed the impotence of Britain's imperial ambitions. Nowhere was this impotence more obvious than in the Conservative Opposition's response. Churchill, hero of the Boer War and a staunch imperialist who consistently opposed Indian Independence before the Second World War, did nothing to obstruct the Indian Independence Bill (1947). Sir Herbert

Williams complained about his party's failure to even vote against the bill, but could do little else. Conservative Associations protested, but their calls for the party to do more to prevent the disintegration of the Empire went unanswered. One young right-wing researcher at the Conservative Research Department later recalled feeling unable to do anything other than bury his head in his hands.

Shock at the size of the 1945 defeat only partly explained this picture of a lacklustre Conservative Opposition. The Conservative Party under Lord Salisbury, facing the demands of extended suffrage in the late nineteenth century, had realigned itself to attract lower-middle and working-class votes. Thereafter, imperialism remained at the heart of Conservatism, contributing to electoral success. Doubtless, there were many right-wing Conservative voters in 1945 who were disgusted at the result. Perhaps, therefore, imperialism could perform a similar role in the mid-twentieth century to win the working class back from Labour. However, the impact of the 1945 General Election was not simply a matter of scale, as Alan Clark noted. Many right-wing Conservative MPs had lost their seats. Progressives now dominated the parliamentary party, determined to avoid connection with any embarrassments of the past. One progressive even advocated the Conservative Party changing its name to the 'New Democratic Party'. What was left of the right wing of the parliamentary party was unable, therefore, to impose their views on their colleagues, hence lacklustre opposition. This explains why there were only a limited number of clashes within the parliamentary Conservative Party over decolonisation. Very few MPs actually disagreed with it. Unlike domestic policy, therefore, this conversion would be more difficult to reverse. The election result was the real 'rout of the right'.

Yet, this image of an ineffective right within a demoralised Conservative Party is not the whole picture. The right was sufficiently strong to propose resolutions at the party conference expressing its dissatisfaction at the lacklustre attack on the Labour Government. The chosen motion was heavily defeated, but it indicated that a repository for such views still existed. Individual Conservative MPs openly attacked their party's ineffective opposition in the *New English Review*. There were even instances of rebellion against the frontbench when the right thought a bill was 'bad socialist business which should be fought every inch of the way'.[7] Moreover, the notion that the *Charter*'s acceptance signalled the complete collapse of the right was misleading. When the leadership responded to unfilled expectations of victory at the 1949 Hammersmith South by-election by issuing a revised policy statement, *The Right Road for Britain*, the *Daily Express*, the *Spectator*, and *Truth* carried articles attacking it for failing to move sufficiently rightwards. This also meant that the Conservative Party was presenting a confusing message to those holding extreme-right views or antecedents, whether in the Conservative Party or not. On the one hand, the leadership and even some MPs appeared to be appeasing Socialism. This was evident in the view of one MP responsible for drawing up the *Charter*, who believed that government was impossible if trade unions were hostile. On the other hand, a body of opinion and representation existed within the Conservative Party that was fundamentally at odds with this position. Individuals and groups opposed to the latter message had to make a choice of whether to act within the party or not. Some fought from within, while others formed outside pressure groups.

There is strong evidence that pre-war consanguinity between some Conservatives and erstwhile fascists continued. The circumstances in which a British Union of Fascists (BUF) leader could claim that thirty MPs and twelve peers were ready to declare themselves Fascists may have gone, but former BUF member Arthur Winn revealed in the *Daily Mirror* that he intended to vote Conservative in the 1945 General Election. The reason Winn gave was that the Conservatives would allow him, and presumably those like him, to 'get away with more than we could with any other party'.[8] The *Daily Mirror* reported that ex-BUF members' first move after the war was to 'throw themselves and their organisation on the side of the Tory Party'.[9] One local paper even argued that Mosley was reforming his organisation to 'keep Toryism alive'.[10] Dorril highlighted this consanguinity by recounting Mosley's interest in an 'anti-alien' campaign in Hampstead in 1945,[11] where the Conservative MP, Charles Challen, had organised a petition against Jewish residents. Dorril described Challen's petition as owing much to an organisation called the Fighting Fund for Freedom (FFF), led by the Conservative MP Sir Waldron Smithers, and intersecting with a similar, national campaign led by the Briton's Vigilante Action League (BVAL), which Lord Kemsley funded. Advising Kemsley was former editor of *Truth* Sir Henry Newnham. Dorril noted that Conservative parliamentary candidate Eleonora Tennant was having meetings with Jeffrey Hamm during which they discussed their mutual anti-Semitism. Hamm was an ex-BUF internee and was instrumental in Mosley's return to politics at the head of Union Movement. These events occurred at the same time, according to Mosley, that friends tried to secure his return to the Conservative fold.

The radical right, in the shape of the British People's Party (BPP), also exhibited anti-Semitism, a fear of communism, and support for Franco, similar to Conservative MPs. The BPP's importance lay partly in its survival of the war intact, despite the internment of its leading political figure, John Beckett. However, the BPP also had a pre-war connection with the Conservative Party via Beckett's association with Lord Lymington in the British Council against European Commitments (BCAEC), which linked it with a number of other extreme-right groups containing Conservatives.[12] Beckett's membership of the British Council for a Christian Settlement in Europe also linked the BPP with the anti-war faction in the Conservative Party. Linking Beckett personally with the Conservative Party was his friendship with Henry Newnham. However, the strongest revelation of the BPP's concordance with some Conservatives was in its regular post-war publications. The Duke of Bedford funded these publications, and sometimes used them personally to attack Jews, albeit using euphemistic language such as 'international finance' to do so. One regular BPP publication, the *Fleet Street Preview*, provided a mine of language that would not have been out of place coming from Sir Waldron Smithers, Charles Challen, Eleonora Tennant and many pre- and post-war Conservatives. This journal lauded Franco for being correct in 'exposing the true nature of the undeviating aims of Stalin and his coterie', and compared the silence of others over Stalin's actions to the outcry over Nazi atrocities.[13] It described immigrants as a 'foreign invasion' coming from the 'refuse of Europe', and as 'trash', 'alien', and 'poison', frequently juxtaposing them with references to 'true-born Englishmen'.[14] These comments were similar to those raised by Conservative MPs after the disembarkation of the *Empire Windrush* brought New Commonwealth immigrants to Britain. The *Fleet Street Preview* also stated that unions were 'holding the country to ransom with impunity', and denounced their members as 'oblivious to anybody's welfare but their own',[15] views that closely resembled Sir Waldron Smithers' denunciation of the Conservative Party's surrender to the left, *Save England*. The *Fleet Street Preview* also implicitly supported a Conservative MP's proposal that a prospective parliamentary candidate disclose his place of birth, and criticised the Conservative Party for failing to expose the Labour Government's shortcomings sufficiently, and for its poor performance at the Hammersmith South by-election.[16]

What can we conclude from this evidence? There is clear consanguinity between the right wing of the Conservative Party and the external extreme right, which extended to connections between a long-standing extreme-right Conservative publication, non-parliamentary groups and even pre-war fascists. It is also fair to surmise that electors holding similar views to former BUF members probably considered that the Conservative Party was the best place for their vote, at least until Mosley's return to politics. BPP supporters probably held this position also, although the BPP did at least contest one by-election, at Combined English Universities in March 1946, where its candidate, G. S. Oddie, lost his deposit. Yet nothing in the evidence outlined suggests that the Conservative Party played a witting role. Mosley's claim of a possible return to the Conservative fold seems barely credible, and possibly no more than exaggeration of casual comments by long-term, or delusional, friends. Instead, Mosley quickly attracted many erstwhile members of the BUF when he made his political comeback as head of Union Movement in February 1948, and also the opposition of left-wing opponents, and organised Jewish movements such as the 43 Group, who were determined to challenge him. These groups monitored Union Movement activity, but failed to reveal any substantial connections with the Conservative Party. This revelation is unsurprising because new recruits to Union Movement were similar to BUF members in the 1930s in their antipathy towards the Conservative Party, despite the comments of ex-BUF members like Arthur Winn. This antipathy towards the Conservative Party is apparent in the attitude of a 1950 Union Movement recruit: 'the party as a whole gave the impression of wandering aimlessly along, picking up discarded bits of Attlee brand Socialism as its main commitment to a post-war policy. To me they appeared a party of old-men, where youth and modern viewpoints were suppressed, especially if you did not wear the old school tie.'[17] Therefore, the meeting of one obscure parliamentary candidate with a fascist is not evidence for all Conservatives generally, or the party machinery specifically, and definitely not for Union Movement members. Rather, the lack of material in the Conservative Party Archive relating to Union Movement suggests that Conservatives avoided it. Thus, all we can conclude from these examples during this period of opposition is that the Conservative Party may have unwittingly attracted extreme-right voters with nowhere else to go. The views and actions of some Conservatives may have resonated with former fascists, but contrasting with this are the Conservative Party's condemnatory comments towards extreme-right organisations. Central Office, for example, dismissed the known racist Britons Publishing Society in an internal memo to all Central Office Agents, and described its proprietor as a 'notorious anti-Jew'.

These examples understandably focus on Conservative links with any recrudescence of fascism. However, they do not adequately consider the markedly different post-war political context, and therefore do not describe events on the right accurately. It would be natural to assume that the electorate would express its fears about the Labour Government's legislation through the Conservative Party. The Conservative Party, however, had produced the *Industrial Charter* in fear of permanent rejection by the electorate. Right-wing Conservative activists and supporters felt betrayed by this response. Their lack of trust in the Conservative Party's willingness to combat Socialism led to a siege mentality among them and produced an unusual phenomenon, one that has remained within the extreme right thereafter. Erstwhile respectable middle-class Conservative voters began to adopt street and platform cultures more usually associated with working-class and extremist politics. They attacked the state interference of the Attlee Government, and defended Conservative principles by invoking sentiments of mass Conservatism and adopting tactics of popular protest. Their decision resulted in a plethora of groups that denounced Socialism vociferously. Not all Conservatives adopted this stance. Some chose less obvious and extreme outlets to achieve their objectives, especially apparent in those that championed individual liberty and economic liberalism, though not exclusively so. However, many Conservatives did adopt a more vigorous stance. The Conservative Party's response to these groups revealed differing refractory attitudes that frequently, though not exclusively, depended on Central Office's perception of their extremism.

Central Office's emerging role

By 1945, the Conservative Party already contained a mechanism for monitoring outside organisations. On 20 April 1944, the inaugural meeting of the Ad Hoc Committee on Relations with Outside Societies of the Central Women's Advisory Committee noted that, 'it had been appointed to consider all matters relating to Outside organisations'. After the war, the Maxwell Fyfe report reinvigorated the Conservative Party organisation, restoring its pre-war health. The Voluntary Organisations Section now replaced the somewhat makeshift Committee on Relations with Outside Societies. It was located within the

Organisation Department of Central Office, and had confidential terms of reference explicitly mandating an intelligence-gathering role focused on extremist elements, which was perhaps not coincidental given that this was a few months after Mosley's political comeback. Although the Voluntary Organisations Section's terms of reference applied to extremists of different political persuasions, there was a specific term charging it with investigation of 'voluntary organisations who are definitely Conservative in outlook or sympathetic to Conservatism'. There was also the command to render regular reports and recommendations, including any need for 'tactical action within these organisations'. Thus, the Voluntary Organisations Section possessed clear instructions to interfere in the activities of right-wing organisations, some of which would undoubtedly be extreme. Details on a number of extreme-right groups are indeed within the files of the Voluntary Organisations Section, some of which would later cause the Conservative Party genuine concern. Central Office also already ran a bureaucracy to which local associations and Area Agents regularly reported items deemed of interest. This bureaucracy complemented the remit of the Voluntary Organisations Section, and included reports of extreme right-wing activity. It is from correspondence involving Central Office and the Voluntary Organisations Section that we can understand the motives of these groups during the Attlee governments, and discern reasons for the Conservative Party's varying attitude towards them.

Compare, for example, Central Office's attitude towards the National Democrats and The Right Party. The National Democrats' manifesto called for reduced taxation, the restoration of individual rights, a return to free trade and the removal of governmental interference in business. The National Democrats' representative who forwarded their manifesto claimed that the motive for the party's creation was 'to give expression to the views of a considerable body of industrialists'. Thus, the National Democrats were a sectional interest. The views in its manifesto, however, were in line with many Conservatives' thinking. In addition, there were no viewpoints, methods or obvious extreme personal antecedents likely to embarrass the Conservative Party. The lack of any evidence of further enquiry suggests that Central Office did not see the National Democrats as a threat. Lord Woolton, the Chairman of the Conservative Party, even expressed willingness to meet the National Democrats' representatives. In contrast, the agent who brought the Right Party to Central Office's attention, a Mr Hopkinson, was concerned at the 'publicity it had received locally'. Hopkinson nonchalantly dismissed the Right Party as probably 'quite unimportant', but nevertheless requested information in case a constituent asked him to provide it. Central Office's reply mirrored Hopkinson's nonchalance. Vice-Chairman Marjorie Maxse provided details on the founder of the Right Party, a Mr A. C. Cann, and at the same time advised Hopkinson that, 'we do not need to take him too seriously'. Nevertheless, Central Office was sufficiently concerned to investigate Mr Cann's background before replying to Hopkinson, which revealed that Mr Cann had applied, in May 1946, to be a Prospective Parliamentary Candidate for the Conservative Party, and secured an interview with a Mr Thomas. Furthermore, as Maxse also reported to Hopkinson, it was after this interview that Cann created the Right Party, and only then that 'we learnt that before the war he had been connected with Sir Oswald Mosley'. We can only guess at what prompted Cann to create the Right Party, but it is unlikely that he would have done so if he felt that he had a realistic chance of gaining the Conservative Party nomination. However, Maxse's comments show that Central Office had been able to discover Cann's fascist antecedents. This revelation makes Central Office's subsequent actions easier to interpret. Maxse removed Cann from Central Office's lists of approved Conservative Party speakers and potential parliamentary candidates, and blocked his receipt of Party literature. Maxse had moved swiftly to terminate Cann's connection with the Conservative Party on discovering his connections with Mosley. Her actions are in stark contrast to Central Office's attitude towards the National Democrats. They reveal a desire to avoid taint by association, and are early evidence of the post-war Conservative Party's intention to block extreme-right groups and individuals. This explanation also chimes with Hopkinson's description of the Right Party as, 'of the extreme right'.

The Conservative Party's perception of an organisation's exact nature was not always immediately apparent, although this did not stop Central Office taking action when it thought that it was required. The Society for Individual Freedom (SIF), for example, championed the cause of individual liberty against the State. Typical of this was the case of farmers in South Woodham, Essex. The Labour Government's concern with unemployment, specifically its uneven geographical spread, had resulted in the introduction of 'Development Areas' and the Central Land Board in 1947. These developments appeared to provide the state with control over private property, which seemed believable as it came from a Socialist government currently nationalising industry. The South Woodham farmers had agreed to the State requisitioning their land during wartime because they understood the measure to be temporary. Many of them had enlisted while the state utilised their property. The decision by Attlee's government to confiscate their property using a compulsory purchase order, however, was a different matter. SIF became involved in the dispute on the farmers' side, and lobbied local MPs, the relevant ministry, and, securing no redress, Winston Churchill. Regular SIF publications carried articles from individuals denouncing the government, such as that from retired Royal Navy Commander Hyde C. Burton, which complained of 'individualness' being 'sacrificed upon the hideous altar of the "Collective"'.[18] SIF's 'News Bulletins' talked about the undermining of free government, the realm, religion, and monarchy, by saboteurs placed in Britain's 'vital offices, in factories, power-plants, railway centres, laboratories and docks, and wherever the nation is most vulnerable'.[19] These views locate SIF to the right of a Conservative Opposition propounding the *Industrial Charter*. However, Central Office included SIF members on its list of approved speakers. This connection had potential for embarrassment, which a Deputy Central Office Area Agent highlighted when he reported the comments of a SIF member during the 1948 Hampstead Borough Council by-election. SIF member Mr Jack Norris had complained about the level of foreigners in the area affecting housing for indigenous residents. Norris spoke from a soapbox adorned with a Hampstead Conservatives' poster, and brandished another poster of the Conservative candidate. At this stage, there is no comment in Central Office's files that reveal its perception of SIF's nature. However, Central Office removed Norris from its list of approved speakers, as it had done to the leader of the Right Party.

There is also evidence that Central Office took a more subtle approach to minimise the impact of outside organisations. After Labour's landslide victory in 1945, many in the Conservative Party realised the need to refocus its literature to attract more working-class voters. Prospective parliamentary candidate Edward Heath, speaking at the 1948 Party Conference, called for more publicity suitable for the workshop, factory, and trade unions. Central Office was understandably interested, therefore, in conservative organisations that attempted to attract this particular electorate. The Workers' Forum (WF), for example, prompted an enquiry to Central Office asking whether it was 'part of our Conservative Organisation'. Central Office denied any connection, declaring emphatically that it did not sponsor the WF. This response, in naming a specific group, arguably leaves open the possibility that Central Office supported some organisations. More definite is the conclusion that Central Office already possessed information on the WF, or that it gathered information once prompted by the enquiry. Having denied a connection with the WF, Central Office advised: 'From what we know of its activities however it is strongly Conservative in outlook and appears to put forward Conservative propaganda.' Central Office's comments show that it was sympathetic to WF, a view in line with Heath's call at the party conference. Subsequent comments suggest that Central Office had not based its opinion solely on its existing files. The initial inquiry had mentioned a Mr Alnutt in connection with the WF. Miss Fletcher at Central Office revealed that the enquiry prompted her to speak to Alnutt, and that she had discovered that his connection to the WF was limited to providing a speech at its behest in 1947. Thereafter, Fletcher stated, Alnutt confined himself 'entirely to work within the Conservative Party Organisations'. It is reasonable to assume, therefore, that Alnutt was a Conservative Party member, and that Fletcher warned him of the possible dangers of being a member of outside organisations, but that Central Office deemed the WF's work acceptable. These assumptions explain why Fletcher's actions contrasted markedly with that meted out to SIF's Jack Norris.

Central Office seemed even less concerned with the activities of the Middle Class Union (MCU). This stance appears surprising as the MCU had the potential for a mass, populist appeal of the radical right. The MCU was anti-Socialist, but did not wish to support vested interest, tradition, or anything reactionary. A Mr H. J. Chapman forwarded the MCU's literature to Lord Woolton asking for Conservative Party support, and warned him of the potential power of the neglected middle classes. Central Office's report on the MCU explains why it was unconcerned. It identified the MCU as a recurrence of a similarly titled inter-war movement that had included two Conservative MPs among its membership. The report noted the patriotism and anti-Communism of MCU members, and suggested that Central Office respond by highlighting the merits of Conservative Party membership in combating a heightened post-war Communist threat. Subsequent correspondence from the MCU did not alter this position. One reason for this is that despite an implicit threat in Chapman's letter, the MCU was not truly hostile to the Conservative Party. Indeed, MCU correspondence with Central Office revealed that its members saw it as a covert means of spreading Conservatism. A Mr Louis Dickens, for example, advised Central Office that the MCU agenda was 'powerfully Conservative without calling itself Conservative', and that the MCU would 'immeasurably strengthen Conservatism' as its members were likely to vote Conservative anyway. Nor did the MCU adopt an extremist posture or populist activities, despite threatening to do so. Consequently, Central Office stuck to the limited action suggested by its report of advising MCU's members that they would better achieve their objectives by joining the Conservative Party. Central Office's advice to its Area Agents included the statement that the MCU did not include anyone of high standing in its leadership, which reinforced its lack of concern. There is even a tone of disdain in the recollection of Central Office's Marjorie Maxse that apart from one piece of correspondence from a Mr D. Cobbett, the only other MCU person she remembered having anything to do with was Commander Hyde C. Burton, 'who is definitely a crank'.

The British Housewives' League (BHL) also sought Conservative Party support. Unlike the MCU, however, the BHL definitely engaged in activities previously thought alien among Conservatives. The BHL emerged during a period of crises and austerity measures. Wartime rationing remained. The Labour Government introduced bread rationing in summer 1946 to avoid famine in Asia and Germany. In January 1947, severe weather, and a fuel crisis caused partly by nationalisation of coal, combined to force the government to restrict energy consumption at work and home. The government banned cooking by electricity for three hours in the morning and two in the afternoon, leading to the headline, 'Shiver with Shinwell and starve with Strachey', a reference to Labour ministers involved. The BHL were thus part of a more widespread, general protest by a sorely pressed public. It appeared spontaneously with this dissatisfaction, striking a chord with many British women. A Miss M. Parsons, writing on behalf of the BHL, expressed to the Minister of Food, J. Strachey, concern at possible further cuts in rations if a dock strike continued. Parsons' letter is typical of BHL complaints about conditions under a Labour government. The appearance at the BHL's Albert Hall rally on 6 June 1947 of Conservative frontbencher David Maxwell Fyfe, MP, as the main speaker suggested the Conservative Party was aware of the BHL's potential to harm the Labour Government. Many Labour MPs, and others, even thought the BHL a Conservative front organisation. The Communist Party, for example, showered the Albert Hall rally with leaflets focusing on Maxwell Fyfe's presence and that of the erstwhile Conservative MP, Mrs Mavis Tate, and implored people to recognise the BHL's true nature. Yet, the Conservative Party actually shunned the BHL, despite it having the potential to spread an anti-government appeal to a mass audience. Central Office consistently rejected appeals from BHL representatives for official recognition and funding by the Conservative Party. Conservative Party Chairman, Lord Woolton, explicitly denied any connection with the BHL, stating in an address to the Conservative Women's conference on 2 July 1947: 'It might save a little of the time of our political opponents if I were to say publicly that the British Housewives League has no connection with nor is it financed by the Conservative Party.' Central Office adhered to this stance rigorously.

There are a number of reasons for Central Office's attitude. A prosaic reason, that will become a consistent theme in examining the Conservative Party's relationships with outside organisations, is that encouraging outside organisations risked damaging the Conservative Party's membership numbers and thus funds. The Conservative Party owed its success with women at a local level mainly because women viewed Conservative Associations as social organisations, unlike the more masculine Labour Party associations. Central Office, perhaps realising the importance of female support, had already accepted the suggestion in the Maxwell Fyfe Report that local Conservative Associations form housewives' committees from among their members to provide coordinated criticism of Labour austerity. Membership of the BHL, therefore, could hamper Central Office's recommendation. Hence, Central Office's comment to the wife of a Conservative prospective parliamentary candidate who sought advice on how to deal with the BHL, that, 'Any association which tends to drain membership and funds from the local association is not furthering the interests of the party in any particular district.' This focus on membership and funds was particularly acute as Lord Woolton was engaged in a party recruitment drive. There is also the possibility that hostility towards the BHL resulted from a belief that its leading figure, Dorothy Crisp, was using it as her personal vehicle to secure election to Parliament. Supporting this possibility is Maxse's comment that voluntary organisations like the BHL were 'used usually for personal motives'. Yet, Central Office's consistently hostile attitude towards the BHL after Crisp resigned the chairmanship casts doubt on this explanation. Crisp offered upon resigning to write to all BHL members and advise them to vote Conservative. Lord Woolton's rejection of Crisp's offer suggests that Central Office's attitude towards the BHL had not thawed.

Central Office's perception of the BHL as an extreme-right organisation that could harm the Conservative Party explains its attitude. A comparison between the BHL and a similar organisation of the time, the National Federation of Women's Institutes (NFWI), explains Central Office's perception. Paul Martin showed that the NFWI sought to promote women's traditional gender roles as part of a wider attempt to secure progressive legislation and recognition of women's contribution to society.[20] Contrastingly, Martin described the BHL as brandishing 'traditional female domesticity as an exclusive weapon wrapped in heavy sentiment which it used to browbeat the Labour government from the right'. Therefore, progressive legislation was not part of the BHL's platform. Thus, while the NFWI argued that the government's omission of sick pay for house-wives in the National Insurance scheme failed to acknowledge the traditional role of women sufficiently, the BHL remained silent. The NFWI's demands for equal pay for women and a greater provision of school meals met the same response from the BHL, or even hostility. Instead, the BHL attacked the welfare state, deriding, for example, the provision of school meals as a state imposition. In addition, whereas the NFWI was, and remains, apolitical, the BHL's alliance with trade associations, as Martin argued, suggests the opposite. Whether these considerations identify the BHL as an extreme-right organisation today is anachronistic. More germane is the fact that Central Office's reports show that at this time it viewed the BHL as acting in a manner that people would associate with the extreme right.

Miss Spencer's report for Central Office on the BHL's June 1947 Albert Hall rally mentioned the typically Conservative preponderance of Union Jacks and the singing of patriotic songs. The following July, Miss Spencer reported on the BHL's Trafalgar Square rally and subsequent march to Hyde Park. These BHL activities were more redolent of Oswald Mosley's pre-war British Union of Fascists. Mosley's Union Movement, formed at the same time as the BHL's 1948 rally, soon engaged in exactly the same activities. Central Office would have been aware of both events. Spencer identified one known Conservative at the BHL rally. Otherwise, Spencer focused on the crowd's reaction to the BHL, noting that hecklers interrupted with shouts of 'Tories' and 'Fascists'. Katherine Wilmot's report on the BHL's Kingsway Hall meeting of 21 June 1948 was more comprehensive and indicated a more formalised approach to intelligence-gathering, which may be a consequence of the creation in May 1948 of the Voluntary Organisations Section.[21] Wilmot circulated her report to senior Central Office officials. Her report identified Conservative individuals, most notably Sir Waldron Smithers MP. However, it is Wilmot's impression of the audience's attitude that revealed the nature of Central Office's concerns. When Wilmot commented on the reception of various topics, she stated that, 'The more extreme right element was well received.' Wilmot's report made it clear that a re-emerging Conservative Party, only recently armed with a much-changed political programme in the shape of the *Industrial Charter*, wished to avoid any connection with the BHL because it drew attention to extreme-right views from which the post-war Conservative Party wished to dissociate.

Central Office's relationship with the BHL is also a more enlightening example of how the Conservative Party blocked the extreme right. The relationship is more comprehensive than that with, for example, the Right Party, and reveals how the Conservative Party implemented its blocking role. On the one hand, there is the obvious intelligence-gathering. The dissemination of Central Office's disapproval of the BHL to other Conservatives is equally obvious. Lord Woolton, for example, wrote to Colonel A. Gomme-Duncan, MP, regarding an invitation to speak at a BHL meeting, stating that it had, 'long been the policy of this office to dissociate itself from this organisation'. There is also a suggestion of underhand activities by the Conservative Party in the remark made from the platform at Kingsway Hall that, 'the Housewives League will carry on their fight for freedom in spite of the vast sums spent by the Opposition to wreck it'. Central Office vehemently denied the inference that it was trying to do so. Frustratingly, neither the report nor the response it generated provides any details. Nevertheless, Central Office's refusal to grant the BHL official Conservative Party recognition, or to supply funds, forced the BHL to operate under its own auspices and therefore subject to full media scrutiny, and without the resources of a financially powerful institution.

Political alienation was also the result of another aspect to the Conservative Party's blocking role. The Conservative Party's apparent acceptance of Attlee's programme opened political space on its right, which the BHL, and others vehemently opposed to Socialism, occupied. Thus, the BHL was indeed one of those Conservative groups that adopted an extreme political culture to attack Socialism and maintain traditional Conservatism. The Conservative Party's adherence to its changed political stance resulted in the BHL quickly changing its position from supporting the Conservative Party and seeking its imprimatur and funds, to criticising it. This quick change is evident in Wilmot's report of the BHL's June 1948 Kingsway Hall meeting, which mentions hostility towards the Conservative Party for the first time. The report refers to the creation of the National Health Service and changes in National Insurance, and the BHL's castigation of Shadow Chancellor R. A. Butler for being 'proud to be a sponsor' of this 'terrible infringement of freedom'. The following day Mary A. Parsons, on behalf of the BHL, sent Churchill a resolution that denounced the Opposition for accepting 'the imposition of the totalitarian Insurance and Health Service'. This resolution was a particularly mordant criticism to level against an individual many saw as responsible for the defeat of fascist totalitarianism, but it also indicated how the Conservative Party's consistent stance had forced the BHL into political isolation. The result for the BHL of isolation from the Conservative Party was dwindling attendances at its meetings and, apart from an isolated attempt at resurrection, political marginalisation before the Conservative Party regained power in 1951.

The Conservative Party's relationship with the Fighting Fund for Freedom (FFF) is more difficult to judge, as there is evidence of both cooperation and attempts to distance itself from it during this period of opposition. The FFF's stated objective was to re-energise the Conservative Party by 'linking the voters with the Conservative M.P.s and the prospective Conservative Candidates'. Furthermore, the FFF's demands for economic liberalism in the shape of denationalisation ran counter to the ethos of the *Industrial Charter* but corresponded with the views many Conservatives who opposed it. Sir Waldron Smithers' leadership of the FFF also placed it within the Conservative Party's orbit. Smithers had been the Conservative MP for Chislehurst since 1924, and remained a Conservative MP until retiring at the 1955 General Election. Moreover, there is clear evidence that Central Office cooperated with the FFF. In December 1945, Smithers, writing as chairman of the FFF, returned a list of Conservative candidates to Colonel S. Pierssene at Central Office. As the

FFF had supported the anti-Semitic campaign of Conservative MP Charles Challen in Hampstead,[22] we could interpret this as Central Office willingness to provide party material to a potentially extreme-right movement. On the other hand, these events occurred in the immediate aftermath of Labour's stunning electoral victory and before the bureaucratic revival of the Conservative Party, suggesting that Central Office was insufficiently aware of events, and possibly still reeling from the scale of defeat. Furthermore, Central Office probably gave the list to Smithers before Challen's anti-Semitic campaign began as it included prospective parliamentary candidates which, given the size of Labour's victory in 1945, was not for an imminently expected election, and thus indicates that it pertained to the July 1945 General Election. The petition to remove aliens from Hampstead did not commence until October 1945, which absolves Central Office from involvement with an extreme-right campaign on the grounds of ignorance. Such an excuse thereafter, however, would not apply. Subsequent Central Office correspondence regarding the FFF is interesting in that it indicates how the Conservative Party's actions helped to create extreme-right groups. More specifically, however, it reveals that although Central Office was willing to engage with the FFF, there was also an undercurrent of wariness and suspicion that degenerated into panic when Central Office feared the relationship was about to be discovered.

The FFF's monthly reports show that it had come into existence because of a belief that the Conservative Party was not acting appropriately. Two FFF organisers reported in June 1948 their experiences within a constituency formerly held by the Conservatives. They found the local Conservative Association abandoned and neighbouring businesses, local people, and even the police, unable to state its new location. When the FFF organisers eventually discovered the correct address, they found a 'private house without poster, plate or any indication to show that the Conservative Party operate from that centre'. Local Conservatives may have thought success unlikely in an area recently made solidly working-class by council housing construction ordered by Herbert Morrison, the Labour leader of the Greater London Council, but this was inertia. The FFF's reporting of this inertia, and determination to redress it, was also a criticism of the Conservative leadership. In July 1948, the FFF's monthly report complained of a lack of effective leadership in the Conservative Party and an absence of 'true Conservatism'. It combined these charges in its demand for the updating of local Conservative Associations when commenting that local committees would 'get nowhere if they are slack, self-satisfied or allow themselves to be dominated by the pale-pinks, the theorists or the half-informed', and in its call for a rejuvenated grassroots to force the Conservative centre to 'revitalise itself'. These sentiments were a common feature of FFF literature, indicating that the FFF was a coalescence of individuals whose views were now on the extreme right compared to the position adopted by the post-war Conservative Party in the *Industrial Charter*. The FFF's coalescence as a group was, therefore, a product of the changed nature of the Conservative Party.

Central Office's initial response to the FFF came in a memo to all of its Area Agents on 24 June 1948. Marjorie Maxse, stating that the memo was Central Office's response to 'so many enquiries about the attitude of the Party towards the Fighting Fund for Freedom', denied that any official association existed, described FFF visits to local Conservative Associations as not sanctioned, and dismissed FFF statements as unhelpful and its actions intended to undermine the *Industrial Charter*. Maxse concluded that there was no need for any MP, candidate or agent to assist the FFF. Yet this attitude appeared to have changed by September 1948. In that month, Lord Woolton, Conservative Chairman and thus head of Central Office, arranged a luncheon meeting with a member of the FFF's executive committee and officials, ostensibly to establish an acceptable relationship. In March 1949, Maxse wrote again to all Area Agents, but with a very different attitude to that of nine months before. Maxse now advised that, 'various negotiations have taken place and the Chairman of the party has been in touch with the Chairman of the Fighting Fund for Freedom with a view to establishing more satisfactory relations between them and Central Office'. Instead of warning all Conservative Party officers and officials to avoid members of the FFF, Maxse advised that the FFF would be providing assistance in constituencies deemed most in need of their help. There are a number of possible reasons for this changed attitude. The FFF openly sought the return of a Conservative government: 'we hope the government of our Country will be placed in the hands of the Conservative Party'. The FFF was not, therefore, likely to provide an electoral alternative to the Conservative Party. Moreover, the FFF had assisted at least one Conservative prospective parliamentary candidate at a time when the Conservative Party machinery was still recovering from wartime decay, and had openly offered support to others wanting it. Additionally, the FFF claimed to have been more active in working-class areas and factories compared to the Conservative Party's canvassers. The FFF's report also highlighted the negative impact on the working class of the Labour Government's legislation and the 1947 fuel crisis, including difficulties in finding the weekly National Insurance contribution, the loss of an additional wage due to the increased school leaving age, and the rising cost of electricity. It is possible, therefore, that a badly shaken Conservative Party saw the FFF as a vehicle similar to the Workers' Forum in that it could influence a section of the electorate that had overwhelmingly contributed to the Labour landslide of 1945.

Nevertheless, we can detect a degree of disquiet over the FFF in Maxse's comment that its organisers in the constituencies would be 'still ostensibly operating on behalf of the F.F.F', rather than the Conservative Party. This disquiet turned to panic when Central Office realised that FFF leaflet No. 67 exhorting the reader to vote Conservative was a potential breach of the Representation of the People Act (1948). Maxse's concern can be seen in her admission to the General Director of Central Office that, 'We are so near an election that I tremble to think of what might happen if a Socialist got hold of leaflet No. 67.' Panic is evident in the pencilled-in note, presumably from the General Director, asking where the envelope and its contents, presumably a reference to the worrisome leaflet, had gone. Central Office's panic may have resulted from fear of charges of electoral impropriety. Yet, Central Office's desire to maintain distance from the FFF predates panic over a possibly dubious leaflet. In addition, the removal of Sir Waldron Smithers from the FFF's letterheads soon after 1945 ends the overt connection between the FFF and Conservative Party. What, then, accounts for Central Office wariness?

A simple but understandable desire for institutional demarcation is a possible explanation, but may be insufficient. On the other hand, the Conservative Party presumably knew of the FFF's anti-Semitism from the 1945 campaign of its own MP. Even if Central Office was ignorant of this particularly damaging FFF association, subsequent evidence made the FFF's anti-Semitism a possible cause for concern. For example, Central Office received a copy of the FFF's monthly report for August 1948, which included a call for a more active campaign in areas where Labour authorities had built council houses in Conservative marginal constituencies. Contained within this call was a clear anti-Semitic reference to a Labour leader, described as a 'Russian Jewess'. Fear of association with anti-Semitism, therefore, could also underlie Central Office's concern over the possible discovery of a close relationship with the FFF. Moreover, this concern could also explain Lord Woolton's cryptic comment when arranging his luncheon meeting with the Chairman of the FFF that the Chairman was, 'the best person with whom to discuss a certain matter that is at present worrying my colleague and me'. There is no further clarification, however, as to what was worrying Woolton, and it could easily be something mundane. Nevertheless, it is difficult to ignore anti-Semitism as a factor in the relationship between Central Office and the FFF, especially considering the propinquity to, and context provided by, the Second World War. In addition, the timing of Woolton's letter, soon after receipt of the FFF's August 1948 monthly report, adds weight to notion of concern over the FFF's anti-Semitism. One possible conclusion is, therefore, that as the Conservative Party approached the 1950 General Election, the relationship between Central Office and FFF had changed. From being distant, Central Office had created a working relationship that subsequently caused deep concern, and that anti-Semitism was a feasible basis for that concern.

Central Office and its Area Agents also showed interest in another organisation prior to the 1950 General Election, The New British National Reform Party, or New Reform Party (NRP). The NRP's prospectus reinforced the notion that the Conservative Party created extreme-right groups by sloughing off individuals whose ideas no longer suited the Conservative leadership. The NRP's leader, P. W. Petter, J.P., identified himself in its prospectus as a lifelong Conservative who had supported many Conservative candidates by speaking on their election platforms, and as someone who enjoyed realistic prospects of becoming a Conservative parliamentary candidate. Nevertheless, Petter made his disillusionment with the Conservative Party clear: 'The Conservative policy of the last few years has been to run along behind the Socialist Party. Indeed they have presented the Socialists with many of the ideas which they have put in practice.'

Petter damned the performance of the Conservative Opposition frontbench. He described their performance over the introduction of the National Health Service as a 'cowardly retreat', and held them responsible for the loss of the 1949 Hammersmith South by-election. Petter also damned Conservative MPs, criticising them for laziness and poor attendance at the House of Commons, and concluding that the Conservative Party was unworthy of support, not to be trusted with government, and ineffectual in halting the Socialist ruination of the country. The only viable solution for the country's ills, Petter stated, was a new party led by a strong man.

It is easy to dismiss Petter as a crank. His views revealed belief in an international conspiracy involving the papacy and Communism. Nevertheless, Central Office thought it worthwhile paying attention to Petter and his new party. The Central Office Agent who forwarded the NRP prospectus advised of its wide distribution, and the Central Office official who received it noted that, 'We are keeping an eye open on the ambitious Mr Petter.' Central Office did gather intelligence on Petter. Maxse responded affirmatively to a Conservative MP's enquiry as to whether Petter was a member of the party, stating that he was 'known to the Yeovil Conservative Association'. Central Office circulated subsequent NRP literature to its General Director, Chief Political Officer, and four other officials. Meanwhile, Central Office Agents continued to request information on the NRP. A memo from Central Office's Agent for the Home Counties South East Area is typical of others in that it asked whether the NRP was 'of importance and should be watched?' However, what harm could the politically miniscule Petter do to the Conservative Party? An internal memo to all Central Office Agents and local associations provided an answer. Attached was a four-page report by Central Office's Mr Stebbings. Stebbings argued that the NRP was a 'mushroom organisation', a type normally ignored by Central Office but for Petter's claim that a vote for the NRP would not harm the Conservatives at the next General Election, which he thought was specious. Yet, Stebbings's view was unrealistic. With just over one year before the next general election, the most that Petter could achieve was a few NRP candidates, most of whom would probably lose their deposits, as shown by Oswald Mosley's attempts to form new parties. In addition, Petter was not a charismatic public figure, but an unknown who operated in a very different political climate to when Mosley's appeal was at its highest. However, if Stebbings's claim was dubious, what other potential harm could Petter pose to the Conservative Party?

The NRP's policies placed it firmly on the right. It demanded reductions in extravagant spending, particularly on social services, limitations on nationalisation, and a call for economic autarky, especially on foodstuffs. The NRP would criminalise lightning strikes and support the Empire. More idiosyncratic, the NRP called for the restoration of the Penny Post. The NRP's desire for the new party to be a party of youth set it at odds with the Conservative Party, and provided a more radical tone. Yet, the NRP's political programme did not have the potential to damage the Conservative Party. Many of its policies were in line with current Conservative thinking, or had some support within the Conservative

Party. However, religious morality was at the heart of the NRP's political pro-gramme, from taxation based on the Bible, to education policies that included compulsory scripture-based teaching in all state schools. This characteristic was definitely not prominent in Conservative policy. Stebbings also pointed out that the headquarters of the NRP was the same as the National Union of Protestants, an organisation that was responsible for disrupting High Church services, and that Petter was a former Governing Director of this organisation. The NRP's prospectus revealed that hard-line Protestantism was the party's philosophi-cal basis. In it, there was an acceptance of democracy and the institutions of Parliament and the Crown, but the NRP promised that if it ever formed a gov-ernment it would exclude from the institutions of the State those that it deemed were not truly part of the nation. Roman Catholics and Communists could certainly expect restrictions. Nor could Central Office miss the implications of Petter's views, as they were ubiquitous in the NRP prospectus. Moreover, it is likely that the Conservative Party, which possessed a strong Ulster Unionist element, realised that a connection between hard-line Protestantism, Ulster loyalists and the extreme right already existed. The British Protestants League, for example, spread virulent anti-democratic and anti-Semitic literature before and after the Second World War. Central Office probably also knew that public perception would link the Conservative Party with Ulster Unionism, without necessarily distinguishing between its various forms. The Conservative Party had a long connection with local Orange Order movements, and their political representations such as the Liverpool Protestant Party. This, and not a belief in the NRP's possible electoral success, explains why Central Office condemned Petter to all Conservative constituencies. Stebbings revealed this when he stated that the Conservative Party would regard 'as reactionary any attempt to fan sectarian feuds particularly where these are calculated to promote political unrest and distract attention from the real issues of national politics', and thus dissociated the Conservative Party from any religious controversy that placed restrictions on a large section of the electorate. To Central Office, Petter was an extreme-right religious bigot, and they wanted no connection with him.

Central Office's concern to avoid association with extreme-right individu-als leading up to the 1950 General Election is evident. Its treatment of one of its own parliamentary candidates, rather than a disgruntled individual on the periphery of the party, provided the clearest example of this. Andrew Fountaine fought for Franco in the Spanish Civil War and served in the Second World War.[23] He became a leading Young Conservative in his constituency, and his performance at the 1947 Conservative Party Conference, attacking the Attlee Government's policy towards Indian independence, earned a standing ovation. The Chorley Conservative Association adopted Fountaine in 1948 as its can-didate for a constituency it expected to gain at the next election. However, at the Llandudno Conservative Party Conference in 1948, Fountaine described Attlee's Government as, 'that group of national traitors, that hierarchy of semi-alien mongrels, and hermaphrodite Communists that have the impudence to call themselves that which they are not – a British Government', thus revealing himself as an anti-Semitic racist with a possibly violent disposition. As a nominated parliamentary candidate, Fountaine was not as easy to dismiss as a mere party member. Nevertheless, Central Office made it clear that such sentiments were not acceptable when Lord Woolton released a statement saying that Fountaine's viewpoint was, 'completely at variance with the attitude of the Conservative party'. The Chorley Conservatives did not find an alternative candidate to replace Fountaine. This situation may reflect tension between Central Office, which had an approved list of candidates, and a local association that was guarding its autonomy, especially concerning selection and treatment of candidates. Alternatively, it may reflect views that were prevalent within Chorley Conservative Association. Central Office had made it clear, however, that Fountaine no longer had official Conservative Party support.

In the 1950 General Election, Fountaine polled 46.9% of the vote, and missed election by a mere 361 votes. His views could just as easily have secured votes as lost. The closeness of the vote may simply parallel that of the overall result of the General Election. Yet, it is equally probable that Fountaine's failure to capture Chorley rested on having to stand as an Independent Conservative. What this episode does show is that Central Office had acted against an individual it deemed potentially harmful to the Conservative Party, and was willing to lose a seat in a close-run election. Central Office subsequently removed all relevant papers from its Chorley constituency file to a private one with strict access conditions, perhaps wishing to limit details of any connection between Fountaine and the Conservative Party. The private file remains inaccessible. More personally, Fountaine's wife divorced him after objecting greatly to his 'desertion of the Tory Party'. As well as being the daughter of Norfolk's Chief Constable, Mrs Fountaine was a former Central Office worker.

After the 1950 General Election

The 1950 General Election alleviated Conservative fears that the party would never regain office. The Conservative Party attracted nearly three million more votes, gaining eighty-five more MPs. Labour's impregnable 145-seat majority became a precarious five, a result that brought the Conservatives tantalisingly close to power. Thus, there was cause for Conservative optimism. Britain no longer had a mobilised electorate eager for the implementation of the Welfare State. This situation favoured the Conservative Party. The Conservatives could also point to the fuel, food, and sterling crises of the late 1940s as proof that Labour's policies were dangerous. Hypothermia, rationing, and devaluation were easily associated with the Labour Government. Labour's manifesto held the prospect of more of the same policies. Moreover, the Labour Government's desire to protect the newly nationalised coal industry from cheaper imports meant that it was quickly in an invidious position when France surprisingly presented it with the terms of the European Coal and Steel Community in spring 1950. The Government's refusal to enter looked as if it was putting ideology before the electorate's comfort by turning its back on the cheaper imports that membership would bring. Furthermore, the Labour manifesto had marked out sugar, cement, and industrial insurance, as the next targets for state control, despite steel nationalisation being incomplete. Sugar nationalisation particularly put a bitter taste in the electorate's mouth. The sugar manufacturer Tate and Lyle responded to Labour's manifesto with its 'Mr Cube' campaign, a pictorial representation of the perils of nationalisation on every sugar packet. Dogma was now affecting the British cup of tea adversely. Churchill, meanwhile, was still an asset for the Conservatives. He had the right credentials should the military manoeuvres occurring between North and South Korea from 1949 escalate into global conflict, as many expected. Moreover, his campaign comments showed that he now desired to face the Soviet Union with diplomacy, not bellicosity, introducing in the process the word 'summit' into the lexicon of diplomacy. Attlee, by contrast, seemed powerless to avoid the split that would occur within his government should the Korean situation and budget deficits either require increased defence spending or welfare cuts, or worse still, both.

Yet the Conservative Party had cause for concern. Austerity was not the whole picture. The Marshall Plan had reversed the negative impact of the USA's sudden end to wartime lend-lease. The positive effects of the 1949 devaluation were yet to appear, but would undoubtedly result in an improved economy. Moreover, this part of the post-war era was not one of unremitting gloom. Hennessy revealed the positive cultural milieu that alleviated the postscript of continuing wartime privations. Billy Butlin exploited provisions in the 1938 Holidays with Pay Act and created holiday camps that provided a safety valve for spending demands that went unrealised so long as rationing remained. Attendances at sports events mushroomed. Parisian fashions returned, albeit beyond the reach of many. The formation of the National Film Production Council and the passage of the Film Act in 1948 may not have helped the British film industry. Yet, Britain's large cinema-going audiences enjoyed a resurgence of British films including David Lean's adaptation of *Great Expectations* (1946), Orson Welles in *The Third Man* (1949), Alec Guinness in *Kind Hearts and Coronets* (1949), and Laurence Olivier in *Hamlet* (1948). Television began to have an impact also. The number of television licences issued in the four years between 1947 and 1950 rocketed from 15,000 to 344,000, a trend that would continue. This new phenomenon increased the potential for variety, but for the Conservative Party it also carried risks. In May 1951, the appearance of *The Goon Show* heralded an explosion of satire and influenced later shows that lampooned stuffy, outdated politicians. The Conservative Party, a status-based, class-ridden party faced the prospect of derision on television becoming a frequent feature of politics. Therefore, it is hardly surprising that Labour's vote had actually increased by over one million in 1950, given these considerations. This increased vote also indicated approval of Labour's radical legislation, rather than rejection. The Conservative Party's acceptance of most of Labour's legislation in its manifesto *This is the Road* implicitly acknowledged the electorate's approval of it, apart from vague comments on halting or reversing the pace of nationalisation. The

Welfare State and governmental intervention were here to stay. However, this acceptance meant that the tensions between the economically liberal and the more collectively minded of the Conservative Party were never far beneath the surface in the post-war years.

This situation had potentially negative consequences for the Conservative Party. Political space on the right of the Conservative Party had opened because of their failure to challenge the Labour Government effectively, signalled in the formulation of the *Industrial Charter*. Confirmation in the manifesto that this would continue to be the Conservative Party's position meant that organisations to the right of the party would remain a problem. Two examples show that Central Office remained keen to avoid any negative associations that resulted from this situation and the Conservative Party's pre-war connections with the extreme right. First, correspondence between Central Office and the Conservative Research Department in March 1950 revealed concern at the association of the epithet 'Conservative' with right-wing European parties by the BBC, the Labour Party and its publications. The Conservative Party of Great Britain clearly wished to avoid association with European right-wing parties whose political alliances with fascism had contributed to fascism's and Nazism's worst excesses. Secondly, Central Office continued to watch the Fighting Fund for Freedom, and collected information on its general opposition to nationalisation and specific commitment to railway denationalisation. Monitoring revealed that the FFF appeared to be attempting to create a cell-structure within the Conservative Party to propagate its ideology. Central Office responded by acquiring reports from a number of constituencies. Yet, Central Office did not want knowledge of any association between the Conservative Party and the FFF to become widely known, and its desire to minimise this came in July 1950 when a Central Office employee released information about the FFF without checking the file for the Conservative Party's official position. Miss Maxse responded with a severe rebuke, which showed that Central Office was unwilling to acknowledge even that it was monitoring the FFF.

Like the British Housewives' League, Aims of Industry (AIMS) sought a positive relationship with the Conservative Party. Unlike the BHL, AIMS secured it. Central Office agreed to Conservative Associations using AIMS speakers during Attlee's first administration. AIMS vigorously denied attempts to elicit from it an admission of their close relationship with the Conservative Party, and reported such attempts to Central Office comprehensively. In doing so, AIMS acted as part of Central Office's intelligence-gathering mechanism. Reinforcing this view was Central Office's agreement to create a Liaison Officer between the Conservative Party and AIMS after the 1950 General Election, which AIMS only made known to its Area Secretaries on a strictly confidential basis. There are a number of reasons for Central Office's positive attitude towards AIMS. AIMS assisted Central Office in intelligence-gathering, albeit marginally. More importantly, AIMS did not promote its objectives in a manner usually associated with extremists. Nor is there any evidence of overt hostility from AIMS towards the Conservative Party. On the contrary, AIMS's objectives complimented those of the Conservative Party. Moreover, increased support for Labour at the 1950 General Election may have meant that the Conservatives could not promise wholescale denationalisation, but that did not mean that Central Office could not cooperate with outside organisations that did. Indeed, Central Office even accepted a financial relationship with AIMS. In October 1950, Central Office accepted 80,000 free copies of *The Road Ahead*. This publication chimed, in title and content, with the Conservative Party's 1949 policy document, *The Right Road for Britain,* and its 1950 General Election manifesto, *This is the Road.* Central Office distributed *The Road Ahead* to all Conservative constituency agents. There is also evidence that Central Office distributed other AIMS publications, including *British Industry at the Crossroads,* which attacked nationalisation in general, and *No Appeasement,* which, like 'Mr Cube', fought the nationalisation of the sugar industry. AIMS did not pose a threat due to embarrassing activities, nor was it likely to present an electoral alternative to the Conservative Party. Its 'extremism' amounted to no more than occupying political space the Conservative Party felt incapable, at the time, of occupying. Therefore, Central Office's action against AIMS was hardly refractory at all, limited to judiciously advising its Area Agents that it was 'better not to over advertise the fact that they are assisting us'.

Central Office's relationship with AIMS contrasts starkly with is its attitude towards The New Crusade (TNC). Central Office's March 1950 report on the TNC included the names of prominent, distinguished members. Among the names is Lady Rennell Rodd, widow of the Conservative and Unionist MP for St Marylebone from 1928–33, Lord Rennell Rodd, who was also a member of the pre-war Nazi-sympathising Anglo-German Fellowship. The Rodd's third son, Peter, married Nancy Mitford. Although Nancy Mitford was not a Fascist sympathiser, many of the Mitfords were. Nancy's parents had supported Mosley's British Union of Fascists, and her sister, Unity, was a prominent Nazi who had resided in Germany before the Second World War and whom British intelligence services watched carefully. Most notable was Diana Mitford, the wife of Oswald Mosley. These facts were in the public domain. Therefore, it is not surprising that the report's author, Miss Fletcher, informed Miss Maxse at Central Office that TNC was a 'fascist organisation' connected to 'Nazi Youth Parties in Germany'. Fletcher also noted that a Special Branch officer had unsuccessfully attempted to meet the TNC's Secretary, a Colonel Miller, on a number of occasions on the pretext of seeking TNC literature. Thwarted, the Special Branch officer revealed to the property owner his identity, having previously claimed to be a Young Conservative. This claim was a reminder to Central Office that others maintained a connection in their mind between the Conservative Party and the extreme right. Fletcher concluded that TNC 'should be investigated', although the lack of further reports suggests that Central Office interest in it petered out.

Central Office took more action in the same year when it once again encountered sectarian and anti-Semitic extremists. The Guild of Good Neighbours (TGGN) seemed typical of the Conservative activism that was anti-Socialist and wished to overthrow the Labour Government. In April 1950, Central Office's Miss Fletcher advised Miss Maxse of arrangements for gathering information on TGGN, and that more information would be forthcoming after further enquiries. In the meantime, Fletcher identified a Mrs Proctor as the TGGN's Assistant Organiser, and noted that she 'wears a Conservative badge' and was 'on the Committee of St. Marylebone'. Fletcher also advised Maxse that TGGN possessed a 'chart' outlining its views, which its leader, a Captain John Hutchings, had forwarded to approximately 800 people. Fletcher subsequently informed Maxse of her inability to 'ascertain to whom this has been sent'. Although further enquiries did produce TGGN's chart, Fletcher decided to visit its headquarters personally, as the information on it was insubstantial. Fletcher's second report revealed that the TGGN had few members, sought wealthy donors, and that Conservatives ran it despite claiming to be non-party political. However, Fletcher also detected a 'strong under-current of anti-Roman Catholic feeling, and also more strongly still, anti-Jewish'. She also reported that, 'the idea was conveyed that the main troubles of the world sprang from the Jews'. Fletcher gave her private address when asked by TGGN's Captain Hutchings to identify herself. Fletcher also informed Maxse that she was evasive when asked if she had any connection with another organisation, and that when Hutchings persisted she replied 'that I interested myself mildly in various organisations, as I was generally interested in women, but had called purely out of interest, privately'. These comments were disingenuous, vague, and designed to hide Fletcher's purpose. Why relate this to Maxse otherwise?

We can also see Central Office's desire to avoid embarrassing associations when its opinion of an organisation changed upon discovering it had links with the Conservative Party. L. N. Tomlinson was a veteran of both world wars. He created Clan Briton, probably after the Conservative Party lost the February 1950 General Election. Clan Briton's emblem was a Union Flag with a superimposed white crucifix. Tomlinson's correspondence revealed that he held extreme right-wing views. Anti-left sentiment is endemic in it. In the *Sunday Express*, Tomlinson stated his belief that the Labour Government was 'devoted to the destruction of the Empire'. He also wrote to Churchill and demanded that it was more correct to refer to all Labour MPs as 'COMSOT (Communistic Socialist)'. Like Burton of the Society for Individual Freedom, Tomlinson thought Britain was under threat from Communist subversives.[24] This view was not limited to right-wing political activists. The Boulting Brothers reflected its wider currency in *High Treason* (1951), a film depicting left-wing plotters including a Labour MP planning to take over Britain's power stations at the same time as a Soviet invasion. Tomlinson probably saw the film as realistic as he made no distinction between Britain's Labour Party and Communists. His writings reflected this, and included racism and anti-Semitism, sometimes mixed with anti-left comments and a belief in decadence, plus anti-internationalism and conspiracy theory. Tomlinson's views became publicly evident when, on 19 March 1951, Labour MP Sidney Silverman read Tomlinson's letter addressed to a Reverend Fielding Clarke to the House of Commons. In the letter, Tomlinson implied that Mr Silverman was unqualified to speak on matters concerning the Church of England because he was Jewish, and castigated Jewish Labour MPs for not serving in the recent war.[25] In a document attached to the letter Tomlinson stated: 'Today our public life is impregnated with the breeders of greed, jealousy, corruption and self-glorification who are all too often non-Christian, of alien blood, interested only very superficially indeed in the well-being of Britain and Britons. Their loyalties are to themselves alone, and the parasite occupations which find them wealth at the expense of the British people who have given them sanctuary.'

Tomlinson continued his campaign in correspondence with Central Office and newspapers. In a number of letters addressing the issue of 'World Government', Tomlinson argued that the United Nations was 'an Anti-Christian Communist conception' that would result in the Union Jack's replacement by some 'international rag'. In these letters, approbation of the 'truly British' and demands of 'Britain for the Britons' frequently ran alongside xenophobic references to 'aliens' and 'anti-Christian Asiatics' and their intentions.[26] There was also a clear desire to limit the electorate according to specific, exclusive criteria. For example, Tomlinson argued that immigrants who were not 'absorbed racially within the British family' remained in Britain solely as guests, and had to accept 'our Christian way of life', and demanded the government of Britain had to be '100% in the hands of Christian British people'. Tomlinson also indicated that disenfranchisement might not have been the limit of his aims in a letter to the Editor of *Reynolds News*: 'all foreigners in Britain should be deprived of their rights'. These 'foreigners' included Jews in Attlee's Cabinet. In September 1951, Tomlinson wrote to Central Office criticising the publisher W. H Allen for publishing a book by Menachim Begin, the leader of Jews in Palestine. Tomlinson claimed that the publisher's action would allow 'the million or so of unwelcome Jews in our Christian Country' to rejoice at Begin's actions. Tomlinson stated that Attlee was colluding with Jewish ambitions because he had placed control of Britain's armed forces 'in the hands of two blood-brothers of this murderer, i.e. Shinwell and Strauss', who had 'NEVER condemned the outrages committed'. Finally, there was more than a hint of violence in Tomlinson's demands. He likened Communists to mad dogs, and argued for their destruction. A journalist at *Reynolds News* even believed that Clan Briton engaged in violence, stating that it was 'an organiser of planned hooliganism'.[27] These views are all characteristics of the extreme right, even of fascism. Expressing them was an individual who claimed that Clan Briton had a 'County Branch Office' and 'members in most of the Counties of Britain'. He was also a member of the Conservative Party.

Central Office's response to Tomlinson is enlightening. An internal party memo revealed that Central Office had some knowledge of Tomlinson. It described him as 'a rather decent fellow, obsessed with flag-waving, a violent patriot, with probably slight fascist tendencies'. However, the memo's author also stated, 'I never encourage the recruiting of this type of person because it tends to a confusion of ideas'. The author's description of an individual having 'slight fascist tendencies' as a 'decent fellow', is intriguing. It is unclear whether this betrays the author's fascist sympathies, a generosity of spirit based on Tomlinson being a double war veteran, or simply careless language. However, it does show that the author believed violence and patriotism to be constituent parts of fascism. What is also clear is that the author either did not realise Tomlinson was a Conservative Party member, or regretted it if he was. It is probable that the author was ignorant of Tomlinson's affiliation as there is no clear indication of membership in this letter or previous ones. What is unarguable is the author's opinion that individuals with such views should not be part of the Conservative Party, even if only for the expeditious desire to avoid 'confusion of ideas'. However, compare this attitude with that Central Office subsequently displayed when it became aware of Tomlinson's Conservative Party membership. Central Office swung into action after Sidney Silverman's exposé of Tomlinson's views in the House of Commons. The next day, one of its confidential internal memos revealed that Tomlinson was an ex-member of the Heston and Isleworth Conservative Association, where he was quite prominent as a member of a Ward Committee, but was now living in Lytham St Annes. The memo also described Tomlinson as having a 'distinct and bitter anti-semitic prejudice which gives the impression of Fascism but,' the author added, 'I am told he is not Fascist'. Putting aside frustration at the author's failure to amplify on what he thought fascism was, this memo reveals a less sanguine attitude, albeit tempered by a belief that Tomlinson had left the Conservative Party. However, Central Office's attitude changed markedly after Tomlinson subsequently advised that he was an 'ardent Tory' and now a member of the Lytham Conservative Club, which he described as a 'very respectable association of Britains'. Central Office's responses became curter, and they quickly reached a decision not to respond to Tomlinson. Their comments had gone from sympathetic to dismissive in six months.

Relations between the Conservative Party and extreme right in the aftermath of the Second World War are not usually as clear as in Tomlinson's case. The extent and content of Central Office material on right-wing groups varies. Nonetheless, there was an identifiable point when Tomlinson became persona non grata as far as Central Office was concerned. However, we must exercise caution in taking this as proof of the Conservative Party's blocking role in the fortunes of the extreme right. We do not know if Central Office tried to remove Tomlinson's party membership, and even if it did not, the autonomous nature of local Conservative associations would need consideration. Furthermore, Clan Briton was but one extreme-right organisation operating to the right of the Conservative Party, and Central Office's attitude towards them may have depended on other factors. Many extreme-right groups were small, often no more than one-man-bands, and therefore not strictly speaking 'groups'. Consequently, it is difficult to judge the extent of the support attracted or repelled by the Conservative Party's treatment of these extreme-right groups. Central Office correspondence revealed disdain for the size of these groups, and therefore we cannot discount this as a factor in the Conservative Party's attitude. There is even an example where the attitude displayed towards an extreme-right group rested on lines that are more obvious. This involved the Conservative Christian League, which employed similar language as Tomlinson, and aims that were in tune with other extreme-right groups. It even boasted the support of that ubiquitous right-wing Conservative MP, Sir Waldron Smithers. Central Office was interested enough in the Conservative Christian League to investigate it, but the decision to have nothing to do with it resulted not from the Conservative Christian League's extremism, but from discovering that its leading figure had a criminal record.

Nevertheless, there was a clear difference in the Conservative Party's attitudes towards specific external extreme-right groups. A determining factor was Central Office's perception of the extreme-right group as fascist or not. The fascist extreme right were clearly cut off. This attitude towards domestic groups of the fascist extreme right is also in line with the party's stated view of its position in relation to contemporary right-wing European parties. The Conservative Party had no wish to be associated with any outside organisation whose stance could link it in any way with the sufferings caused by aggressive, racist right-wing extremism. Central Office also investigated non-fascist extreme-right groups. It tolerated some and nipped others in the bud. It is reasonable to suggest, therefore, that individuals within these groups were often amenable to the Conservative Party and probably supported it electorally, and that those repelled by such groups sought other areas for their support. If so, then the Conservative Party had acted as a barrier to the development of some extreme-right groups almost by de facto incorporation. However, it had also sloughed off individuals whose views it deemed anathema, forcing them to act without the assistance of the Conservative Party. This role remained constant when the Conservative Party regained office and came under pressure from extreme-right movements that were more highly organised and better supported.

Notes

1 C. Hollis, 'The Conservative Opportunity', *New English Review*, XI (June 1945), 109.
2 See p. 3.
3 See pp. 17–18.
4 *Conference Report*, 1947, 49, quoted in J. D. Hoffman, *The Conservative Party in Opposition, 1945–51*, MacGibbon & Kee, London (1964), 165.
5 M. Edelman, 'A Day with the Tories', *New Statesman and Nation*, 11 October 1947, 284, quoted in Hoffman, *Conservative Party*, 166.
6 Hoffman, *Conservative Party*, 166. See also 161–166.
7 *The Star*, 22 January 1947, referring to a rebellion over the Statistics of Trade Bill vote, 21 January 1947.
8 *Daily Mirror*, 28 June 1945.
9 *Daily Mirror*, 29 June 1945.
10 *Hastings Observer*, 4 August 1945.
11 For the following, see S. Dorril, *Blackshirt: Sir Oswald Mosley and British Fascism*,

Viking, London (2006), 549–550.

12 F. Beckett, *The Rebel Who Lost His Cause: The Tragedy of John Beckett*, London House, London (1999), 153–155. Participating in the BCAEC were Beckett (BUF, BPP), James Joyce (BUF, NSL), Arnold Leese (IFL), and members of the Anglo-German Brotherhood, Nordic League, White Knights of Britain, the Militant Christian Patriots, British Vigil, the Britons, and English Array.

13 H. Alexander, 'When Red is Black', *Fleet Street Preview*, 24 April 1948, 1:6, 2. See also H. Alexander, 'Prophets Without Honour', *Fleet Street Preview*, 15 May 1948, 1:9, 1.

14 H. Alexander, 'Britain Importing Labour', *Fleet Street Preview*, 8 May 1948, 1:8, 1.

15 H. Alexander, 'The Press Strike', *Fleet Street Preview*, 14 August 1948, 1:22, 1–2.

16 'Background News', *Fleet Street Preview*, 18 September 1948, 1:27, 2. H. Alexander, *Fleet Street Preview*, 5 March 1949, 1:51, 1.

17 J. Bean, *Many Shades of Black: Inside Britain's Far-Right*, New Millenium, London (1999), 60.

18 *The Individualist*, 1950.

19 *News Bulletin, the publication of The Society For Individual Freedom, incorporating The Society of Individualists and National League for Freedom*, 21, September 1948, 1.

20 P. Martin, 'Echoes in the Wilderness: British Popular Conservatism, 1945–51', in S. Ball and I. Holliday, *Mass Conservatism: The Conservatives and the Public since the 1880s*, Frank Cass, London (2002), 122.

21 Seepp. 17–18.

22 See p. 15.

23 For the following on Fountaine, see S. Taylor, *The National Front in English Politics*, Macmillan, London (1982), 61ff, and 'Tories "Skeleton"', *Manchester Guardian*, 9 March 1959.

24 See p. 19.

25 'Another Letter Shock for MPs – "Privilege" Ruling', *Daily Mirror*, 20 March 1951. Tomlinson's letter was dated 14 March 1951.

26 Letter from L. N. Tomlinson to the Editor, 'First-rate, Mr Shinwell', *Sunday Express*, 27 August 1950, and to Mr Rossiter Esq., 14 October 1951.

27 Letter from L. N. Tomlinson to the Editor, *Reynolds News*, 14 August 1951.

2

Consensus Conservatism and extreme right revival, 1951–57

Defeat at the 1950 General Election went some way to exorcise the Conservative Party's shock at the 1945 defeat, and held the promise that success was near. Labour's 145-seat majority was now a mere five. A number of high-calibre individuals among the 1950 intake of new MPs reinvigorated the Conservative parliamentary party. Some quickly formed the One Nation Group, which was a modernising organisation that played a pivotal role in reshaping Conservatism. Not that the Conservative leadership lacked advantages; Eden's war record meant he was the expected and accepted successor to Churchill, which meant that the Conservative Party succession looked settled. This situation compared favourably to a tired Labour leadership damaged by the resignations of left-wing Bevanites, and assailed by a concerted campaign by the Conservative Opposition to counter its political programme. In contrast, the Conservative Party leadership's apparent clearer stance in the 1951 General Election manifesto of anti-Communism, commitment to competition and denationalisation, assuaged its right wing. The Conservative's machinery and organisation remained prepared for an expected General Election, with opinion polls in 1951 moving decidedly in the party's favour. By-elections showed swings towards the Conservatives of 4%, and there were many gains in local elections. The Conservative Party also looked set to benefit from the Liberal Party's weakness. When the election came, the Liberal Party only fielded 109 candidates, compared to 475 in 1950. The result was still close. The Conservatives under Churchill won, but Labour actually polled more votes. Moreover, the Conservative majority of seventeen depended on the nineteen seats won by National Liberals who had allied to the Conservative Party in the Woolton-Teviot Pact of 1947. Nevertheless, the Conservative Party had regained office only six years after a seemingly catastrophic defeat.

Churchill's administration was the first overtly Conservative government since 1929. However, the less than convincing nature of its victory meant that it was not a government suffused with confidence. Churchill's Government had an obvious need to reach out to that part of the electorate viewing the Labour Party as more likely to deliver its requirements, especially as Labour had polled 1.2 million more votes than the Conservatives had, and 2 million more than in 1945. Therefore, Churchill's Government adopted a cautious approach. It did not embark on wholesale reversal of Labour's legislation, and left untouched virtually all nationalisation. Indeed, so similar were the policies of Chancellor Butler and his Labour predecessor, Gaitskell, that commentators conflated the two to form 'Mr Butskell'. Henceforth, 'Butskellism' became synonymous with consensus. It is doubtful that right-wingers acknowledged the impact of political reality behind this term. Instead, they opted to question just how 'Conservative' the new government was. On top of this criticism was the added problem of an ageing leader whose interest in domestic issues paled beside foreign ones and gave the impression of lethargy. The 1952 Conservative Party Conference reflected this situation, containing many complaints of apathy and discontent just one year after election victory. Nevertheless, Churchill's Government did have some successes. The Chancellor's introduction of emergency economic measures in late 1951 and early 1952 ameliorated poor economic conditions. Consumer goods became more plentiful and diverse at the same time as a staged abolition of rationing. The national budget increased and thus so did the amount of public expenditure. House building was a great success, with the Housing Minister proudly delivering the election promise to build 300,000 new homes. By-elections contrasted favourably with the period of opposition. A general swing to the Conservatives meant that no by-elections were lost, and one, Sunderland South, even gained from Labour in 1953. Consequently, the Conservative Party's electoral prospects looked bright when Anthony Eden succeeded Churchill in April 1955, and the following month's General Election confirmed this by producing a 60-seat Conservative majority. This was the first time since 1841 that a party had improved its performance in three successive General Elections.

In less than two years, Eden had resigned. Eden proved incapable of a firm hand in Cabinet appointments. The decision to promote quickly the most promising of the 1950 intake of Conservative MPs drew criticism from Conservative newspapers. In addition, the first stages of imperial decline marked foreign policy, most obviously in the decision to withdraw British forces from east of Suez. However, economic and industrial concerns initially caused Eden's popularity to decline. Eden's popularity slumped by 30% even before the Suez Crisis due to the necessity of higher and more widespread taxes in the 1955 Autumn Budget, further deflationary measures the following year, and a number of strikes, most noticeably in the docks and railways. Poor by-election results reflected his declining popularity, and one protester physically attacked him at Bradford. In February 1956, the Liberals reduced the Conservative majority at Hereford by over three-quarters, while at Taunton Edward du Cann barely won with a majority of 657 votes. The Walthamstow by-election in March produced a 7.5% swing to Labour. The Tonbridge by-election of June 1956 appeared to presage electoral disaster when a Conservative majority of 18,000 fell to 1,600. Eden received wide criticism as an ineffective leader causing the malaise pervading much of the Conservative Party. The only probable remedy, save an unlikely party coup, was a serious international crisis that would enable Eden to unite party and country behind him. Eden's poor handling of such an eventuality when it occurred in the guise of the Suez Crisis was, therefore, the final straw.

The impression derived of this period of Conservative government is one of steady success built on a consensual approach, followed by acute leadership failure. Yet, unease among the Conservative Party's right wing about the party's direction was always present. Churchill, working with a small majority, had attempted on becoming Prime Minister to form a Conservative–Liberal government rather than a purely Conservative one. His government contained National-Liberals, although the Liberal Party leader refused a Cabinet post. Churchill's attempts to include even more Liberals in Cabinet resulted in the 1922 Committee of Conservative backbench MPs voicing their suspicions. His appointment of individuals to key ministries whose sympathies were in keeping with the spirit of the *Industrial Charter* would have reinforced these suspicions. The Conservative Right's long-standing perception of Butler, with his acceptance of Keynesian economics, was that he was little better than a Socialist. They viewed 'Butskellism' as synonymous with Socialism. Similarly, the appointment of Walter Monckton to the Ministry of Labour, a politician known to be on the left of the party and preferring to be above party description, would not have reassured the Right in their desire to counter trade unions. Likewise, the decision to entrust the Ministry of Housing to Harold Macmillan concerned those who equated increased government spending with Socialism because of his pre-war advocacy of government controls and economic interference as seen in his book *The Middle Way* (1938). Macmillan had even proposed changing the Conservative Party name to 'The New Democratic Party'.[1] In contrast, right-wingers were notably absent from Churchill's Government. Moreover, this apparent favouring of progressives over right-wingers appeared to extend to the party bureaucracy. Formed in 1951, for example, the Bow Group became swiftly one of the most prominent progressive Conservative groups. By August 1952, Central Office viewed the Bow Group's work as 'an asset to the Party'. The Bow Group's Annual Report for 1952 acknowledged that Central Office assisted it, and named the individuals concerned. Thereafter, Central Office entered into a 'Memorandum of Agreement' with the Bow Group, a legal document outlining the financial and publishing terms under which it distributed Bow Group publications. Right-wingers may have been ignorant about the Bow Group's legal relationship with Central Office, but they can hardly have failed to notice the distribution of its progressive material, which they considered left-wing.

Churchill's reputation probably muted the degree of right-wing criticism because it remained an electoral asset. However, the right wing was never silent.

As early as 1952, there were complaints that the government was not carrying out a 'Conservative policy'. Monckton's settlement of the 1953 railway dispute on terms favourable to the unions drew criticism from Conservative MPs into the open. Butler's utilisation of the 'peace dividend' to produce tax cuts and increase spending avoided criticism from the right becoming too serious, but did not remove it completely, as seen in right-wing Conservative MPs' opposition to pension increases. New circumstances provided other avenues for the right to criticise the government. The docking of the *Empire Windrush* in 1948, which symbolised that Britain was no longer simply an exporter of people to the Empire, had introduced into British politics the issue of New Commonwealth, i.e. black, immigration. At the end of 1952, Churchill raised the issue of immigration in Cabinet, but delusions of Empire and concern not to disrupt the nascent Commonwealth meant that no policy emerged. The complacency of Conservative ministers over immigration contrasted with restiveness among Conservative supporters. Concerns had grown. A change of leader did not alleviate them. Continuing restiveness among Constituency Associations after Eden became Prime Minister, including complaints that his government failed to tackle trade union power while the middle class increasingly bore the financial burdens of government. Stephen Pierssene, Central Office General Director, warned Eden of the possible consequences in the wake of the March 1956 West Walthamstow by-election, stating that the middle class had not had a fair deal and were looking for alternatives to the Conservatives.

Concerns existed in imperial and foreign policy also. Churchill's staunch support for Empire failed to stem criticism of imperial policy. His anti-Communism was a matter of public record since his 'Iron Curtain' speech, but it failed to prevent criticism over foreign policy. Conservative local associations castigated the government for a perceived lack of emphasis on the Empire and 'Britishness'. The government, lacking support from the USA to maintain a military presence in the Middle East, commenced negotiations to withdraw British forces from east of Suez. This decision seemed to justify local associations' complaints. The parliamentary right reacted by forming the Suez Group in December 1953. Among the Suez Group's members was Enoch Powell, the dejected Conservative Research Department member who had buried his head in his hands at the granting of Indian Independence.[2] In December 1953, forty-one Conservative MPs signed an Early Day Motion rejecting their own government's policy. Their belief that the government propounded policies that moderate Labour MPs deemed 'Bevanite' a mere twelve months ago, showed the anger they felt towards their own government. Ramsden identified this period as the 'moment at which the Conservative right started to move away from the front bench's international policy',[3] a fracture within the Conservative Party that would continue for the remainder of the century. However, the number of Conservative rebels actually declined to twenty-eight when the bill proposing British withdrawal from Egypt appeared in the House of Commons in October 1954. Right-wing Conservative MPs' objective of halting this ignominy seemed even more remote when Foreign Secretary Anthony Eden succeeded Churchill because he was the individual most closely associated with withdrawal from east of Suez. To those outside the parliamentary party, Imperial decline probably appeared the policy of collusive frontbenches.

Conservative governments of 1951–57 were clearly not ones of Conservative reaction. They were centrist administrations that realised that the electorate approved of Labour's post-war programme, which meant that there was little prospect of a substantial return to the Conservatism of the inter-war years. They were also governments with a leadership apparently unable to deal with domestic and foreign affairs. Both situations alienated the Conservative Party's right wing, who joined groups attacking the government from the right. Discontent over domestic policies led Conservatives to seek redress in movements that promised economic liberty. Die-hard imperialists occupied the space on the Conservative Party's right flank as the government 'scuttled' from empire. The Conservative leadership's objective was to remain in power, regardless of these right-wing critics. Its decision to maintain a consensual economic policy so as not to alienate the electorate, and to seek disentanglement from costly overseas commitments, were difficult policies for a party that contained supporters of laissez-faire and imperialism, but essential for one that had decided to adapt to new circumstances. However, this decision also meant that the Conservative Party could not afford to let the extreme right succeed.

Central Office remained the leadership's foremost agent in meeting its objective of limiting the extreme-right's impact. It continued to collect information on groups that it had investigated while the Conservative Party was in opposition. Sometimes, this action resulted in Central Office deciding that a group was 'extreme' rather than just right-wing. New groups emerged. Some enjoyed a positive relationship with Central Office, especially if they could assist the Conservative Party to disseminate views on economic policy that remained inexpedient for the government to endorse openly. In contrast, Central Office had a negative relationship with those groups that openly and vociferously sought to cajole the Conservative leadership into adopting economically liberal policies. Central Office commissioned reports on these groups and took measures to counter their impact. However, Central Office saved its strongest countermeasures for those individuals or groups that it believed had fascist antecedents, or advocated policies that the Conservative Party's opponents could portray as characteristics of fascism or Nazism. These individuals and groups could rekindle memories of the Conservative Party's inter-war association with the extreme right, especially if they exhibited the anti-Semitism or racism commonly associated with right-wing extremism. The emergence of skin colour as a phenomenon in British politics exacerbated these fears. Consequently, Central Office blocked the political career of at least one former member of Mosley's British Union of Fascists. It strongly advised party officers and members not to join groups with connections to Nazism, no matter how tangential these connections were. Central Office mobilised the party bureaucracy against these groups and sometimes openly accused them of fascism. This was an especially risky strategy when some of these groups contained Conservative Party members.

Existing concerns

Central Office correspondence makes it clear that its desire to avoid association with the extreme right remained consistent and overrode fears of alienating its own right wing. In February 1952, a Central Office Area Agent requested information on the Fighting Fund for Freedom. This desire for information could have been be due to ignorance on the Agent's part. Alternatively, it may have reflected Central Office's successful avoidance of too obvious an association with the FFF, as seen in the rebuke of an official disseminating incorrect information on it.[4] Central Office's response to the new request showed that its opinion of the FFF had now hardened, and why. Mr Watson at Central Office advised a colleague that he would not respond in writing to the Agent, as he would 'prefer the matter to be dealt with verbally'. This is a reminder that written comments were only one medium by which Central Office blocked the extreme right. Watson felt sure that his colleague had 'the necessary information in your files which, together with your own recollections', would enable him to provide the Agent with the information requested. A memorandum attached to Watson's communication explained his circumspection. It advised that, the FFF was an 'Extreme Right Wing Organisation', which supported the Conservative Party but was 'likely to compromise us in their zeal'. This is the first time that Central Office revealed clearly its opinion of the FFF's political nature. It is perhaps not coincidental that Sir Waldron Smithers was no longer associated with the FFF.[5]

Central Office continued to monitor others it had already deemed either incorrigible or too extreme, as well as those it was initially unsure about like the FFF. Central Office noted the *Daily Mail's* report of Andrew Fountaine's attempted formation of a National Front Movement in 1952. This action suggested that Central Office remained concerned about Fountaine. Central Office anxiety is also evident when the British Housewives' League reappeared. BHL members were angry at Chancellor Butler's imposition of Purchase Tax on household and kitchen articles in the autumn Budget of 1955, and threatened a revival in Rochdale. Central Office instructed the informing Agent to 'watch this carefully in your Area and, if you find evidence of activity of this kind in any constituency, perhaps you would let me know', which suggests that Central Office had not altered its opinion about the BHL.

However, it is not always possible to be definite about the reasons for Central Office's attitudes towards certain organisations. For example, Central Office continued to receive reports of, and material from, The Society for Individual Freedom. SIF had maintained a benign position to the right of the Conservative Party in opposition, with a stated objective of coordinating an attempt to resist the drift towards collectivism. Now that the Conservative Party was in Government, SIF criticised it when it felt it did not fulfil SIF's aims. Marjorie L. A. Franklin, for SIF, forwarded in February 1952 a SIF article regarding the 1951 General Election titled, 'For the enlightenment and disillusionment of such members of the Conservative Party as may be disposed to be complacent regarding the result'. The SIF article chided the Conservative Government for failing to promise tough enough measures in its manifesto, such as repeal of the Trades Dispute Act, and warned that the economy was a tottering ruin. It also condemned the Conservative Government for failing to curb the National Coal Board and the unions. Central Office might have thought SIF's attitude towards the government already fixed because the article appeared a mere four months after the 1951 General Election. Those that the article named as responsible for the Government's failure would have reinforced Central Office's view, identifying Monckton and Butler as appointments that were 'enough to force the most docile and house-trained eyebrows to elevate in surprise'. SIF had specifically attacked cabinet members identified as being on the Conservative Party's left wing, with Butler's emergency Budget attracting particular criticism.

Central Office responded to SIF's attack on the government with only minimal counter-measures. When SIF's Director General requested assistance in approaching Conservative members six months after their critical article, Central Office Area Agent Brigadier Rawcliffe replied that Conservative Associations might see such an action as harmful to their interests and thus as unhelpful. Rawcliffe informed Central Office of his reply, and stated that, 'I am inclined to feel that we have enough troubles of our own and that if we encourage our own supporters to join we might lose them'. Rawcliffe's comments support three possible conclusions: a basic desire not to lose members; a belief that SIF would bring problems; and that SIF's objectives appealed to Conservative members. Rawcliffe's correspondence typified many between Central Office and its Area Agents regarding SIF. However, there is little evidence of any stronger counter-measures by Central Office, save for an anodyne response after Eden became Prime Minister that identified SIF as a 'small right wing association'. The problem facing Central Office, apart from concern over the impact on party membership, is that the ubiquitous Sir Waldron Smithers MP consistently promoted SIF and was one of its leading members. Smithers had instructed Franklin to forward SIF's warning to the newly elected Conservative Government. He wrote personally to John Hare at Central Office lauding SIF's activities, and asked Hare and his friends to become members, and requested a donation. Smithers also requested that Central Office distribute a SIF-sanctioned publication that addressed the world's spiritual and moral crisis. Central Office could not afford to denounce SIF as extremist when a Conservative MP was a prominent member and while the government only had a slim majority. Therefore, it acted cautiously. The Chief Publicity Officer requested 7,500 copies of the publication that Smithers had asked Central Office to distribute, enquiring how many would be free of charge. However, SIF had not actually written this publication, and Central Office files do not contain any 'Memorandum of Agreement' setting out a formal relationship with SIF, unlike that with the Bow Group.[6] Nevertheless, the Chief Publicity Officer's request does show that Central Office was prepared at this stage to have a relationship with SIF that was similar to the one it had with Aims of Industry.[7]

Central Office's relationship with Aims of Industry, if anything, became closer. AIMS continued to assist Central Office's intelligence-gathering, although the material was hardly secret. For example, AIMS Director Roger Sewill forwarded to Central Office positive media responses to Government legislation. Central Office also accepted the results of AIMS's research into industry. Its General Director informed a colleague of a conversation he had with AIMS's Roger Sewill, stating that he welcomed 'any research into industry which his organisation could undertake'. The General Director's comment was a reference to AIMS's 'Industrial Information Service'. When Central Office accepted use of this service, it once again entered into a financial relationship with AIMS. AIMS also embarked on a campaign explaining the country's problems to the electorate in simple terms. The first plank of this campaign was the production of explanatory films. AIMS requested permission to use in a film a quotation from one of Churchill's wartime speeches. AIMS's request resulted in the Prime Minister's office asking Central Office for 'your observations on the standing of the organisation and your advice on whether the Prime Minister should allow them to use this quotation in the way suggested'. This request showed that the Prime Minister's office knew that Central Office was the accepted repository of information on outside organisations. Whether Churchill acceded to AIMS's request is unclear, but Central Office unarguably supported AIMS's films. In October 1952, Central Office arranged for senior officials, including Chairman Woolton and General Director Pierssene, to view AIMS's production *Point of No Return*. Woolton and Pierssene were unable to attend on the day, but Central Office nevertheless sent representatives. These representatives reported to the General Director and Chief Publicity Officer that the film was 'first-class propaganda from our point of view'. However, AIMS's laissez-faire views were just a little too much to the right of a Conservative government that had accepted much of the Attleean settlement. Therefore, Central Office ensured that AIMS was removed from the credits in the public showing of *Point of No Return*, and stipulated that 'we should not be connected with it in any way ourselves at this stage'.

Nevertheless, Central Office was unarguably more positive towards AIMS than other group to the right of the Conservative Party. AIMS's objectives and methods resonated with the views of many Conservatives who realised that their party had to adapt to the new paradigm revealed by Labour's victory in 1945, not just with those like Smithers who wished to return to pure laissez-faire. Prominent among Conservatives that understood the need to adapt was the One Nation Group. E. H. H. Green described the One Nation Group as seeking 'to construct a distinctive Conservative position on the role of the State which avoided "me-tooing Socialist solutions" … to blend judicious Statism with strong inflections of liberal market, laissez-faire ideas'.[8] It was far from being extreme. Central Office gathered information on the One Nation Group in accord with its remit, but its attitude towards it was benign from the beginning, even positive. This was because the One Nation Group attempted the acceptable objective of demonstrating how Conservatism met post-war Britain's demands. In early 1952, Central Office supported the 'One Nation Campaign', a countrywide tour in which the One Nation Group disseminated its views on how the Conservative Party could remain relevant in post-1945 Britain. Central Office also supported the One Nation Group because its members worked with Central Office. Angus Maude, founder member of the One Nation Group, worked at the Conservative Political Centre within Central Office. Central Office's General Director, S. H. Pierssene, asked Maude for his fellow One Nation Group member's reactions to the 'One Nation Campaign'. Maude's response revealed that the One Nation Group members put themselves at the disposal of the Speaker's Department at Central Office, and went where that department instructed. Pierssene responded encouragingly to the One Nation Group's actions, and suggested meeting to discuss further arrangements. However, Maude also identified a problem. He stated that most audiences were bad because they were mainly Conservative supporters, and argued that there was no point in going to strongly Conservative constituencies, whereas the One Nation Campaign had achieved a positive reaction on the few occasions it ventured into Labour areas. However, Maude's 'problem' accorded with Central Office's own objective of disseminating the Conservative Party's message to a section of the electorate that had voted heavily for Labour after the Second World War. That the One Nation Group complemented its work also explained Central Office's positive attitude toward it.

This similarity of objectives also explained Central Office's positive attitude towards AIMS. AIMS also organised a series of meetings, known as the 'Brains Trust'. AIMS ostensibly formulated these meetings to provide audiences with a broad range of opinion. These meetings attracted Central Office attention. Mr Hearn at Central Office deputed a Mr Chandler to attend the Brains Trust meeting at Nottingham in 1954. Hearn concluded from Chandler's subsequent report that the meeting was 'probably too broad to be partisan', but nevertheless advised that, 'it is predominantly right-wing and Aims of Industry always make sure that is the majority view of the platform'. Reports provided to Central Office by AIMS showed that the audiences' questions supported Conservative views. This was a consistent feature of Brains Trust meetings, which local newspapers reported. In Rochdale, the dominant topic was strikes unsupported by unions.[9] Such strikes were occurring in the docks and railways at the time. At the Cardiff meeting, restrictive practices that adversely affected Cardiff and Bristol docks generated most interest.[10] At the Wigan meeting, negative comments on Attlee's argument that China should control Formosa vied with condemnation of poor road conditions.[11] At Stirling, the audience discussed strikes, housing, and local government,[12] as did audiences in areas as diverse as Falkirk and Grangemouth.[13] Therefore, AIMS provided the valuable service of propagating Conservative Party thinking to a polarised people. Hearn revealed awareness of this service when he said that, 'From our point of view the hope is that floaters, particularly, will be convinced by the majority arguments of the Aims of Industry platform and when they hear something similar from a Conservative platform also will take our side.' Furthermore, there is also a hint of collusion between AIMS and Central Office. Mr Horton at Central Office commented on the locations of future Brains Trust meetings and wrote that, 'I am glad to know that the Aims of Industry are running their next season's Brains Trust in our marginal areas.'

Indeed, the location of AIMS's Brains Trust meetings provides the key to Central Office's positive attitude. Butlins holiday camps had mushroomed after the Second World War. New sites at Skegness and Clacton added to pre-war camps at Filey (1945), Pwllheli (1947), Ayr (1947), and Mosney (1948). In the 1950s, Billy Butlin acquired hotels in Blackpool, Brighton, and Cliftonville. Northern towns decamped virtually en-masse for holiday activities that went far beyond the 'knobbly-knees' contests of popular memory. Butlins in the 1950s provided middle- and even highbrow entertainments to a clientele that was more diverse than subsequent ones. As represented in *Hindle Wakes* (1951), when almost the whole town's inhabitants went on holiday to Blackpool and its factory workers mingled with managers and even owners, social interaction between different classes often ensued. Therefore, Butlins potentially provided a sizeable audience for AIMS's propaganda, and thus the Conservative Party's, away from the divisions of the factory and shop floor. In April 1954, AIMS's Roger Sewill boasted to Lord Woolton at Central Office that its Brains Trust meetings had been successful, and a further eighteen were already arranged at Butlins holiday camps. This, Sewill indicated, meant that the Conservative message would reach many people, with 'audiences of 1000 per time guaranteed', which Sewill underlined for emphasis. Woolton forwarded this information to Mr Chapman-Walker at Central Office, showing his interest by his terse but revealing comment: 'You ought to see this.' The press was soon reporting the impact of using Butlins for Brains Trust meetings. The *Recorder* mentioned Billy Butlin's decision to become involved, focusing on the audiences' response to specific questions. It referred to the adverse effects of nationalisation, and opined, 'It might be thought that to make such remarks in front of an audience, the majority of which must have been Labour-inclined, would be flaunting with the possibilities of a riot.'[14] Nor was the positive response of Brains Trust audiences limited to domestic issues. Sewill forwarded to Central Office a report by a Mr Hunt, Head of Public Relations at AIMS, which focused on a particular audience's response. Hunt also thought that the audience was 'predominantly Labour supporters', but reported that the answer given by a right-wing panellist to a question regarding the impropriety of a visit by Attlee and other Labour leaders to the newly Communist China, received a tumultuous response. Central Office's political exploitation of the cultural phenomenon provided by Billy Butlin also explains its positive relationship with AIMS.

This does not mean that Central Office took no counter-measures against AIMS. An AIMS representative in Lowestoft sought assistance from the local Conservative Association in contacting local industrialists. He offered to disseminate propaganda useful to the Conservative Party in return. However, the representative's additional offer to contribute to the local association from funds he had collected for AIMS caused concern. The Secretary of Lowestoft

Conservative Association informed the Central Office Area Agent, Brigadier Rawcliffe, that, 'This scheme would be quite unofficial and known only to the Officers of the Association and one or two leaders in local industry'. However, the Secretary thought the offer might be improper, and asked Rawcliffe if such a scheme was advisable or operated elsewhere. Rawcliffe sought Central Office clarification, adding that it was, 'a pity to encourage organisations which collect subscriptions from people who might otherwise support us and which make no comparable contribution to the maintenance of our own organisation'. General Director Piersenne replied that as, 'Aims of Industry professes to be a non-political organisation it would not be right for it to make money-raising arrangements with Conservative Associations', and added that AIMS's actions could deflect money from the local Conservative Association, as they were 'in some sense in competition'. These comments show that Central Office placed definite limits on the relationship it was prepared to have with AIMS.

It is unlikely that Piersenne was unaware of the existing financial relationship with AIMS. So, what explained Central Office reluctance to help the AIMS representative? Acceptance of cash rather than services in kind may have been a step too far. On the other hand, political circumstances had changed. Hitherto, most contact between Central Office and AIMS occurred during a Labour government with a large majority, or a Conservative one with a small majority. Piersenne, however, was writing after the 1955 General Election, when Eden had increased the Conservative majority to a comfortable fifty-nine. It is therefore possible that opportunism and necessity played a role in Central Office's previous decisions, and now that the Conservative government was more secure it wished to distance itself from this external right-wing organisation. For, although AIMS had proved useful in the objective of appealing to Labour voters when the party's hold on power was not secure, its particular form of 'extremism' was still problematic for a Conservative government that had adopted the consensual approach to domestic issues. Even when Eden removed R. A. Butler from the Chancellorship, he made no philosophical change to domestic affairs, and the consensual approach remained. Quite simply, the Conservative Party no longer needed AIMS and therefore Central Office did not want to draw attention to its connection with AIMS. There is evidence to support this. Central Office's Chief Publicity Officer wrote to Pierssene on the same day that Pierssene rejected the Lowestoft offer. He enclosed a draft letter to all Constituency Agents, Central Office Area Agents, and Assistant Publicity Officers, advising that he intended to accept an AIMS offer to supply literature to the Conservative Associations. The Chief Publicity Officer had consulted AIMS about such a possibility before the General Election. He advised Piersenne that, 'we are very short of material that we have produced ourselves for the use of the Constituency Associations,' and stated that this literature would be useful without the Conservative Party incurring any costs. This position was no different to previous cooperation between AIMS and Central Office. However, this time Piersenne declined the offer, justifying his decision by pointing out that 'Aims of Industry are at pains to proclaim themselves non-political and I don't think it would do them or us any good if we were distributing their material from here.' This comment suggests that a changed political context had altered Central Office's financial and possibly collusive relationship with this particular right-wing organisation.

Other organisations remained beyond the pale as far as Central Office was concerned. The Anti-Communist Guardian (ACG) was the resurrection of the Conservative Christian League, despite purporting to be a new organisation.[15] Central Office based its decision to shun the ACG on the knowledge that its proprietor, a Mr George De Courtenay, was a crook with convictions for larceny, false pretences and house breaking. Central Office noted that De Courtenay had ceased to use the title 'Conservative' in his bogus organisations after Parliament and the press exposed his convictions. Central Office also noted that De Courtenay continued his criminal activities despite public exposure, citing a conviction in January 1954. However, De Courtenay included an element of plausibility in his schemes like all good confidence tricksters. He claimed that prominent Conservatives supported the ACG, including them in its literature. These names included Sir Waldron Smithers MP. Central Office responded by denouncing De Courtenay and attempting to entice him into legal action against the Conservative Party. The main determinant of Central Office's position in the ACG's case was De Courtenay's disreputable character. Yet there is evidence that Central Office also used political criteria when it judged the ACG. It noted that the ACG had a possible association with anti-Semitism. Mr Gill at Central Office referred a colleague to the ACG publication *Voice of Freedom*, and stated, 'I would draw attention to the advertisement on page 3 for the Britons Publishing Society, an extreme anti-Semitic body which publishes scurrilous attacks on Jews.' The fact that the Britons Publishing Society also printed the *Voice of Freedom* emphasised the connection between the ACG and the Britons Publishing Society. Gill's comments are consistent with previous Central Office comments regarding the Britons Publishing Society.[16]

Stopping individuals with embarrassing antecedents from joining the party was not always possible, partly because of the autonomous nature of local Conservative Associations. This autonomy was particularly problematic for the Conservative Party at this time because former members of Mosley's British Union of Fascists had expressed their intention to vote Conservative immediately after the Second World War.[17] It was likely that some joined the Conservative Party. They may have explained membership of the BUF as misguided youthful indiscretion, attracting little attention if they were at the margins of Mosley's fascist party. John Charnley, however, was not a peripheral BUF figure.[18] All four of the Charnley brothers had joined Mosley's BUF. When the authorities banned the BUF's publication *Action* in 1940, it was John and a few others who had kept Mosley's message alive by publishing an eight-page booklet, *British Freedom*. By this stage, John had risen within the BUF, becoming its prospective parliamentary candidate for a Hull constituency at the next general election, expected in 1940. However, instead of becoming a politician, Charnley spent the bulk of the war years as an internee, keeping company with fellow

Mosleyites and members of other extreme-right organisations like Admiral Sir Barry Domvile. Charnley resumed his bakery business after the war, and soon became prominent in his local chamber of trade. He mixed with civic leaders and even enjoyed the hospitality of Conservative MP Ernest Maples on the House of Commons Terrace. Charnley also became involved with Union Movement, Mosley's post-war attempt at a political comeback. He claimed that he 'did not play a very active part in Union Movement affairs', but spoke at Union Movement meetings and contributed to the 'Small Shopkeepers Front' section in Mosley's publications *Union* and *Action*. Charnley understood that his continued support for Mosley meant that he had to be 'circumspect in the expression of my views', but soon experienced problems nonetheless. He had continued to receive the monthly 'Mosley News Letter' and attended meetings with Mosley from 1946. One meeting received press coverage and became public knowledge. This revelation forced Charnley to defend his actions before his local chamber of trade, which he described as keen to avoid depiction as a platform for neo-fascists. However, Charnley seems to have survived the revelation as his local Chamber of trade elected him President in 1952, perhaps proving that his connections with Mosley were no bar to civic advancement.

Indeed, by 1950 the local Conservative Association considered Charnley a pillar of the community. The Conservative Party had regained Ormskirk, the constituency in which Charnley lived, at the 1950 General Election. Ormskirk's Conservative MP, Sir Ronald Cross, had tried enticing Charnley into joining the Conservative Party on a number of occasions. Charnley believed Cross's actions were a precursor to his eventual adoption as a parliamentary candidate for the Conservative Party, and thus accepted an invitation to visit the home of the treasurer of the Ormskirk local Conservative Association. Charnley did not name the Treasurer, but described him as well-known and influential. Charnley also claimed that the Treasurer was aware of his support for Mosley, and hinted that the Treasurer was a Mosleyite too, but thought Mosley's political prospects were nil. The Treasurer offered Charnley the chairmanship of the Burscough and Latham Branch of the Conservative Party, plus support should Charnley seek parliamentary nomination. Charnley accepted the offer, and cited that he had done so to enable him to further Mosley's cause 'through less obvious channels.' Thereafter, Charnley helped successive Conservative Ormskirk MPs and stood as a Conservative in a local council election. As in civic life, it appeared that Charnley's support for Mosley was no barrier to political advancement. Therefore, Charnley applied to become a parliamentary candidate for the Conservative Party on 5 June 1954, after securing the support of three sponsors.[19] Central Office invited Charnley to an interview after he had also gained the support of Area Office in Manchester. Here, however, Charnley's political career met a Central Office roadblock. Asked at the interview whether he 'did not consider that my earlier commitment might be a deterrent against my acceptance', Charnley, perhaps unwisely, responded by pointing out that Churchill had changed allegiance during his political career. Central Office rejected Charnley's candidacy.

Why did Central Office reject Charnley? His comment about Churchill was a faux pas, but was this sufficient to disbar him, especially as Churchill's political career was not a secret? Moreover, the Conservative Party machine was quite capable of ensuring that a candidate avoided making such comments in public. That is, provided Central Office wanted the individual in the first place. So why did Central Office interview Charnley if they never wanted him as a candidate? It would have been difficult for Central Office to refuse Charnley the courtesy of an interview as he had gained acceptance at a local level, both in business and politics, and secured nominations from prominent members of the party. Central Office may also have been intrigued, and possibly even used the interview to elicit intelligence on former Mosleyites and their intentions, especially as immigration from the New Commonwealth was rising and Conservative MPs and Prospective Parliamentary Candidates (PPCs) had previously embroiled themselves in Mosley's 'anti-alien' campaigns immediately after the war.[20] Therefore, it is likely that when Central Office interviewed Charnley they had two objectives, one a matter of form, the other consonant with its role in gathering intelligence on extreme-right groups and individuals. That Central Office never intended to sanction Charnley's parliamentary candidature is easy to surmise. It did not even bother to inform him of their rejection. Charnley's subsequent failure to secure nomination to a safe council seat further proved that Central Office was determined to block his political career. This determination was evident when Central Office had the final decision over a local council nomination, and rejected Charnley despite the local Conservative Association previously having considered him suitable to be a parliamentary candidate. Charnley was in no doubt about the reason for persistent rejection: 'This small example of inside jiggery-pokery to prevent the election of a one-time Blackshirt rather dismayed me, and at the first suitable opportunity I withdrew from local politics.' Thus, not only had Central Office acted to prevent any national association between Charnley and the Conservative Party becoming widely known, it had additionally thwarted his local ambitions, and thereby minimised his connection with the party at a local level. It is hard to disagree with Charnley's claim that his attempt to become a Conservative Party parliamentary candidate 'must have been a dead duck from the start'. Also hampered thereafter was Charnley's civic career. Asked to serve as a local magistrate, Charnley was the only individual nominated by his sponsor ever denied this position. Nor, despite working for many trade associations and NHS Tribunals, did Charnley receive any official recognition, which Charnley later ascribed to 'behind-the-scenes chicanery'.

New concerns

The Conservative Party's information network continued bringing new organisations to Central Office's attention. A Mr Lee, the Chief Agent of the Bradford Conservative and National Liberal Association, wrote to General Director

Stephen Pierssene at Central Office in February 1952 requesting information on a group called Common Cause. Common Cause had invited one of Lee's ward secretaries to become one of its local secretaries. Lee included a Common Cause leaflet outlining its objectives and asked whether Conservative members should support this new organisation. The events that he set in motion showed how Central Office interest in an outside organisation developed, and why. Central Office ascertained that people interested in combating Communism had attended Common Cause's inaugural meeting in November 1951, where they agreed to hold a six-day conference in London in May 1952. The General Director saw little cause for alarm regarding party members, and advised Lee that, 'I feel that at this stage we should not give active party support to the movement, although there does not seem to be any reason why individual Conservatives should not join it.' Yet, Piersenne's caution about potential for embarrassment to the Conservative Party remained, which meant that he advised a slightly firmer line regarding the ward secretary. Pierssene stated that, 'the position of the ward secretary of your Association may be a little difficult if he is to become secretary of the local branch of Common Cause as well, and if I were you I should tactfully discourage him from accepting the office'. Nevertheless, Piersenne was initially nonchalant towards Common Cause. However, his attitude changed within a month. Lee had continued to supply Central Office with Common Cause literature, plus information on its leadership structure. Piersenne circulated the literature to others within Central Office. The Chief Publicity Officer now suggested that Central Office should make unofficial enquiries about Common Cause and deferentially ask its aristocratic Chairman for his comments before providing advice to all constituencies. Pierssene agreed, and added that, 'it would be just as well to see the lines on which it is developing and what its plans and prospects are'. What explains this altered attitude?

The method by which Common Cause created its 'groups' questioned its claim of political neutrality. A Central Office report described how 'prosperous and leisured people' initially gathered as a 'group'; but only transformed into a 'branch' when supporters of all three political parties joined it. This gave Common Cause a class perspective as well as a status one. Some of the names associated with Common Cause, such as Major-General Richard Hilton and Field Marshall Wilson, supported the notion that status was an important factor in its composition, but the existence of trade unionists provided the possibility of socialist influence. In March 1952, Piersenne expressed the fear that Common Cause could become another Fighting Fund for Freedom or Society for Individual Freedom, but in August 1952, a Central Office Area Agent reported concerns over the presence of two socialists acting as organisers of Common Cause's Sheffield branch. Central Office's decision to send two observers to Sheffield raises the possibility that it decided to investigate Common Cause because it believed it was a vehicle for the left wing. This is a confused picture, although Piersenne's comments suggest that Central Office was more concerned about the extreme right rather than the left.

Yet, Common Cause's aims did not seem extreme. The Common Cause literature forwarded to Central Office welcomed 'all who support political democracy, cultural freedom and the rule of Law against totalitarianism and dictatorship'. Common Cause claimed that it had many regional, and professional, branches, plans for an information centre, and that the creation of a parliamentary group was imminent. However, its requests for assistance and funds negated these grandiose claims, while its claims of various political and religious affiliations seemed to lessen the possibility of sectarianism or sectional interest. Thus, Central Office was unlikely to fear that Common Cause was a sectarian, potential rival. Moreover, Common Cause declared its opposition to fascism, and sought to distance itself from the pre-war British right and its links with fascism. It represented fascism as an alien ideology, proclaiming that it opposed 'fascism of every hue (whether black, brown or red) and of every nationality (whether Italian, German, Russian, Spanish or British).' Yet, this was simply special pleading, a self-serving smokescreen behind which Common Cause attempted to hide its embarrassing pre-war antecedents. It is unlikely that Common Cause's statements fooled Central Office for long. The address it provided to forward funds to, 66c Elizabeth Street, London, SW1, may have alerted Central Office. Central Office possibly knew that the proprietor of this address was Hugh Grosvenor, the Second Duke of Westminster. It may or may not have known that Grosvenor provided this office free of charge, or that Common Cause shared this address with an organisation assisting a known Nazi collaborator. However, it is inconceivable that Central Office was ignorant of Grosvenor's pre-war connection to the extreme right and the suspicion that he was a fifth columnist.[21] Moreover, Central Office definitely did know that Lord Malcolm Douglas-Hamilton was the Chairman of Common Cause. The Chief Political Officer had identified Douglas-Hamilton as such when he responded to the circulated Common Cause material. Recently released MI5 documents show Lord Douglas-Hamilton secretly flew aircraft to assist Franco in the Spanish Civil War.[22] It is feasible to assume that the Conservative Home Secretary knew this, and that senior Central Office officials did so too given their well-known connections to the intelligence services. Therefore, the fact that Lord Douglas-Hamilton was also a Conservative and Unionist MP could hand the damaging information to the Conservative Party's enemies. If so, Westminster's involvement would only have added to Central Office concern. This explained Central Office's change of attitude, which by the end of January 1953 had become one marked by vigilance, action, and discouragement. Central Office's Miss Fletcher now personally questioned a member of Common Cause as she had with The Guild of Good Neighbours.[23] Although Fletcher concluded that Common Cause's aims were unexceptionable, she stated that she had 'gained the impression that this is an organisation which we would be unwise to ignore, and I think we should do well to watch it'. Central Office consequently altered its advice not to join Common Cause to include all Conservative Party supporters, not just its officials.

The contrast between Central Office's negative attitude towards Common Cause and its positive stance towards another newly formed organisation further supports the idea that its perception of their nature shaped it. The organisation's name was Drake's Drum, in line with the dawn of a new Elizabethan Age. Elizabeth II had succeeded George VI on 6 February 1952. The name 'Drake's Drum' referred to the time of Elizabeth I, an earlier English golden age. It also possessed connotations of palingenesis, which Griffin argued was one characteristic of fascist groups.[24] Later theories cannot be attributed retrospectively to the thinking of 1950s Central Office officials, but it is likely that Central Office recognised Drake's Drum as a right-wing organisation from its name. As usual, Area Agents requested information on the organisation, the first record of such being in March 1952. The signature of Drake's Drum leader, Mary Parsons, matched that of the Mary Parsons of the British Housewives' League. Therefore, Central Office wariness about Drake's Drum would be understandable. However, requests for information about Drake's Drum consistently attracted the minimally refractory comments usually given to officials, or simple denials of its affiliation with the Conservative Party. Although Central Office stated that the Conservative Party was 'not in any way officially (or even mildly unofficially) connected with it', it had 'no objection to individual Conservatives supporting this effort if they so desire, in a private capacity'. Indeed, Central Office even appeared to sanction Drake's Drum when its Chief Publicity Officer described it as 'a perfectly respectable organization and one of which we approve'. This was far from the hostility that Central Office exhibited towards the British Housewives' League.

Again, expediency and opportunism explained Central Office's attitude towards Drake's Drum. Churchill's administration lacked confidence and, realising the true message of the 1951 General Election, sought to widen its appeal. However, instantaneous electoral change was unrealistic. Proving this was the electorate's rejection of the Conservative Party by nearly 57% in 1950 and 52% in 1951, despite ideological change in the *Industrial Charter*. The anti-Conservative vote appeared substantial and recalcitrant, which presented the Conservative Party with a problem of how to attract them. These voters would not switch to the Conservative Party if they were unconvinced by its acceptance of the Attleean settlement. As the Conservative Party's own appeal alone was insufficient to attract these hitherto hostile voters, it had adopted a covert strategy of using friendly organisations such as Aims of Industry to complement its realignment of party literature.[25] Like AIMS, Drake's Drum fitted this approach. Drake's Drum attempted to spread an anti-Communist appeal to the working class, and used Conservative trade unionists to distribute its literature because it believed that, 'through them we reach the most vital fields for our activities'. It described the realities of Communist rule in the Soviet Union, identified 'Moscow stooges' in the trade unions and warned of 'Soviet laws' coming to Britain unless the workers 'fight Communism – and win!' Thus, Drake's Drum provided Central Office with a useful and non-attributable medium for achieving their objective of spreading the Conservative Government's message.

Numerous comments supported the existence of this positive relationship, and the reasons for it. A Mr Chapman-Walker at Central Office secured for Drake's Drum adequate paper supplies at a time when it remained in short supply. In April 1952, Parsons thanked Chapman-Walker for his 'generous help in supplying paper'. Central Office reassured Conservative officials that it had legally vetted all of Drake's Drum literature. Parsons promised not to use the Conservative Party organisation to spread Drake's Drum literature. Central Office revealed Parson's promise not to implicate the Conservative Party 'in any way' despite doing 'some quite useful propaganda work in our interests', and denied the existence of any institutional connection. Parsons stressed to distributors that Drake's Drum 'must remain entirely unofficial and dissoci-ated from Conservative Party activities'. The Chief Publicity Officer, mean-while, revealed that Drake's Drum could reach 'people whom we cannot get at in the normal way'. These comments explain why Central Office applied its least refractory stance towards Drake's Drum: regardless of Parson's previous affiliations and the name of her organisation. Drake's Drum was useful to the Conservative Government.

Fear of Communism also lay behind the emergence of the League of Empire Loyalists (LEL), an extreme-right group that focused on Communism's impact on the British Empire. Churchill and Eden's Government had adopted a harsh line towards imperial tensions, which suggested a desire to maintain overseas possessions. British forces brutally crushed the Mau Mau rebellion in Kenya and contained Communist insurgency in Malaya. Opposition to British involve-ment in Cyprus resulted in the jailing of the Greek Cypriot leader Archbishop Makarios in 1956. However, this picture of a government determined to with-stand threats to the Empire was illusory. In June 1952, Eden presented his assessment of Britain's overseas commitments to the Cabinet, highlighting Britain's inability to meet current demands and recommending transference of these burdens. In the same year, Britain withdrew its Governor from the Gold Coast, allowing Kuame Nkrumah to become Prime Minister only one year after the British released him from prison. Imperial prospects in Asia also looked bleak, with a solution to racial tensions between Malays and Chinese unlike-ly against a background of an increasingly powerful Communist China plus recent Indonesian independence and colonial war in Indo-China. In Europe, the jailing of Makarios had only served to provide the Cypriot Independence movement, Enosis, with a martyr barely one year after its creation in 1955. The Conservative governments may have tried to give the impression that they pos-sessed the stomach to fight and were not retreating from Empire, but it is un-likely that the extreme right saw it this way because it was already suspicious at the direction of domestic policy.

Only Cabinet secrecy prevented public knowledge of Eden's recommen-dations and the confirmation of the extreme right's suspicions. However, the coronation oath of Queen Elizabeth II in 1953, which contained far vaguer claims to imperial domination than that of George VI in 1937, had set the tone. Additionally, the government's policy towards Egypt provided tangible proof of imperial abandonment, and reinforced right-wing fears. In 1953, Churchill had stressed that Britain's actions in Egypt would set the pace for us all over Africa and the Middle East, but did not elaborate on what the 'pace' was.[26] He realised Egypt's strategic significance. The Suez Canal provided access to the Red Sea and Britain's eastern territories. Thus, when Churchill acquiesced in the agreement that Foreign Secretary Eden forged with Egypt removing all British soldiers by June 1956, it seemed that the Empire was truly ending. Eden's failure when Prime Minister to secure Egypt's signature to the Baghdad Pact of February 1955 as a quid pro quo for British removal looked weak. The Pact's objective was to prevent the spread of Communist Russia's influence to the Middle East and North Africa by forming a buffer comprised of Iran, Iraq, Pakistan and Turkey, but it now lay in shreds. The Conservative Government looked like it could neither maintain the Empire nor counter the left's most extreme ideology. It had confirmed the imperial right's worst fears by abandoning the Conservative Party's link with imperialism, and in doing so opened political space on its right flank. The League of Empire Loyalists stepped into this space.

The LEL presented a more serious threat to the Conservative Party than all the other extreme-right movements hitherto. Founded in 1954, it operated on a firmer basis than any other right-wing or fascist movement since Mosley's pre-war heyday. This was mainly because an expatriate living in Chile financially assisted the LEL's founder, A. K. Chesterton, allowing him from 1953 to produce a regular publication, *Candour*, and attract a substantial membership in his quest to save the British Empire. Chesterton focused on the Empire, conflating the Soviet Union and America as the cause of its decline. His explanation appealed to many Conservatives' fear of Communism and cultural anti-Americanism. Chesterton's military and literary credibility also appealed. He had served in both world wars and gained the Military Cross in the process, which attracted many military figures to the LEL. Chesterton's employment at senior levels in Conservative publications provided him with an air of respectability. From April 1953, Chesterton was the literary advisor and personal journalist to Lord Beaverbrook and a senior writer for the Daily Express group. His co-authorship, with the Jewish writer J. Leftwich, of *The Tragedy of Anti-Semitism* (1948), added to the LEL's image of respectability. So, too, did the presence of establishment-sounding individuals on the LEL's Grand Council, such as Field Marshall Lord Ironside, The Earl of Buchan, Elizabeth Lady Freeman, and Lieutenant-General Sir Balfour Hutchinson. However, the Conservative Party bureaucracy was hostile towards the LEL from the beginning. Central Office commissioned substantial reports that detailed the LEL's membership and collected intelligence material that far outstripped those it had acquired for any other outside organisation, and made it clear that membership of the LEL by any Conservative was unacceptable.

The LEL's written attacks and publicity stunts help to explain Central Office increased interest and action. Chesterton produced a series of publications titled '*Sound The Alarm*' to accompany the LEL's launch in 1954, at the height of concerns over withdrawal from east of Suez. These publications overwhelmingly attacked the Conservative Government's imperial policy. Chesterton exonerated Churchill of treasonable intent, but accused him of self-delusional culpability. He stated that, 'Sir Winston, after all his brave words, now presides over the liquidation of the British Empire, but so potent is the alchemy of his mind that no doubt he persuades himself that the process is really one of wafting the Empire to the sunlit uplands of his wartime imagining.'[27] Chesterton did not extend any leniency to other government leaders or the Conservative Party. The Labour Government may have lost Ceylon and Burma, weakened Britain's position in Malaya, and negatively affected Britain's oil supplies by abnegating Britain's sphere of interest in Persia, but it was the Conservative Party's acceptance of these policies in Opposition, and their continuance of them when in power, that had resulted in the 'rot at the core of Churchillian Conservatism'. Chesterton described Conservative leaders as collectively giving 'every appearance of working for the abrogation of our national sovereignty as their supreme political objective', thereby levelling a charge of treachery. Nor did the parliamentary party fare any better. Chesterton portrayed the Conservatives as giving the Empire away as quickly as the Socialists had done, and noted there had been 'only one or two protests from those whom some have supposed, too charitably, to be the custodians of the imperial cause'. Thus, Chesterton argued, all Conservative MPs were complicit in this treachery. This was a particularly odious and irritating charge to put while memories of the Second World War were still fresh, and was a recurring theme in Chesterton's *Sound The Alarm* series.

However, this charge was not as irritating or embarrassing as the LEL's publicity stunts. Churchill's resignation in April 1954 had triggered a wave of LEL protests focused on his successor, Anthony Eden, the man most closely associated with the policy of 'scuttle' from Empire. The LEL protested against the first visit of Soviet leaders in April 1956, delivering a wreath in memory of those killed under Communist rule and a 10-foot long silver spoon to Eden at 10 Downing Street. In the following month, LEL member John Bean interrupted Eden at a Conservative gathering at Warwick Castle, presenting him with a black scuttle and loudly declaring that it was 'in view of the development of your Empire policies'. In August 1956, Bean was one of the LEL protesters who gatecrashed the Suez Conference at Lancaster House. A female LEL member hid backstage at a Young Conservative meeting at the Royal Festival Hall in late 1956, and walked straight on to the platform while Eden was speaking and protested against suppression of the recent Hungarian uprising, with John Bean shouting slogans from the rear of the hall before stewards removed him. The individual who attacked Eden at Bradford was an LEL member,[28] and Bean was the 1950 recruit to Mosley's Union Movement who had rejected the Conservative Party as not reflecting his views.[29] Bean had joined the League of Empire Loyalists in 1955 in desperation at Union Movement's tactics, but only after a two-month spell in the Conservative Party in 1953 had confirmed his earlier views. The publicity stunts that Bean and his LEL colleagues engaged in occurred in an increasingly televisual age, and thus brought into the living rooms of millions of voters the image of Conservatism divided and a government assailed by many erstwhile voters irritated at imperial betrayal. It made Eden look a fool.

Central Office's adoption of more stringent counter-measures proved how seriously it took the LEL. Urgent, negative replies replaced nonchalant advice that individual members were free to join outside organisations. In May 1955, a Colonel Harrison of Eye Division informed Central Office that he had met a constituent whom the LEL had placed on its Council. Central Office responded with the formulation of a 'short but forceful brief' for Harrison enabling him to show the constituent why the Conservative Party 'do not approve of their activities'. The description of the task of formulating this brief as 'top priority', and the command to produce it at the 'earliest possible moment', revealed Central Office's sense of urgency. In the same month, the Conservative Parliamentary Prospective Candidate for Darlington, Sir Fergus Graham, sought elucidation from Central Office of the full case against the LEL after discovering that his 'most eloquent and able' lieutenant was a supporter. The General Director feared legal action and did not give extensive comments. The LEL's willingness to use legal action when it felt defamed, winning at least fourteen libel cases during its existence, explained the General Director's reticence. However, the General Director also referred to the 'full case against the League', which revealed that Central Office was indeed making 'a case'. He also inferred that this 'case' was stronger than that usually constructed, and that Central Office would probably disseminate it more widely than usual. The existence of press articles reporting party officials' comments about the LEL within Central Office files supports the idea of a coordinated campaign against it. This is unsurprising as the LEL's publications and actions had angered Central Office. The General Director failed to understand how any Conservative member could have any connection with an organisation engaged in the 'violent denigration of the Prime Minister'. Central Office correspondence also reveals a tangible sense of alarm over the LEL's potential impact on the Conservative Party, not least the 'careful scrutiny' of membership applications when it feared that the LEL was attempting infiltration of the Conservative Party. Yet, no matter how irritating or embarrassing the LEL comments and stunts were, they do not explain adequately Central Office's increased activity, especially not the fear of legal action by the LEL and concern that it was acquiring a foothold within the Conservative Party. This is because these comments mask the main reason for Central Office's attitude.

The LEL's earliest publications revealed that anti-Semitism was central to its philosophy. They portrayed Jews as systematically setting about the destruction of national institutions, countries, and empires, and the creation of internationalist organisations in pursuit of their objective of world dominance via one-world government. Thus, the Jews were the hidden hand behind all the wars and revolutions that had resulted in the fall of monarchies, and any subsequent disingenuous attempts at collectivist guarantees against their repetition. They had removed the Bourbons by means of the French Revolution, while the Habsburgs, Romanovs, and Hohenzollerns fell during the Jewish-financed First World War. However, these publications argued that the British monarchy had proved resilient to the anti-monarchism unleashed across Europe by the Jews. Thus, as the League of Nations, the initial vehicle of one-world government, had proved incapable of delivering their objective, the Jews set about destroying the British monarchy at its periphery, i.e. the British Empire, and instigated the Second World War to cripple Britain financially. However, to ensure that there would be no repetition of the League of Nations failure, the Jews created a frightening post-1945 scenario of two opposed ideologies that possessed nuclear weapons and struggled for world domination. Therefore, American capitalism and Soviet Communism were the twin pillars of a bogus contest, the Cold War, containment of which the Jews provided for in the shape of new international organisations that were more powerful than the League of Nations, including the United Nations, NATO, SEATO and the Common Market. Chesterton concluded that nations' eventual subservience to these internationalist organisations would enable the Jewish denouement of one-world government. He claimed that there was substantial evidence that supported his conclusion. Churchill had become Prime Minister as an ardent opponent of Nazism and supporter of Empire. Yet he had succumbed to American pressure and commenced dismantling the Empire in return for American assistance in the 'Lend-Lease' programme. The American president who had pressurised Churchill was a Jewish emplacement, as were many American presidents. The 'New York Money Power' had provided American finance for 'Lend-Lease', abruptly ending it at the end of war in Europe, thereby forcing Britain to borrow heavily from America to finance domestic war damage and its military commitments in the unfinished conflict in the East. This, Chesterton said, had increased the advantage of the Jews' nominee, the American president, in securing further concessions from British Prime Ministers to dismantle the Empire. Should there be any doubt as to the real identity of the 'New York Money Power', the names of institutions and individuals that Chesterton identified were all Jewish.

Moreover, the LEL engaged in violent language and actions, and possessed the capacity to escalate it in search of its objectives. The LEL operated in a political milieu very different to that existing before the Second World War, one that eschewed political violence due to inter-war Fascism and Nazism. Nevertheless, the LEL advocated policies that necessitated violent solutions. Indian Independence had already provided a substantial impetus for colonies desiring independence. The LEL's objective of maintaining the Empire would require substantial force to deny aspirations that this impetus had fuelled. The LEL also condemned the decadent parliamentary democracy that it perceived as incapable of halting imperial decline. Its comments implied the possibility of limiting the franchise to those patriots who agreed with LEL objectives. Disenfranchising a part of the electorate also implied the requirement of force. More direct was the charge of treason levelled at the Conservative Government. Chesterton argued that dismantling the Empire was, 'treason, beyond doubt it is treason, to dissipate the heritage of a thousand years: to destroy the values which those thousand years have created, and prepare to hand over the sovereign right to our obedience'. The sentence for treason was capital punishment, and remained so until 1998. However, the gravity of this charge within a decade of the end of an existential conflict carried more weight. It is unlikely that Chesterton did not realise this, or that those he accused, or his readers, failed to notice. Less ephemeral were the LEL's actual activities. Violence frequently ensued. The LEL's protest against the visiting Soviet dignitaries in April 1956 resulted in its Organising Secretary, Leslie Greene, and her fellow protester receiving criminal convictions.

Thus, Chesterton held Jews responsible for the British Empire's collapse as part of a wider conspiracy to secure world domination less than a decade after a war against a regime that exterminated Jews as the cause of Germany's and the world's ills, and propounded remedies that were at least implicitly violent. His conspiracy theory and solutions smacked of Mosley's BUF. The antecedents of individuals in the LEL supported the view that it was a 1950s British throwback to right-wing extremism. Chesterton epitomised this personally. After leaving the BUF, Chesterton had maintained his extreme-right credentials by joining the Nordic League and becoming the editor of Lord Lymington's *New Pioneer* in 1939. Chesterton was also responsible for the failed attempt to form the National Front after Victory, a coalition of extreme-right organisations including the British People's Party. There were others in the LEL with fascist connections too. Leslie Greene's husband, Ben, was a former member of the British People's Party. Anthony Gittens was a partner in Clair Press, the printers of the LEL's *Candour*, but also provided a link with the Britons Publishing Society. P. J. Ridout, founder of the extreme-right British Empire Party that contested one seat in the 1951 General Election, was also a former member of the pre-war Imperial Fascist League.

Nor was the LEL's connection with the pre-war extreme right limited to these individuals. Historians have depicted members of the LEL as Colonel Blimp types determined to preserve a fast-disappearing world who gingered up the Conservative Party into preserving the Empire. The cartoonist David Low created Colonel Blimp as a symbol of foolish, reactionary right-wing establishment, but the subsequent film *The Life and Death of Colonel Blimp* (1943) sanitised Blimp into a confused but essentially harmless patriot. The LEL membership is replete with names fitting the 'Blimp' epithet, but they were often far from the sanitised film version. Major-General Richard Hilton was a member of Common Cause. Air Commodore G. S. Oddie was a pre-war member of the British People's Party, and stood as its candidate in the Combined Universities by-election of March 1946.[30] Furthermore, in Field Marshall Ironside, the LEL risked rekindling the link between the Conservative Party and a possibly treacherous pre-war extreme right in a way similar to Common Cause. Ironside's involvement with the pre-war Nazi-sympathising Anglo-German Fellowship countered any benign Blimp-type characterisation.[31] At a meeting on 12 November 1939, Major-General J. F. C. Fuller had revealed to Admiral Barry Domvile that Ironside supported the attempts of extreme-right groups like the Anglo-German Fellowship to halt the war with Nazi Germany. Domvile was a member of many extreme-right organisations, and the government subsequently interned him under Defence Regulation 18B during the war as a potential threat to national security. His recollections are therefore open to dismissal as confused, justificatory recollections. On the same basis, so could Fuller's as he was as a member of the Nordic League and involved in Lymington's *New Pioneer*. Pugh described 'Boney' Fuller as Britain's 'most remarkable Phoney War fascist', and argued that he was more a candidate for internment than promotion.[32] Nevertheless, Ironside attempted to have Fuller appointed his deputy Chief of the Imperial General Staff. The War Cabinet overruled Ironside, no doubt aware of Fuller's sympathies. Yet Ironside had supported Fuller at the highest political level. Therefore, it is difficult to accept that Fuller's claim to Domvile of Ironside's support was idle gossip. It is hardly credible that Fuller would intentionally harm such a powerful patron. Fuller was an LEL member. Even if Central Office was unaware of these connections and their potential for embarrassment, which seems unlikely, there was always Chesterton. As the post-war Deputy Editor of the Conservative publication *Truth*, Chesterton was also an example of the remaining nexus between the Conservative Party and the extreme right.

Regardless of whether the LEL as a whole was fascist, the actions, activities, and antecedents of its members, plus its racist philosophy, made it possible to suggest that it was. Its multifarious connections with the Conservative Party made it potentially extremely embarrassing. Central Office's actions revealed its awareness of this potential. It commissioned a report on the LEL and *Candour* in the same year that Chesterton launched them that highlighted fascist antecedents and anti-Semitic connections, and identified members of the LEL's National Council and National Executive. The report concluded that Chesterton's publications contained 'the familiar strain of Fascism and anti-American Semitism'. The consequence of Central Office's investigation was a circular to all Conservative MPs, PPCs, Constituency Agents, and Central Office Area Agents, stating that all enquiries about the LEL should receive the comment that the Conservative Party could not recommend it because of its fascist 'outlook'. It was LEL's fascist antecedents that most troubled Central Office. Party Chairman Lord Woolton responded to a Captain Duncan's concerns about the LEL's publicity stunt during the Soviet leaders' visit advising that, 'The driving forces behind these attacks are former members of Fascist and anti-Semitic organisations.' Herbert Lee, the Chief Conservative Agent for Bradford, informed the *Yorkshire Post* that the LEL appeared 'to be of similar character to that of the pre-war British Fascist Movement'. The Right Honourable Sir Reginald Dorman-Smith, former Governor of Burma, complained that the LEL had 'raped my Young Conservative Branch', and described it as 'being almost more Fascist than Oswald's lot'. These comments were both ironic and credible because Dorman-Smith had been a member of Lord Lymington's pro-Nazi English Array before the war.[33] However, proof that Central Office desired to avoid association with any post-war manifestation of fascism did not come from Conservative Party officials alone, but from Chesterton too. Chesterton denied he was a fascist and complained that Central Office was engaged in a deliberate smear campaign. He also publicly turned the accusation back on the Conservative Party by dismissing his former membership of the British Union of Fascists as an 'ancient fact', and adding that he was considering 'publishing a list of Tory candidates and Members of Parliament who had also been members of the movement'.

Central Office had to deal with another organisation it considered fascist at the same time that it was dealing with the LEL. Its correspondence reinforces the idea that it based its comments and actions on perception of an organisation's extreme right-wing nature. However, in this instance Central Office also revealed some methods it deemed acceptable to determine an organisation's nature and potential threat. The Elizabethan Party possessed, like Drake's Drum, a name evocative of a previous golden age. It operated in the West Country and presented itself as a new type of political party that stood against the established ones. It placed adverts entitled 'England Expects' in the 'personal columns of local newspapers seeking individuals willing to stand as Elizabethan Party candidates in their own constituencies, unlike the strangers often adopted by the Conservative, Labour and Liberal parties'.[34] The information that the Elizabethan Party produced for these putative members placed it to the right of the Conservative Government. The literature demanded reductions in direct and indirect taxation and the size of the civil service, restrictions on price and wage increases, a reversal of nationalisation, and the need for increased productivity. However, it also revealed imperialism similar to the LEL when it blamed all post-war governments for the loss of 'vast tracts of the Empire which are vital to our future existence'. The accusation that all post-war governments were treacherous for ceding British territory revealed that the Elizabethan Party was another manifestation of extreme-right reaction to the dismantling of the Empire. Additionally, the Elizabethan Party claimed to be 'recognised as the centre of resistance to all that is rotten in the policies of the old parties'. This claim was particularly redolent of Oswald Mosley.

Central Office thought that the Elizabethan Party was similar to the LEL, and made its view known in the same communication that alerted Conservative Party officials to the LEL's nature, and with the exact same wording. However, Central Office lacked the detailed knowledge on the Elizabethan Party that it possessed for the LEL. Consequently, it decided to act on the Elizabethan Party's request for local candidates. In July 1956, Vice-Chairman Donald Kaberry MP responded to an Area Agent who had forwarded an Elizabethan Party advert for candidates by asking, 'I wonder if you could arrange for some suitable, reliable person to reply to the advertisement.' The Area Agent fully understood Kaberry's comments and advised that he had immediately arranged 'for someone to reply to the advertisement'. The insouciant language does not hide what Kaberry wanted the 'suitable' and 'reliable' person to do. This person, a Mr Lewis, acquired the material that revealed the Elizabethan Party's right-wing nature. Kaberry's action was similar to that taken regarding the Guild of Good Neighbours; only in this instance, distance from London necessitated the use of a local investigator. However, unlike earlier examples, Central Office had arranged for someone to pose as a supporter of an extreme-right party. Central Office's intelligence-gathering had developed into an increasingly adept and bold machine capable of gaining information on extreme-right organisations in a number of ways.

However, it would be incorrect to assume that Central Office's only important concern was imperialist extreme-right wing organisations occupying the political space vacated by the Conservative Party. Admittedly, most attention from July 1956 was on foreign matters after Egyptian President General Nasser nationalised the Suez Canal Company. Britain commenced a military attempt to seize the Canal within five weeks of Nasser's action. American financial pressure halted Britain's action, an ignominious failure of such magnitude that Eden swiftly resigned early in January 1957. However, during this period Central Office also watched right-wing organisations that were angry at the Conservative Government's domestic policies. The Middle Class Alliance (MCA) and the People's League for the Defence of Freedom (PLDF) attracted Central Office attention, the latter of which worried it considerably. Central Office's investigation of the MCA and PLDF revealed just how formularised and systematic its surveillance of right-wing organisations had become. Central Office created a 'Committee of Investigation', which the General Director instructed to discover the history, methods, and prospects, of the MCA and PLDF. This committee possessed specific terms of reference to discover both organisations' activities, strength, and geographical spread. In addition, Central Office requested details of policies and methods, chief personalities, and the type of people the MCA and PDF appointed as officials. Central Office's request for a judgement of the potential impact on support for the Conservative and Liberal parties, and the probable reaction of the press, showed that it was concerned about possible adverse consequences. Finally, Central Office requested advice on how to improve the Conservative Party's intelligence on both organisations in the lead-up to the next General Election.

The MCA seemed a recurrence of irritated sectional interest akin to the earlier, similarly titled Middle Class Union.[35] Its formation was due to the actions of one person, Henry Price, Conservative MP for Lewisham West since 1950. In July 1954, the Labour Party-dominated London County Council sought the compulsory purchase of Price's home to build new council houses.[36] Thus, Price had a personal axe to grind. He also believed inefficient unions were behind such schemes.[37] In April 1956, Price announced the MCA's formation.[38] This announcement coincided with a period of acute middle-class irritation, which was unfortunate for the Conservative Government. The Conservatives had performed badly at the West Walthamstow by-election in the previous month. This result had prompted General Director Stephen Pierssene's warning to Eden that the middle class was deserting the Conservative Government.[39] With portents for the June 1956 Tonbridge by-election so poor, the local Tory-owned *Kent and Sussex Courier* vied with the national press in criticising Eden's Government. The result at Tonbridge was a 90% drop in the Conservative vote while the Labour vote remained static, suggesting that Pierssene's warning was correct. *The Times* printed letters that praised the Tonbridge voters for refusing to support a party that implemented socialist policies. The middle classes had had to pay higher interest rates on mortgages without the benefit yet of annual reviews of salary and clearly resented government policy. It is in this context that Price launched the MCA, stating that its objective was, 'to preserve the middle classes for the service of the nation'.[40]

Central Office's Committee of Investigation reported in November 1956 that the MCA had a membership of approximately 50,000. This is not surprising as many Conservative MPs attended MCA meetings. The report recounted Price's claim that over forty MPs supported the MCA. However, although Central Office considered whether MCA members deserved expulsion from the Conservative Party, it rejected the idea and decided to limit counter-measures to discouraging financial or official support so as not to antagonise members of the MCA. Central Office based its decision partly on a belief that the MCA was an amateurish organisation without 'a single person on its Executive Committee of any consequence'. More charitably, it believed that the MCA was not the personal vehicle of an ambitious right-wing individual, the Conservative Government having chosen Price to give the Loyal Address to the Queen's Speech in 1952.[41] This choice was traditionally the role of a rising backbencher, not a troublemaker. Moreover, the MCA possessed essentially the same objectives of the Conservative Party. It would decline as the economic situation improved. These considerations informed the Committee of Investigations' recommendation of a benign response to the MCA, and its specific instructions that local Constituency Agents should befriend individual members of it in their area.

In some senses, the PLDF appeared to pose less of a threat from the right than the MCA. Founded in 1956, the PLDF's leaders included former Liberal Party parliamentary candidates and office holders, and only three Conservatives sat on its eleven-man National Committee. Central Office Area Agents' investigation of the PLDF revealed that it had made little headway among leading local Conservatives. However, the PLDF's existence troubled Central Office more than the MCA, despite nearly 40% of the PLDF's Area Convenors being non-Conservatives. The Committee of Investigation believed that as the PLDF had Area Convenors, it signified that it intended to 'create branches in all Parliamentary constituencies'. This belief probably raised doubts in Central Office about the intentions of the PLDF's leadership. Either the PLDF represented an attempt to form a new party, or it sought to influence the Conservative Party by infiltrating it at local level using its Area Convenors. The PLDF also had a regular newspaper and publishing company with which to disseminate its views in the shape of *The People's Guardian* and the Free Press Society respectively. Moreover, the PLDF leader's ambiguous denial that he intended to form a new party 'at the moment', would not have assuaged any concerns within Central Office.

The PLDF's philosophy and methods also probably contributed to Central Office's wariness. It possessed a libertarian economic philosophy that nevertheless countenanced the use of extreme interventionism to weaken the power of organised labour. This viewpoint logically necessitated the creation of a strong, even authoritarian, government that was prepared to crush those rights that workers had gained despite decades of employers' reluctance as democracy expanded. Therefore, the PLDF's objectives carried an implication of violence, and were only 'Liberal' in the sense that it was like European 'Liberals' who operated on the right. In this regard, the PLDF appeared to be an example of the 'ethnocratic perversions of liberalism' that Griffin identified as one of the 'ideological mutations' taken by the 'fascist species of the radical right' in a hostile post-war milieu.[42] The PLDF's leadership had definitely travelled towards an extreme-right destination The presence of a former Mosleyite in the PLDF's leadership supported the suspicion that it was at least an extreme-right organisation, and possibly a nascent fascist one.

Furthermore, the PLDF's leader Edward Martell was potentially a greater threat than the MCA's Henry Price was. Martell initially attracted public attention by campaigning for a fund to celebrate Churchill's eightieth birthday in 1954, and subsequently gained prominence for strike-breaking activity. He acquired *The Recorder* in the mid-1950s and appealed for £10,000 to maintain production during the 1955 press strike. Martell secured double the amount asked for, which enabled him to create the Free Press Society from which the PLDF sprang. In the summer and autumn of 1956, Martell held PLDF meetings before large audiences in Liverpool and Edinburgh respectively that arguably smacked of 1930s British Union of Fascist meetings. They suggested that Martell was willing to make a populist appeal. Martell's actions probably influenced Party Chairman Oliver Poole's decision to attack fringe organisations in July 1956, in which he singled out the PLDF. If so, it backfired. Nearly 800 letters poured into Central Office from Conservative Party voters and members, the overwhelming majority supporting Martell's activities. The Committee of Investigation's synopsis of the letters revealed that the letter-writers were predominantly dissatisfied with the Conservative Government's failure to curtail trade union power effectively, and provided only limited comfort in that only twenty stated that they had ceased subscribing to the Conservative Party. Martell clearly appealed to a section within the Conservative Party, but the Committee of Investigation warned that the Conservative Party should have nothing to do with him or the PLDF. Although the PLDF subsequently blunted its own appeal by patriotically supporting the Government over the Suez Crisis, Central Office would continue to be wary of it, and Edward Martell, long after the main political casualty of Suez, Prime Minister Anthony Eden, resigned in January 1957.

Indeed Central Office maintained surveillance of right-wing organisations and individuals whether they were inside or outside the Conservative Party, regardless of what prompted their actions. However, it would do so in a society that was different to that when the Conservative Party formed the Voluntary Organisation Section to investigate such organisations and individuals. On the positive side, rationing had disappeared and consumer choice increased. More people took annual holidays at resorts like Butlins. New fashions in clothing displaced wartime drabness. Electrical appliances had mushroomed, revolutionising work and home. Opportunity for social mobility had increased, notably referenced in the Kingsley Amis novel *Lucky Jim* (1954) that charted the career of Jim Dixon as he attempted to take advantage of the new possibilities available in a wealthier society. Yet there were negatives too in this changed society. Not everyone appreciated the changes. To some right-wing individuals, Jim Dixon epitomised much that was wrong about these changes, having attained a position in society to which he was simply unfit. Additionally, a denuded and fading empire had replaced the image of the heroic imperial power that had triumphed over Hitler. Suez had laid bare Britain's imperial impotence. Deference had declined as criticism of the still dominant social structure and establishment that many thought were responsible for Suez increased. Mid-1950s Britain was a time when the imperial verities of British world power no longer held sway. Literary representations of this changed Britain, such as John Osborne's *Look Back in Anger* (1956), attracted for their authors in the summer of 1956 the soubriquet 'Angry Young Men'. These literary voices reflected perceptions of the everyday realities that this transformed society posed for ordinary people. Many of them became films. However, they also presaged the realism of the 'New Wave' in literature and the 'kitchen sink dramas' of television, a cultural phenomenon that reflected a less deferential attitude which would become increasingly prominent during the premiership of Eden's successor.

Notes

1 See p. 14.
2 See p. 14.
3 J. Ramsden, *An Appetite for Power: A History of the Conservative Party Since 1830*, Harper Collins, London (1998), 332.
4 See p. 32.
5 See p. 27.
6 See p. 41.
7 See pp. 32–33.
8 E. H. H. Green, *Ideologies of Conservatism: Conservative Political Ideas in the Twentieth Century*, Oxford University Press, Oxford (2002), 247.
9 *Rochdale Observer*, 20 October 1954.
10 *Western Mail*, 27 October 1954.
11 *Wigan Observer and District Advertiser*, 30 October 1954.
12 *Stirling Journal and Advertiser*, 18 November 1954.
13 *Falkirk Sentinel*, 19 November 1954, and the *Grangemouth Advertiser*, 20 November 1954.
14 'The Story of the Aims of Industry Brains Trust Programme', *Recorder*, 11 September 1954.
15 See p. 37.
16 See p. 17.
17 See p. 15.
18 For the following see J. Charnley, *Blackshirts and Roses: An Autobiography by John Charnley*, Brockingday, London (1990), unless stated.

19 Charnley's sponsors were D. Glover, Conservative MP for Ormskirk, R. Fleetwood-Hesketh, Conservative MP for Southport and John Heynes, Chairman of the Ormskirk Conservative Association.

20 See p. 15.

21 See p. 3.

22 'Franco's British Friends', *Document*, BBC Radio 4, 29 January 2007.

23 See p. 34.

24 R. Griffin, 'The Concept that Came Out of the Cold: the Progressive Historicization of Generic Fascism and its New Relevance to Teaching Twentieth Century History', *History Compass*, 1: 1 (2003), 1–41.

25 See p. 33.

26 Quoted in N. Ferguson, *Empire: How Britain made the Modern World*, Penguin, London (2004), 355.

27 The following information on the LEL derives from A. K. Chesterton, *Sound The Alarm! A Warning To The British Nations*, Candour Publishing Company, Croydon (1954), or Bean, *Many Shades of Black*, *unless* stated.

28 See p. 40.

29 See p. 16.

30 See p. 16.

31 See p. 3.

32 Pugh, *Hurrah for the Blackshirts!*, 297.

33 See pp. 2–3.

34 *Exeter Express & Echo*, 10 July 1956.

35 See pp. 20–22.

36 'Compulsory Order Sought for MP's Home', *The Times*, 23 July 1954.

37 'Parliament', *The Times*, 22 February 1956.

38 'Formation of 'Middle Class Alliance'', *The Times*, 24 April 1956.

39 See p. 42.

40 'Middle Class Alliance', *The Times*, 25 April 1956.

41 'Dinner Parties for the Government', *The Times*, 31 October 1952.

42 R. Griffin, 'Interregnum or Endgame? Radical Right Thought in the 'Post-fascist' Era', *Journal of Political Ideologies*, 5: 2 (2000), 163–178.

3

Macmillan and Home: 'pink socialism' and 'true-blue' Conservatism, 1957–64

When Harold Macmillan succeeded Eden in January 1957, he advised the Queen that his new government might not last six weeks. Macmillan said this only half in earnest, which revealed his nervousness after the Suez fiasco. His first objective was to steady the Conservative Government after Suez, and he could not afford to lose many by-elections. Therefore, Macmillan maintained his predecessors' cautious economic policies and avoided confrontation with organised labour. The economy continued to grow. After losing three by-elections early in 1958, the Conservative Party did not lose any more. Macmillan appeared to be a more languid version of previous Conservative leaders. However, Macmillan was more progressive than either Churchill or Eden. He gave some indications of where his sympathies lay from the beginning of his premiership. In public, Macmillan supported progressives, whilst in Cabinet he preferred government spending to tackling inflation and favoured accelerating decolonisation. Macmillan's progressive views came to the fore after the Conservatives secured an increased majority at the 1959 General Election. Domestically, this meant a turn leftwards, with Macmillan introducing policies that provided a larger role for the state. In imperial affairs, Macmillan made his views clear in a dramatic speech that warned the South African government to accept the inevitability of decolonisation.

Macmillan's policies had continuities with those of previous Conservative governments. State interventionism occurred under the Conservative-dominated National Governments of the inter-war years, and arguably harked back to earlier Tory paternalism. Decolonisation was underway from the later 1940s and continued under Churchill and Eden. However, the scope and extent of Macmillan's policies suggested that he was more left-wing than any previous Conservative leader. Many increasingly disgruntled Conservatives viewed Macmillan and his government this way, with those favouring economic liberalism attacking his government from the right. Conservative governments had effectively marginalised such groups before the 1959 General Election by working with some, such as Aims of Industry and Drake's Drum, and by opposing others such as the PLDF. Now, the PLDF returned and coalesced with others into a sizeable pressure group. Existing imperialist groups such as the LEL maintained their attack on a 'treacherous' Conservative leadership, and new ones emerged often opposing decolonisation in openly racist terms. A group even formed within the Conservative Party containing all of these attacks from the right. This group, the Monday Club, also appeared to include skin colour among its concerns.

Initially, there was little detectable change in the Conservative Party's relationship with the extreme right under Macmillan's leadership. Central Office continued to investigate extreme-right groups, and its agents provided intelligence. Yet, there was a change. Central Office took more vigorous action against the extreme right than hitherto. It interviewed leaders of extreme-right groups, and attempted to identify Conservative members involved in them and pressurised them to desist. Central Office acted proactively when the extreme right contested by-elections, inferring that these groups had links with fascism and devising strategies that limited their chances of success. Central Office was even prepared to extend such charges to the PLDF, a group whose 'extremism' was of the economic kind, not racial. Its actions are unsurprising given the circumstances in which Macmillan succeeded. However, these were not isolated incidents. Central Office watched economically right-wing groups like AIMS and Drake's Drum particularly closely and persistently. It defended the party stewards' physical attack on extreme-right protesters. Central Office rebuffed the Conservative Party's own extreme right when it asked for assistance, while at the same time assisting the party's progressive groups. Nor was action against the extreme right limited to Central Office. Macmillan's Government marginalised that part of the extreme right that was concerned about immigration by enacting legislation that appealed to their voters without ever conceding to their demands fully. The result was that the extreme right could do little to affect the Conservative Party's electoral fortunes during Macmillan's leadership.

In 1959, Macmillan secured the Conservative Party's third successive electoral victory. In July 1957 he had commented, 'indeed let us be frank about it; most of our people have never had it so good', which the media subsequently paraphrased into, 'You've never had it so good.' This phrase summed up the Macmillan Government's appeal to an electorate that was like the characters in John Braine's *Room at the Top* (1957) and Alan Sillitoe's *Saturday Night and Sunday Morning* (1958), contemporary 'New Wave' fiction produced after Macmillan's accession and subsequently turned into films, in that they had indeed never had it so good. The Conservative Party reminded the electors of this with their election slogan, 'Life's better under the Conservatives', and increased their vote for the third successive General Election. This was the first time that a governing party had achieved such a feat since the mid-nineteenth century. Macmillan now had a majority of over one hundred. The press dubbed him 'Supermac', the unflappable leader. However, this electoral success was misleading. It obscured an increasingly divided Conservative Party. It also obscured the fact that the extreme right had become a much more vociferous, organised, and potentially dangerous entity than any time since the Second World War because Macmillan's Government had opened space for it by following progressive policies. This was especially so in areas such as decolonisation, immigration, the economy, and trade unions, and less so over Europe, the USA, and defence. Consequently, the extreme right was an increasingly prominent phenomenon in British politics.

The Conservative Party's left-wing leader

Many originally viewed Macmillan as the right-wing candidate in the battle to succeed Eden, but he was probably slightly to the left of Butler in a contest with no obvious right-wing candidate. He openly supported the Bow Group as Prime Minister and quickly made his 'progressive' sympathies apparent. In July 1957, the Bow Group invited Macmillan to the launch of its new periodical *Crossbow*. Although Macmillan had substantial engagements, his Secretary believed that Macmillan 'may feel that the Bow Group is so worthy of support that he should come up especially in order to help them', and sought Lord Poole's advice at Central Office as to whether Macmillan should accept. Poole advised 'that if Mr. Macmillan could manage to go to their meeting it would be a very good thing'. On 1 October 1957, Macmillan publicly launched *Crossbow*. Central Office officials also attended. This support for the Bow Group would have irritated right-wing Conservatives and disillusioned those who viewed Macmillan as Eden's right-wing successor. However, right-wing Conservatives' irritation and disillusionment would have been far greater if they knew just how extensively Central Office assisted the Bow Group. In August 1958, Earl Woolton sought Central Office advice about a Bow Group invitation to become Patron of its appeal fund. Lord Poole responded that although he thought groups of this kind should stand on their own feet and remain independent from Central Office and had always refused to give any assistance from Conservative Party funds, the Bow Group nevertheless did valuable work for the party, and therefore advised Woolton to become its patron. Poole's comments reflect the standard Central Office position disclaiming any association with other organisations, which it stuck to rigidly. For example, when the Secretary of *Crossbow* sought confirmation of the way in which Central Office would be promoting it, Deputy Chairman Sir Toby Low advised of the need to include wording approved by Central Office highlighting the separate identities of both parties. This disclaimer may have been correct legally, but Central Office's publishing relationship with the Bow Group limited the reality of it.[1] Moreover, Central Office was also complicit on at least one occasion in securing funds for the Bow Group. It was Low who advised the Bow Group's Chairman to seek funding from the United Industrialists Association (UIA). The UIA and its later guise, the British United Industrialists, supported AIMS, the Progress Trust, Central Office, and the wider Conservative Party. They were organisations that channelled funds through seemingly neutral sources.

Central Office clearly favoured the Bow Group. Many invitations to attend Bow Group functions are included within Central Office files. These files also include evidence of Central Office collusion with the Bow Group, particularly regarding the Bow Group's areas of investigation. Macmillan's Government might even have used the Bow Group as an instrument of policy over decolonisation. Iain Macleod's identification of the Bow Group as an organisation from where the Conservative leadership could fly 'useful kites' regarding the Commonwealth and Colonies supports this idea. So too does the presence within Central Office files of a Bow Group Memorandum supporting government policy that was timed to coincide with the release of the critical Devlin Commission Report on events in the Central African Federation. However, to most Conservatives the exact relationship between Central Office and the Bow Group was obscure. This did not necessarily stop some voicing their opposition to it. T. P. Tierney, an active member of the party since 1945, responded to the Bow Group's advocacy of comprehensive education in 1957 by threatening to leave the party if it adopted the policies of a group whose only method of combating socialism was 'by absorbing large doses of socialism into official Conservative policy'. Some party members even raised their suspicions about the relationship. Major Becket, Chairman of the North Dorset Conservative Association, identified the printing of Bow Group publications by the Central Office's Conservative Political Centre as probable evidence of a financial relationship, but he asked a series of easily evaded questions rather than query whether there was any organisational or financial relationship of any kind.

However, Macmillan's support for the Bow Group was obvious, and enough evidence existed to suggest that Central Office acted accordingly. Just after the 1959 General Election, the *Observer* referred to the Bow Group as an example of 'that secret and unacknowledged alliance between the leadership and the younger progressives'.[2] This description of the Bow Group was important because it was exactly how many contemporaries saw it. Even non-Conservative newspapers thought the Bow Group was another phrase for the Tory Left. This view of the Bow Group was especially prevalent among right-wing Conservatives. T. E. Utley thought the Bow Group 'hardly to be distinguished from radical liberalism and sometimes even from socialism'.[3] The extreme right agreed. Edward Martell of the PLDF stated that, 'It is obvious that the Bow Group speak mainly for a clique of people who should really be in the Socialist party. And yet the Prime Minister, who has the final say in these matters allows them to continue their disastrous sway over the fortunes of the Conservative Party'.[4] When already disillusioned Conservatives responded to Macmillan's leftward turn, which his support for the Bow Group exemplified, it revealed an increasingly divided party.

The clearest sign of Macmillan's leftwards turn came in a rush to decolonisation, which the Bow Group had advocated in *Race and Power* (1956). Such a policy would unarguably anger the right wing of the party. Macmillan informed the Cabinet within days of becoming leader that he intended to accelerate de-colonisation, perhaps realising that Eden's resignation provided an opportunity to pursue a policy that many in the Conservative Party would find unpalatable. Abstentions and resignations during the Suez Affair indicated that Macmillan should exercise caution, but Macmillan also realised that implementing faster decolonisation would be difficult if he allowed the divisions revealed by Suez and other imperial disentanglements to widen. Therefore, he acted to isolate Lord Salisbury, the probable head of any revolt against this new policy. Robert Gascgoyne-Cecil, Lord Salisbury, symbolised High Tory imperialism. He was the grandson of the Conservative Prime Minister who had consolidated the Conservative Party's association with Empire, and the scion of the Cecil family whose connections with the Conservative Party and Conservatism reached back over four hundred years. Moreover, Salisbury knew that Macmillan had minimised opposition in Eden's Cabinet to the military attempt to recover the Suez Canal, only to be one of the first critics when it failed. He had been Macmillan's partner in ensuring the Cabinet's acquiescence. Moreover, Lord Salisbury was dangerous to Macmillan in a party that was deferential to the aristocracy. Therefore, Macmillan had to act adroitly to limit the harm that Salisbury could inflict on his decolonisation policy. First, Macmillan margin-alised Salisbury by instructing the civil service to brief the press on his limited importance to the Government. He then orchestrated Salisbury's isolation in Cabinet over the less contentious issue of the release of the imprisoned Greek nationalist leader Archbishop Makarios in March 1957, knowing that Nasser was about to reopen the nationalised Suez Canal. Nasser reopened the Canal the following month, by which time Macmillan had succeeded in putting dis-tance between his government and Eden's over the Suez embarrassment, at the cost of Salisbury's resignation as Lord President of the Council.

Macmillan's actions made swifter decolonisation possible. In 1957, Ghana and Malaya gained independence. Swift decolonisation provided the context for Anthony Burgess's Malayan Trilogy (1956–59).[5] Literary representations like Burgess's depicted not only a deflated and worn down imperial ideal, however, but also the mother country too. This view was unacceptable to many on the right. Macmillan's lack of circumspection after gaining an increased majority for the Conservative Party, and a large mandate personally, inflamed right-wing anger. Six days after the General Election, Macmillan replaced the right-wing Colonial Secretary, Alan Lennox-Boyd, with the more liberal Iain Macleod. The Bow Group's actions also irritated the right. It published *Africa – New Year 1960* calling for Kenyan independence, just prior to Macmillan's departure on a month-long tour of African colonies early in 1960. On 3 February 1960, Macmillan addressed the Parliament of South Africa and left no doubt about his intentions by proclaiming that, 'The wind of change is blowing through this continent. Whether we like it or not, this growth of national consciousness is a political fact.' These comments signalled that Macmillan had decided to abdi-cate Britain's imperial role in Africa. Historians have debated the reasons behind it ever since. Right-wing reaction to it hardened immediately, both outside and within the Conservative Party.

Macmillan had also signalled that a similarly liberal attitude would prevail in the Home Office by making R. A. Butler Home Secretary in the January 1957 reshuffle. Thus, it is unlikely that right-wing individuals who demanded restrictions on immigration were hopeful of success. Although all citizens of the Empire technically had a right to reside in Britain, immigration did not become a serious issue until post-war decolonisation began. The Churchill and Eden governments unwisely ignored it. A combination of not wanting to antagonise the Commonwealth, the desire to present an image of enlightened Conservatism, limited experience of domestic issues, and the Suez Crisis, meant that these governments left concerns over immigration to fester. Their inertia created a vacuum that the extreme right exploited, as seen when tensions over immigration erupted a year after Macmillan became Prime Minister. Two weeks of race riots in Nottingham in 1958 foreshadowed more notorious rioting in Notting Hill in August. Oswald Mosley stepped into this trouble. He used the propensity of 'Teddy Boys', youths who supported the new cultural phenomenon of American 'rock and roll' and who were identified with violence and racism from the start, to form gangs and fan racial hatred against immigrants. Conservative MPs raised the issue of immigration at the October party conference. Sir Cyril Osborne's motion calling for entry controls gained the delegates' support. The Government bought time by limiting its response to negotiating with Commonwealth countries. Mosley's failure to secure election at Kensington North in the 1959 General Election, despite being confident of success in the constituency containing the worst of the rioting, indicated that the Government was correct not to act precipitately.

The hostility of local Conservative Associations to immigration, and the persistent raising of it to the party's agents, meant that Macmillan's Government lost the option of doing nothing about it, despite omitting immigration from the 1959 General Election manifesto. The actions of its own MPs and councillors after the 1959 General Election reflected the Government's limited room for manoeuvre. Newly elected Birmingham MPs formed a committee to secure controls on immigration, as did local Conservatives in Brixton and Birmingham. The Conservative Party bucked the national trend by taking control of Smethwick Council on a platform calling for immigration restrictions. This result reflected a fear of immigration that the film *Winds of Change* (1961) portrayed in its tale of Teddy Boy violence in Notting Hill. Demands for action became increasingly prominent at party conference as immigration and unemployment increased, resulting in the Commonwealth Immigration Bill of 1961. However, Party concerns were not the only considerations that Butler faced as he drafted the government response. Immigration restrictions would limit Britain's moral authority as leader of the Commonwealth, especially if seen to be racist. The creation in 1958 of the Institute for Race Relations ensured that race-related legislation had an international perspective, meaning that Butler could not consider immigration a purely domestic issue. Thus, immigration problems gave Butler an opportunity to present a multi-racial Commonwealth to the world. Butler presented this enlightened view of Conservatism in the Commonwealth Immigration Act of 1962. However, as the Act did not preclude further increases in the rate of immigration, or plan effectively for its consequences, it still left some political space on the right for the dissatisfied to exploit.

Compounding this situation was the confused relationship Britain had with Europe and the USA, both of which were inherently associated with lost Empire and defence issues. Britain had lost an Empire, impoverishing itself in the process, and now sought a new paradigm that would allow it a leading role while maintaining its defensive integrity. Large defence spending was impossible in peacetime, especially if Conservative governments were to honour commitments to the Welfare State. The Commonwealth, with its emerging nationalisms, would not necessarily prove a vehicle for this new role, leaving Europe or the USA as the only viable alternatives. Both presented problems. Britain was ambivalent to Europe from the time of Monnet's ECSC proposal.[6] Membership of the European movement would also have affected the Conservative Party because influencing its MPs was the National Farmers Union (NFU), which bitterly opposed EEC agricultural policies. Iain Gilmour was Conservative MP for Central Norfolk from 1964, and thought that the NFU influenced approximately eighty Conservative MPs, with up to fifty of them actively opposing entry into the Common Market.[7] Central Office officials watched the local Conservative Associations for signs of anti-Common Market revolt. Meanwhile, monitoring of external Conservative organisations revealed worrying beliefs, including the Common Market as another Popish Plot by Catholic Europe to undermine Protestant England. Entry into the EEC risked revealing party divisions, but procrastination was also risky as unfavourable economic comparison could result in the electorate returning a Labour government. This outcome could magnify Conservative Party divisions because many of its MPs represented rural constituencies with large majorities, which meant that they would be among the last removed in a Labour election victory, thus leaving them with a disproportionate influence in the parliamentary party. It is unsurprising that Macmillan later justified his initial vacillation over Europe by citing fears of splitting the Conservative Party. The combination of this fear and Macmillan's belief in a special relationship with the USA, plus the electorate's view of Europe as a troublesome continent that had unnecessarily embroiled Britain in two vast conflicts, resulted in the Government looking to the USA as the alternative focus to Empire.

However, Conservatives were not necessarily positive towards the USA. Many Conservative MPs had voted against American financial aid after 1945 because they suspected its negative impact on the Empire. After 1945, the USA initially adopted an isolationist nuclear policy, forcing Britain to seek an independent nuclear deterrent in economically straitened circumstances. Moreover, the USA wanted Britain to join and lead Europe as it was hostile to the British Empire and thought that the Commonwealth evinced a continuing colonial mindset. American hostility towards British military intervention in Suez had amply demonstrated its position. In 1962, former USA Secretary of State Dean Acheson rubbed salt into British imperialists' wounds when he claimed that, 'Britain has lost an empire and has not yet found a role'. Nevertheless, Macmillan desired to maintain the 'special relationship' and sought the USA's approval prior to applying for membership of the Common Market. However, Macmillan's action indicated Britain's unwillingness to put Europe before its relationship with the USA, which resulted in de Gaulle vetoing Britain's application in 1963. To many Conservatives, the USA must have seemed at best a conditional ally, and at worst an untrustworthy one. Nowhere was this relationship more evident or more troubling for Macmillan than over a failed defence policy in 1962. On 19 December 1962, the USA unilaterally jettisoned the air-launched ballistic missile Skybolt, leaving Britain with no credible nuclear deterrent. Britain seemed reliant on an ally with its own national interests at heart, not those of the fading British Empire. The Nassau Agreement of December 1962, wherein Britain leased its submarine base at Holy Loch to the USA in return for the promise of nuclear-armed Polaris missiles, amplified the unequal relationship with an ally apparently determined to weaken the remaining British Empire.

Unfortunately for Macmillan, his political troubles coincided with declining deference. The 'Angry Young Men' movement in literature and film,[8] and satire in theatre, television, and radio, exemplified this change. The stage revue *Beyond the Fringe* satirised the impotent government that the Nassau Agreement had revealed. It attacked the Conservative establishment mercilessly, and to a vastly increased audience than its precursor, *The Goon Show,* and influenced future television satire such as *That Was The Week That Was.* The issuing of over 10 million television licences meant that satirical representations of the Government reached more people than ever before. Peter Cook's portrayal of a hapless Macmillan reminiscing about his discussions with President Kennedy at the Nassau Agreement was particularly biting. Cook showed Macmillan saying 'We talked of many things, including Great Britain's position in the world as some kind of honest broker. I agreed with him when he said no nation could be more honest, and he agreed with me when I chaffed him and said no nation could be broker.' The Conservative Government's apparent incompetence in economic matters and geo-politics seemingly confirmed the right's fears that it was ready to ditch the Empire and compromise British sovereignty. Unsurprisingly, the government's right-wing critics raised these issues.

However, the right attacked the Government even more consistently over its economic policies and attitudes towards trade unions. Its criticisms continued attacks during Churchill and Eden's administrations, but became more vociferous and increasingly included suspicions of Macmillan's true political persuasion. Macmillan's Government tried to avoid industrial unrest in the immediate aftermath of Suez, probably fearful of a collapse in sterling, but failed. It encouraged employers' resistance only to swiftly back down, which resulted in more strikes in 1957 than for over thirty years, and angered Conservatives in the process. In addition, Macmillan's failure to support Chancellor Thorneycroft's demands for expenditure cuts resulted in the resignation of the whole Treasury frontbench on 6 January 1958, which exposed division over economic policy within the party leadership. Many party activists made known their support for Thorneycroft. The loss of three successive by-elections, at Rochdale in February, and Glasgow Kelvinside and Torrington in March, signalled a party in disarray. The fact that Labour's vote held or dipped proportionately on a reduced turnout highlighted the Government's slump as irritated supporters abstained. However, the defeat in summer 1958 of a poorly executed London bus strike raised the Government's popularity. As the inflationary impact of the Government's economic policies had yet to materialise, it secured five by-election victories on 12 June 1958, which heralded a reversal of fortunes that Macmillan carried through to the 1959 General Election. However, this was a temporary respite.

A doubling of strikes in the decade to 1960, 90% of them unofficial, provided commentators with material on a unionised Britain. Socially realistic 'British New Wave' films focusing predominantly on the working classes' reality of living in a changing society in which strikes loomed large flourished between the late 1950s and 1964. Strikes were thus a particularly worrying undertone to general election victory. Thereafter, the inflationary nature of Macmillan policies led to price increases and fears of more to come. Macmillan was unwilling to contemplate using unemployment as a fiscal measure; a position based on his pre-war experiences of unemployment as MP for Stockton-on-Tees and revealed in his book *The Middle Way*. Instead, Macmillan adopted the 'New Approach' in 1961 of aiming to forge harmony between government, industry, and the unions. The New Approach was essentially the reinforcement of state intervention, planning, and controls, which was anathema to the right. In 1962, the formation of the National Economic Development Council (NEDC) and National Incomes Commission (NIC) symbolised Macmillan's corporatist approach, as they appeared to institutionalise trade unions' role in the economy. This development grated with many in the party. Party activists passed resolutions at local and national level, and revealed an increasingly hard-line approach to unions after the 1959 General Election. An Area Chairman reported defeatism among party workers and identified the Government's taxation and trade union policies as the culprit. Some Conservatives questioned whether Macmillan or the party leadership was truly Conservative, arguing that there was little difference between the Government and opposition, especially in areas such as the Welfare State. Macmillan's search for economic consensus had divided the Conservative Party in a similar manner as his attempts to deal with decolonisation, immigration, relations with Europe and the USA, and defence. It was against this background of a bifurcating party that Central Office contended with existing and new extreme right-wing threats from both outside and within the Conservative Party, threats that materialised quickly after Macmillan became Prime Minister.

Outside right

Macmillan faced a by-election at Lewisham North barely one month into his premiership. The Conservatives had won the constituency in 1955 on a 77% turnout. Labour won the 1957 contest with a virtually unchanged vote on a still healthy 70% participation. Its victory was understandable in the immediate aftermath of Suez. The Conservative's second place with a loss of over 4000 was hardly disastrous, especially as three candidates stood instead of the two in 1955. However, the third candidate was not a Liberal, but Leslie Greene of the LEL. She gained 1,487 votes, which exceeded Labour's majority. Therefore, it is probable that the LEL had damaged the Conservative Party at the ballot box by attracting disgruntled right-wing Conservatives. This by-election was arguably the first time that an extreme-right group had affected the Conservative Party in this manner since the Second World War. Central Office correspondence during the contest suggested that it realised the possible harm that the LEL could inflict in the by-election, and led to consideration of counter-measures during the campaign.

Sir Reginald Dorman-Smith visited Central Office on 4 January 1957 and presented to the General Director, Sir Stephen Pierssene, some notes on the LEL should they contest the Lewisham North by-election. He warned of the need to brief the Conservative candidate, and described the LEL as a 'thoroughly reactionary semi-fascist organisation'. Dorman-Smith commented on the LEL's pre-war connections to Oswald Mosley, and drew attention to anti-Semitic, anti-black, white supremacist views in its literature. Pierssene believed that a response from the Conservative Party provided such opponents with sought-after publicity, and so advised that it was 'generally better to ignore freak candidates and not to attack them'. However, he acknowledged Dorman-Smith's argument that the LEL might fight Lewisham North as it came so soon after Suez, and accepted his suggestion of a 'carefully worded and well-timed letter to the Times or the Telegraph, or indeed one of the Express newspapers'. Pierssene requested a Mr Adamson and two other officials to consider this action and report back. By 17 January, Deputy Chairman Oliver Poole was sufficiently concerned about the by-election to inform Macmillan of the possible harmful effect on the party of losing the seat. Poole argued that the LEL's attraction of 'a certain amount of dissident middle class vote and some right wing extremists' complicated the issue. Poole also advised that Henry Price, Conservative MP and leader of the Middle Class Alliance, had promised support for the Conservative candidate. This information, together with details of reinforcements that Poole had drafted into the constituency, suggested that it was concern over the possible non-democratic actions of extremists within the LEL that worried Central Office most rather than middle-class dissidents.

The following day, 18 January, Mr Adamson reported to Pierssene the results of his considerations, agreeing with Dorman-Smith's suggestion of placing a letter in the newspapers. Adamson also suggested that Dorman-Smith should attack the LEL's campaign as futile and likely to result in the Socialists winning.

However, Adamson suggested a more circumspect stance when it came to commenting on the LEL's nature. While Adamson advocated questions about the LEL's anti-Semitism, he emphatically warned against mentioning Oswald Mosley and fascism. His reasoning provided insight into how Central Office's perception of 'fascism' and an organisation's nature shaped its position. Adamson initially justified his stance by describing Mosley as inconsequential, but also suggested that the term 'fascism' had altered: 'The man does not count today and the term has a changed connotation.' Unfortunately, Adamson did not elaborate. However, genocide had indelibly imprinted fascism with anti-Semitism in public perception. The Conservative Party wanted to forget its pre-war connections with fascism. If Central Office could highlight the LEL's anti-Semitism but avoid accusing it of fascism, it would associate the LEL with Nazi brutality without raising potentially embarrassing questions for the Conservative candidate. This is possibly why Adamson warned at the same time that mentioning Mosley and fascism only provided the LEL's leader, Chesterton, with the opportunity to counter-accuse that, 'there are Members of Parliament in the House who were nearer Mosley than he was and then goes on the attack against the Tories'. Central Office had quickly learned that attempts to describe the LEL as fascist rebounded against the Conservative Party,[9] and adopted instead a more subtle approach that smeared opponents while distancing the Conservative Party from any prior connections. It is in this context that we should see the *Daily Telegraph's* description on 28 January of Greene as a 'crackpot candidate'.[10]

By the end of January, one of the Central Office employees with whom Adamson had concocted this approach felt confident that it was working, and advised Pierssene that the LEL was not making much headway. However, two days after losing Lewisham North on 14 February, this official, Mr Bagnall, reported to Pierssene the conclusions of a post-mortem meeting held at the local Conservative Association. Bagnall identified Labour's misrepresentation of the recent Rent Act as the main reason for loss, but thought that the LEL candidacy was the second cause. He described this as an 'interesting new development', and highlighted the LEL's anti-American comments and posters as particularly important. There was also a jolt for those who thought that the LEL would attract votes equally from both main political parties in Bagnall's comment that, 'Most of those present this morning were convinced that the Independent Candidate took most of her votes from us.' Even more worrying was Bagnall's claim that, 'It was even known that members of our own association in Lewisham stated that after Suez and the abortive action they were going to give Miss Greene a vote to show what they thought of the Tories.' The report's comments made clear that Central Office's counter-measurers against the LEL were insufficient in the immediate post-Suez circumstances. However, Macmillan was intent on accelerating decolonisation and could not tolerate the existence of an organisation that exploited the vacuum of imperial disgruntlement on the right of the Conservative Party.

Publicity stunts remained the most obvious aspect of LEL activity during Macmillan's premiership. In March 1957, an LEL protester interrupted Macmillan's first major public speech. At the October 1957 Party Conference John Bean tolled a bell for an empire that the Conservative Party had allegedly betrayed. The LEL even managed to break into the BBC's programmes in 1958 and denounce the Government's decision to integrate Britain's forces with NATO. Meanwhile, the Conservative bureaucracy continued to gather intelligence on the LEL. One report identified the Branch Chairman of the Cambridge Conservative and Unionist Association as an active member of the LEL. An internal report highlighted other Conservative's connections with the LEL, including Field Marshal Lord Ironside and Major-General Richard Hilton, the former an erstwhile President of the Conservative Central Norfolk Area until 1954, the latter involved in the Young Conservatives. One Area Agent noted the simultaneous nature in many Yorkshire constituencies of LEL protests on the morning of government proposals for Cyprus in 1958, which raised the possibility of a coordinated campaign fuelled by inside knowledge. These are but a few examples. The Conservative Party and Central Office's reactions revealed that they were increasingly prepared to use tougher measures against the LEL. For example, the Area Agent responsible for the Cambridge and Unionist Association reported that party members had attempted to oust the Branch Chairman and members of his family for their LEL sympathies. The author of the internal report that identified Ironside and Hilton, although not wishing to commit firm instructions to paper, made it clear that, 'Area Agents should be informed and asked to make the point known' that membership of the LEL was incompatible with Conservative Party membership. Central Office demanded that Conservative organisations identify LEL sympathisers within their ranks. Its response to the LEL's stunts provide the best evidence of how far it was prepared to go to thwart this particular extreme-right organisation.

Mr G. E. Higham of Stockton Heath, Warrington, encapsulated alienation from the Conservative Party. He was angry about the Conservative Party's actions against the LEL, and wrote to Oliver Poole at Central Office in June 1957 identifying himself as 'a lifelong Conservative, by birth, upbringing and inclination'. Higham highlighted manhandling and threats of violence and asked Poole how Conservatives could act in this manner towards individuals whose principal loyalty was to 'her Majesty, The Empire (or what is left of it), and the White British way of Life'. Higham compared the actions Conservatives had meted out to LEL members to the leniency he claimed to have witnessed to 'Communist TRAITORS' at Conservative Party meetings, expressing anger in similar terms to Clan Briton's Tomlinson.[11] He also stated that many others shared his views and warned Poole of the consequences for the Conservative Party unless it returned to 'the ordinary common decencies and Loyalties which people like me have been brought up to believe in'. This letter was the first of many between Higham and Central Office spanning more than twelve months. Poole initially responded by implying that Higham was misguided due to ignorance. He set out the errors of the LEL's disruptive activity at Conservative events and denied that Conservative stewards had been violent. Higham comprehensively rebuffed Poole's interpretation and elaborated on his claims, and in the process expanded upon extreme-right characteristics evident in his initial letter. He reiterated disgust at the Conservative Party's treatment of LEL activists compared to their tolerance towards Communists, claiming that officials at a Warrington Conservative Association meeting, at which he was present, granted permission to a 'Communist interloper' to question the platform and distribute copies of the *Daily Worker*. Higham interpreted this as evidence that the party did not adhere to true Conservatism and was becoming soft on socialism. While admitting that he did 'not altogether agree' with the LEL's actions, Higham saw no other way that people could 'protest against the behaviour of a so-called Conservative Government which is perpetually letting the country down and behaving in the Liberal-Socialist-Fabian manner which was expected of its predecessors'. When Higham complained about the futility of writing to MPs, ministers, newspapers, and even the BBC, and of the consequent lack of an alternative, he revealed his frustration with contemporary democracy. Thus, Higham implied that only by making non-parliamentary protests like the LEL's could he and likeminded individuals achieve their objectives. Higham showed just how far to the right of the Conservative Party he had become when he demanded redress for injuries that it had perpetrated or accepted. These injuries included, 'The Liquidation of the Empire under the supervision and influence of the U.S.A.', 'The appalling influx of Coloured people into the country', 'The perpetual subservience to the U.S.A. in all matters', 'The European Free Market', and 'Taxation'. Higham's correspondence was a futile exercise. Central Office stuck to Poole's position of blaming the LEL and denying Conservative violence. Nevertheless, Higham was another example of how the Conservative parliamentary party isolated an extreme-right supporter sufficiently enough for him to consider leaving it.

Despite Poole's denials Conservative violence occurred. Many witnessed its apogee at the 1958 Blackpool Conservative Party Conference where an LEL interruption to proceedings resulted in assaults on the individuals concerned. Centre-right publications were outraged. Bernard Levin, writing under the pseudonym 'Taper' in the *Spectator*, condemned the Conservatives for the punching and kicking of a defenceless LEL protester who was on the floor. Levin said there was only one conclusion: 'There lies perilously close to the surface in some of the members of the Tory Party a layer of brutal, Fascist thuggery that breaks through at the sign of resolute disagreement.'[12] Levin's comments touched on how far Central Office was prepared to go in smothering the Conservative Party's association with any organisation that rekindled its erstwhile association with fascism. The legal consequences of these events support this interpretation. Media coverage of the violence was extensive, and the LEL identified Conservative member George Finlay as the chief culprit and sued for assault. The judge acquitted Finlay and awarded him costs,[13] a decision that vindicated Poole's assertion to Higham that the LEL caused trouble to peaceful Conservatives. Finlay may have been innocent. The Conservative Party may not have organised the violence. However, Central Office was prepared to defend it. It received numerous letters from Conservative witnesses supporting the LEL's version of events. Despite possession of this contrary evidence, Central Office made a legal deposition denying the LEL's claims. If Central Office disclosed the letters supporting the LEL, it would have meant contradicting individuals who by their attendance indicated some level of support for the Conservative Government. However, nothing in its files showed that Central Office disclosed these letters, which showed that it was prepared to alienate more supporters to defeat the LEL. It also meant that Central Office was possibly prepared to distort evidence when it made its legal deposition. If correct, Central Office was prepared to go to extraordinary lengths to harm the LEL.

The LEL declined from 1958. This was because the Conservative hierarchy had made it known that membership of the LEL 'meant political death' to any Conservative with ambitions. Complaints in *Candour* of actions against the LEL supported Thayer's assertion. These actions included the removal of the Cambridge Conservative Association chairman and the expulsion of a member of the Conservative Hackney Association.[14] *Candour* also highlighted negative employer reaction and a general social exclusion, which it categorised as 'silent treatment, vituperation, ridicule and abuse'.[15] In this climate, it is not surprising that a Conservative parliamentary candidate felt compelled to resign his candidacy because of his association with the LEL.[16] It is not possible to attribute these incidents solely to Central Office, as it did not run the likely places in which the LEL members experienced 'social exclusion', such as the workplace, golf club, and other organisations. However, these were socially conservative avenues, and it is likely that party activists channelled warnings about LEL membership to aspirant Conservatives. The Conservative Party employed stewards from 1960 onwards with instructions to block LEL attempts to disrupt the party conference, a development noted by national newspapers.[17] Its attempt to disrupt the 1962 Party Conference failed and received little press coverage,[18] showing that the LEL's ability to harm Macmillan's Government had lessened.

The LEL failed partly because the post-war electorate was lukewarm about the British Empire. Prosaic cultural symbols of empire such as Camp coffee and 'Empire Made' toys formed part of day-to-day existence in the 1950s, but by the time decolonisation had been achieved, Empire was already virtually forgotten. Nowhere was this indifference more obvious than in imperial commemorations. The Empire Day Movement, founded in 1903 by an ardent supporter of Edwardian patriotic movements, advocated annual celebration of Empire. From 1916 onwards, Britons throughout the Empire celebrated 'Empire Day'. It was a major event involving school parades, the BBC, Church and Crown, and reached its apogee in 1925 when 90,000 attended a thanksgiving service held at Wembley Stadium as part of the Empire Exhibition. Thereafter, interest in Empire Day declined and state institutions' support for it diminished. Britons had rejected the imperial ideal even before the Suez Affair, save for a brief resurgence during the 1953 Coronation. However, they were even less interested in the Commonwealth. Ministers were aware of the people's lack of interest in or knowledge of the Commonwealth, and vigorously supported changing 'Empire Day' into 'Commonwealth Day' in 1958. When the change came in 1959, it was to a 'Commonwealth Week', not merely a day, with a touring exhibition visiting British cities. When the exhibition failed to shake British apathy by 1962, the government abandoned 'Commonwealth Week', which the Empire Day Movement meekly accepted before dissolving itself the same year.

The failure of other imperialist right-wing groups to make any headway supported this apathetic image. In November 1957, internal Central Office correspondence reported again on the Elizabethan Party. It noted Central Office's previous highlighting of the Elizabethan Party's anti-Americanism and fascism, and dismissed claims of extensive membership. It also highlighted anger at Conservative policy towards India, Sudan, and Suez, and a fear of unchecked communist infiltration within the establishment and trade unions. Central Office's E. S. Adamson interviewed the leader of the Elizabethan Party, Frederick Guest, indicating that it took this extreme-right organisation seriously. Adamson's report quoted Guest's belief that 'the wretched' Conservatives were 'too cowardly to work for anyone or even have a policy of their own', a typically extreme-right belief that there was little difference between Conservative and Labour. Guest also claimed that there was a deliberate attempt to hinder the Elizabethan Party by a 'news blackout imposed by the party newspapers and the State controlled B.B.C.'. If true, Guest's accusations revealed that the Conservative Party had used a new, more extensive method to marginalise the extreme right, but evidence is lacking. More substantial was the Elizabethan Party's irritation at Conservative policy under Macmillan. Its demands for reductions in the cost of living and taxation, offset by increased production, showed that the Elizabethan Party was angry at government economic policy, and its calls for the removal of nationalised industries as the first stage in improving industrial relations indicated that it thought that the Government pandered to the trade unions. However, the Elizabethan Party's overwhelming focus on a foreign policy based on the Empire and British interests alone, closer Empire ties, restricting NHS access to British citizens, and an independent nuclear deterrent with the Empire as a defence polity, revealed that imperialism was at its heart. Yet, not one single Elizabethan Party candidate stood for election in 1959. This is unsurprising considering that domestic issues remained the focus of the overwhelming majority of people. Its inability to mobilise an electorate apathetic to imperialism meant increasing marginalisation for organisations that were already marginal.

The Conservative Party had played a part in this marginalisation by opposing the LEL and investigating the Elizabethan Party. It continued to do so when LEL members defected to Edward Martell's People's League for the Defence of Freedom, an extreme-right wing group that was not anti-Semitic but focused on issues that more obviously affected the electorate. This meant that the PLDF arguably posed a greater threat than the LEL. Its prominence early in Macmillan's Government had also resulted from contesting a by-election. This by-election, at East Ham North in July 1957, revealed Central Office awareness of the PLDF's threat, and that it had learned from the LEL's challenge at Lewisham North

Edward Martell, the PLDF's chairman, believed that political trends made it impossible for the Conservative Party to overturn a Labour majority exceeding 5,000 at East Ham North, but nevertheless thought that, 'an anti-Socialist not tied to the Conservative Party might conceivably deprive the Socialists of the seat'. He argued that the Conservatives stood no chance in the by-election, and suggested to Conservative Party Chairman Oliver Poole that he should allow the PLDF to challenge Labour instead. Martell sought Conservative Party co-operation, unlike the LEL. Indeed, while Martell admitted that the PLDF was often critical of government policy, he proposed a meeting to Poole to discuss a coordinated anti-Socialist campaign. General Director Pierssene acted according to the conclusions of prior Central Office investigations into Martell,[19] and curtly advised him there was no point in further discussion as selection was a matter for the local Conservative Association. Martell's subsequent attempt to gain the cooperation of the local Conservative Association received the same curt response. Central Office was suspicious of Martell and determined not to have any association with the PLDF. Some of its Area Agents saw an opportunity to 'follow out the excellent North Lewisham arrangements without too much difficulty when it comes to fighting East Ham'.

Martell reacted to these rebuffs on 13 March with a populist appeal in the PLDF's newspaper, *The People's Guardian. The People's Guardian* was always replete with letters and articles that criticised trade unions and their leaders, articulating the views of a large section of the electorate and at the same time implicitly criticising the Government. The 13 March edition of *The People's Guardian* was no different, and it is easy to see why it would concern Central Office. It listed PLDF meetings throughout the country, including verifiable details of venues, attendees, and platform speakers such as Commander Hyde C. Burton, and thus reflected the countrywide extent of PLDF support and Conservative alienation. It also printed Martell's correspondence with Central Office over the East Ham North by-election, and portrayed the PLDF's candidature at East Ham as, 'An opportunity to show both Tories and Socialists that the public has had enough of party antics'. This article suggested that Martell actually intended to harm the Conservative Government despite his attempts to secure Central Office cooperation. Martell's request that readers participated in a referendum to support a PDLF candidacy in East Ham North supported this suggestion, and indicated a worrying ability to harness disillusioned Conservative populism to attack Conservative Government policies. Finally, Martell used *The People's Guardian* to increase PLDF membership and activism, which gave the impression that he wanted to create a new political party on the right of the Conservative Party. Such a party would undoubtedly harm a Macmillan government following a centrist path, and could potentially harm the Conservative Party permanently if it failed to counter socialism.

By 20 March, Central Office was exhibiting a resolve that was swifter and firmer than during the LEL challenge at Lewisham, even before confirmation of a PLDF candidacy. General Director Pierssene was part of a triumvirate coordinating the Conservative Party's response to the PLDF. He stated to his two colleagues his belief that, 'I think we should go ahead at once and prepare a plan of action and a line of attack', and that he did not think 'that this is a case where the best policy would be to ignore them altogether', a position that contrasted with his usual nonchalance towards 'freak candidates'. The responses of Pierssene's colleagues, P. Cohen and E. S. Adamson, mirrored this more proactive attitude. Cohen viewed a PLDF candidacy as likely to exploit present industrial troubles, and raised the possibility that East Ham North was only the beginning of a concerted PLDF campaign by arguing that whoever the PLDF candidate turned out to be, they might only be 'a guinea-pig in order to judge whether future by-elections should be contested'. He advised caution until the PLDF revealed the identity of its candidate and until Central Office knew 'whether any prominent local Conservatives are to be associated with him', suggesting that until then Central Office rely on its Area Agents' reports on any PLDF developments in the constituency, and that it 'should have an observer there throughout the campaign'. Cohen identified four duties of this observer: to study tactics; provide the Conservative candidate with information and guidance; report regularly to Central Office and other interested departments; and draft questions to be put at PLDF election meetings. He ended by stating that focus at all elections should be the defeat of socialist candidates, but that he was in favour of systematic and coherent counter-measures against the PLDF challenge. Adamson's comments reinforce the image of Central Office acting proactively. Adamson referred to the LEL's use of outside supporters in the Lewisham by-election and raised with Pierssene the probability of similar methods by the PLDF. He acknowledged that any action against the PLDF 'in respect of this by-election must be taken within the Constituency', but considered 'whether some action on our part is necessary to curtail an ingress of League supporters from the Home Counties'. Adamson was not kite flying, but making a serious recommendation about how Central Office could counter the PLDF. He also considered tougher measures and looked to the future when he concluded that, 'One most important point is whether now, or after the by-election, the attention of Conservatives should not be drawn to the departure of the League from its original stated intentions, and inferring that Conservative Members of the League must consider the question of loyalties.'

Central Office was also aware of developments within the PLDF. The same day that Adamson sent his comments, Pierssene received intelligence from Harold Soref, an unsuccessful Conservative candidate at the 1955 General Election. Soref reported that a meeting to determine the PLDF candidate was occurring that morning and wagered that Martell would secure the nomination, a view that Pierssene immediately forwarded to Chairman Poole. Poole responded quickly with a report to Macmillan that highlighted the Government's failure to enforce secret ballots on trade unions and end their restrictive practices, and warned Macmillan that it was 'inevitable that Martell will take away a number of Conservative votes'. Poole understood Martell's appeal to Conservative voters. He recommended that the party put 'a considerable effort into fighting this by-election', but instead of focusing on the Labour candidate, Poole argued that Conservatives should 'devote most of our attentions to the People's League candidate, as we cannot in any circumstances win'. This was not a counsel of despair, but a reasoned appraisal of the likely result and from whence damage to the Conservative Party would come. Nor was it defeatist, as Poole requested that Macmillan allowed two Cabinet ministers to participate in the by-election, and subsequently referred to the assistance of hundreds of party workers. Just how seriously Central Office intended to counter the PLDF, and by what methods, soon became clear.

On 27 March, R. Bagnall, the Central Office's Chief Organisation Officer, explained to Pierssene that an un-proofed letter sent to the Chairman and members of the local Conservative Association in the East Ham North constituency was an administrative error. Nevertheless, the content of the letter, which asked recipients to resist the PLDF's attempts to secure enough support from Conservatives for their candidacy, showed that Central Office tried to strangle the PDLF at birth. Subsequent events showed how. On 1 April, Cohen forwarded further information to Pierssene and Adamson, pointing out that Martell was bound to use the strikes that were occurring as proof of his warnings about trade union power and Conservative government weakness. He developed his earlier comment that East Ham was a springboard for future PLDF challenges, and warned that Martell intended to use East Ham as the pilot scheme for these putative challenges if he saved his deposit. Cohen had acquired further intelligence on Martell's intentions. He was aware that Martell had rejected LEL assistance, which made it more difficult to level the same charges against Martell as those levelled at the LEL candidate at Lewisham. However, Cohen nevertheless advocated that Conservative activists used the accusation of fascist connections against the PLDF. He called for the preparation of reasoned criticisms of the PLDF's demands and heckling material for Martell's meetings, arguing that if they detected any LEL involvement, 'our line might be to hint, through hecklers, that Martell has Fascist allies'. This was an orchestrated personal attack on Martell. The resignation of the chairman of the Young Conservatives in East Ham, a Mr Bell, proved that a personal attack on Martell formed part of Central Office's campaign in the by-election. Bagnall forwarded to Pierssene a report on the resignation, with a *Daily Telegraph* cutting that described Mr Bell's disgust at the conduct of the campaign, quoting him saying that, 'it would appear that Mr. Bangay [the Conservative candidate] is preparing to conduct his campaign in the form of one long attack against Mr. Martell'.[20]

There was also evidence that Central Office implemented a greater degree of activity against Martell and the PLDF in the constituency. In the month of the poll, Central Office unsuccessfully attempted to enlist Churchill's support with Macmillan's backing. Undaunted by its failure, Central Office continued to seek to control the situation by importing intelligence officers into the East Ham constituency. Pierssene noted the recruitment of a James Hankey who had 'undertaken to perform some intelligence duties', in a letter to the Central

Office Area Agent responsible for East Ham North. He demanded that Hankey consulted with officials involved in the Lewisham campaign, and requested information from the Area Agent, Mr Horton, of what plans had evolved and whether Hankey had begun preliminary investigations. Horton responded that Hankey had already read the report on the Lewisham defeat and had visited East Ham on a number of occasions. Moreover, when Horton advised that he would endeavour to carry the 'additional expenditure' caused by Hankey's activities, he revealed that this was beyond the activities normally borne by Conservative constituencies or areas. Whether these actions affected the result is difficult to judge. The Conservative vote halved and Labour gained a similar sized majority. However, the PLDF's saving of its deposit meant that Central Office would continue to watch Martell.

Central Office's actions during 1957 also reflected the political tenor of the new Macmillan Government and his two primary objectives. In line with Macmillan's comments to the Queen, the first objective was ensuring the Government's survival. This meant maintaining distance from 'extreme' organisations and individuals. A change in Central Office's attitude towards the SIF confirmed that this was its aim. It had previously identified the SIF as a small, right-wing organisation,[21] but in March 1957 Central Office stated that it was 'very right-wing in character'. This was a small, but significant, difference indicating that the tenor of the leadership had changed when Macmillan became Prime Minister. It is a view supported by the candidacy of former Conservative parliamentary candidate Andrew Fountaine at the Norfolk South West by-election of March 1959. The Conservative Party had disowned Fountaine in 1950, but his candidacy still caused worry within Central Office. Central Office probably wished to avoid embarrassing connections with an individual who was now openly operating on the extreme right. The evidence that Macmillan achieved his second objective is clearer: a three-figure majority at the 1959 General Election. This result may have limited the extreme right's potential to harm the Government, but it did not mean that it would meekly acquiesce. On the contrary, Macmillan now faced an extreme right that the government's policies alienated to an extent unequalled by any other post-war Conservative prime minister, and the society it represented.

Moving right?

In *A Kind of Loving* (1960),[22] sexual desire conflicted with social mores. The lead actor, Victor, is from a solidly blue-collar working-class background, but apprenticed in a white-collar occupation. He gets the lower-middle-class Ingrid pregnant and marries her. Financially forced to live with Ingrid's mother, Victor is soon bored with their gossiping, game show-watching vacuity, and irritated at the elder woman's criticism of striking busmen and miners. Almost inevitably, Victor walks out, but, receiving short shrift from his parents, returns to Ingrid and settles for 'A Kind of Loving' in dingy premises away from her mother.

A Kind of Loving reflected late-1950s and early-1960s continuity and change. Victor's parents envisioned better jobs, even social advancement for their three children. Ingrid and her mother lived in a semi-detached house with modern amenities, especially the television set, a house that was typical of many built when Macmillan was Housing Minister. Yet, predominantly working-class football supporters still attended matches in suits, and men and women working for the same company remained segregated on the shop floor and canteen. Victor's decision to marry Ingrid reflected surviving conventions of shame and honour, which the registrar hilariously captured by intoning the marriage service as if a prison sentence, while his sister's incredulity when he admitted marrying Ingrid only for the sake of the baby mirrored changing attitudes. *A Kind of Loving* was a snapshot of a society undergoing change, with Victor struggling against contemporary society's constraints and long held mores, yet standing at the gate of the 'permissive society'. *A Kind of Loving* typified other works of the time, such as John Braine's *Life at the Top* (1962), which was a sequel to *Room at the Top* (1957). Braine's main character prospered in this changing, affluent society, but he was not necessarily contented with the results it afforded him. For many right-wing individuals these changes were not necessarily for the better and the society portrayed by authors like Barstow and Braine was alien and troubling.

New groups reflected this alienation from society generally, and the Conservative Party particularly. Major-General Richard Hilton, formerly of Common Cause and the League of Empire Loyalists,[23] formed True Tory in 1960. He complained that a lack of religious instruction had left students with 'practically no knowledge of right and wrong',[24] and implicitly accused the liberal-minded Home Secretary, Butler, of failing to redress the situation. Hilton reflected a wider concern about juvenile delinquency, as seen in films such as *No Trees in the Street* (1958), *Violent Playground* (1958), *And Women Shall Weep* (1960) and *Some People* (1962), which associated juvenile degeneracy with the period's lazy prosperity. He highlighted the soft punishments that the judiciary meted out to offenders, and decried, 'No wonder our standards of morality have gone to pieces, and with them our British character'. Hilton also argued that there was 'a general lack of courage in tackling the evil trends of post-war society'. He blamed these 'evil trends' on the 'positive poison, mostly from America, which is poured into the minds of Britons by almost every form of propagandist machinery – the cinema, television, sound radio, cheap books, the "gutter press", and above all by that American device for destroying juvenile minds – "the comic strip"'. Here, Hilton identified many prominent social features of society under the Conservatives that the literature and films in this period referenced. When he called for a return to the 'unalterable principles upon which British greatness was established', which he identified as 'a robust religious faith' and 'healthy moral standards, dependent on rigid distributions between right and wrong', he showed that he was utterly opposed to the society that had emerged under Conservative governments.

Hilton opposed imperial decline just as Colonel Renfrew, wistfully remembering the end of empire in India, did in John Osborne's *Look Back in Anger*

(1957).[25] However, unlike Colonel Renfrew, Hilton did not simply pine for long-gone imperial grandeur. Nor did Hilton accept the apathy of an electorate that contentedly watched comic depictions of imperial bureaucratic impotence in films such as *Carlton-Browne of the FO* (1959) and *The Mouse That Roared* (1959) while minimally participating in commemorations of Britain's overseas role. Instead, Hilton attacked. He held Conservative governments responsible, especially that of Macmillan. Hilton began by stating that the Conservative Party was formerly without question 'traditionally the patriotic party', in the True Tory Political Manifesto of 1961. The Conservative Party's return to power in 1951 had reassured right-wing patriots who believed that it would avert the fall of the British Empire, restore Britain's prestige, and redress the decadence affecting society, he added. However, Hilton argued that this had not happened because, 'appeasement of anti-British agitators, the betrayal of Her Majesty's loyal subjects abroad, and a general lack of courage in tackling the evil trends of post war society … continued unabated throughout the Conservative period'. He went further, commenting that despite its 'unchallengeable size', the Conservative Government after 1959 'surpassed its predecessors in the shameful characteristics of appeasement and betrayal, which are the hall-marks of "official" Conservatism to-day'.

However, the True Tory manifesto was more than a generalised attack on Conservative governments. It denounced the Commonwealth as a 'spineless agglomeration of nations, no longer, even on paper, under British leadership', and thus revealed a specific belief that Conservative governments were trying to obscure the reality of decolonisation. Hilton cited the treatment of Archbishop Makarios as an example. Makarios was the charismatic leader of Greek Cypriot attempts to gain independence whom Eden had exiled as a troublemaker. However, in 1959 the Queen welcomed Makarios as an honoured guest. Although the Queen's action was part of a wider process to resolve conflict in Cyprus, Hilton nonetheless saw it as similar to the appeasement of anti-British agitators who terrorised British subjects, as occurred before Ghana gained independence in 1957, and was occurring in the Kenyan Mau Mau uprising. Hilton contrasted this 'appeasement' with the Government's treatment of the Central African Federation, a penumbra of white colonial rule formed in 1953 by a coalition of Nyasaland and South and North Rhodesia. Macmillan's Government believed that independence was inevitable and, under pressure from the United Nations and the Organisation of African Unity, it pressurised the Central African Federation's constituent parts towards decolonisation. Hilton believed that the Conservative Government was willing to appease 'a few anti-British Commonwealth politicians'. He argued that this was unsurprising because it was white settlers that Colonial Secretary Macleod threatened with force if they did not 'accept Whitehall's betrayal with good grace', not 'black demagogues'. When Hilton bemoaned Britain's lack of any fighting forces worthy of the name and claimed that its existence was now dependent on a 'none too genuine ally or upon the condescension of the United Nations', he also revealed anti-Americanism and anti-internationalism.

Nor did Hilton miss changes that occurred at home, especially those within organised labour. Leader of the London bus strike in 1958 was Frank Cousins, General Secretary of the Transport and General Workers' Union. Cousins's election in 1956 heralded a changing of the guard from moderate to left-wing leadership. Hilton specifically criticised the Conservative Government's handling of tensions like the London bus strike in the True Tory 1961 'Manifesto', and pointed to its failure to prevent victimisation or unofficial strikes by enacting legislation as an example of appeasement. The Manifesto also highlighted rising living costs in general and the Welfare State in particular. Hilton deemed the former most detrimental to those on fixed incomes, but less so to the industrial worker who he described as the 'pampered child of socialism and false toryism alike'. The Welfare State attracted Hilton's condemnation for appeasing the 'idle and feckless at the expense of the industrious and enterprising'. Hilton also attacked the Conservative Government's corporatist economic policies. However, his irritation did not end at economic matters. R. A. Butler's five-and-a-half-year tenure of the Home Office had brought a liberalisation in categorising homicide, resistance to the reintroduction of corporal punishment and a relaxation of laws governing licensing hours, betting and gambling, and obscene publications. Butler's actions brought the opprobrium of party activists upon his head annually at party conference. Hilton's views accorded with many of these activists. He pointed to violent crime levels, and described Butler's refusal to comply with calls for tough measures as appeasement of 'a few cranky psychiatrists at the cost of flouting those who put him in office'. Hilton made many such criticisms of contemporary society that mirrored many Conservatives' alienation and anger. His True Tory Manifesto was a directed attack on the specific policies of Conservative governments, but Macmillan's in particular.

The remedies suggested in the True Tory Manifesto of 1961 were extreme. They included social service cuts in order to fund an independent national defence, heavier penalties for violent crime, penalising young offenders' parents, and allowing police to kill certain criminals on sight. Yet, the Manifesto was more than the demands of an extreme-right individual. It also showed that Hilton was on a rightwards journey. The methods that Hilton suggested revealed this journey. Hilton was formerly a Conservative Party member, and claimed that the initial objective of True Tory at its inception in 1960 was the 'gradual re-education of the Conservative electorate, as a whole, in the temporarily forgotten principles of "true toryism"'. He believed that a reawakened Conservative electorate that pressurised the leadership by their votes and withdrawn funds would bring the party 'back into the path of patriotism'. However, by the time that Hilton wrote the True Tory Manifesto in 1961, his attitude had changed due to the commencement of Macmillan's New Approach. Hilton now described his initial plan as unworkable due to the leadership only being in touch with the electorate at election time. He accused Macmillan's Government of holding the electorate in contempt, especially on crime and black immigration, and argued that, 'Right-wing patriots must, therefore, bring *pressure* on this obstinate leadership in the legitimate ways that are open to us.' Despite using the word 'legitimate', Hilton's appeal did not quite rule out other means. Moreover, although Hilton mentioned democratic measures such as letter-writing and cancelled subscriptions, his emphasis of 'pressure' indicated he was an individual who at least contemplated the possibility of non-democratic measures. In his opinions, remedies, and methods, Major-General Richard Hilton was an example of a wider trend in which the Conservative Party alienated right-wing individuals by adopting policies and a political stance they considered was hitherto associated with the left. The Conservative Party's action against the extreme right in this instance was that it forced such individuals into the political spotlight without the comforts of belonging to a powerful mainstream political party, and had no relationship henceforth with them whatsoever. However, the Conservative Party's opposition to Hilton and True Tory was more than mere repulsion. In this instance, attraction played as great a part.

Skin colour was central to Hilton's weltanschauung. He advocated the creation of a new British Empire and denounced the vagueness of the Commonwealth in the third True Tory leaflet of 1960, 'Who are the British?' This new empire would become one economic and defensive unit united under one monarchy, in which British minorities enjoyed the protection of Her Majesty's Government. Therefore, being British conferred substantial privileges regardless of domicile in this new empire. Whom did Hilton regard as 'British', however? Hilton stated that the term British 'should be reserved for those whose home country is the United Kingdom', but added a caveat that 'even here caution is needed'. He posed the question of whether a Jamaican living in Britain was British because of his residence, and answered emphatically: 'Obviously not, say True Tories, if there is any meaning at all in race'. Even if the individual concerned was the most loyal subject, who for Hilton included those who adhered to the proper rules and mores of British society, 'this does not, and never can, make him "British" by race'. It is clear from this alone that race would be the determining characteristic in Hilton's new British Empire. However, Hilton also made a clear distinction between being 'British', as determined by race, and being a 'British subject', which he saw as applicable to all within the Empire. Hilton stated that both terms had become indistinguishable due to lax language and attitudes, and argued that this gave rights of entry to individuals with no real loyalty to Britain, as they were not British by race. He believed that this laxity threatened Britain's existence: 'True Tories insist that such laxity is illogical, suicidal and must be stopped at once'. By 'suicidal', Hilton meant the dilution of the 'white race', a contemporary racist view that the film *Sapphire* (1959) successfully portrayed in which a 'respectable' white mother killed the mixed-race fiancée of her son. Hilton called for a colour bar on all immigration to avoid the consequences evident in *Sapphire*, along with an immediate end to non-British immigration, repatriation of immigrants arriving in the last five years, and an end to the betrayal of white settlers. Unfortunately for any political ambitions that Hilton harboured, a colour bar on immigration was exactly what the Conservative Government provided.

The Conservative governments from 1951 onwards had avoided immigration. By 1955, the Eden Government was increasingly aware of the protests from local Conservative Associations regarding immigration's effects on housing and public health, and concluded that controls were inevitable, but then decided that the time was not ripe. This dithering reflected divisions within the Conservative Party hierarchy over immigration. Lord Salisbury urged Eden to take action before it was too late, but the Commonwealth Relations Secretary, Lord Home, countered effectively by warning that immigration was a sensitive issue within the Commonwealth that the Government must avoid if possible. Additionally, Suez had made it unlikely that a government that needed allies would wilfully antagonise potentially separatist parts of the Empire. Thus, the Conservative Government avoided the immigration issue for foreign and domestic reasons. Nevertheless, grassroots concerns about immigration remained. In 1958, Sir Cyril Osborne angrily told the press that, 'it was time someone spoke out for the white man in this country'. Party Conference supported his call for entry controls. The Government did gain some respite when negotiations with Commonwealth countries ensured that immigration remained off the agenda at the 1959 General Election. Oswald Mosley's failure to convert exploitation of the 1958 race riots into electoral success in 1959 provided additional respite. Polling 8.1%, Mosley lost his deposit in Kensington North, an area badly affected by the riots. However, respite was minimal.

The 1959 General Election produced the paradoxical effect of a Prime Minister with a much increased majority but also potentially far more hostility from the right. Some newly elected Birmingham Conservative MPs united and pressed for action against an issue they claimed that the electors had raised during the campaign. In January 1961 Harold Gurden, Conservative MP for Birmingham Selly Oak, arranged a meeting to campaign for immigration controls that was comprised of party backbenchers who represented areas where immigration was keenly felt. The following month, Osborne put a motion to the Commons that provided seemingly coherent and reasonable arguments in favour of immigration control. However, coherence and reasonableness disappeared when Osborne explicitly identified black immigrants as the major problem. His comment, 'This is a white man's country and I want it to remain so', was more in tune with Hilton. Debate within the Commons was openly racist at times, with Norman Pannell, Conservative MP for Liverpool Kirkdale, especially prominent. This debate presented the Government with a dilemma. If the leadership granted immigration controls, they would be open to the charges of racism and risk refreshing memories of embarrassing pre-war connections with fascism. However, if the leadership failed to act it would inflame the right wing, which seemed to be coalescing and more organised. The comments of David Renton, the government spokesman in the debate, reflected this dilemma. Renton was the Joint Under-Secretary of State for the Home Office. He denied or minimised every problem that those seeking immigration controls raised, and assured the Commons that the Government was against discrimination. Yet, paradoxically, Renton argued that immigration would become a more severe problem if it continued. Renton's admission that the Government was indeed considering possible solutions questioned his conclusion that the motion was impractical and the Government not ready to act.

Late in 1961, the Government introduced the Commonwealth Immigration Bill. Rising unemployment, which was especially severe among New Commonwealth immigrants, contributed to this decision. Worsening economic conditions would result in the Government's poor performance in four by-elections in spring 1962 and culminate in the shocking loss at Orpington on a 27% swing to the Liberals. The Commonwealth Immigration Bill was largely a response to the electorate's economic fears that led to these startling by-election losses. However, there is also little doubt that immigration per se also increasingly concerned the electorate. Investigations revealed that the number of those thinking immigration too high had increased; it would reach 84% of those polled by 1963. Therefore, in one sense the decision to introduce the Bill after many years of delay was a consequence of pressure exerted from outside the Government and party. Yet, internal pressure also played a powerful role. Many letters from party members in the Conservative Party Archive support this view. The actions of Conservative MPs Gurden, Osborne, Pannell *et al.*, add weight to this view. More cynically, the Bill allowed the Conservative Government to appease its grass roots. It may also have pacified those Conservative MPs alienated by the extent and speed of decolonisation.

However, the Commonwealth Immigration Bill also had implications for the Conservative Party's relationship with the extreme right. The Bill did not place limits on future immigration, or address the issue of repatriation. Both omissions allowed the Government to combat charges of racism and memories of painful pre-war associations from resurfacing. However, the Bill's implementation of a colour bar, made clear by exempting Southern Irish immigrants from stringent entry requirement, did meet one of the extreme right's most substantial demands. In doing so, the Government had extended its reach into extreme-right political space it had hitherto avoided. This presented the extreme right with problems. The politically involved like Hilton may have understood the Bill's limitations, but its enactment in 1962 provided those who were considering supporting extreme-right groups with a dilemma. Should they vote for a Conservative government that had passed a law addressing their fears of black immigration, despite some Conservative MPs obvious distaste for the Bill, and despite extensive and swift decolonisation? Alternatively, should they cast their vote for a miniscule group such as the LEL or True Tory? The lack of any electoral breakthrough in any by-elections in the 1959–64 Parliament suggests that extreme-right voters stuck with the Conservative Party, even if reluctantly. Thus most of these voters undoubtedly knew that their objectives had more chance of realisation by voting Conservative. Therefore, the Commonwealth Immigration Act of 1962 cut the feet from under True Tory and further limited the appeal of the LEL, regardless of its intent.

Many people in Britain may have shared Hilton's views on immigration. Some undoubtedly shared his views on race. Few shared his imperial ambitions, especially after 1945. Inter-war parties that advocated the imperial cause had achieved respectable levels of support. However, between the Second World War and Hilton's launch of True Tory in 1960, these parties' electoral results were derisory. The Empire Free Trade Crusade (1929–31) and the United Empire Party (1930–31) secured votes of 24–37% at by-elections in 1930 and 1931. In contrast, the British Empire Party of P. J. Ridout (1951–52) gained only 3.4% in the one constituency it contested in the 1951 General Election. The subsequent vehicle for Ridout's views, the League of Empire Loyalists, secured only 4% at Lewisham North in February 1957. Those parties that focused their British Nationalism domestically rather than imperially faired no better. While Mosley was performing badly at Kensington North in the 1959 General Election, the erstwhile member of Mosley's Union Movement and the League of Empire Loyalists, John Bean, unsuccessfully campaigned for the National Labour Party candidate at St Pancras North, gaining just over 4%. These results support the view that the electorate was apathetic towards a moribund Empire, but there was other evidence too. Contemporary observers believed that traditional working-class entertainments such as music hall were declining. Instead, people watched the modern equivalent of these declining entertainments in the isolation of their homes, television productions such as *Saturday Night at the London Palladium* and game shows like *What's My Line*, just as Barstow depicted in *A Kind of Loving*. In 1960, the same year that Hilton formed True Tory, the film version of *The Entertainer* based on John Osborne's play of 1957 coincidentally premiered. Osborne used the disappearing music hall genre as a metaphor for the declining Empire in *The Entertainer*. He portrayed Britannia naked save for a trident and helmet, which represented cinematically Britain's imperial weakness just as Hilton represented it politically. It was a view that Britons themselves increasingly voiced.

Not all groups alienated by societal changes focused on immigration and race. Fears about the changing morals that *A Kind of Loving* exemplified provided an impetus to Moral Re-Armament, a group that emerged from the Oxford Group founded in 1938 by Reverend Frank Buchman, intending to bring Christian values to the fore in political and social issues. This objective was acceptable to many Conservatives. However, in 1946 prominent Labour MPs had highlighted the Oxford Group's associations with leading members of the Nazi Party.[26] Therefore, any connection with Moral Re-Armament was dangerous for the Conservative Party, and Central Office and progressive Conservatism could not tolerate it. In April 1962, a Conservative MP narrowly missed de-selection for his membership of Moral Re-Armament, and received the instruction to spend more time with his constituency.[27] Central Office objected to Conservatives using party platforms to make Moral Re-Armament speeches. It objected to the religious bigotry inherent within an exclusively Christian political organisation that promoted just one religious creed, as it had objected to R. W. Petter and his New Reform Party. Some Conservatives complained that Central Office issued directives warning local associations against associating with Moral Re-Armament, and sought clarification. These brought the by now standard

Central Office reply that denied any connection or association with such organisations, but its internal correspondence revealed a belief that Moral Re-Armament was 'ultra right wing'. However, if extreme-right individuals such as Hilton were backing an imperial horse that the electorate now considered lame, Moral Re-armament was flogging a dead one, as revealed by massive sales of *Lady Chatterley's Lover* after jurors acquitted its publishers of indecency charges on 2 November 1960.

This failure of morality as an issue for the extreme right added to the impotence of imperialism as a mobilising force, and Mosley's failure to exploit the issue of race. Race was the issue most central to the extreme right's thinking, as seen in Hilton's comments, but if Mosley could not harness genuinely held concerns about immigration, what chance had those with much less public recognition? The failure of these issues was due to economic considerations being far more pressing for the electorate. The ubiquitous nature of economic concerns affected all electors, not just right-wing extremists. However, ubiquity made this issue potentially far more problematic for the Conservative Party and Government. Two factors provided the extreme right scope to attack Macmillan's Government on this front after the 1959 General Election: poor economic management and a failure to counter increased trade union militancy.

The Right to work

Chancellor Amory's 1959 give-away Budget might have helped Macmillan win the 1959 General Election, but it also increased the trade gap and inflation as imports increased to meet consumer demand. Macmillan baulked against harsh remedial measures. Amory realised the necessity of overturning the pre-election Budget and offered to resign, but Macmillan refused. Amory consequently produced a neutral Budget in April 1960. When Amory eventually resigned in June 1960, Macmillan made Selwyn Lloyd Chancellor, a promotion that Sandbrook thought indicated Macmillan's determination to run the Treasury himself. However, when Lloyd's measures also appeared to be failing, evidenced by the shattering loss of Orpington in March 1962, Macmillan quickly sacked him. Macmillan's mishandling of the resulting reshuffle destroyed his public image of unflappability. His sacking of one-third of the Cabinet earned the soubriquet the 'Night of the Long Knives'. However, Macmillan's effective takeover of the Treasury in 1960 had identified its policies with the Prime Minister personally, which is important when considering the opinions of the right wing. Viewed in this light, the New Approach of 1961, a turn towards corporatism and state planning,[28] becomes even more a product of Macmillan's political philosophy. Macmillan's advocacy of state intervention and consensus with labour was unacceptable to many on the right. His actions would increase right-wing suspicions about a Prime Minister that they held responsible for the staggeringly swift dismantling of the British Empire, as they revealed to them a Prime

Minister incapable of managing the economy due to a personal penchant for socialistic economic theory.

Macmillan's apparent appeasement of organised labour exacerbated right-wing suspicions. Many right-wingers viewed organised labour as Communism's domestic vanguard, but they were not alone in this view. The Boulting Brothers produced *I'm All Right, Jack* (1959), a film satire of union selfishness and incompetence that the left viewed as an unpardonable assault on the Labour movement. The film depicted ostracism, a Lenin-worshipping shop steward who refused to accept a union member's incompetence as sufficient grounds for dismissal, a wildcat strike that spread throughout British industry, and a government minister who was incapable or unwilling to become involved. The film struck a chord with many due to the increased incidence of such action in the real economy. The film's composition of those demonstrating against the unofficial action was also revealing when considering the right's opinion of the government's inertia towards organised labour. The only groups identified among protesters supporting the right to work are the British Housewives' League and the LEL. This suggested that the Boulting Brothers knew exactly who was prepared to confront the unions when the Conservative Government would not. Much harder-hitting was *The Angry Silence* (1960), winner of the 1961 BAFTA Award for Best British Screenplay. The film opened with a pre-arranged meeting between a naive union official and an imported Communist agitator, making clear that what followed resulted from Communist design. The Communist manipulated the union man to escalate petty grievances into a wildcat strike. Tom Curtis, an employee struggling to make ends meet with two children and a pregnant wife in an inadequate flat and faulty television brought on hire purchase, ignored the unofficial strike because it was unpaid. The union official accepted the agitator's plan to utilise Curtis's stance, unaware that the agitator worked under instruction from his political masters to disrupt the factory's contribution to the Cold War effort. His actions resulted in Curtis's ostracism and intimidation, and sympathy strikes in other factories. National press and television became involved. Alan Whicker devastatingly interviewed juvenile strikers, and revealed the ignorance and callousness of those who tormented Curtis. Meanwhile, schoolchildren attacked Curtis's son. Curtis lost the sight in one eye when two of Whicker's interviewees attacked him. Conservative newspapers praised *The Angry Silence* for dealing with an issue many thought that the Government ignored, although the left-wing press vilified it. *The Angry Silence* was simplistic, inaccurate, and even paranoid. British unions were much less active than their European counterparts and many British workers held long-standing grievances in an unequal society. However, that is to miss the point. The film succeeded because it resonated with an electorate that personally or vicariously experienced the effects of union action. The criticism of union excesses by those who wrote, filmed, directed, and starred in *The Angry Silence* reflected this experience, many of whom deferred their salaries to make their point.

The fact that the British electorate only experienced British circumstances minimises charges that industrial relations were worse elsewhere. It is unlikely that many electors soothed their irritation by comparing British industrial relations with those in Europe, Japan, or America. Instead, what they saw was a government incapable or unwilling to act against increased industrial action. The average number of strikes lost in the decade to 1964 increased by nearly 50% on the previous decade, and working days lost nearly doubled. Wildcat strikes increasingly predominated. Macmillan's Government submitted to union demands or introduced poorly thought out policies. Soon after the 1959 General Election, Macmillan agreed a 5% rise for railway workers to avoid a crippling strike. It did not work. Strikes occurred in the docks, car, and construction industries, and the Post Office, in 1960 and 1961. Similarly ineffective were Chancellor Lloyd's attempts to curb economic pressures that led workers to strike. His 'pay pause' of July 1961 to March 1962 applied only to public sector workers and had no statutory enforcement. It outraged the unions. The 'pay pause' failed dismally as pay awards simply ignored it. Such was the level of concern over these events that *The Stagnant Society* (1961), which attacked the restrictive role played by unions in achieving a more prosperous society, became an unlikely best-selling book for the Industrial Editor of the *Financial Times*. *The Stagnant Society* reflected Macmillan's views in *The Middle Way*, favouring planning as a remedy for economic malaise and intellectual torpor. It was in this atmosphere that Macmillan had openly turned corporatist and introduced the National Economic Development Council. However, regardless of whether the Conservative Government's response was a product of benign inertia, woolly-minded appeasement, or something more sinister, the effect was similar to that which had favoured the emergence of Hilton and True Tory in that it opened political space on the right. This was similar to the Government's handling of immigration in that it forced disillusioned extreme-right figures to choose whether to operate beyond the comforts provided by party membership or accept party discipline. As one right-wing MP who unsuccessfully attempted to remain inside the Conservative Party subsequently put it: 'Into the vacuum of political leadership thus created … stepped the dynamic personality of Edward Martell.'[29]

Since the 1957 East Ham by-election, Edward Martell's People's League for the Defence of Freedom (PLDF) had been quiescent. Redundancies at Martell's printing presses and reduced publications of *The People's Guardian* suggested that Martell's political star was declining. However, disgruntled Conservatives continued to voice their discontent in Martell's publications, and in April 1960 Martell felt that the circumstances were propitious enough to re-enter the political spotlight and therefore launched *The New Daily*. This newspaper advocated a return to Christian principles, and persistently criticised the Government's failure to counter inflation, union strength, falling moral standards, and its spending. Martell also tapped into the morality debate that was a particular phenomenon of the time, just like Moral Re-Armament and Hilton's True Tory. However, Martell's comments focused almost exclusively on domestic issues, and soon took an exasperated and irritated tone. Martell responded to the Government's justification of its non-intervention in industrial action by stating, 'If this is the best that Tory intellectuals can do in their approach to the menace which trade unionism in its present form presents to the nation we might as well put our money on the London School of Economics and be done with it.'[30] He argued that the current Conservative Party leadership was too entrenched to effect the necessary changes, suggesting its removal in *The New Daily*.[31] When regional Conservative newspapers, such as the *Hornsey Conservative News*, extolled the Government's achievements, *The New Daily* retorted that the Government was failing in areas including independent defence capability, trade union power, crime, transport, inflation, and productivity.[32]

Theoreticians who focus on the primacy of culture see harking back to a golden age and the seeking of a charismatic individual to run the country as hallmarks of fascism. These features were present in Martell and *The New Daily*. When Sir Cyril Osborne decried that Protestantism's lost influence had resulted in a soft generation unwilling to endure the discipline necessary to withstand communism's challenge to Christendom, *The New Daily* agreed.[33] Osborne's comments reflected sharply declining attendance at Protestant services, but they also tapped into the Orange strand within Conservatism that other extreme-right figures such as Petter of the New Reform Party had displayed.[34] For *The New Daily*, the solution to the country's problems was obvious. It lauded Oliver Cromwell as the epitome of Englishness and, although it bemoaned that no such leader was currently available, it stated that, 'he certainly exists and may we hear from him very soon'.[35] Whom did *The New Daily* mean? Additionally, although it did not advocate, like Hilton, the restoration of a British Empire based on skin colour, Martell's publication embroiled itself in the immigration issue. It identified 'coloured immigrants' as the source of problems in housing, vice, crime, unemployment, and the Welfare State.[36] *The New Daily* called for a check on 'coloured' immigration while denying it was prejudiced, which resembled right-wing Conservative MPs rather than Oswald Mosley. Nevertheless, it is unsurprising that *The New Daily* had to deny charges of fascism from the outset,[37] or that it was 'secretly backed by Sir Oswald Mosley and his so-called "Union Party"'.[38] The author of the article that denied these accusations described Mosley as a 'demagogue' and was incredulous that anyone would think *The New Daily* 'would ever accept support of any kind from a Fascist source', and concluded that malice lay behind these rumours. Yet, it was *The New Daily's* comments on immigration that had made such an accusation credible.

Frustratingly, *The New Daily* did not identify its accusers. However, the accusation was the same damnation by inference that Central Office suggested its activists use on Martell's PLDF at the East Ham by-election.[39] Martell's literature continued to circulate within constituencies, and enquiries about the PLDF to Central Office received the same emphatic denial of support as hitherto. Central Office possessed both the means and opportunity to act against Martell's organisations. Moreover, Central Office possessed a motive for describing *The New Daily* as fascist because of the similarity of Martell's views and those of right-wing Conservative MPs who were increasingly at odds with the party leadership since the 1959 General Election.[40] If effectively made, the inference of fascist connections would diminish the credibility of *The New Daily's* attacks against the Government. It would also remove an avenue of support to dissident Conservative MPs. Thus, while it is unclear whether Central Office or any other Conservative organisation made the specific accusation against *The New Daily*, or whether it resulted from their previous inference at East Ham, their involvement would be unsurprising. Unfortunately for Macmillan's Government, the accusations appeared not to stick as *The New Daily* and Martell prospered. The frequency of *The New Daily's* comments on immigration declined after the introduction of the Commonwealth Immigration Bill in 1961, which was perhaps not coincidental considering the Bill's probable impact on *The New Daily's* readers. The Bill's passage may even have helped Martell's publication as it reduced the likelihood that *The New Daily* would comment on immigration, the one issue that its opponents could link with fascism. However, this left Macmillan's Government with an even bigger problem. It could no longer simply smear *The New Daily* as a fascist or racist organisation, which now presented coherent arguments on less contentious issues from the right that resonated with irritated Conservative MPs and voters.

Commander Hyde C. Burton was a regular contributor to Martell's publications who epitomised Conservative irritation. *The New Daily* serialised Burton's comments under the heading 'The Great Betrayal: An Indictment of a Decade of Conservative Socialism, 1952–1962'.[41] Burton was a retired naval officer and veteran of both world wars with commercial interests in Malaya. However, his concerns about decolonisation had not led him to the imperialist stance of Chesterton or Hilton. Instead, Burton criticised from the direction of the 'Freedom Right'. He believed in economic liberalism, which placed him and those of similar views outside the position of contemporary Conservative governments. Burton also understood that many dissident Conservative and extreme-right groups existed because of Conservative governments' actions in other areas. He included the Elizabethan Party with the Society for Individual Freedom, Middle Class Alliance, Fighting Fund for Freedom, and Aims of Industry, as examples of this dissidence. However, Burton's articles overwhelmingly focused on Conservative governments' mishandling of domestic and economic issues rather than imperial ones. In January 1961, Burton lambasted 'weak Conservative governments' for betraying the country by their failure 'to protect the general community against the demands of the militant trade union leaders and semi-Communist shop stewards who call the tune'. In September 1961, he described Chancellor Lloyd's 'pay pause' as a panic measure, claiming that this was the 'direct and inevitable result of ten years of Socialism administered by so-called Conservative Governments', which had 'sold the country down the river' instead of proving the trustees of private property and individual liberty. Burton threw the Prime Minister's words back at him, arguing that Macmillan had duped the electorate with phrases such as 'You have never had it so good' while unscrupulously pursuing socialist policies that were 'bringing us to national bankruptcy'. He condemned Chancellor Lloyd as Macmillan's puppet for giving in to threats by the President of the Electricians Trade Union, a surrender he viewed as proving the pay pause's impotence as it revived 'an inflating wage spiral'. If readers missed Burton's inference of political cowardice, or what was required, he made it clear by comparing 'Our weak-kneed "Conservative" politicians' who never have 'the "guts" to throw down that challenge', to de Gaulle and Roosevelt who had made strikes in nationalised industries illegal. Successive Conservative governments had 'run away every time a national industry has put in a wage claim', and the 'latest surrender' to the electricians had finally squashed any hopes that the 'correct and resolute action' of implementing a true free market economy would ever occur. By the end of 1961, Burton wondered whether, 'after ten years of Socialism administered by pseudo-Conservatives, free enterprise in Britain has come to an end'.

What Central Office thought of these attacks in *The New Daily* is unknown. However, it was sufficiently concerned by November 1961 to ascertain Martell's financial situation. Martell was plainly operating in fertile soil, echoing views held by many Conservatives. On 1 January 1962, he responded to their perception that Conservative governments had failed by forming The National Fellowship. Martell claimed that 2,000 people backed him.[42] This included Conservative MPs Dr Donald Johnson and Captain Henry Kerby, both frequent speakers at large meetings of The National Fellowship. The National Fellowship's funds appeared plentiful. Martell seemed to be making a significant move.

Martell used *The New Daily* to spread The National Fellowship's views. It reached a circulation of approximately 100,000, and was therefore capable of making an impact. This meant that Commander Burton's criticisms of the Conservative Government's economic mismanagement and adherence to what he perceived as socialist philosophy reached a wider audience. In February 1962, Burton warned that Macmillan's establishment of the National Economic Development Council heralded Britain moving towards 'an era of governmental dictatorship'. The following month, Burton attacked 'the present left-of-Centre leadership which continues to impose Socialism on both Parliament and the country'. He believed that the Government had failed to recognise the significance of the by-election defeat at Orpington, and explained his position by claiming that, 'the true Conservative feels that he has to revolt against what he considers to be the Government's mischief and unwisdom'. Burton also believed that Macmillan and the rest of the Cabinet would 'not be deflected from their Socialism', and denounced the Conservative Party's failure to do anything to stop them. He did reveal some racist sentiment when he called the Conservative Party 'a party of expediency, a party of retreat, the party of cowardice, the party of surrender to the blackmail of organised trade unions at home and to the black demagogues abroad', but there was little substantial that suggested racism akin to that of Hilton. The summer of 1962 brought the Conservative government some relief from Burton's offensive as he thought that the 'Night of the Long Knives' Cabinet reshuffle of 13 July presented an opportunity to fight the forthcoming General Election on: 'Conservative principles and not on Socialist expediency'. However, whatever relief summer brought was gone by the autumn. On 3 October 1962, *The New Daily* carried an open letter from Burton to Macmillan. A rail strike had inconvenienced Burton, who once again levelled the charge of cowardice against a government that failed to deal with organised labour. He ended by claiming that Macmillan was doing as much harm domestically as he had in Africa, implicitly calling for a revolt to remove him. The National Fellowship threatened the Conservative Government as it provided critics like Burton with a regular platform to attack it from the right.

Central Office kept The National Fellowship at arm's length and monitored it throughout 1962. Donald Johnson MP explained this attitude towards The National Fellowship when he stated that official disapproval of his link with it was 'virtually guaranteed' because it was 'considered dreadfully Right-Wing to be with the National Fellowship'.[43] More specifically, Johnson continued that in 1962 it was still 'considered to be the extreme of Right-Wingism to criticise the trade unions even for their most irresponsible actions'. Additionally, Johnson made it clear that disapproval of his links with The National Fellowship came specifically from Central Office. A Central Office warning to the Conservative candidate at the July 1962 Leicester North East by-election against involvement with Martell supported Johnson's view. Johnson's memoirs are admittedly frustrating. His claim that official disapproval was 'perhaps natural on account of the type of support it attracted', was unexplored. Nor can we ignore the possibility that official disapproval of Johnson resulted from his own actions. Johnson engaged in personality clashes and supported awkward parliamentary Motions, which would not have endeared him to Central Office. Yet, these considerations do not lessen Johnson's belief that Central Office frowned on membership of The National Fellowship because it viewed it as extremist. Indeed, Johnson's comments simply confirmed the view that Central Office was the Conservative Party's vehicle for counter-measures against perceived extremists, which Central Office had also demonstrated in official attitudes towards Martell's earlier vehicle the PLDF. The word 'vehicle' appropriately explains Central Office's caution. For in 1962, Martell joined the Conservative Party. His aim was to make his views dominant within the Conservative Party by 1975, according to Johnson. Martell may have desired political advancement, and he did swiftly become a ward chairman in the Hastings Conservative Association. If so, Central Office faced an individual using an organisation to enter the Conservative Party from the right, possibly with the intent of dominating it. Support from Conservative MPs made countering Martell problematic. Central Office could not make insinuations of fascist connections when The National Fellowship had two Conservative MPs on its National Executive. However, Central Office understood the need for careful and subtle handling of The National Fellowship.

The events of 1963 proved how careful Central Office needed to be. Martell brought his various organisations together under the umbrella title 'Freedom Group', and increased his campaign against Macmillan's Government. Mass, organised Freedom Group meetings provided evidence of the scale of Conservative discontent. The Freedom Group orchestrated letter-writing campaigns that ensured ministers were aware of this discontent. Unofficial referendum campaigns organised via *The New Daily* and mainstream newspapers targeted unpopular policies and ministers. These referendums enjoyed front-page prominence in *The New Daily*. Their results made it clear that Conservative irritation focused on the Government's 'pink-socialism' and those who administered it. These referendums were radical methods aimed to effect radical policies, both of which were anathema to traditional Conservatives. Martell held them at a time when the Government looked increasingly inept. In January, President de Gaulle ended Macmillan's hopes of Britain entering the EEC, and at a stroke removed his chance to deflect attention away from domestic concerns. In June, the Profumo Affair erupted, dealing the Government and Macmillan a severe blow. Macmillan's support for Profumo did not reflect the public's sense of scandal, and therefore reinforced the notion of an increasing disconnection between the Government and the electorate. As well as creating political space on the right of the Conservative Party, Macmillan had also created a political vacuum at the head of government.

Martell commenced 1963 with an article in *The New Daily* titled 'A Year of Great Activity For Us All'. Having placed comprehensive adverts in the previous day's *Times* and *Daily Telegraph*, Martell launched an 'Independence Campaign' urging rejection of the Nassau Agreement.[44] He advocated a staged letter-writing campaign that would involve successively the reader's MP, Chairman of the local Conservative Association, national newspapers, and the Prime Minister, and tapped Conservative anti-Americanism to reinforce demands for an independent British nuclear deterrent. However, perhaps more worrying for Central Office was Martell's intention to increase the Freedom Group's potential impact with a recruitment drive, and the publication of *A Book of Solutions* that looked like a rudimentary political manifesto. Central Office did not wait to see if Martell's action heralded a new party or not. On 8 January, it decided that all Chairmen of Conservative local associations had to provide the names of constituents who had joined Martell's organisation. Local association Chairmen acted quickly on this directive, as indicated by a letter of 9 January from a Chairman in the North West Area asking Martell for the names of constituents in his area as a 'gesture of goodwill'. Central Office's action was more vigorous than the attempted identification of members of the LEL within the Conservative Party as that did not include constituents. This does not prove that Central Office intended a witch-hunt against Freedom Group members, but it is evidence that it attempted to counter Martell's impact on the Conservative Party at the local level. Central Office's directive to local association chairmen, when added to its previous comments about Martell's organisations and Donald Johnson's views regarding The National Fellowship, indicated that Central Office saw Martell's Freedom Group as a viable extreme-right organisation that posed a potential threat to the Conservative Party. If so, Martell's subsequent actions suggested Central Office was correct.

The year 1963 did indeed prove to be a year of 'Great Activity' for the Freedom Group. At the end of January, *The New Daily* began a referendum on Cabinet changes that asked readers which members they trusted, which they wished to see promoted, and which they wanted demoted.[45] Shortly after this referendum began, some evidence of Freedom Group influence in the citadels of traditional Conservatism emerged. Under the liberator-pseudonym of 'Brutus', a regular contributor to *The New Daily* highlighted an article in *The Daily Telegraph* titled: 'Is It Too Late For The Tories?'[46] The use of the soubriquet *Daily Torygraph* reflects the common view that the *Daily Telegraph* is the Conservative Party's 'house-paper'. The article that 'Brutus' highlighted was written by Colin Welch, an advocate of Freedom Group policies. 'Brutus' requested that *The Daily Telegraph*, 'adopt Mr. Welch's policy and campaign for it with all the undoubted authority they possess'. The request showed that Welch's views were not the paper's official stance, but 'Brutus' saw the article as a positive step and pointed to another encouraging sign. 'Brutus' identified two Motions at the 16th Annual Conference of the Surrey Young Conservatives as especially noteworthy under the sub-heading 'Light Is Breaking Through', one calling for tough anti-union measures, the other critical of the lack of 'Conservative' policies under the current government. 'Brutus' thought 'The fact that the powers-that-be which control such Conferences have allowed two such Motions to get on the Agenda is quite as important as the wording of the Motions themselves.'

In February, *The New Daily* criticised the Government's handling of the steel industry. Macmillan's Government had supported two nationalised steel companies, Richard Thomas, and Baldwins, in their attempt to purchase the privately owned Whitehead Iron and Steel Company. *The New Daily* referred to Labour MP Michael Foot's *Tribune* article claiming that the Conservative Party now had no argument should a future Labour Government nationalise the steel industry completely, and agreed.[47] Conservative writers also contributed articles to *The New Daily* criticising the Conservative Research Department's inability to counter the assumption that progress was synonymous with being left wing. Anthony Lejeune argued that, 'It is surely possible to present radical Right-wing policies which would seem more exciting to young people than the conventional fussiness of the Left'.[48] The same edition of *The New Daily* proposed another letter-writing campaign, this time to support the parliamentary Motion that Conservative MP Harold Gurden had tabled that called for a Royal Commission to investigate the causes of strikes and disputes. *The New Daily* described Gurden's action as 'an attempt to make the Government face up to a matter which they have consistently avoided since they came to power eleven years ago', thus tarring all post-war Conservative governments with the brush of industrial appeasement.[49] It also reinforced the message that it represented the views of disgruntled backbenchers as well as ordinary party members by listing the names of Conservative MPs who supported Gurden's Motion. The following day, *The New Daily* colourfully combined an attack on governmental inertia over strikes with a warning about the damage government inaction caused by stating that the 'maggot of inactivity has eaten its way into the organisation of the Tory Party until it has become one of the main reasons for a malaise which threatens the Party's very existence'.[50] Less than a week later, *The New Daily* claimed that its letter-writing campaign was responsible for the increased support for Gurden's Motion from Conservative MPs, and exhorted its readers to step up their campaign.[51] Considering the political context and that Martell was already the subject of one comprehensive report,[52] it is highly probable that these activities increasingly concerned Central Office.

March provided no respite in Martell's actions. *The New Daily* reported a Freedom Group meeting in Canterbury and focused on Martell's comment about a Conservative leadership that imposed Socialism on the party and country.[53] More troubling was the inclusion of a two-year programme of Freedom Group activity that indicated its organised criticism would not cease before parliament ended in 1964.[54] The next day *The New Daily*'s Editorial attacked Iain Macleod, whom the right viewed as the chief proponent of the Government's socialist tendencies and blamed for the failure to counter trade union abuses.[55] The week following, *The New Daily* announced a new style Freedom Group campaign, dubbed the 'Hastings Experiment'.[56] The 'Hastings Experiment' aimed to swamp a single constituency with the Freedom Group's political material, and included a series of four conferences. Martell exaggeratedly portrayed it as a response to grassroots demands, but the 'Hastings Experiment' was simply a product of his organisational and publicity skills. Nor was it an experiment, but a carefully prepared event to further the Freedom Group's role and Martell's own ambitions. *The New Daily* published its lead article about the 'Hastings Experiment' before its occurrence. Its favourable reporting of the second meeting cannot hide the fact that this only amounted to sixty individuals and possibly included Freedom Group officials, despite claiming that it attracted twice the expected audience. These facts bear out the impression that the Freedom Group was Martell's personal vehicle more than the product of grassroots Conservative revolt. So, too, do *The New Daily*'s reports of the Hastings Experiment. *The New Daily* noted that all audience members wished to keep the Labour Party from power and stated the consensus view that, 'there is not much hope of doing so if things are allowed to go on drifting as they are at present'. Thereafter, it portrayed the audience's view that the Conservative Party was not the vehicle for such ambitions, and made it clear that, 'they feel there is no incentive to work for the Conservative cause because traditional Conservative policies have been abandoned, their complaints and suggestions are ignored and evaded, and pink Socialism pervades the Party more and more'. If the Conservative Party was not the vehicle to keep Labour out, then what was?

The New Daily's article concluded by stating that it believed Central Office was interested in the 'Hastings Experiment', and promised to forward its full results to the Party Chairman. Central Office probably knew about the 'Hastings Experiment' as it was in the public domain. It probably viewed it in its true light: a contrived event from an extreme-right individual possibly aiming to attract sufficient Conservative discontent to replace or take over the Conservative Party. However, Central Office could not afford to ignore the Freedom Group's potential impact on the Conservative Party, regardless of the limited attendance at its events. The result of the Colne Valley by-election three days later on 21 March 1963 would not have eased any fears Central Office had about Martell's potential impact on the party. The Conservative candidate polled less than 50% of the vote in the previous General Election and came a poor third. *The New Daily* judged that this by-election result was the 'writing on the wall for the coming General Election', and proclaimed that 'The Macmillan Revival Has Failed' and demanded that 'MacLeod Must Go Now.'[57] Martell's subsequent comments lent weight to fears that he was prepared to act in ways contrary to the leadership's views and not necessarily in conjunction with the Conservative Party. He argued that there was no evidence of a change for the better, and stated in italics for impact, *'unless somebody makes it happen'*. Martell concluded that if Conservative leaders could not be made to understand that ordinary members had a right to play their part in preparing for the next General Election, and failed to improve their ways, 'they must not be surprised or resentful if we attempt to do it for them – and ourselves'. Finally, if the Conservative leaders ignored the results of the 'Hastings Experiment', Martell menacingly hinted that, 'we must try some other way'. These were not merely glib words, as Martell led an organisation of alienated and irritated Conservatives that now claimed to have 160,000 members.

In May, Anthony Lejeune identified the impact of a philosophical/ideological divide on the political system and the organisation of the Conservative Party, as key factors in right-wing alienation.[58] He argued that new political paradigms had re-orientated British politics, moving the fulcrum of politics steadily leftwards as epitomised by trade union collective bargaining where employers merely lost out at slower rate rather than ever actually won. The Conservative leadership appeared to right-wing voters to be collaborating in an inexorable leftwards drift by participating in this process. Lejeune argued that whereas this process usually satisfied the left of the Labour Party as a step in the right direction, it was always a step away from the position of right-wing Conservatives. This meant that right-wing individuals who maintained their political stance became increasingly isolated from an ever-receding centre, thus turning them into extremists. Lejeune argued that as the mass of these right-wingers were in the constituencies, they were physically isolated from the counsels of the party, making it more difficult for them to affect the party's actions in government. He implied that the autonomy of local Conservative Associations further isolated these right-wing individuals, and provided an organisational distance between party members and leaders. Thus, Lejeune concluded that Conservative governments' acquiescence in policies opposed by right-wing party members impotent to do anything about them resulted in feelings of betrayal of true Conservatism, alienation and anger. Consequently, some members would abstain at the next General Election, while those that voted Conservative only did so reluctantly to stop Labour winning. Lejeune had explained the Conservative Party's alienation of its own right wing, if not quite taking it to the conclusion that some newly dissident Conservatives would consider voting for extreme-right parties, such as the League of Empire Loyalists, or even form them, like Hilton of True

Tory. If Lejeune argued correctly, subsequent events would see the number of alienated Conservatives increase.

Labour surged into an 18.5% opinion poll lead in the weekend after Lejeune's article, prompting more criticism of Macmillan and his administration in *The New Daily*.[59] The following week, the Profumo Affair shook Macmillan's Government to its core. Martell used his position as Editor of *The New Daily* to produce front-page banner headlines that denounced 'Degeneracy And Indolence In High Places' and 'The Collapse of Leadership',[60] putting the blame firmly at Macmillan's door. He asked readers to look back over the previous two years to see what had gone wrong, and identified declining moral standards, especially increasing gambling, drinking, and vice, as a product of Macmillan's lack of leadership. Nor did anybody seem to care, most notably the Prime Minister who had remained on holiday while his government was 'rocked by one of the greatest Parliamentary scandals there has ever been'. The answer, Martell stated emphatically, was to stop the harm the current government and Prime Minister were doing: 'Somehow they must be stopped.' Who was going to affect this? Martell did not advocate a solution enforced from the top. Instead, he stated that, 'the people must give their leaders leadership, and teach them that no nation can live that does not maintain certain standards of behaviour that should not need defining'. Thus, Martell's use of the Profumo Affair was no different from other government failings he had identified in that the solution he suggested involved a pivotal role for ordinary Conservatives, i.e. those in the Freedom Group that Martell led.

However, what was this role to be? Whether Martell aimed to usurp the Conservative Party by creating a new party or merely sought to alter its ideological position is difficult to deduce. On the one hand, public events such as the 'Hastings Experiment' and thinly veiled hints that the Freedom Group would have to act if the Conservative Party failed to, suggested that the Freedom Group could become a political party. On the other, Martell wrote openly to all Conservative MPs offering assistance in marginal seats, which suggested that he wanted Conservative Party success. Yet, in one sense, the question is immaterial. For, if Martell's objective was to change the Conservative Party's ideology, the fact is that if he succeeded it would effectively result in a new political party after many years of Conservative acceptance of post-war consensus. Martell's Conservative Party would certainly not be the same as that led by Macmillan. This consideration warrants a brief re-appraisal of Central Office's role outlined earlier,[61] especially vis-à-vis right-wing organisations. There is a perception that Central Office simply provides a range of services to the leader and to the party, and maintains efficient contact between the two. As such, Central Office is a reflection of the political philosophy and ideology of the leader and the views of the membership, which implies an equal relationship. However, when the members' views clashed with those of the leader it was the leader's views that prevailed in Central Office, as was the case with those who supported the Freedom Group and indeed all other extreme-right groups. It was most emphatically not Macmillan's wish that Edward Martell should take advantage of his current troubles to replace his political views with those represented by the Freedom Group. More generally, Central Office's role included avoiding embarrassing connections, and the monitoring of the extreme right and effecting counter-measures where necessary. Central Office had monitored Martell for some time by this stage, and it was probably considering very carefully what Martell's intentions now were. Martell's subsequent actions suggest Central Office was right to do so. One month after the Profumo Affair, Martell explicitly outlined a coherent Freedom Group plan to combat the Labour Party at the next General Election and capture the Conservative Party from within.

On 5 July, *The New Daily* carried details of the Freedom Group's plan to thwart Labour. It reported Martell's boast that the Freedom Group 'has now developed into the most powerful organisation of its kind in Great Britain' under the headline 'The Plan To Keep The Socialists Out'.[62] Martell stated three reasons why he believed the Freedom Group was capable of achieving its objective. First, with over 100,000 members and growing, the Freedom Group had sizeable support that the leadership could mobilise at short notice, all noted on a 'Master-Index' including constituency details and special interests. Secondly, Martell possessed a non-unionised printing works that he had built into a public company with £½ million in capital, which meant that the Freedom Group enjoyed a propaganda machine immune to hostile trade unions and with potential access to funds. Thirdly, the Freedom Group had a means of communicating its objectives to its members six days a week in *The New Daily*. Martell's boasts may have been completely hollow, but Central Office took them seriously, as shown by its attempt to elicit details of Conservative members of Martell's groups. Its action is unsurprising considering that Martell had announced that, 'The task of every Supporter of the Freedom Group is thus to become an active leader in the Conservative Party in his or her area' so as to push Freedom Group policies and root out 'Semi-Socialist MPs and prospective candidates … as quickly as possible'. Martell's comments and activities were much more than the adoption of street and platform cultures as seen in the British Housewives' League and other extreme-right groups by an angry but hitherto compliant Tory-voting middle class. Instead, they were a plan for infiltration of the Conservative Party. It was possibly even more. Martell now acknowledged that the Freedom Group had the potential to become a new party, adding that, 'Nobody is going to deny that there is a need for such a party.' These are not isolated words taken out of context. They were also in the public domain like the 'Hastings Experiment'. Suspicion that Martell intended infiltrating the Conservative Party or forming a new one to challenge it must have increased, and Martell's subsequent move into a political vacuum created by Conservative Party inaction would have seemed part of this 'plan'.

The Conservative Party opted not to contest the Bristol South East by-election, as it was simply a result of the incumbent, Tony Benn, renouncing his peerage. Martell's decision to stand as a 'National Fellowship-Conservative' candidate put him and his organisation in a position whereby they could portray themselves as a right-wing alternative to an absent Conservative Party.

The Times certainly thought so, reporting that Martell campaigned in front of blue posters with 'Conservative' in large letters and 'National Fellowship' in smaller ones, as well as Martell's brandishing of his party membership card in refutation of the claim that he had no connection with the Conservative Party.[63] The probability that the public would connect Martell with the Conservative Party was extremely high. Central Office opposed Martell very actively. First, it monitored The National Fellowship's selection process, and was aware that three candidates were under consideration. Secondly, Central Office asked Conservative supporters to abstain from the election, which would deny Martell support.[64] Finally, it attempted to portray Martell's candidacy as obscure and ir-relevant. The Chairman of the Bristol Conservative Association, Sir Kenneth Brown, declared that, 'I have only heard of the National Fellowship in name. I know nothing of them.'[65] The General Director at Central Office dictated to the Deputy Central Office Area Agent an official 'line' that those standing against Benn had 'no connection whatever with the Conservative Party and are receiving no support from me'. Central Office instructed that all queries were to receive the response that the Conservative Party was 'in no way con-nected with the present by-election'. However, Central Office claims were not credible. It is hard to believe that Central Office did not know that in 1961 Martell had become a Ward Chairman of the Hastings Conservative Party, es-pecially as they were so concerned about him to commission a 'Committee of Investigation' into his activities. Moreover, Sir Kenneth Brown's knowledge of Martell's organisations may well have been zero, but that does not mean that he did not know that they, and Martell, were the object of Central Office's counter-measures. As Chairman of the local Conservative Association, Brown would have received and acted upon the Central Office directive of 8 January that sought the names of Conservative Party members and voters who had joined the Freedom Group.[66] Moreover, Central Office had previously instructed offi-cials to make dubious comments to hinder an extreme-right organisation, and it is understandable that officials wished to limit Martell's organisation given the severity of the political context. However, what makes this scenario more likely was the simultaneous emergence of an internal extreme-right organisa-tion that threatened to combine alienation over the Conservative Government's domestic policy with anger at its imperial policy.

Inside right

Lejeune's argument that Conservative governments forced right-wingers onto the extreme right applied somewhat to the Monday Club. Formed in 1961,[67] the Monday Club was a response by young Conservative Party members to rapid decolonisation, and took its name from the day of the week that Macmillan made his 'winds of change' speech.[68] Its explicit questioning of decolonisation alone placed the Monday Club on the extreme right vis-à-vis the Conservative Government. In its mockingly titled pamphlet *Wind of Change or Whirlwind?*, the Monday Club stated that the Macmillan Government's desire to appear progressive had resulted in 'a Hasty Abandonment of British responsibilities in Africa', a policy it described as 'Abdication and appeasement'.[69] In the pamphlet, the Monday Club claimed that the government's action had 'put Kenya on the verge of bankruptcy and resulted in a loss of confidence in the Rhodesias that undermined its Federation, and the driving of South Africa from the Commonwealth'. The Monday Club's alternative was a return to 'Conservative principles', and not the abandonment of Britain's civilising role, as this was the only way to stop the creation of weak states prone to 'exploitation by the forces opposing us in the cold war'. These were the traditional calls of the alienated imperialist right wing in that they exhibited racial chauvinism, criticism of the Conservative Government, and fear of left-wing ideology. However, the Monday Club was much more than simply the Conservative Party's version of the LEL or True Tory. When the Monday Club called for an independent nuclear deterrent, tougher measures on crime, action on wildcat strikes, a rationalised welfare state, reduced taxation, and expressed concerns over entry into the Common Market,[70] it camped firmly in the political space of other organisations like the Freedom Group too. Moreover, as the Monday Club was unarguably within the Conservative Party, the comprehensive nature of its criticism made it potentially a far more potent threat to Conservative governments than other right-wing organisations.

Initially, Central Office appeared relaxed about the Monday Club. An early Central Office report on the Club focused insouciantly on the involvement of Young Conservatives, perhaps reflecting the predominant influence of the middle-aged within the Conservative Party. This does not mean that Central Office neglected its role of investigator of right-wing organisations. On the contrary, the report showed that Central Office maintained its intelligence-gathering role by identifying four Young Conservatives who had attended a Monday Club meeting at the Onslow Court Hotel on 25 September 1961. Similarly, on 29 November the Chief Organisation Officer wrote on a letter from the Secretary and Agent of the Wirral Conservative Association requesting information on the Monday Club, 'Do we know anything about this outfit? If not can we get a line on it?' Outwardly, the Chief Organisation Officer maintained a carefree, even dismissive air. He responded to the Wirral Conservative Association's request for information on the Monday Club denying any organisational link between it and the Conservative Party, and confidently stating that Monday Club circulars to Divisional and Young Conservative chairmen would not win it any support.

Nevertheless, Central Office continued to monitor the Monday Club. Its officials wrote two documents on the same day that the Chief Organisation Officer replied to the Wirral Conservative Association. The first document was a more detailed report on the Monday Club by E. S. Adamson. It revealed what Central Office thought the Monday Club's objectives were and who backed it. Adamson highlighted the role of youth in the Monday Club's formation, and noted that its first chairman, Paul Bristol, had failed to become a Conservative parliamentary candidate. He stated that requests for information about the Monday Club were now coming in 'from all over the country'. Adamson thought that this reflected an attempt by these young party members to 'set up an organisation along the lines of the Bow Group'. If so, then Adamson thought it possible that the Monday Club intended to create an intellectually coherent body of opinion to influence policy from within the Conservative Party as the Bow Group had. Adamson stated that, 'It would be interesting to know who is behind the movement or who is putting up the money for the printing etc.' He identified 'John Dayton and his True Tories' as one possibility, justifying his suspicion by stating that Dayton 'seems to have plenty to spend and this sort of attack would fit with his ideas'. Adamson also commented that the only mention of the Monday Club in the press was in *The New Daily*, and that the Free Press, 'which is Martell's', printed the Monday Club's literature, but added that this connection was 'purely fortuitous for Martell has no money to spare nor is this his line of country'.

Adamson's comments may have allayed suspicion that the Monday Club was another Martell organisation, but some were not so sure. This suspicion is evident in Central Office's second document on the Monday Club, written by Area Agent A. S. Garner on 30 November 1961. The document was a response to a request for information about the Monday Club from the Unionist MP S. Knox Cunningham, who had received their literature. Cunningham was also Macmillan's Parliamentary Secretary. He telephoned Central Office to enquire about the Monday Club, and then wrote from 10 Downing Street requesting further information. Garner referred to the Martell connection and thought that, 'It may be that they get their money from there.' Garner's letter also revealed how Central Office viewed the Monday Club. He advised Cunningham that Central Office had sent an 'unofficial observer' to the Monday Club meeting of 25 September, who reported that the Monday Club was 'formed by former members of the Bow Group who held extreme-right views'. Garner passed on the view that the Monday Club members held 'extreme right wing views' to Cunningham, but dismissed their importance as a very small organisation of 'a few enthusiastic young members'. The significance of this second document is that it revealed Central Office thought the Monday Club was an extreme-right organisation from the beginning.

On 4 December 1961, Central Office instructed its Area Agents to respond to all inquiries with the common line that there was no organisational link between the Conservative Party and the Monday Club. Area Agents swiftly acknowledged the directive, acutely aware of the need for loyalty as Macmillan attempted to implement contentious decolonisation. Meanwhile, Central Office tried to appear nonchalant about the Monday Club, basing its attitude on a belief that the Monday Club was a product of temporary upper-middle class youthful exuberance. A report to the General Director in January 1962 describing the Monday Club as, 'a group of young people of extreme right wing views who operate in Chelsea/South Kensington and hold their meetings at the Onslow Court Hotel by way of roughing it', confirmed this air of nonchalance. However, on 24 January, 'Peterborough' announced in the *Daily*

Telegraph that ten Conservative MPs and Lord Salisbury would be attending that day's Monday Club meeting on Rhodesia.[71] 'Peterborough's' news would have punctured any nonchalance within Central Office because it was a credible Conservative source. Two days later, the *Daily Telegraph* confirmed Salisbury's attendance. Worse, Salisbury had become the Monday Club's patron, beginning his tenure with a salvo aimed directly at Macmillan's Government when he said that, 'There never was a greater need for true Conservatism than there is today'.[72] This news changed matters. Salisbury would undoubtedly attract party critics to the Monday Club. On the same day that 'Peterborough' revealed these events, Patrick Wall, Conservative MP for Haltemprice, visited London Area Agent Garner and asked him for Central Office's view of the Monday Club. Garner concluded that Wall had decided to support the Monday Club, and warned Central Office that this would result in other MPs joining it and thus increasing its strength.

Any residual indifference that may have existed within Central Office now disappeared. Central Office ordered its own Young Conservatives' department to cease contacts with the Monday Club in February 1962. Area Agents continued sending intelligence reports to Central Office. Meanwhile, Central Office monitored attempts to create new Monday Club branches, and was probably alarmed to note that any negative aspects did not hinder its success. It was disappointed that the Monday Club's lack of clarity over aims in a presentation in February did not, according to the Central Office Area Agent for the Western Area, dampen the interest of two vice-chairmen, two vice-presidents, the Divisional Chairman of the Young Conservatives and two other office holders of the St Ives National Liberal and Conservative Association. Central Office attributed the Monday Club's success despite this lack of clarity to it containing 'the essence of the considerable dissatisfaction with recent Party policy which has been evident throughout the country'. Central Office's Area Agents and those working for them continued to try hindering the Monday Club. In February 1962, Central Office Agent Mr Welch rejected the Monday Club Chairman's request for a discussion group in Durham by claiming that the Conservative Political Centre met such needs. Welch showed that he knew the remit of the December directive precisely by passing all the correspondence on this matter to the Area Agent Mr Livingston, who in turn forwarded it to Central Office. Area Agents did not limit their activities to ordinary party members. In April, the Conservative MP for Yeovil asked the Chairman of his local Conservative Association for the names and addresses of Young Conservatives whom he thought would be amenable to an approach by the Monday Club. The Area Agent, Mr Slinn, told the Chairman that the Monday Club was not part of the Conservative Party and ordered him to withhold the details requested. Slinn forwarded the enquiry to Central Office, including his instruction to deny information to a sitting Member of Parliament. The Chief Organisation Officer thanked Slinn and made plain that in April 1962 Central Office viewed the Monday Club as an 'extremely right wing' organisation, which 'obviously are not to be trusted'.

Martell's activities may have diverted dissatisfaction from the Monday Club, but that does not mean that Central Office ignored it. Central Office could not afford to do so, especially when considering the Monday Club's actions and comments in the difficult year of 1963. Between 1 April and 15 July, 24 new members brought the Monday Club's membership to 198, at a time when a large Labour poll lead and the Profumo Affair rocked the Government.[73] Leading Monday Club members hoped that a reorganisation and embarkation on a number of operations would give the Club 'a firm place in Conservative politics'.[74] They planned an 'Annual Dinner' for October, which lent the Monday Club respectability, and by August Lord Home was among distinguished guests at its functions. Meanwhile, the Monday Club had sought funds to cover production costs of a pamphlet that they intended to distribute at the October Party Conference, *Conservatism Lost? Conservatism Regained*. Behind the scenes, Monday Club leaders continued to criticise Macmillan's policies, particularly foreign and imperial, and revealed views similar to Hilton of True Tory. In September, Salisbury expressed to Patrick Wall his fear that the Government's current policy of decolonisation would cause 'the old White Commonwealth countries' to abandon Britain's sphere of influence, leaving only 'the blacks, who have no sympathy with Britain and all that Britain stands for'.[75] This language was not simply reflective of contemporary discourse, but was also the result of a personal credo of imperialism sunk deeply in the roots of the Cecil family, and in which 'race' justified British dominance. For Salisbury, if the Government abandoned imperialism it would have dire consequences. He believed blacks to be 'our problem', and the likelihood of a 'future white versus black racial world conflict' to be 'very great' if the policy of swift decolonisation continued. As these comments came from such a high profile individual, it was also likely that Central Office saw race as crucial to the Monday Club's existence from virtually the beginning. It is hard to believe that Central Office was ignorant of these views.

If anybody in Central Office was ignorant of the Monday Club's views, the publication of *Conservatism Lost? Conservatism Regained* just before the party conference in October 1963 would have removed it. The pamphlet touched on many areas. It saw decadence as rife in a Britain where material wealth uneasily coexisted with declining religious and moral standards,[76] and a powerful, centralising state eroded individual liberties. The pamphlet claimed that the machinery of government, economy, business, taxation, and nationalised industries all needed reforming. Yet, its real focus was Britain's colonies. The pamphlet stated that the Government had allowed British colonies their independence, and bribed the electorate into acquiescence 'with promises of greater affluence and materialism'. Further, 'Nothing can be more destructive of Britain's good name than certain aspects of the Government's African policy since 1960', where, the pamphlet implied, the Government had been less than honest in its actions. The Monday Club held Macmillan responsible. Criticism of 'Too much of the old school-tie, of nepotism' transparently referred to the over-representation in the Cabinet of the major public schools, particular

Macmillan's alma mater, Eton, and the preponderance of Macmillan's relatives in the whole government. Ironically, the pamphlet quoted Lord Home. He said, 'I think the greatest danger in the world today is that the world might divide on racial lines', and thus revealed the centrality of skin colour to early Monday Club thinking. The pamphlet was a rallying call to 'new leaders', for distribution at what looked liked being a very difficult party conference. Martell's Tileyard Press printed it.

Right turn homewards?

Perhaps fortuitously for Macmillan, he did not attend the 1963 Party Conference at Blackpool. Ill health forced his sudden resignation and absence from party conference. Alec Douglas-Home, another Etonian, surprisingly succeeded Macmillan rather than the expected R. A. Butler or Lord Hailsham. In some respects, Home's succession to Macmillan reinforced existing political alignments as the Conservative Party replaced an ersatz anachronism for a real one. Home was the fourteenth earl of a family first ennobled in the fifteenth century, whose maternal ancestry connected him to the late Stuart and early Hanoverian aristocracy. Home was barely an early renaissance figure, let alone a contemporary one, and therefore contrasted poorly with the dynamic scholarship boy from Huddersfield leading the Labour Party since early 1963, Harold Wilson. Exacerbating the contrast between the two leaders was a phenomenon that did not trouble Home's forebears. On television, Home's voice, personality, and even physiognomy, reinforced the idea that the Conservatives had turned in desperation to its aristocratic core. It did not help the Conservatives that television ownership was thirteen times greater than when it regained office in 1951. Moreover, in other respects the political context had changed. Home had been a loyal lieutenant of Neville Chamberlain, unlike his three predecessors as Conservative leader. Supporting Home's candidacy was the hierarchy of the 1922 Committee of backbench Conservative MPs, who deplored decolonisation and believed that the Government had moved far too far to the left domestically. Home was unequivocally the candidate of the party's right wing, unlike Macmillan. His succession presented both Central Office and alienated right-wing Conservatives with a new situation for the post-war era, and changed the Conservative Party's relationship with some of the extreme right.

Unlike Macmillan, Home did not have the luxury of over three years before having to call a General Election. Only a bare twelve months were available to him. This consideration may also have influenced a clear change in the attitude of some extreme-right organisations and their relationship with the Conservative Party. A definite change was detectable in the Freedom Group. Martell's activities at the Bristol South East by-election in August had probably not allayed Central Office fears that he intended to infiltrate the Conservative Party or launch a new party. He had appeared on national television twice and secured 19% of the vote, which allowed Martell to claim that 'millions' had now heard of his organisation.[77] On his becoming Prime Minister, Central Office warned Home against contact with Martell because it believed that Martell would use any contact to portray himself as a confidant of the new Prime Minister. However, the Freedom Group's attitude towards the Government had altered. On 21 October 1963, *The New Daily* announced that Home's accession had restored its belief in a future Conservative election victory.[78] It also welcomed the removal of R. A. Butler from domestic policy and Iain Macleod's resignation from the Cabinet and party chairmanship, claiming that 'The Conservative Party's dangerous drift to the left has now been halted.'[79] *The New Daily* declared that Home's promotion of right-wingers demonstrated 'that progress and development need not be leftwards'. Perhaps significantly, the Area Agent for the South East reported to the Chief Organisation Officer the positive reception given to Home's accession at a public meeting in Martell's constituency.

Central Office's stance towards Martell and his organisations now changed. Somewhat disingenuously, Central Office claimed to Home's Constituency Secretary in November 1963 that it had never 'set out to dissuade any of our supporters from joining Mr. Martell's movements', and stated its pleasure at Martell's support. Central Office now argued that Martell's current position could 'do nothing but good', and denied ever taking any inimical action towards him. A reformulation of Central Office's position towards Martell was clearly under way, and as Martell embarked on yet another referendum to influence government policies in January 1964, the General Director ordered another dossier on him and his organisations. The result was much different to earlier ones in one vital respect. Innuendoes of fascism were absent.[80] Instead, the new dossier described *The New Daily* as 'anti-fascist'. However, this does not mean that Central Office ceased monitoring Martell's activities. A subsequent report summarised the extent of contact with Martell's organisations within Areas and local Conservative Associations.

Nor had Central Office necessarily had a collective change of heart regarding Martell. Its correspondence about him contained too much grudging language and qualifying comments indicating that old opinions had not really gone. Central Office described the Freedom Group's views as 'fair enough ... as it stands at the minute', suggesting that it thought this new situation was only temporary. Additionally, Central Office's new stance does not mean that it had suspended its suspicions of Martell's ultimate intentions. Martell attempted to stop the removal of his Association Chairman in March 1964, a Central Office Area Agent reported. The Agent forwarded his report to the General Director, and the Chief Organisation Officer wrote on it, 'You see how right we were. This is the "encounter battle." I suspect we shall now have "a struggle for full control" and no Queensbury rules!' This was evidence that Central Office still took seriously Martell's intention to infiltrate and take over the Conservative Party, which he had expressed in July 1963.[81] Nevertheless, Central Office's stance towards Martell during Home's premiership was different to that exhibited while Macmillan was Prime Minister. Moreover, it was a change that removed one of the most substantial barriers to an organisation's chances of having a relationship with the Conservative Party: a perception of fascist connections. Unlike previous Martell organisations, the Freedom Group proceeded to form a relationship with the Conservative Party.

At the end of April, the *Yorkshire Post* announced that the Freedom Group intended to become involved in the Huyton constituency of Labour leader Harold Wilson.[82] Martell announced that thirty-eight Conservative MPs supported the Freedom Group and the beginning of a 'decapitation strategy' to defeat Wilson in case Labour won the expected autumn General Election. On 2 May, Martell extended the Freedom Group's offer of assistance to all Conservative Associations, claiming that he had informed Party Chairman Lord Blakenham of his actions. Two days later, as Freedom Group adverts proclaimed in *The Times* its involvement in the Huyton constituency and requested donations,[83] Martell wrote to Blakenham and offered the Freedom Group's cooperation to the Conservative Party, including use of *The New Daily*. Martell received a polite, but non-committal response. Martell wrote to Blakenham once more, this time including a copy of his letter to the Chairman of the Huyton Conservative Association, Mr R. Bradley, which made it clear that the two men had recently met. If Central Office wanted to stop Martell in his tracks, this was the time to do it as no working relationship had yet developed. Central Office was perfectly capable of doing so as it had previously issued prohibitive directives concerning Martell.[84] However, at the end of May the *Observer's* report on events in Huyton quoted Martell as saying, 'We are very ready to conform to the conditions proposed by the Huyton Conservative Association',[85] which made it clear that Central Office had not issued any such directive or stopped Martell's contact with the association. What followed proved that this was not simply a case of a local association exercising its autonomy. The following day, *The Daily Telegraph* covered the story. It downplayed Martell's likely impact, but did not deny his involvement, which was perhaps a reflection of Central Office's wishes.[86]

In mid-June, Blakenham admitted privately to Conservative MP Joan Vickers that Martell was indeed assisting the party in Huyton. He justified Martell's cooperation in Huyton, and elsewhere, by stating that it was acceptable 'providing it is on our terms and not on his and if it is made quite plain that any of his members working for us agree to do so under the control of the Constituency Officers and Agent in support of our policy'. Blakenham had revealed the existence of a working relationship with an individual whom Central Office had previously been prepared to smear with accusations of fascism. In September, Martell wrote to Blakenham and enclosed the instructions given to Freedom Group workers assisting in Huyton. The instructions were completely in accordance with the remit Blakenham outlined privately to Joan Vickers. Even if these events had not raised awareness of this relationship, the campaign poster would. For, although Blakenham forced Martell to remove the Freedom Group's name from the initial version, the printing press acknowledged on the final one included the name of Tileyard Press, which belonged to Martell. Central Office knew this from its earlier investigation of Monday Club literature.[87] If it had forgotten, one call to the phone number given for Tileyard Press would reveal that it had the same telephone number as the Freedom Group.

Why had Central Office changed its attitude? Opportunism is a possible answer. The Conservatives had been in power for thirteen years and looked staid compared to Labour. Alternatively, did Central Office believe that the Freedom Group had changed? The 'Freedom Group's General Election Policy', printed in the May editions of respectable publications such as *The Times* and *Spectator*, said that immigration restrictions should not be based on skin colour.[88] This removed one of Central Office's most consistent post-1945 dividing lines in determining relations with extreme-right groups, and made association with the Freedom Group less risky. Central Office may also have believed that by using Martell they lessened his potential to harm the Conservative Party. Martell had continued criticising the Government's apathy during the summer, which Central Office may have viewed as evidence that he retained personal ambitions, whether inside the Conservative Party or not. This would explain why Blakenham stressed in his letter to Vickers that he would not be happy to see 'his group take over even the smallest section of our organisation', a comment that did not rule out Central Office using Martell to keep him within the Conservative fold and yet at arm's length. However, the explanation that Martell had become the victim of the problem facing the leaders and supporters of extreme-right organisations is just as likely. The Conservative Party seemed to have changed its orientation under Home, and thus appeared more attractive to Freedom Group members. If so, Central Office was simply reflecting this change.

In one sense, the Conservative Party's dual role is difficult to detect under Home. This is because Home effectively played Macmillan's hand with such a short space of time available. Extensive changes were injudicious in election year, and would leave the Government open to the question, why were the policies it followed for thirteen years no longer suitable? Nevertheless, Home's Government did proffer olive branches to the right. A promised inquiry into trade-union practices and legislation directly answered the Freedom Group's demands for a Royal Commission.[89] The forcing through of the abolition of Resale Price Maintenance appealed to right-wing advocates of economic liberalism, even if it did irritate many traditional Conservatives. Just as in the Commonwealth Immigration Bill, the Conservative Party was extending its reach rightwards and denying political space to those seeking to exploit it, in this instance Edward Martell and his Freedom Group, while also attracting his supporters. This rightwards move makes Central Office's changed stance towards Martell more understandable. By allowing the Freedom Group's participation in the General Election, specifically in Huyton and generally elsewhere, Central Office increased the probability that these formerly alienated supporters would vote Conservative in the General Election. However, by doing so Central Office was also driving a wedge between Martell and his supporters. It offered just enough to Martell's supporters to win them over and thus limited his ability to use them as a vehicle for his personal ambition. Blakenham's justification for using the Freedom Group revealed that this consideration was a factor. Blakenham reassured the Conservative MP that Central Office only accepted Martell's assistance after he had given 'very specific undertakings that he will not make his co-operation prior to the Election an occasion for pursuing policies in which he and his Group believe but which are not accepted by us'. Proof that this strategy worked came during the General Election campaign, when Martell acknowledged that Freedom Group members now felt that 'no extraordinary measures are needed', and abandoned a secret plan to field fifty Freedom Group candidates. The reason was obvious. Martell had conceived the plan when a 'sweeping Labour victory in the General Election was a certainty',[90] but this was no longer the case. The reason why Martell no longer believed a Labour victory was certain was that the Conservative Party under Home was again an attractive proposition to formerly alienated right-wing Conservative supporters. However, the reason why Martell abandoned his plan was as much to do with Central Office's actions.

There was a definite change in the attitude of the Monday Club too. A leading member noted that the press considered *Conservatism Lost? Conservatism Regained?* 'an attack against the leadership'.[91] The fact that the Monday Club pamphlet had quoted Lord Home's intemperate words on race made before he became Prime Minister made its publication impolitic.[92] It caused recriminations within the Monday Club and a reassessment of what it stood for. Sir Patrick Wall MP told Lord Salisbury that he thought that the problem arose from the Monday Club's young Chairman and his friends using it as their personal vehicle.[93] Furthermore, Wall thought that whereas consensus existed within the Monday Club regarding Africa, diverse views existed on other subjects, and concluded that the Club needed an effective machinery of consultation. These events show that the Monday Club was still rudimentary in its policy formulation, dissemination, and position. Senior figures like Wall also saw the Monday Club's comments as irresponsible now that Home had replaced Macmillan, the catalyst for its formation. The ensuing furore over the pamphlet within the wider Conservative Party soon caused the resignation of the Monday Club's Co-Chairman and Vice-Chairman. The Monday Club sought to repair any damage by issuing a swift explanation and a reassuring statement. It claimed that the offending publication was an expression of 'what we felt to be lacking in the Conservative system of government', but added that there was now 'already a welcome new atmosphere in the conduct of our affairs, nor is the present Prime Minister unaware of the truth about Africa'.[94] It concluded that the Monday Club henceforth 'must and will offer constructive suggestions to the Government as to how it can develop Conservative principles into practical policies'.

The Monday Club's damage limitation had immediate consequences. The minutes of its General Meeting on 14 November 1963 recorded the Chairman's disappointment at the poor attendance, despite noting that one hundred new members had joined in the previous year.[95] Patrick Wall ensured that the Monday Club discussed its orientation and function at the next meeting on

Monday 9 December 1963. However, the circular proposing the discussion showed that one embarrassing publication had not cowed the Monday Club, nor that it was prepared to settle for obscurity. Instead, this ambitious organisation remained intent on pursuing its policies. The circular pointed to the Club's focus on African and Commonwealth affairs, and admitted that the Club 'attracted an ultra-right label,'[96] but justified this as an inevitable consequence of focusing on areas that attracted most criticism of the Government. It also noted that a proposal at the recent Annual General Meeting that the Monday Club 'cease to be the exclusive preserve of the Right and should attract and embrace every colour of opinion in the Conservative Party', had received short shrift. The circular's author stated that there was 'no virtue in this', arguing that the consequence of such a move would be the Monday Club withering away 'into complete ineffectiveness'. Instead, the Monday Club should be a 'vocal conscience of Tory Principles', which counterbalanced left-wing clubs like the Bow Group. When the circular stated that the Monday Club should function as the 'nagging conscience and a spur to the Party or Government to act on true Tory principles', it identified the Club with other post-1945 extreme-right champions of Conservative ideals. However, by organising itself into specific departments, the Monday Club presented a far more realistic and coherent prospect of dealing with 'specific aspects of policy where these Tory principles have either been abrogated or not yet realised', than external groups. When the circular called for an enlarged parliamentary group that liaised with a small 'action group' backed by a team of letter-writers, it was proposing an effective mechanism for disseminating Monday Club views similar to Edward Martell's organisations. The method it outlined held greater promise of success as it advocated switching the Monday Club's vigorous attacks away from the Conservative Government to the Labour Opposition. The circular stated that this switch would legitimise the Club's policies and thus increase their chances of acceptance. However, its comment that the Monday Club should do this regardless of how 'much they were disapproved of by the pinker and less resolute Conservatives', showed that the Club would continue to operate on the extreme right of the Conservative Party. The Monday Club's members intended its function to be a 'rallying point of the Right rather than the somewhat inert refuge of the Right'.

This picture of a refocused, policy-developing organisation eager not to alienate the party leadership continued throughout election year 1964. The relationship between Central Office and the Monday Club was therefore predominantly positive. In February, the Monday Club's Annual General Meeting rejected another call for greater representation across the Conservative Party, and welcomed instead the removal of those it thought were ideologically unsound.[97] The minutes of the meeting record the cooperation of the Conservative Political Centre at Central Office in publishing the Monday Club pamphlet *Strike Out or Strike Bound*. In April, the Monday Club's Council attacked the more left-wing Bow Group, and determined on a clearer definition of the Club's domestic policy to increase the chances of their inclusion in the forthcoming manifesto.[98] In July, the Conservative Political Centre decided not to publish the Monday

Club pamphlet, *Automation*.[99] This may have resulted from a desire to avoid contentious issues near the General Election or annoyance towards a group that attacked progressives within the party. Central Office may have simply used the Monday Club's publications to attract alienated supporters, cherry-picking its acceptable literature while ignoring those deemed too contentious, using the Monday Club as an attracting agent in the Conservative Party's alienation/attraction role vis-à-vis the extreme right. The Monday Club does not appear antagonistic towards Central Office at this stage. On the contrary, its determination to 'Improve our standing with the Party Organisation' and resolution that, 'all our efforts should be towards helping the Party over the next few months', suggests that the Monday Club's aim during Home's leadership was not to 'rock the boat'. Its publication of *The Handmaidens of Diplomacy* in summer 1964 supported this picture. It comprehensively outlined deficiencies in Britain's strategic political warfare aims and focused on areas where criticism of previous Conservative governments was possible, but made none. The pamphlet instead reserved its negative comments for the traditional targets of Conservative ire such as the civil service and the BBC. It received favourable comments in *The Times*,[100] and 'an almost unprecedented number of inquiries and requests for copies'. This publication arguably attracted dissident Conservatives back into the fold. Therefore, it is unsurprising that the Monday Club offered to provide Central Office with a canvassing squad at the General Election, or that Lord Blakenham specifically asked for Monday Club assistance as the General Election loomed.[101]

Central Office's more positive attitude towards the Monday Club does not mean that it ceased to be hostile towards right-wingers. Donald Johnson MP admitted holding views that Central Office considered extremely right wing.[102] Johnson was a Monday Club member, as well as being on The National Fellowship's National Executive. He believed that his criticism of the Government's health policy had resulted in counter-measures by the party organisation: 'Platforms throughout the country were fenced in by the Party machine.'[103] He was in little doubt that Central Office received reports from within his local Conservative Association of the criticisms he made of the Government. Johnson also questioned whether Central Office was neutral in disputes within a constituency, surmising that it made its views known by a 'discreet phone call from Chairman at Headquarters to Chairman of Constituency Association', and stated that the supposed autonomy of the local Conservative Associations was a myth. He said that Association chairmen deserved their well-known nickname of the party's 'hatchet-men'. In this instance, Johnson spoke from bitter experience.

Johnson's local Association deselected him as Conservative candidate for Carlisle on 14 October 1963. His account needs cautious usage as it is partial. Additionally to be borne in mind is the trouble that Johnson caused his government, and his constituency. Johnson's case is also opaque. It does not definitely prove Central Office involvement in his removal. Nevertheless, some incidents suggested that Johnson had a point when he suspected central orchestration in his removal. It is probable that the Carlisle Conservative Association decided to deselect Johnson before Macmillan resigned. Constituency files reveal that Central Office knew that the Carlisle Association considered deselecting Johnson at least one year before it happened. Moreover, there is evidence of suspicious contact between Central Office and the Carlisle Conservative Association before Johnson's de-selection. Johnson pointed to some events at the party's 1963 Blackpool conference, during which Macmillan resigned. He cited the contact between the Treasurer of the Carlisle Conservative Association and Sir Toby Low, Vice Chairman at Central Office, especially the strange occurrence of the Treasurer personally driving Low to his hotel. The Treasurer was not a senior party official in the Blackpool area, so it is hard to explain why he undertook this task. It could be innocent. Johnson's inference was that Low helped the Carlisle Association to engineer his removal. It is unlikely that the two men did not discuss the problem presented by Johnson, particularly at this difficult time for the Government. The events of the extraordinary meeting that Johnson forced on the Carlisle Conservative Association in June 1964 to air his grievances are also suspicious. The local press reported doubts over the right of some of the attendees to vote on the issue or even be present.[104] It probably did not help Johnson that Edward Martell was among those that most vocally pointed out suspicions of sharp practice. Therefore, it was possible that Central Office guided or advised the Carlisle Conservative Association in removing Johnson, and maybe even in countering him afterwards. However, in one sense the question of Central Office's agency in these events is irrelevant. Regardless of who was culpable, the Conservative Party had ensured the de-selection of an extreme-right MP. It was unlikely that Home wished to worsen party divisions by reversing a decision that had occurred amidst the turmoil of his succession as he had only just become Prime Minister. Having a more right-wing leader in this instance was, thus, irrelevant.

Nevertheless, Home's accession clearly did have an impact on the extreme right. Some policies of the Freedom Group and Monday Club were now either in accord with those of the Conservative Government, or nearly so. The Freedom Group and the Monday Club still operated along the Conservative Party's nebulous right-wing border, but were now more firmly within it. This change tempered the nature and extent of their extremism when judged by the political position of the Conservative Party. It also presented a problem for right-wing extremists who criticised Conservative governments prior to the Home administration. Should they remain loyal to the Conservative Party? Did they believe that Central Office's cooperation with the Freedom Group reflected the Conservative Party's true opinions or not? Had the Conservative Party at last returned to 'true Conservatism'? The accession of Home and the emergence of the Monday Club would have strengthened the views of any extreme-right voter who thought that the Conservative Party was truly Conservative again. Some probably still abstained. Others probably remained loyal. Loyalty was now the position of Commander Hyde C. Burton, a vocal and persistent critic of the recent Conservative Party. Interestingly, the family firm of Donald Johnson MP,

Johnson Publications, was Burton's publisher. Burton now stated that there was little alternative to voting Conservative.

Other voters probably remained immune to Burton's argument and voted for extreme-right parties. Major-General Richard Hilton formed True Tory into the Patriotic Party in 1964 and contested two seats at the General Election, while the LEL contested three. All five candidates provided an outlet for extremist views, but polled less than 2% of the votes and lost their deposits. Former LEL member John Bean was another outlet for these views when he contested Southall and attracted just over 9%. Bean's performance aside, these were miniscule rewards. Yet, they were also informative. They support the idea that the Conservative Party attracted the extreme-right vote, although far too limited to be definitive. A Conservative candidate did openly campaign on the extreme-right's political space and proved that the Conservative Party attracted extreme-right voters. Peter Griffiths notoriously used the slogan 'If You Want A Nigger For A Neighbour Vote Labour', and bucked the national swing to Labour, turning a Labour majority of 3,544 into a Conservative one of 1,774 at Smethwick. He may have attracted Labour voters, but Labour's vote remained virtually static at only 0.3% higher than at the 1959 General Election. Therefore, it is feasible that Home's accession had attracted some formerly alienated supporters away from extreme-right parties to an extent unlikely under a continued Macmillan leadership. The result of the General Election was a four-seat Labour majority.

Notes

1 See p. 41.

2 R. Rose, 'The Bow Group's Role in British Politics', *The Western Political Quarterly*,14:4 (1961), 865.

3 *Daily Telegraph*, 18 February 1960, quoted in J. Barr, *The Bow Group: A History*, Politicos, London (2001), 68.

4 'Helping Mr. Gaitskell', *The New Daily* (nd, but probably 1962 as it refers to the Liberal revival seen at the Orpington by-election).

5 *Time for a Tiger* (1956), *The Enemy in the Blanket* (1958), and *Beds in the East* (1959).

6 See p. 30.

7 I. Gilmour and M. Garnett, *Whatever Happened to the Tories: The Conservatives Since 1945*, Fourth Estate, London (1998), 161.

8 See p. 67.

9 See p. 63.

10 *Daily Telegraph*, 28 January 1957.

11 See pp. 36–39.

12 'Taper', 'Violence at Blackpool', *Spectator*, 17 October 1958.

13 Obituary, 'George Irvine Finlay', *Herald*, 5 January 1999.

14 *Candour*, 12 April 1957, 120; and 9 June 1961, 184.

15 *Candour*, 1 January 1954; and 30 January 1959.

16 'Case of Major Friend', *Daily Mirror*, 13 October 1958. Confirmed by Adrian FitzGerald, author interview, 20 May 2008.

17 *Daily Mail*, 13 October 1960.

18 *Candour*, Interim Report, October 1962, 8.

19 See pp. 65–66.

20 'Chairman Quits: East Ham Young Conservatives', *Daily Telegraph*, 25 April 1957.

21 See p. 45.

22 Made into a film in 1962, it is part of a trilogy covering Vic Brown's life, the other two novels being, *The Walkers on the Shore* (1966) and *The Right True End* (1976). They form part of the 'Realism' movement of the 1960s, which also included John Braine, author of *Room at the Top* (1957), and later a convert to the Monday Club.

23 See pp. 153, 161.

24 The information on True Tory derives from their publications, held at the British Library, unless stated.

25 J. Osborne, *Look Back in Anger*, Faber, London (1957), 70.

26 'Return of the Prophet', *Time*, 13 March 1946.

27 'Victory for Mr. Wolridge Gordon', *Daily Telegraph*, 26 April 1962.

28 See p. 177.

29 Donald McIntosh Johnson, *A Cassandra at Westminster*, Johnson, London (1967), 110.

30 'Whose Freedom?', *The New Daily*, 12 July 1960.

31 'The Cross Bowmen', *The New Daily*, 12 October 1960.

32 'Comfort and Joy!' *The New Daily*, 19 October 1960.

33 'Unto Caesar', *The New Daily*, 28 November 1960.

34 See pp. 27–29.

35 'Unto Caesar', *The New Daily*, 28 November 1960.

36 'A Problem That Can No Longer Be Avoided', *The New Daily*, 7 December 1960.

37 'An Experiment in Independence: Our Policy and Why', *The New Daily*, 3 May 1960.

38 'Our True Colours', *The New Daily*, 3 November 1960.

39 See p. 186.

40 See pp. 92–93.

41 The information on Burton, and his comments, derive from the subsequent publication, *The Great Betrayal: An Indictment of the Conservative Governments' Departure from Conservative Principles, 1951–1963*, Johnson, London (1963), unless stated.

42 'Anti-Socialist Movement: 2000 Supporters', *The New Daily*, 1 January 1962.

43 Johnson, *Cassandra*, 111. Johnson's following comments and views derive from this account, unless stated.

44 See p. 176.

45 'How Would You Change The Cabinet', *The New Daily*, 26 January 1963.

46 'Brutus', 'Right Thinking Grows In Tory Circles', *The New Daily*, 30 January 1963.

47 'Incredible Stupidity', *The New Daily*, 4 February 1963.

48 'Any Thinking Going on at the Tory Top?' *The New Daily*, 13 February 1963.

49 'Campaign to Promote a Royal Commission on Industrial Disputes', *The New Daily*, 13 February 1963.

50 'Hammer It Home!' *The New Daily*, 14 February 1963.

51 '22 MPs Have Now Signed the Gurden Motion. HAS YOURS?' *The New Daily*, 20 February 1963.

52 See pp. 65–66.

53 'Tories Must Drop Socialistic Tendencies Says Martell at Canterbury', *The New Daily*, 11 March 1963.

54 *The New Daily*, 11 March 1963, 14.

55 'Mr. Macleod's Chimera', *The New Daily*, 12 March 1963.

56 'Growing Interest In The Hastings Experiment', *The New Daily*, 18 March 1963.

57 'The Writing On The Wall', *The New Daily*, 23 March 1963.

58 'Tory Party Organisation', *The New Daily*, 29 May 1963, 6. What follows is a précis.

59 'Big Shock For The Prime Minister', *The New Daily*, 3 June 1963.

60 'Thus Fell Rome', *The New Daily*, 8 June 1963.

61 See pp. 6–8.

62 'The Plan To Keep The Socialists Out', *The New Daily*, 5 July 1963.

63 'Mr. Benn Has Ideas on Drying up Peerages at Source', *The Times*, 16 August 1963.

64 'Tories Urged: Do Not Vote Anti-Labour', *Yorkshire Post*, 8 August 1963.

65 *Bristol Evening Post*, 7 August 1963.

66 See p. 102.

67 R. Copping, *The Story of the Monday Club*, Monday Club, London (1972), 5.

68 *Policy and Aims of the Monday Club*, Monday Club, London (1961), 1.

69 *Wind of Change or Whirlwind?* Monday Club, London (1961), 2.

70 *Policy and Aims of the Monday Club*, 1–2.

71 'Peterborough', 'Breath of Youth', *Daily Telegraph*, 24 January 1962.

72 'By Our Political Staff', *Daily Telegraph*, 26 January 1962.

73 'Membership Position and Recruiting Campaign', Private Papers of Sir Patrick Wall, Monday Club: 1961–89, 40/1, November 1961–February 1964, University of Hull.

74 John Howe to Major Patrick Wall, MP, 'The Monday Club', 27 August 1963, *ibid.*

75 Lord Salisbury to Patrick Wall, 17 September 1963, *ibid.*

76 *Conservatism Lost? Conservatism Regained*, Monday Club, London (1963).

77 'Success at Bristol', *The New Daily*, 22 August 1963.

78 'Now the General Election Can Be Won', *The New Daily*, 21 October 1963.

79 'Dangerous Drift to the Left Comes to an End', *The New Daily*, 21 October 1963.

80 See pp. 86, 98–99.

81 See p. 107.

82 'Freedom Group Plans to Oust Mr. Wilson: "Conservatives Need Gingering Up"', *Yorkshire Post*, 30 April 1964.

83 'This Man Can Be Unseated', *The Times*, 4 May 1964.

84 See pp. 66, 101.

85 'Tories Take Help From Martell', *Observer*, 31 May 1964.

86 '"Get Wilson Out" Campaign by Tory Constituents', *Daily Telegraph*, 1 June 1964.

87 See p. 113.

88 'The City had Better Make Up its Mind if it Wants a Socialist Government', *The New Daily*, 12 May 1964.

89 See p. 103.

90 'The Secret's Out So Here Are The Full Details', *The New Daily*, 5 October 1964.

91 Sir Patrick Wall to The Rt. Hon. The Marquess of Salisbury, 29 October. Private Papers of Sir Patrick Wall, 40/1.

92 See p. 113.

93 Sir Patrick Wall to The Rt. Hon. The Marquess of Salisbury, 29 October. Private Papers of Sir Patrick Wall, Monday Club: 1961–1989. 40/1, Nov. 1961 – Feb. 1964. University of Hull.

94 *Monthly Newsletter*, Monday Club, November 1963.

95 'The Minutes of the General Meeting of the "Monday Club" held on Thursday 14th November at 7 p.m. at the Onslow Court'. Private Papers of Sir Patrick Wall, 40/1.

96 Circular titled 'The Monday Club', 1., *ibid.*

97 Minutes of the Annual General Meeting of the Monday Club, 24 February 1964. Private Papers of Sir Patrick Wall, 40/2, November 1963–December 1964.

98 Minutes of the Monday Club Council Meeting, 23 April 1964, *ibid.*

99 Minutes of a Monday Club Committee Meeting, 13 July 1964, *ibid. Automation* was eventually published in January 1965.

100 Minutes of a Monday Club Committee Meeting, 24 August 1964. Private Papers of

Sir Patrick Wall, University of Hull. Monday Club: 1961–1989. 40/2, Nov. 1963 – Dec. 1964.

101 *Monthly Newsletter*, Monday Club, September 1964.

102 See p. 101.

103 Johnson, *Cassandra*, 102. Johnson also mentions the Speaker's repeated failure to allow him to speak in debates in which he had a personal interest. Also mentioned are the preponderance of Etonians and the necessity of possessing the right social cachet as prerequisites for success. The Speaker was an old Etonian. 33–55ff.

104 'Now MP Challenges City Tories' Chairman on Votes', *Cumberland Evening News*, 22 June 1964.

4

Edward Heath: a rightwards turn and the coalescence of the extreme right, 1964–70

In some respects, Britain in 1964 differed greatly from when the Conservative Party was last in opposition. Earnings had increased, prices appeared stable, unemployment remained low, and consumer goods were plentiful. Affluence had replaced austerity as the country's leitmotif: according to one Nye Bevan obituary, the hum of the spin-dryer drowned the sounds of class warfare.[1] Computers were beginning to impact on British business too, leading to fears about jobs. Art was finding new expression in Pop and Op Art. The Public Libraries and Museum Act (1964) had precipitated an explosion in reading that continued throughout the decade. The opening of Terence Conran's first Habitat store in 1964 began an emphasis on stylish living that reflected this affluent society. Increased affluence had also resulted in a greater emphasis on youth culture, shaped largely by American influences such as the new musical phenomenon of rock and roll and a growth in nightclub culture. The advent of The Beatles proved a watershed in British popular music, widening generational differences and presaging change for decades to come. Films, books, and television reflected the passage of another watershed to a less deferential society. By 1964, kitchen sink dramas, social realism, and satire, had entered the literary and visual mainstream. Religion and morality likewise appeared changed. Church attendances continued falling. The Wolfenden Report (1957) had tentatively commenced moves towards a more tolerant society when it came to sexual mores by calling for the legalisation of homosexuality, but the most famous example of this change had occurred in 1960 when jurors acquitted Penguin Books of obscenity for publishing *Lady Chatterley's Lover*. Consequently, Britain in 1964 had a more questioning and liberal attitude towards morality, which Philip Larkin summed up by claiming that sex began in 1963, between the Chatterley ban and The Beatles first LP.[2]

The long-standing superstructure of British society had also changed. The Empire, apparently robust in 1951, was virtually over, and increased black immigration visually reminded people of it as former colonial subjects claimed little-tested rights of citizenship. Black immigration was a far more important phenomenon of British life by 1964 than in 1951, and found increasing representation. Some earlier films had presented a positive image of black immigrants. *The Proud Valley* (1940) told the story of Welsh villagers who accepted a musical black miner from West Virginia, but this was the exception. By 1964, there existed a marked focus on the negative impact of black immigration in films such as *Flames in the Streets* (1961), which highlighted white anxieties over black immigration. Similarly, Colin MacInnes had portrayed areas of high black immigration and the race riots of 1958 as un-English in his book *Absolute Beginners* (1959). This negative attitude towards black immigration continued after 1964. In 1965, the vice-president of the Empire Day Movement described such immigration as 'the gravest social crisis since the industrial revolution'.[3] Winston Churchill died and received a State funeral in the same year. The death of this imperial soldier and war leader symbolised the passage of an imperial age, just as increased black immigration presaged the dawn of a multicultural one.

Yet, continuities existed. The Nassau Agreement ensured that Britain remained dependent on America for nuclear technology and weaponry. The New Towns Act (1946), which Attlee's Government intended to relieve overcrowding in industrial areas, had resulted in fourteen new developments in the 1940s and 1950s. Conservative and Labour governments continued this policy throughout the 1960s, which television programmes set in New Towns, such as the police series *Z Cars* (1962–78) and the soap opera *The Newcomers* (1965–69), reflected. Changes in fashion and social mores were often slow to reach parts of Great Britain. Many changes were limited to an unrepresentative London-based coterie of the educated and wealthy. However, even changes that occurred usually possessed strong antecedents. Violence in Easter 1964 between Mods and Rockers prompted shocked and condemnatory headlines. Yet this episode was simply a more virulent form of endemic youthful violence stretching back via Teddy Boys in the 1950s, Spivs in the 1940s, Biff Boys in the 1930s, to the late Victorians who coined the word 'hooligans' for working-class boys who engaged in violence during the August holiday. Nor was the 'Permissive Society' an established fact. Capital punishment continued in 1964, while abortion, homosexuality, and suicide, were still criminal acts. Divorce remained a painful and unjust process. Moreover, the Empire may have been dying, but many in the colonies and in Britain had not accepted this. Nor had any new organisations challenged the dominance of the three main political parties.

However, some did not perceive this image of continuity. When Christopher Booker began working on *The Neophiliacs: The Revolution in English Life in the Fifties and Sixties* (1969) in autumn 1965, he intended to provide a clearer perspective on 'that bewildering tidal wave of change which had been sweeping through Britain and the Western World' from the early 1950s.[4] Booker was not alone in seeing Britain in 1964 as very different from the 1940s and early 1950s, or in criticising it. Paul Johnson in the *New Statesman* deplored Britain's obsession with modernity.[5] Even satirists took a break from lampooning politicians and poked fun at popular music instead. In *Forty Years On* (1969), Alan Bennett acknowledged the inevitability of change while paying due cognisance to the past, and was probably nearer the mark. The 1964 General Election was certainly both similar and different to an earlier contest in some important respects. Just as Attlee had caught the mood of an electorate that demanded radical change in 1945, so Harold Wilson sensed a desire to break free from the image of post-imperial decline in 1964. Wilson consequently sought a modern, classless society, a 'New Britain', and landed on the slogan 'White Heat of Technology' as the means of capturing the zeitgeist. However, Wilson only had a four-seat majority, unlike Attlee, which meant that Britain's first Labour Prime Minister for thirteen years would almost certainly have to seek a greater majority soon.

In government, Wilson continued to condemn 'thirteen years of wasted government' under the Conservatives, and consequently his government enjoyed the goodwill that had resulted from the simple but effective demand of 'time for a change'. Unfortunately, for Wilson, the picture of economic stability that the Conservatives presented during the election campaign proved chimerical, leaving the new government to face severe economic problems. Yet, Wilson turned an 8% Conservative lead in the polls in August 1965 into a Labour lead of 7% in September, despite economic problems and a reduced majority due to losing the Leyton by-election and the opposition of two right-wing Labour MPs to steel nationalisation. Thereafter, Labour maintained a 7% lead throughout winter 1965/66. Thus, when Wilson sought a stronger mandate to deal with problems at the end of March 1966, the electorate accepted his claim that the Conservative governments were responsible for the problems and gave him a 97-seat majority. However, a larger majority did not solve Britain's deep-seated economic problems. On 18 November 1967, the Labour Government devalued the pound, and swiftly fell eighteen points behind the Conservatives. Labour's position improved under new Chancellor Roy Jenkins, regaining a poll lead one week after his April 1970 Budget. However, this was illusory. Wilson's Government irretrievably lost economic credibility when it devalued the pound, and consequently lost the 1970 General Election.

Concerns over the economy were a large stick with which to beat the Labour Government. However, the Conservatives attacked the Government in many other areas too. Handling of industrial relations was the most obvious area. Unofficial 'wildcat' strikes proliferated from 1966. Industrial action coincided with severe economic problems, while the emergence of radical union leaders Jack Jones and Hugh Scanlon revived fears of Communist subversion. In June 1966, Wilson denounced the strike by the National Union of Seamen as inspired by Communists. The dockers struck in autumn 1967, just as irresistible pressure for devaluation mounted. Working days lost continued to soar after devaluation, which led *The Times* to dub 1968 'The Year of the Strike'.[6] On 16 January

1969, Wilson's Government published arguably the most famous government White Paper, *In Place of Strife*, which proposed placing statutory obligations on trade unions and other measures to limit industrial unrest. However, *In Place of Strife* failed, caught between economic necessity and the political expediency of not alienating the Labour Party's main source of funding. A divided Cabinet faced opposition to *In Place of Strife* from the unions and its backbenchers, plus a bitter dispute at the Ford motor plant in Dagenham. Therefore, it ditched the penalties in its White Paper and accepted a vague promise that the unions would seek the advice of the Trades Union Congress (TUC) on wildcat strikes. The promise proved baseless almost immediately. Wildcat strikes erupted in the docks, the Post Office, British Leyland, and in the National Health Service. The 7 million working days lost in 1969 easily outstripped the previous year's record high of 4.7 million. Meanwhile, the Conservative Party's policy statement *Fair Deal at Work* (1968) balanced obligations and rights, contrasting favourably with *In Place of Strife* to provide a viable prospect to halt apparently endemic industrial unrest. Newspapers across the political spectrum supported *Fair Deal at Work*. By-election victories after its publication in June 1968 at Oldham West and Nelson and Colne, and the following March at Walthamstow East, indicated that voters thought that the Conservatives possessed answers to an seemingly intractable problem.

Nor did Wilson's Government appear to make much progress solving the country's social ills, unlike Attlee's administration. Here, Wilson was in one sense unlucky. Conservative governments had sporadically faced popular representation of social issues in television series such as *Armchair Theatre*. However, *The Wednesday Play*, an anthology series that devastatingly highlighted social problems, ran conterminously with the Labour governments from 1964–70. A larger television audience than when the Conservatives were in government watched this series of plays reveal shocking conditions. *Up the Junction* (1965) portrayed lives dominated by petty-thieving, illicit sex, and back street abortions. *Cathy Come Home* (1966) depicted unemployment and homelessness, concluding harrowingly with scenes of the State removing children from their hapless mother's care, and swiftly acquired iconic status. Dennis Potter linked issues of social mobility and class. In *Stand Up, Nigel Barton* (1965) and *Vote, Vote, Vote for Nigel Barton* (1965), Potter recounted one man's journey from respectable, working-class grammar-school boy into the cynical world of party politics. However, Potter's Nigel Barton plays were more than a portrayal of social mobility and class betrayal. He depicted Barton's Labour Party Agent advising him to put party before principles, thus suggesting the contemporary political scene's moral turpitude. Wilson thought the BBC was biased and determined to undermine the Government, but implicit criticism of the Government was not limited to BBC plays. In 1968, Ted Lewis published *Jack's Return Home*, a tale of corruption, pornography, provincial crime, gambling, and revenge. When work on the film version, *Get Carter*, commenced in the last months of Wilson's Government, the producers set it in Newcastle. The leader of Newcastle Council, Labour councillor T. Dan Smith, epitomised local corruption. Illegal building contracts led to his subsequent imprisonment. Smith made a factual mockery of Wilson's ambitions for a 'New Britain' forged in the 'White Heat' of technology as much as Potter's play mocked it fictionally. However, a much more frightening symbol of Labour's failure was Ronan Point, a high-rise tower block commenced in 1966 and finished on 11 March 1968, which the Government intended to provide affordable housing for the working-class. Ronan Point collapsed on 16 May killing four and injuring seventeen. The resulting investigation found serious shortcomings and irregularities behind the façade. This judgement seemed a fitting allegory for Wilson's 'New Britain'.

However, the Labour Government's problems were not necessarily comfortable issues for the Conservative Opposition either. Society's ills presented problems for a broad-church party that included progressives and reactionaries because morality was often at the heart of debate. Films, books, and newspapers made it difficult to ignore the fact that society's trends had changed and continued to do so. In the Oscar-winning *Darling* (1965), Julie Christie portrayed an amoral single woman who used sex to achieve success. Murder and, for the first time in British cinema, full-frontal female nudity, were the main features of *Blowup* (1966). Teenage marriage, domestic abuse, and a life degenerating into prostitution formed the plot of *Poor Cow* (1967). Lindsay Anderson's *If...* (1968), surreally reflected subversion in the ultra-Establishment surroundings of a public school and questioned the existing social structure. At the other end of the social spectrum Ken Loach's *Kes* (1969), which depicted a dysfunctional family and a boy's futile attempt to break free from the confines of an inadequate education system and avoid becoming a miner, highlighted the potential for challenging the status quo. For many traditional Conservatives, these films reflected a troubled decade in which a Church of England Bishop questioned God's existence, youths fought openly on British beaches, church attendances continued to decline, and drugs, sexual immorality, and other social problems appeared far more prevalent. Yet, the Conservative Party had to appeal to this electorate too. Its reaction to the 1968 Wootton Report indicated their dilemma. The Conservatives opposed the report's conclusion, which stated that the danger of cannabis smoking was overstated. This position no doubt pleased some party members, but it also risked alienating both the young and libertarians. Meanwhile, other events called the 'Permissive Society' into question. Newspapers and television covered the trials of the Richardson Brothers and Kray Twins, bringing tales of organised crime, protection rackets, torture, and cold-blooded murder to the public's attention. Unarguably most shocking was the Moors Murders. These were not new phenomena, but the abolition of the death penalty, easing of divorce laws, and the decriminalisation of abortion, homosexuality, and suicide, were.

Great Britain's role was even more problematic for the Conservative Party, predominantly because of Britain's international position, which involved unresolved questions about its relationships with the USA, Europe, and the Commonwealth. Each relationship highlighted Conservative Party fault-lines.

Support for America had damaged Macmillan's attempt to join the Common Market, which in turn highlighted divisions between pro-EEC and imperial-ist Conservatives. Meanwhile, any focus by the Conservative Party on Britain's remaining imperial possessions was problematic for two reasons. First, divi-sions existed among Conservative MPs over whether to support the remaining white-minority governments that were resisting moves to majority, black rule. This issue resulted in the parliamentary party dividing three ways in 1965, when the Labour Government imposed oil sanctions on Rhodesia after its white-mi-nority government declared unilateral independence rather than grant conces-sions to the black majority. Secondly, support for white-minority governments risked exacerbating the tensions that surrounded black immigration and would allow opponents to portray the Conservative and Unionist Party as the party of division within the United Kingdom. Such views could limit Conservative Party fortunes if Great Britain became multi-racial, as seemed increasingly likely. Yet, the Conservative leadership risked dividing the party and presenting the extreme right with political space in which to thrive if it failed to address concerns over immigration. The Conservative Party leadership faced the quan-dary of dealing with immigration while maintaining party unity. In April 1968, Shadow Cabinet member Enoch Powell brought this to the fore spectacularly when he warned of 'rivers of blood' if black immigration continued.

Moreover, questions of unity were not simply issues of skin colour. On 14 July 1966, Plaid Cymru gained its first parliamentary seat when Gwynfor Evans overturned a large Labour majority in Camarthen. On 2 November 1967, Winnie Ewing performed the same feat for the Scottish National Party in Hamilton. These events may have reflected deep-seated economic concerns, but they were also evidence of a strengthening separatist nationalism, and proved not to be ephemeral blips in the United Kingdom's history. An increas-ingly polarised Northern Ireland similarly questioned the Union, if from a dif-ferent perspective. The Republican-Catholic ambition remained the reunion of Ireland, which blatant discrimination by gerrymandered Protestant authorities stoked. Unionists, on the other hand, felt isolated and were suspicious of acts of conciliation towards the Republic by Westminster. They opposed Civil Rights movements and divided into conservative and die-hard loyalists. Hardliner un-ionists even spoke of declaring unilateral independence similar to Rhodesia. These events also presented problems for the leaders of a party that supposedly stood for British union.

A reaction to these changes occurred, most notably among hitherto left-wing literary figures. In 1967, Kingsley Amis wrote 'Why Lucky Jim Turned Right' in the *Sunday Telegraph* to explain his conversion to the right wing. John Braine joined the Monday Club, which published *A Personal Record* (1968), Braine's explanation of his political journey from left to right. One Labour MP formed his own political party and espoused views that found favour with the Conservative Monday Club. These were high-profile conversions, but not necessarily welcome to the Conservative Opposition because the issues that prompted them were often difficult for it too. Additionally, the Conservative

Party leadership alienated many of its supporters by failing in varying degrees to oppose 'progressive' measures. This failure once again left political space on the Conservative Party's right flank for others to exploit. Conservative groups emerged to fight in areas that the party appeared unwilling to, just as in the late 1940s and early 1950s. The National Viewers and Listeners Association (NVLA), led by Mary Whitehouse, was the most famous of these groups. Whitehouse was a long-standing member of Moral Re-Armament and had fought the consequences of modern consumerism and mass culture by attacking the BBC in a 'Clean-Up TV Campaign' in 1963. However, when Whitehouse launched the NVLA in spring 1965, she no longer simply targeted the BBC. Instead, Whitehouse focused on the areas of change that the Conservative Party either ignored or accepted, and inveighed against the Welfare State, consumerism, working-class affluence, and the power of the unions.

In contrast, extreme-right groups appeared to be in decline. The membership of the LEL and True Tory fell markedly. Financial irregularities discredited Edward Martell and made the Freedom Group defunct. However, this was an illusory picture. Black immigration remained a potent issue in British politics, and an especially difficult one for the Conservative Party. 'Residents' Associations' emerged, demanding an end to black immigration. Edward Martell joined the bandwagon, supporting an anti-immigration candidate in a 1966 by-election. In early 1967, a large section of the extreme right used its racist anti-immigration views to coalesce into the National Front, Britain's first credible extreme-right party since the Second World War. More troubling for the Conservative leadership was the existence of views similar to the National Front's within the Conservative Party, particularly in the Monday Club. Admittedly, the Monday Club was far more than a single-issue movement. It contained traditionalists and neo-liberals who engaged in a wide variety of topics. However, the Monday Club also contained members whose views on immigration resembled those of the external extreme right very closely. In this period, the immigration issue increasingly dominated Monday Club activity. This was a far more dangerous time for the Conservative Party than at any period since 1945. Racism had provided the extreme right with a unifying ideology and presented extreme-right voters with a home for their votes away from the Conservative Party. Moreover, Powell's entry into the immigration debate in 1968 placed racism centre-stage in British politics and risked splitting the Conservative Party between liberals and racial-nationalists. There was even the possibility that Powell would take over the Conservative Party if it failed to win the next election.

However, the party leadership stuck to its policy of countering the extreme right. In 1965, Edward Heath replaced Home as party leader. As Heath came from a lower-middle class grammar school background like Harold Wilson, he seemed the appropriate person to oppose the Labour Prime Minister. He was the first leader that Conservative MPs elected by secret ballot. Heath was difficult to categorise. Some viewed him as the right-wing candidate in the contest to succeed Home. This was possibly because Heath had forged a reputation as a tough parliamentary operator as Macmillan's Chief Whip. Alternatively, it was because Heath had forced the Resale Price Maintenance Bill onto the statute book against the wishes of many Conservatives. However, Heath was no right-winger. He had entered parliament at the 1950 General Election and quickly became a member of the One Nation Group, which had supported the post-war consensual approach and Macmillan's leftist policies, and was not at all extreme. Therefore, Heath had identified himself with Conservative Party progressivism from the beginning. He saw trade unions as an estate of the realm with whom cooperation was both desirable and necessary, an opinion he adhered to even when industrial action increased. He also rejected racism.

Heath ensured that the party bureaucracy reflected his own stance by replacing the Chairman that Home had appointed. This resulted in Central Office's attitude towards the Monday Club becoming unambiguous. Central Office was henceforward complicit in the Monday Club's consistent failure to gain representation in party organisations, while at the same time it continued assisting the Conservative Party's progressive groups. Heath combined these internal manoeuvrings against the extreme right with a rightwards shift in the Conservative Party's political orientation, without ever totally acceding to the extreme-right's views. He continued to reject the extreme-right's racism, but adopted a tougher stance towards immigration. Heath also moved towards the views previously espoused by the 'freedom right' on the economy and industrial relations, which appeared to culminate in a programme declaration at the Selsdon Park Hotel in January 1970. Right-wing Conservatives such as Norman Tebbit believed that the Selsdon Declaration was genuine, describing it as the Conservative Party's 'first repudiation of the post-war Butskellite consensus', and believed that it showed that 'Heath was committed to the end of that corporate consensus and to the new liberal economics'.[7] However, it is doubtful that Heath was sincere in this rightwards shift. His actions were probably little more than political expediency, a reflection of the difficult political context in which he led the Conservative Party. Yet, Heath presented the extreme-right wing with a problem by placing the Conservative Party firmly in its territory. His actions, and those of the bureaucracy that served him, continued to present the extreme right with the same dilemmas that the post-1945 Conservative Party had consistently posed.

Right, left, right

Views expressed by extreme-right groups reflected this period's difficult context. In 1965, the leader of the LEL A. K. Chesterton, complained about the destruction of the White Commonwealth, and stated that Britain had lost its independent nuclear capability due to the Nassau Agreement.[8] He particularly criticised 'coloured' immigration: 'The supreme treason in the British Isles, however, is the creation of a colour problem in a White nation where no such problem has existed throughout hundreds of years of its existence.' Chesterton reiterated these views at the LEL's twelfth annual conference in October 1965, at which he also scorned American materialism, the churches' betrayal of Christendom, the horrors of decolonisation, and Britain's reliance on foreign debt.[9] However, Chesterton's problem by 1965 was that the LEL was a fractured rump damaged by splits, departures, and adverse publicity. In 1956, Colin Jordan had left and formed the more overtly Nazi White Defence League. John Tyndall and John Bean left in 1957 and created the National Labour Party to counter black immigration. Consequently, the LEL appeared little more than a training ground for neo-Nazis and neo-fascists; this added credibility to Central Office claims that it was a fascist organisation. Chesterton continued to voice his views of a Jewish conspiracy to control the world, which alienated many people and gave the impression of fanaticism, which also added further weight to Central Office claims. Chesterton's world-view was especially obvious when he chose the Britons Publishing Company to distribute the book outlining it, *The New Unhappy Lords* (1965). However, the LEL's membership had declined from 3,000 at the height of the race riots in 1958 to around 300 by 1961, and nothing indicated that this fall had reversed by 1965. Also, Chesterton had lost the main source of LEL funding when expatriate Chilean R. K. Jeffery died in 1961. All three LEL candidates in the 1964 General Election had lost their deposits. Thus, Chesterton was venting his spleen to a dwindling audience. The Conservative Party and those newspapers that supported it simply ignored the LEL, probably because they considered it irrevocably damaged.

Edward Martell elicited a different response from the Conservative Party. Martell's companies had experienced financial difficulties by 1965, and he had failed to repay the loans that he had requested in *The New Daily*. Disgruntled creditors wrote to MPs. On 18 June 1965, Labour MPs demanded an inquiry and public protection 'from this kind of racketeer whose personal guarantees are worthless'.[10] Martell responded the following day with hand-delivered letters challenging Labour MPs to repeat their accusations without parliamentary privilege.[11] Four months later, Martell won an apology and retraction,[12] but this did not mean that his financial troubles had ended. In January and February 1966, Martell faced bankruptcy petitions.[13] In September 1967, the *London Gazette* secured a receiving order against Martell.[14] The following month, the Official Receiver estimated Martell's debts at over £100,000.[15] By March 1968, the London Bankruptcy Court estimated that Martell's debt had increased to £179,600, and ordered him to submit a full statement of affairs within twenty-one days or face serious consequences.[16] This process was an unedifying spectacle for Martell.

For Conservative Central Office, Martell's problems presented an opportunity. Central Office now developed selective amnesia. It claimed to have 'always refused to have any working arrangement with any of his organisations', and recalled 'that in 1957 Mr. Martell contested East Ham as a People's League Candidate', rather than remembering his National Fellowship Conservative candidacy at Bristol in 1963. Internal Central Office files correctly claimed in August 1966 that Martell's failure to honour loans was 'nothing to do with us'. However, Central Office was incorrect when it replied to a Conservative MP's request for assistance in recovering money from Martell in November 1966 with the claim: 'The Party has always made it clear that we would have nothing to do with the Freedom Group and all offers from the Group as such have been refused.' Reaction within Central Office to the MP's request revealed why it made this claim. Craig noted that Martell appeared to be 'getting under way with the New Daily' again, which presented 'a good opportunity of nipping him in the bud by drawing attention to his unpaid debts, perhaps by a letter to the Telegraph or the Express', and finally deal with Martell.

Central Office officials maintained their stance of denying its past connection with Martell even when corresponding with its own Party Chairman Edward du Cann. When Mr Webster received a complaint in December 1966 from du Cann about money lent to Martell, he suggested to Mr Craig that, 'I think we should reply that the Freedom Group has no connection with our Party at all, nor are we in any way responsible.' Webster's conclusion is debatable, but his use of the present tense may be significant. Perhaps equally significant, however, was the fact that du Cann was a Home appointee. Edward Heath disliked du Cann. Both men had discussed an appropriate time for du Cann to leave Central Office. This discussion occurred before the March 1966 General Election. By the time that du Cann complained to Webster in December 1966, it was common knowledge that Heath planned to remove him. Press rumours to this effect circulated at the October Party Conference. It is improbable that Central Office officials were ignorant of du Cann's expected removal, and therefore decided not to reveal the full extent of the relationship with Martell to a right-wing chairman whose days were numbered. Central Office's attitude towards Martell had returned to one of hostility, which was not surprising considering that the new party leader was a member of the One Nation Group and detested right-wing extremism.

Publicly, Central Office continued to deny a corporate relationship with Martell. On one occasion, it did admit to having played a role in Martell's association with the wider Conservative Party. It revealed in a confidential letter to a Conservative MP that it had previously insisted that any Freedom Group assistance 'must be done on an individual basis by joining the local Association'. However, this was an exception, and the tougher stance remained. It is possible to argue that Central Office based its position on a desire not to be associated with Martell's financial irregularities alone. However, its willingness to publicise Martell's difficulties argued against this. What else, then, had precipitated this change? Central Office had reverted to a more negative stance towards Martell after the brief hiatus of Home's leadership, meaning that its role of reflecting the leader's wishers provides an obvious explanation. However, it is also possible that Central Office remained convinced that Martell still intended infiltrating the Conservative Party or forming a new party.[17] If so, the Nuneaton by-election of March 1967 may have influenced Central Office. The National Party's candidate at Nuneaton was decorated war veteran, Air Vice-Marshall 'Pathfinder' Bennett. Bennett was briefly a Liberal MP in 1945, but like Martell had long since travelled rightwards. His candidature included demands that reflected the contemporary context, including a call for 'True British Honour, Integrity and Loyalty', especially towards Rhodesia's white-minority government.[18] Bennett blamed the Conservatives as much as the Labour Government for events in Rhodesia. He rejected the Treaty of Rome and suggested that Britain remained outside the Common Market. Bennett advocated trade union reform, reduced taxation, abolition of the rating system, and cutting welfare spending. He emphasised that his demand for a five-year suspension of immigration applied to all races. However, when he justified this on the grounds of increased housing problems and unemployment, Bennett implicitly identified that section of immigrants most likely to experience such conditions, which meant blacks. Bennett's election literature was typical of contemporary extreme-right material, and the Conservative Party leadership did not want to be associated it. In small print at the foot of the last page of the literature was the attribution, 'Printed and Published by E. Martell, Election Agent to Air Vice-Marshall Donald Bennett.'

Exactly when Central Office knew of the connection between Martell and Bennett is unclear. Its files do not clarify the issue, but they do show awareness of his involvement. The committee overseeing the Nuneaton by-election convened on 15 September 1966. The secret minutes of the meeting for the section titled 'Running of the Campaign' recorded that, 'It must be made quite clear in future that the Central Office Agent was in charge of the running of the campaign.' This may have reflected a difficulty peculiar to the Nuneaton Conservative Association, but this seems unlikely due to the absence of any comments or evidence to this effect, plus the supposed autonomy of Conservative Associations. However, it is possible to suggest that Central Office intended to maintain effective reporting channels at Nuneaton because of Martell. For, although there is nothing in these particular files suggesting there were problems in the Nuneaton Conservative Association, there is material relating to Martell. On 9 February 1967, Bryan Edgell, an Agent in the Reading Conservative Association, wrote to du Cann revealing confidential information imparted to him by Martell. Edgell acknowledged many years' acquaintance with Martell, and recounted Martell's claim of an approach by a number of 'big boys' from the Freedom Group who were willing to fund a new party. Martell had acquiesced, forming the National Party to fight the next five elections until Heath and du Cann left the leadership of the party and Central Office. The National Party operated from the address of 'Modern Organisers', one of Martell's other groups, and appeared a more extreme reprise of the Freedom Group. Central Office may have initially thought that Martell's financial difficulties made this venture less feasible, but in May 1968, he revealed in court that nearly 90% of his 748 creditors were not making a claim against him.[19] The bulk of these creditors were probably disgruntled Conservatives who had responded to Martell's appeals in *The New Daily*. Their refusal to pursue Martell freed him to pursue his political objectives. It also confirmed continuance of grassroots irritation towards the Conservative Party.

Major General Richard Hilton's activities should have concerned Central Office more than those of the financially embarrassed Martell. Hilton was now Vice-President of the British National Party, and Chairman of the Patriotic Party that had contested two seats at the 1964 General Election, as well as leader of True Tory. Hilton was also Honorary President of the National Youth League, a group that claimed to be Britain's only 'one hundred percent' patriotic youth movement confined to those of British ancestry.[20] From these positions, Hilton occupied political space to the right of the Conservative Party, believing that the 'wide divergences between the Conservative front bench and the Conservative electorate' provided him with opportunities. Hilton attempted to exploit divisions within the Conservative Party over issues such as immigration and Rhodesia, arguing that it was 'seething with discontent against its present leadership'. Hilton also appeared to have a plan to take advantage of these divisions. He claimed to have abandoned elections and now openly advocated infiltrating the Conservative Party, particularly via the Young Conservatives. The aim of this plan was the familiar refrain of the alienated extreme right: 're-converting the Conservative Party to patriotism'. Hilton believed that the Conservative leadership had so severely discontented their supporters that it would remain in opposition for at least ten years, and outlined a two-stage 'Ten Year Plan' to accomplish his objective of infiltration. Hilton wanted True Tory members to infiltrate Conservative Associations via activism in local issues and then, having secured sufficient influence, dominate the voting in them. Hilton even set up a central Headquarters in London to coordinate the True Tory campaign.

However, Hilton and True Tory did not worry the Conservative leadership and Central Office. True Tory were an old movement, notwithstanding Hilton's connection with the National Youth League, which constrained a movement that sought to infiltrate the Conservative Party via the Young Conservatives. The seventy-two year old Hilton realised this when he attempted to form a working committee of young patriots aged between twenty and thirty-five to take over the leadership of True Tory. There was little evidence that this committee ever existed. Nor had Hilton enjoyed any obvious success in his aims to bring the Conservative Party back to 'True Toryism'. This was because while the leadership's position on many issues undoubtedly irritated some Conservatives, at least as many were probably reluctant to oppose it actively, while others agreed with it. Hilton unwittingly acknowledged this situation when he said that rank-and-file members of the Conservative Party had 'blindly allowed themselves to be led by a gang of doctrinaire Left-wing intellectuals'. These comments helped to explain why Hilton's True Tory had run out of steam by 1966. Hilton seemed incapable of forming a sizable following, unlike Martell, and membership of True Tory was probably less than half of its peak of 3000 by 1966.

Therefore, at this stage there seemed many reasons why the Conservative Party should be unconcerned about the extreme right outside the party. Since the 1964 General Election, the external extreme right had proved its limitations. This does not mean that the Conservative Party ignored it. Intelligence-gathering continued. The Conservative Party also monitored the opportunities afforded to the extreme right. Of particular interest was the impact of black immigration on local communities, which had resulted in the emergence of protesting 'residents' associations' in the early 1960s. Their membership came from the three major political parties, but especially the Conservative Party. They were often schismatic. This was because local Conservatives determined that no single body should emerge from the residents' associations that would be strong enough to jeopardise the Conservative Party's chances of attracting the anti-immigrant vote. In Birmingham, for example, Conservatives were involved in an argument within the Birmingham Immigration Control Association that resulted in the formation of an additional two residents' associations. Local factors and the presence of members of other political parties no doubt played a role in these schisms too. However, if this view of the local Conservatives' action is correct, then their determination to stop residents' associations from uniting into a single body was one that deliberately intended to hinder the extreme-right's development. This was an opportunistic attitude, best seen when Peter Griffiths took advantage of residents' fears of black immigration in Smethwick and delivered a victory for the Conservative Party in the 1964 General Election.[21] John Bean later claimed that the Birmingham Branch Organiser of Mosley's Union Movement invented Griffiths's election slogan.[22] Griffiths put racism at the forefront of his campaign and accepted the assistance of British National Party (BNP) members in his campaign. His actions once again raised the fear that the electorate would remember the Conservative's pre-war associations with fascism, a view supported by Bean's claim that, 'In some respects Griffiths' victory was a victory for us'. However, the Smethwick result was also a victory for a Conservative candidate who took advantage of the tensions caused by anti-immigrant residents' associations, and the divisions in them. In reality, Griffiths had reduced the extreme-right's chances by operating in their space, evidenced by the BNP's failure to field a candidate.

Nor was it only Griffiths or a few local Conservatives that crowded the political space of residents' associations and extreme-right parties. From the 1950s, Conservative Party MPs had expressed concerns about black immigration.[23] The manner in which they did so had ensured that the public knew that a repository for their fears existed within the Conservative Party. However, Conservative MPs did not limit their concern to public pronouncements. Just after the 1964 General Election, a Mr R. F. Beauclair wrote to Conservative MP Sir Patrick Wall. Beauclair stated that his family were 'certainly not racists in any way', then likened 'coloured' immigration to the invasion planned by Hitler which he had fought against, and described 'coloured' immigrants as unsuitable to Britain's climate and modern political system as they were 'by nature simple indolent people, who thrive in a simple country environment'.[24] Beauclair did not have in mind the green pastures of Wall's Yorkshire constituency. Wall replied that although he was not personally opposed to the immigrants, he too was 'extremely concerned' about it.[25] He also believed that the present problems caused by these immigrants would be 'nothing compared to the problems we shall face in a generation's time' when their children would be competing 'directly with our own British people'. These comments made it clear that Wall did not see black immigrants as British, or ever likely to become so, just like Hilton of True Tory and many others of the extreme right. Beauclair agreed with Wall's comments and claimed that there was no need for immigrant labour, that the true number of immigrants was higher, and warned that when these immigrants were on the electoral roll and voting Labour, the Conservative Party could soon cease to exist.[26] Beauclair was wrong. The Conservative Party was not acquiescing in its own demise, but providing a more viable alternative for those voters sympathetic to the residents' associations who might otherwise be tempted to vote for extreme-right parties.

However, Conservatives' attempts to stop residents' associations from forming into one coherent group faced a challenge. The belief that the Conservative Party leadership was unaware of the dangers that immigration posed to its continued existence resulted in the formation of the Racial Preservation Society (RPS) in 1965. It sought to galvanise residents' groups into a coherent movement to play a wider political role, and Beauclair was a member. The RPS focused its attention on a wider stage rather than limit itself to local issues, demanding a national referendum on immigration. More pertinent perhaps to an electorate that increasingly watched television was the RPS's attack on what it perceived as a cultural acceptance of 'mongrelisation'. When the soap opera *Coronation Street* began in 1960, Granada Television intended it to run for only thirteen episodes, but its popularity caused a reassessment. By 1964, *Coronation Street* regularly attracted an audience of over 20 million people. In 1965, the RPS attacked a *Coronation Street* storyline involving the adoption of a mixed-race child, describing it as a cynical attempt to soften up the viewers into accepting race mixing. The RPS accused other television programmes of brainwashing their audience too. It also published lists of Conservative MPs it thought 'sound' on immigration. This list was potentially very embarrassing for the Conservative Party, as leading figures in the RPS included former members of Mosley's British Union of Fascists. However, by publishing the list the RPS was also acting against its own interests, as the names of sympathetic Conservative MPs simply increased the likelihood that potential supporters of extreme-right parties would vote for these 'sound' Conservatives rather than waste their vote on miniscule parties.

More problematic for the RPS was that on immigration the Conservative Party actually faced both ways. For, although some Conservative MPs and probably many party members were hostile to immigration, they could do little about it in the House of Commons. Apart from the obvious problem of being in opposition, anti-immigration Conservative MPs were at odds with their own parliamentary leadership and much of the wider party. In 1965, for example, the Conservative frontbench acquiesced in the Labour Government's Race Relations Act. At the 1965 Conservative Party Conference, platform speakers did not advocate anti-immigration measures. This resulted in some dissent from the conference floor, but when Reg Simmerson, who represented the

London University Graduates Association, argued that 'To allow in immigrants is madness; to allow in coloured immigrants is double madness', he received jeers as well as cheers.[27] The case of Peter Griffiths, the new Conservative MP for Smethwick, typified the Conservative Party's split over immigration. Some sections of the Conservative Party warmed to Griffiths, and he received invitations to speak at local associations and Young Conservative meetings. The attitude of the leadership was very different. Edward Heath may have dismissed anti-immigration Conservative MPs with the nonchalant comment that, 'Every party has its extremists',[28] but he also recorded that many treated Griffiths with particular opprobrium: 'Griffiths was a severe embarrassment to us and he was rightly shunned in Parliament when he arrived.' In this instance, 'us' probably meant the party leadership and those progressive Conservatives who baulked at the anti-immigration stance of some of their fellow Conservative MPs. In a party where the leadership determined policy, this situation was sufficient to stymie those who wished for harsh anti-immigrant measures. It also suggested that the leadership was willing to act against the extreme right even within the parliamentary party.

The wider Conservative Party's ambiguous stance on immigration went right to the heart of the dilemma faced by the RPS and all extreme-right movements. The Conservative Party contained members who were sympathetic to these groups' aims and thus attracted their potential voters. Yet it also alienated extreme-right activists by offering little probability of actually delivering their objectives. The Conservative Party caught the RPS in its jaws of attraction and repulsion, as it did to all other extreme-right groups. As ever in this process, Central Office acted as the agent of repulsion since it reflected the leadership's wishes. Central Office was at best evasive when replying to RPS questions. On at least one occasion, all participants in an RPS letter-writing campaign received from Central Office the same stereotyped reply. If Central Office's evasion stemmed from its desire to avoid embarrassing connections, then a subsequent comment from an RPS member suggested this was a wise position. A 'Mrs L' wrote: 'I have been a member of Sir Oswald Mosley [sic] and his party for years, but in this great democracy of ours, only Communists get the voice.' Mrs L was irritated that the Conservative Party had sponsored two immigrant councillors. In December 1967, the RPS tacitly acknowledged that the Conservative Party had the ability to thwart its aims when it argued that someone should hang above Central Office the legend 'Abandon Hope All Ye Who Enter Here.'

From 1967, the RPS declined and the majority of its members joined the National Front, leaving only a rump. One remaining member, Dr David Brown, attempted to arrest the RPS's decline. In 1966, Brown had formed his own party, the National Democratic Party (NDP). Now, Brown tried to maintain the RPS message by merging his NDP with other small extreme-right groups, including the British Defence League (BDL). John O'Brien led the BDL. He was a member of the Shrewsbury Conservative Association. In April 1969, the RPS and BDL produced a combined bulletin, which suggested that the RPS rump was struggling to survive as a separate entity. The bulletin's demands reflected contemporary social issues. It criticised the Wootton Report (1968) for its liberal attitude towards drugs, and argued for measures that were more repressive instead.[29] However, the RPS's position here was indistinct from that of the Conservative Party. This showed that the Conservative Party, having created political space for the extreme right to exist in, could also occupy it and thus deny the extreme right space in which to operate. The bulletin had racism at its core and unsurprisingly blamed non-white immigrants for society's ills. It highlighted the imprisonment of three drug-smuggling Pakistani men at Sowerby Bridge in 1968. However, the bulletin also supported Conservative MPs who opposed the parliamentary leadership on issues such as immigration and the Common Market, and named them. It attacked progressive Conservative MPs in the familiar tones of the extreme right. The bulletin particularly criticised Sir Edward Boyle MP and pledged to 'support any opposition to this man, from whatever source it comes. Let us purify and purge the Tory party, and relieve the parliamentary scene of this strange person.' There was even a comment that suggested that Conservatives withheld party subscriptions due to their irritation at the leadership.

The bulletin also threatened violence. Initially, this threat seemed implicit and directed at the left. The bulletin stated that failure to redress the electorate's concerns would lead it to turn further rightwards and warned of 'dire consequences … for all the motley crew of unpatriotic citizens whose allegiance is to a foreign creed, not their own country'. It believed that progressives dominated the Conservative Party, and, as the party was likely to gain power at the next general election, argued that Edward Heath would be 'putty in the hands of the centre faction of the Tory party'. This was the post-1945 extreme-right's constant refrain. The bulletin argued that the result would be the electorate's disillusion with all mainstream parties, which was reminiscent of the claims of inter-war fascists who sought to sweep away the political 'old gangs'. The consequences that the bulletin identified next suggested that violence was not just implicit in the RPS, and revealed the possibility of beliefs even more worrying. The bulletin argued that since both mainstream parties had failed the nation, 'the stage will be set for a resurgence of the forces that produced extremist governments in Italy and Germany in the twenties and thirties. The left and centre will have brought it on themselves AND IT WILL SERVE THEM DAMN WELL RIGHT.' Admittedly, this may reflect concern within the RPS rump that Britain faced a rise in neo-Nazism; a possibility supported by the RPS belief that those who left it in 1967 had joined a party tainted by neo-Nazism and fascism. The presence of former fascists in the RPS before 1967 argued against this, however, as did an obvious racist ideology and the use of violent terminology, and casts serious doubts on whether the RPS's conclusion was a warning or a wish. What is certain is that Central Office watched the RPS, and that the Conservative Party contributed to its fracture and decline by providing an alternative to it.

These examples do not mean that Central Office focused solely on groups and individuals that always operated on the extreme right. Central Office was also alert to the possibility of political parallels to Amis, Larkin, and Braine, literary figures who had renounced their socialism in favour of the right. One such example in this period was Desmond Donnelly, Labour MP for Pembroke West since 1950. Although Donnelly originally aligned himself with Aneurin Bevan, as a consultant to engineering firms and merchant banks he was passionately anti-Soviet and thus an incongruous member of the Labour Party's left wing. Donnelly had embarked on a rightward journey like Edward Martell and Donald Bennett, albeit one that started further left on the political spectrum. Donnelly proceeded to support the moderate Hugh Gaitskell for the Labour leadership and oppose his more left-wing successor Harold Wilson, and was a thorn in the side of the Labour Government by the mid-1960s. Donnelly was one of the two Labour MPs who opposed nationalisation of the steel industry during Wilson's first administration.[30] His action was particularly difficult for Wilson because the Conservatives' unexpected victory at the Leyton by-election on 21 January 1965 left his government with a parliamentary majority of three.

However, at this stage Central Office appeared to have had little interest in Donnelly. He was, after all, simply a rebellious Labour MP. Yet coincidentally, the events that Donnelly was peripherally involved in add to our understanding of the relationship between the Conservative Party and the extreme right, particularly the Leyton by-election. Central Office was deeply anxious during the by-election campaign. In November 1964, C. A. J. Norton, the Central Office Agent responsible for the Greater London Area, provided a preliminary report on the constituency. Norton noted the likelihood of a BNP candidacy and a proliferation of 'Keep Britain White' slogans, and that one-third of people canvassed raised the 'colour question'. One reason why this might have worried Central Office is obvious. Harold Wilson had appointed Patrick Gordon Walker as his first foreign secretary. However, Walker's defeat in the 1964 General Election meant that an unelected individual held one of the highest offices of state. The Labour leadership imposed Gordon Walker as their candidate in Leyton to secure his swift return to the Commons. Gordon Walker was also the candidate that Griffiths defeated at Smethwick in the 1964 General Election by playing on fears of immigration. The Conservative Party thus risked becoming embroiled once again in the divisive issue of race and possible identification with right-wing extremism.

On 4 January 1965, the Chief Organisation Officer informed the General Director at Central Office that the extreme right had disrupted a Labour press conference at Leyton, noting the role played by a Mr Colin Jordan. The Chief Organisation Officer visited Leyton with Area Agent Norton, and reported his findings to the General Director. He stated that there was 'a great deal of rowdiness owing to Mr. Colin Jordan and I hope we shall not get the backwash of some of this'. There were two reasons for this worry. Jordan was a former member of the British People's Party and the LEL's Midlands Organiser before it expelled him for his blatant neo-Nazism in 1958. Thereafter he launched a number of openly Nazi movements and amalgamated with other extremists to form new parties such as the BNP. Jordan was thus a link between the Conservative

Party and neo-Nazism thanks to his membership of the LEL. Secondly, if the Conservative candidate at Leyton ran a racist campaign similar to Griffiths's at Smethwick, which included assistance from the BNP, there was a real risk that this would further taint the Conservative Party. Indeed, there is some evidence that the Conservative Party candidate at Leyton, Ronald Buxton, colluded with the BNP. The BNP's John Bean claimed that Buxton promised that he would 'call for a moratorium on all further immigration for two years' if he withdrew from the contest.[31] Bean did withdraw, and later claimed that Buxton willingly accepted BNP assistance, including the distribution of 8,000 of its 'Stop Immigration' leaflets. Buxton's small victory margin, a mere 205 votes, led Bean to claim that the Leyton result was a victory for the BNP. However, he was shocked to see Buxton abusing the BNP after the result. Buxton's behaviour may have been little more than opportunism. It also showed that the Conservative Party could overpower a much smaller extreme-right movement, use it, attract its supporters and then disdainfully dismiss it. If Bean's claims are correct, Buxton had acted in a very risky manner, which would explain the Chief Organisation Officer's comments. Knowledge of Buxton's behaviour and the involvement of the BNP would magnify Central Office anxiety. It is unclear whether Central Office played any role in Buxton's behaviour. It had proved capable of manipulating individuals to the Conservative Party's interest, as seen with Martell, but that instance did not involve blatant racism. The reasons for the Chief Organisation Officer's concerns are clear, however.

What is also clear is that Central Office was more concerned with the Leyton by-election than with Desmond Donnelly. However, this changed as Donnelly became more alienated from the Labour Government. In February 1965, Donnelly expressed views on Britain's industrial relations that later found resonance in the Conservative Party's *Fair Deal at Work*. Donnelly argued that Britain could not 'survive as a leading industrial nation if it accepted that three men should do two men's jobs or that out-of-date practices are sustained'.[32] Donnelly also called for an elimination of waste in the Welfare State and a refocusing of priorities and expenditure limits. The following month, Donnelly rebuked the Government for failing to support the USA wholeheartedly in its conflict with Vietnam and denounced the 'present cacophony of Anti-Americanism'.[33] Three months after the 1966 General Election, the Government faced the prospect of devaluation. Donnelly questioned whether Britain had a government with sufficient courage and competence to deal with the crisis.[34] In 1967, Donnelly became the *News of the World*'s chief political correspondent, from where he continued to criticise the Labour Government. The power of the trade unions was a particular target of his, similar to Martell in *The New Daily* beforehand.[35] The final breach with the Labour Party came when devaluation in 1967 resulted in reduced defence spending and the Government's withdrawal from its commitments east of Suez. On 18 January 1968, Donnelly resigned the Labour Whip, and the party expelled him two months later. Donnelly responded by writing *Gadarene '68* (1968), a biblical reference to the Labour Government's headlong flight towards suicide. In the same year, Donnelly received a two-minute standing ovation from the Monday Club after he had addressed them. He also formed his own political party, the United Democratic Party.

Given the terms of reference presented to it regarding outside organisations,[36] it is no coincidence to find that Central Office's interest in Desmond Donnelly also commenced in 1968. On 29 November 1968, Donnelly wrote to a Mr Eastwood enclosing a leaflet that claimed that the crisis facing Britain was 'essentially political as well as economic'. The leaflet, *Through the Barriers*, revealed Donnelly's beliefs that society was decadent, government overspent, especially on the Welfare State, individual and business taxes were excessive, the need for private provision, the need for government to cease interfering in the economy and industry, and a nationalistic foreign affairs stance. Conservatives sympathised with many of these demands, but the leadership by no means accepted them all. Some of the demands mirrored those found in the literature of groups to the right of the Conservative Party. Eastwood forwarded this material to the Conservative Party, presumably his local Conservative Association, from where it found its way to the Central Office Area Agent. On 16 December 1968, the agent forwarded these documents to Mr Webster at Central Office, and stated that he 'thought you would like to have this in case you had not already seen this'. These are the earliest extant documents in Central Office's file on the United Democratic Party, although it is probable that Central Office already knew about Donnelly's activities, including his appearance before the Monday Club.

In this instance, it is how the documents arrived at Central Office that is interesting, not just their content. It shows that Central Office's intelligence network was not limited to its own agents as the documents originated from a businessman. This leads to two important conclusions. First, the demands of the party leadership took precedence. The leadership demanded that Central Office handle carefully issues that could divide the party, and, as many of these potential divisions during Heath's leadership centred on the Monday Club, Donnelly's presence at one of its meetings meant that monitoring of the United Democratic Party also became a requirement. The second conclusion is that Central Office had an extensive reach. If Eastwood was simply a member of a local Conservative Association, Central Office had a great reach within the Conservative Party. However, Central Office's reach extended even deeper into society if Eastwood was not a member of a local Conservative Association. Considering that Central Office had positive connections with some right-wing groups, such as Aims of Industry, this last scenario is likely. It seems that Central Office's intelligence-gathering went far beyond its own bureaucracy.

Central Office continued to gather intelligence on Donnelly and the United Democratic Party. In May 1969, this activity included acquiring the first issue of *Opportunity*, the United Democratic Party's newspaper. The following month, J. Galloway, the Central Office Area Agent for the West Midlands, placed observers at a Keele University meeting where Donnelly spoke in support of the United Democratic Party's candidate in the Newcastle-under-Lyme by-election. Galloway's report mentioned some Conservatives's alarm at the similarity of

Donnelly's views to those of the Conservative Party. The result of the by-election on 3 October suggested that these Conservatives were justifiably concerned. The Conservative candidate, Nicholas Winterton, came second to the Labour candidate by 1,042 votes. The United Democratic Party candidate secured 1,699 votes. The Conservative Party had arguably lost a by-election because a former Labour MP had journeyed into the political space just to its right. In June 1969, the Central Office Area Agent for Wales and Monmouthshire forwarded a cutting from the *West Wales Guardian* in which Donnelly criticised the Conservative Party leadership's poor performance.[37] In his attached report, the agent stated that, 'There are members of our Party who view Donnelly as all but Conservative.' No political party could afford to ignore events like these. Yet, there seemed to be little consternation within Central Office. There were no comments written on these documents, and there are no revealing internal memos within the file. Donnelly's views were not too far to the right, which probably explained Central Office's attitude. Nor did the United Democratic Party have any connections with pre-war fascism or any evidence of racism, unlike some other organisations. Thus, although Central Office was probably irritated at the by-election loss and interested by the ovation given by the Monday Club, it was not as disconcerted by Donnelly as it was by extreme-right groups.

Another reason Central Office was not as concerned about Donnelly was that he attacked the Labour Government, whereas nearly all extreme-right movements saved their most vitriolic comments for the Conservative Party. The Conservative leadership probably welcomed this. This notion is supported by a cartoon in the Conservative Party's 'house paper', the *Daily Telegraph*, which depicted Donnelly as a shop proprietor standing in front of a window display offering 'Taxes Slashed', 'All Goods Guaranteed Denationalised' and 'Fantastic Cuts in Welfare'. Behind Donnelly stood Harold Wilson outside 'Harold's Super Duper Market', obviously irritated by Donnelly's claim that 'Our customers are always right.' Donnelly reproduced this cartoon in the first edition of *Opportunity*. However, the *Daily Telegraph's* positive portrayal of Donnelly also pointed to another reason for Central Office's attitude. Donnelly's policies were very close to those of a Conservative Party that had also moved rightwards since 1967. Thus, while Donnelly's political position obliged Central Office to monitor him and his party, other groups posed far more problems for the Conservative Party and required its attention, both outside and within the party.

In 1967, the extreme right moved to overcome the weakness that it had displayed since the 1964 General Election. The catalyst was the 1966 General Election. Chesterton had already created 'Candour Leagues' to run sanction-busting petrol convoys to Rhodesia. These sanctions would remain because Labour now possessed a large majority. Chesterton believed that the General Election result made it a propitious time for the extreme right to unite. The Conservative Party leadership had provided it with the political space to do so by accepting the Labour Government's immigration legislation.[38] However, this was a very small space in which to operate. Mosley had proved just how difficult this was either side of the Second World War, failing first with the British Union of Fascists and then with Union Movement. Chesterton's LEL and the myriad neo-Nazi and neo-fascist groups it spawned had failed too. Nevertheless, Chesterton decided to begin negotiations with the BNP, RPS, and a number of smaller extreme-right groups, soon after the 1966 General Election.

These negotiations resulted in the formation of the National Front on 7 February 1967. This was Britain's first coherent extreme-right political party since the Second World War, and it possessed the potential to make an electoral impact. The National Front included members of the LEL, the RPS, and the BNP. Chesterton was the party leader, but it also included figures such as Major-General Hilton, Air Vice-Marshall Bennett, Andrew Fountaine, and R. F. Beauclair. It initially excluded individuals whose comments or actions more easily categorised them as Nazis or fascists, such as Bean, Tyndall, and Jordan. However, this proved to be temporary. The National Front soon included Bean and Tyndall, and attracted others in time, including John O'Brien of the British Defence League. Only Colin Jordan of the prominent extremists remained outside the National Front. Although inchoate, the National Front quickly provided the previously fractured extreme right with a common focus. It emerged in a context that included fears about immigration and Europe and became Britain's largest extreme-right party. It presented the Conservative Party with its biggest challenge from the external extreme right since Mosley in the 1930s.

On 2 October 1967, Anthony Royle, the Conservative MP for Richmond, forwarded National Front literature to the new Chairman at Central Office, Anthony Barber, advising him of its distribution in Beckenham. Royle was a progressive Conservative. He clearly thought it his duty to forward this material and information to Central Office, and his comment that 'I thought that the appropriate department of Central Office might be interested,' is revealing on a number of counts. What Central Office read would have confirmed that the National Front was an extreme-right party. The National Front's literature called for repatriation of black immigrants. It announced the formation of a 'Free Speech Defence Committee', which included former Conservatives Andrew Fountaine and Henry Newnham, to champion the cause of those charged under the Race Relations Act (1965). It opposed Britain's membership of the Common Market. The National Front also demanded an end to overseas aid unless it clearly benefited Britain's interests, the establishment of a strong national government that restored the nation's pride, honour, and greatness, and the replacement of the 'coloured' Commonwealth with a new political unit based on the economic and strategic union of Britain and the White Dominions. Unsurprisingly, the Britons Publishing Society published at least one of the National Front's leaflets and shared the address of the National Front's Free Speech Defence Committee. Perhaps more troubling was the realisation that works by individuals connected with the Conservative Party appeared in the attached literature list of 'Kinsmen Books', the National Front's publishing section. This included *The Puppeteers*, written by erstwhile Conservative parliamentary candidate Harold Soref and his fellow Monday Club member Ian

Greig, and *The Defeat of Communism* and *No Vision Here*, written by another Monday Club member, D. G. Stewart-Smith. Alongside these works was the notorious *Protocols of the Learned Elders of Zion*.

The official who received Royle's correspondence immediately asked his colleague, Miss Varley, whether Central Office had any 'knowledge or contact with the National Front'. Varley responded that Central Office did indeed have such knowledge, and showed Central Office's disdain for the National Front when she described it as 'an amalgamation (or should I say unholy alliance?) between John Bean's British National Party and the League of Empire Loyalists'. She identified Bean as Colin Jordan's 'first lieutenant' in his 'fascist organisation' before 'striking out on his own', which showed that Central Office not only associated the National Front with fascism, but that it had watched the political careers of those that it thought fascist. Varley also thought that the component parts of the National Front were 'too discredited to prove a real threat to us', but admitted that it could attract the support of 'some of our extreme right-wing members', and stated that Central Office would 'certainly advise any of our people approached to have nothing whatsoever to do with them'.

Barber summed up Central Office's attitude to the National Front when he replied to Royle that, 'They all seem to be a pretty dangerous crowd!' Central Office continued to monitor the National Front for the remainder of the 1966–70 Parliament. A. S. Garner, the Area Agent for the North West, requested information about the National Front from Central Office in 1968. His request suggested that either Central Office's intelligence-gathering had not performed effectively in the North West, or that the National Front's impact was limited there. An inquiry from an associate in the insurance industry had precipitated Garner's request, which provided further evidence of the social reach of the Central Office intelligence-gathering system. Central Office may have been dismissive about the National Front's prospects, but it warned Garner that its attempt to project an image of respectability 'could be a bigger nuisance' than its constituent parts had so far proved. Central Office had a point. In 1969, the Conservative Party's opponents noted that the National Front included Admiral Sir Barry Domvile on its National Council.[39] Domvile was a former BUF member interned during the Second World War. His presence posed a potential problem should the Conservative Party ever become associated with the National Front. Hence, the Conservative Party's vigilance towards the National Front as the 1970 General Election approached. An example of vigilance came on 4 May 1970 in the response of Mr Carrick at Central Office to material forwarded by the Conservative MP for Petersfield, Miss J. M. Quennell. Carrick thanked Quennell for the 'opportunity of discussing this organisation with you in view of the immense amount of work you have done'. Admittedly, this was a cryptic comment, made more so by the absence of Quennell's material from the file. However, Quennell's correspondence reinforced the notion gained from Anthony Royle that some Conservative MPs actively opposed the National Front, and knew that Central Office did too.

Yet, although Central Office was aware of the potential harm the National Front posed, there was not yet any acute anxiety. By 1967, Central Office had investigated extreme-right organisations under the remit provided in 1948 for nearly twenty years. All of these extreme-right organisations had collapsed, with a few exceptions. Some had produced parliamentary candidates, but they all fared badly as the electorate easily identified them with Nazism or fascism. Arguably, only the LEL candidature at Lewisham North in 1957 had harmed the Conservative Party. Yet, the Conservative Party had effectively rebuffed the LEL at the 1958 Party Conference at Blackpool, and thereafter watched it fracture. Therefore, Central Office's apparently relaxed attitude in this period is understandable. The National Front's poor performance since its inception also warranted Central Office's attitude. Just before the 1970 General Election, Central Office received a report on the National Front's performance in recent municipal elections from the Board of Deputies of British Jews. Central Office informed the sender that it had forwarded the report to the other political parties, which was perhaps a diversionary manoeuvre to minimise linking the National Front with the Conservative Party alone. The report showed that the National Front possessed the potential to deprive the Conservative Party of council seats. In 1969, for example, the National Front polled over 10% in Cardiff Cathays, and the next year at Huddersfield South Central its vote far exceeded Labour's margin of victory over the Conservatives. However, these results were really of little concern. Seats where the National Front may have deprived the Conservatives of victory were few, while the unknown previous loyalties of its voters made firm conclusions difficult. Nowhere did the National Front win a council seat. Nor would the National Front's dismal by-election performance have unduly worried Central Office. On 28 March 1968, former Conservative parliamentary candidate Andrew Fountaine stood at Acton, the only seat that the National Front contested in the period 1966–70, and gained a mere 5.6% of the vote. At Acton, a Labour majority of 4,941 turned into a Conservative one of 3,720, so Fountaine's candidacy did not cause much concern. Yet, there was another reason for Central Office's apparent lack of concern about the National Front. Within the Conservative Party, an extreme-right group was posing far more problems than the National Front.

The internal extreme right

The official history of the Monday Club described its first five years as 'The Years of Struggle'.[40] Membership was small, possibly caused by a confusing attitude towards the Monday Club by the Conservative Party leadership and bureaucracy. Central Office had attempted to block the Monday Club when Macmillan was party leader, but appeared to adopt a more positive stance under Home. That changed again after the 1964 General Election. Pressure mounted quickly for Home's resignation, and Edward Heath replaced him on 27 July 1965, which meant that the leader of the Conservative Party once again was a person unsympathetic to its right wing. Moreover, there was little prospect of Heath's early removal, as he was the first Conservative leader elected by the party's MPs, and another general election was expected soon.

The Monday Club responded to these circumstances by transforming itself into a mass organisation. In 1965, the Monday Club removed restrictions that limited membership to Conservative Party members less than thirty-five years old. Membership increased considerably, more than fivefold between 1964 and 1969 according to the most cautious estimates. Sixteen Conservative MPs were Monday Club members after the 1966 General Election, including Harold Gurden and Patrick Wall. The Monday Club looked increasingly like a party within a party. It adopted a political platform attacking the 'liberal establishment' for its involvement in the decline of British society and the abandonment of loyalists abroad. The Monday Club included the Conservative Party leadership in this 'liberal establishment', a stance similar to many post-war external extreme-right groups. However, its development was more dangerous than that of other groups for two reasons. First, the Monday Club had a higher calibre of member than other extreme-right groups. Therefore, their concentration on society's divisions threatened to exacerbate existing tensions to a degree that other groups could not achieve, most notably over immigration. Secondly, the Monday Club was unarguably of the Conservative Party and operated within it, unlike virtually all of the other extreme-right organisations Central Office had faced since 1945. Therefore, it threatened to identify society's divisions explicitly with those of the Conservative Party.

An early sign of the Monday Club's changed intent after the 1964 General Election came in November 1964 when Paul Williams replaced Paul Bristol as chairman. Williams had been a Conservative MP for Sunderland South from 1953 until 1964, but sat as an Independent MP from 1957–58 after resigning the party whip in protest over the decision to withdraw from Suez. His appointment as Chairman of the Monday Club was probably a result of the fallout after the publication of *Conservatism Lost? Conservatism Regained*.[41] Under Williams, the Monday Club's more concerted and outspoken opposition to the Labour Government frequently also put it at odds with the Conservative leadership. We can see evidence of the Monday Club's opposition to the Conservative frontbench in an internal memorandum on immigration by Tim Hardacre of December 1964. Hardacre cited Griffiths's success at Smethwick and that of other similarly minded Birmingham MPs, and argued that this was a consequence of 'the grave problems caused by the post-war influx of coloured workers from the Commonwealth'.[42] This was a clear criticism of Conservative governments that had held power for thirteen of these nineteen years. Hardacre continued in same vein, identifying the continual 'failure to appreciate the present and future difficulties caused by the 500,000 new immigrants in our country', and their deficiencies in hygiene, social behaviour, customs, language, and consequent impact on housing, education, and jobs, which, he concluded, made racial discrimination 'understandable in the present state of affairs'. Hardacre suggested that the Monday Club should note how MPs like Griffiths had made use of black immigration. Many of these MPs were now in the Monday Club.

Hardacre's comments were a harder line than hitherto, and the language he employed redolent of the extreme right. Whether the party leadership or Central Office was aware of this memorandum is unclear, but a copy of a similar memorandum in the Conservative Party Archive date-stamped 15 February 1965 by the Conservative Research Department, suggests that they were. In February 1965, the Monday Club's pamphlet, *Immigration Into the U.K.*, tempered this language by including some progressive measures. Moreover, its stated objective was the assimilation of all immigrants, which seemed laudable. However, the method it proposed to achieve its objective showed that the substance of Hardacre's memorandum remained. The pamphlet proposed tighter administration of the colour bar inherent in the 1962 Immigrant Act to keep numbers to a minimum.[43] Other recommendations included the establishment of hostels for single black immigrants, clearer information on immigrant unemployment levels, and regular checks for incidence of venereal disease and tuberculosis. These measures directly addressed the fears raised by extreme-right parties such as the BNP. In doing so, the Monday Club reduced the space available to the BNP, but also brought its motives into serious question as it had based its immigration policy solely on skin colour. Nowhere was there criticism of white immigration. The Monday Club memorandum received by the Conservative Research Department proved this when it claimed that, 'Colour exaggerates differences. Competition for housing, education and health services cause resentment.' This would have left the party leadership and Central Office with little doubt about the Monday Club's views and objectives regarding black immigration.

Also issued early in 1965 was the Monday Club pamphlet, *The Role of Subversion in Foreign Affairs*. It criticised previous Conservative governments more explicitly. The pamphlet focused on the threat posed by Communism and stated that, 'When last in office Conservative leaders appeared to many of their supporters to be providing an inadequate defence to this threat.'[44] However, this pamphlet also targeted the current Conservative Party leadership as much as previous ones. It warned that, 'the party leaders would be well advised to assure their supporters that they appreciate the contemporary threat to the British Commonwealth and state unequivocally that they intend to do something effective about it'. Here, the Monday Club implied that the Conservative Party leadership remained insufficiently anti-Communist. More ominously, the pamphlet threatened that, 'unless steps are taken and are seen to be taken, many otherwise loyal Conservative supporters will become increasingly disillusioned: may refuse to vote for the party and may even become more swayed by extremist groups because their fears have not been allayed'. All Monday Club publications carried the caveat that they did not represent its collective view, but we cannot dismiss the comments in this pamphlet as simply one individual's view. For, although its author, Geoffrey Stewart-Smith, was anti-Communist and active in groups that attacked communism, all Monday Club pamphlets required the approval of the chairman, and the National Executive where possible, before publication.

The Conservative Party leadership could neither ignore this criticism from its right wing, nor exaggerate divisions within the party given the proximity of a General Election. However, Central Office still made its view of the Monday Club known. Lord Salisbury requested Central Office help to acquire office space and £1000 funds for the Monday Club in November 1964. The General Director responded: 'Not bloody likely.' When Sir Robert Renwick donated £250, a Miss Yonge made it clear that Central Office would not provide the rest, and informed the Chairman that, 'As a matter of interest I gather that this is about 6% of what the Bow Group gets.' These examples contrast markedly with previous assistance to the Bow Group. They also revealed that Central Office remained hostile to the Monday Club, and suggested that the positive attitude it adopted while Home was party leader was more apparent than real. Nevertheless, at this time only low-level blocking of the Monday Club occurred, such as the comments by the General Director and Miss Yonge.

However, there was also obstruction of the Monday Club's literature. On 6 April 1965, a meeting of the Monday Club's Executive Committee agreed that chairman Williams should seek to meet the Party Chairman 'with a view to correcting the discrimination in the Research Department and Conservative Political Centre against Monday Club publications'.[45] Both departments were within Central Office. Williams duly requested 'fair recognition for the work of the Monday Club in the Research Department and the C.P.C.' and suggested a meeting to Chairman du Cann. Mr Craig at Central Office thought that Williams's request was a complaint about the allegedly preferential treatment it afforded to the Bow Group. In July 1965, the Monday Club's Council discussed Central Office's alleged preferential treatment of the Bow Group. The minutes referred to 'instances of discrimination against Monday Club publications by the C.P.C., in particular in a recent advertisement in the Sunday Times'.[46] In the same month, Williams reported that Party Chairman Edward du Cann had provided assurances that there was no question of any bias against the Monday Club within the party organisation.[47] The Monday Club may have accepted the good faith of the Chairman's assurances. Du Cann was loyal to the still incumbent party leader and fellow right-winger Alec Douglas Home. However, du Cann's assurance did not allay the Monday Club's suspicions. The Council members to whom Williams reported agreed that, 'in view of certain specific instances, such as the fact that no Monday Club Literature was ever on display at Swinton, a file should be compiled giving examples of bias which should then be shown to Mr. du Cann'. This decision reflected the Monday Club's suspicion that even with Home as party leader, 'the pink miasma of the Bow Group continued to overshadow conservative policy. The leftists were deeply entrenched.'[48] The 'Swinton' referred to is Swinton College, the North Yorkshire establishment where the party leadership provided political education for its members. Members of the Bow Group were prominent among those attending

Swinton College, where they engaged in a deliberate strategy of forming political relationships with other members and the party leadership.

Du Cann's assurances bore fruit when Central Office printed a small review of a Monday Club pamphlet and the Conservative Political Centre (CPC) agreed to publish a toned-down *Immigration Into the U.K.*[49] The Monday Club Council considered 'Bias at Central Office' again in September 1965, but decided that, 'no complaint should be made at present as the attitude was becoming more favourable'.[50] CPC's agreement to publish the Monday Club's pamphlet on Europe and display the Club's literature in its bookstall at the forthcoming Conservative Party conference at Brighton influenced the Council's decision. CPC's decision did not prove that Central Office approved of the Monday Club. The Conservative Party faced the prospect of Prime Minister Wilson calling a General Election at any time. Therefore it is unsurprising that Central Office tempered its obstruction of Monday Club literature. However, this is not quite the whole picture. Central Office's decision to publish *A Europe of Nations: A Practical Policy for Britain* was not difficult as this Monday Club pamphlet reflected the more pro-European stance of Edward Heath. Nor did the apparent change in Central Office's activity mean that it, or the wider party organisation, truly welcomed the Monday Club's interventions. For example, when the Monday Club's Council again considered Central Office's bias, Harold Soref complained that no member was 'ever selected in a winnable seat'.[51] It is possible to dismiss this as sour grapes as the agreement to stock Monday Club literature did not include Soref's *The Puppeteers*, although this publication's subsequent appearance on the National Front's approved literature list suggested that any Central Office concern about it was well founded.[52] Nevertheless, Soref's claims pointed to a wider obstruction of the Monday Club. Central Office compiled lists of acceptable candidates and one of its officials attended candidate selection meetings, so it could have influenced proceedings. More clearly, the actions of Edward Heath confirmed the obstruction of the Monday Club. Immediately after the 1964 General Election defeat, Home appointed Heath to mastermind the biggest policy review since the *Industrial Charter*. Heath managed over thirty working groups investigating a broad spectrum of policy. His election as leader strengthened his control over these groups. The result was the policy statement *Putting Britain Right Ahead*, published in time for the 1965 Party Conference. Heath maintained these policy groups and control over them after he was heavily defeated at the 1966 General Election. Heath never appointed any of the Monday Club's nominees to these policy groups, even though they submitted names for consideration.

Rhodesia was the issue that most obviously highlighted the Monday Club's difference from progressives, and its position on the right of the Conservative Party. After the disintegration of the Central African Federation, two of its three constituent parts, Zambia and Malawi, had adopted black majority rule. The white minority rulers of the other member state, Rhodesia, refused to accept such an outcome, and elected a hard-line government led by Ian Smith. The British government applied pressure on the new Rhodesian government to compromise, but failed. On the eve of the 1964 General Election, Smith threatened to unilaterally declare independence rather than accept subordination to majority rule. This situation caused acute problems for the Conservative leadership. The Conservative leadership could not condone an illegal act, but the party's right wing would not accept any abandonment of what it saw as its 'kith and kin'. Initially, these right-wingers formed the Friends of Rhodesia, a group that initially caused little concern at Central Office because its perceived extremism deprived it of funds. However, money from Rhodesia allowed this group to launch the Anglo-Rhodesian Society on 9 September 1965, a development that changed Central Office's stance. The Anglo-Rhodesian Society's existence promised concerted pressure on the Conservative leadership as its patron was the Monday Club's patron, Lord Salisbury. As the issue at stake concerned skin colour, Rhodesia threatened to inflame racial tensions in Britain and once more identify the Conservative Party in public perception with divisive issues both at home and abroad. The Monday Club involved itself prominently in the question of Rhodesia. While right-wing Conservative MPs did not agree on all topics, the Monday Club used the Rhodesia issue to give the right wing a coherent organisational force with which to assail Heath. The division of the Conservative Party in parliament into three distinct groups over the imposition of sanctions against Rhodesia embarrassed the party leadership and made Heath appear weak. However, the Conservative leadership's actions show that it was quite prepared to meet the Monday Club's challenge on this issue.

With a declaration of independence increasingly likely, Heath's Shadow Cabinet released a statement on 6 October 1965. It announced the parliamentary Conservative Party's opposition to Rhodesian independence, and its desire to see Rhodesian government based on majority rule, a statement that Heath's Opposition intended 'to be helpful to the Government in a very difficult situation'.[53] The *Daily Telegraph's* editorial of the same day mirrored the Shadow Cabinet's statement, and indicated that the Conservative leadership would go further if necessary. It stated that there was little difference between the positions of the Government and Opposition, and implied that there would be little dissent from the Conservative leadership if the government imposed sanctions on Rhodesia.[54] Sanctions included an oil embargo, which Chesterton's Candour Leagues subsequently tried to break.[55] The *Daily Telegraph's* editorial was a warning to the Monday Club about just how far the Conservative leadership was prepared to go to oppose it.

However, letters to the *Daily Telegraph* showed how far the views of Monday Club members were from that of the Conservative leadership. Patrick Wall suggested modification of the Rhodesian constitution 'to ensure that power does not yet pass to the majority race'.[56] Wall's qualified statement was in line with the Monday Club's professed agreement with the idea of eventual black majority rule and a solution that was 'just to all races'.[57] Monday Club pronouncements never said when black majority rule would be viable, always placing it some time in the indefinite future. Some Monday Club members made comments that suggested 'eventual' was synonymous with 'never'. Wall's comments to Beauclair in 1964 had revealed a chauvinistic belief that some individuals were unfit to govern themselves by dint of skin colour.[58] His view was more in line with the leader of the LEL than with the Conservative Party leadership, but it is unlikely that Wall was a lone voice in the Monday Club. It is possible that the Monday Club opposed a unilateral declaration of independence on purely legal grounds, not skin colour, and that it based its opposition to any sanctions on a belief in their ineffectiveness. This was certainly the Monday Club's position, but it was inconsistent to oppose independence because it was illegal, and then to oppose legally imposed sanctions. The Monday Club's inconsistency made its support for Rhodesia's white minority look similar to that of the LEL, leaving it open to charges of racism. However, the Monday Club in 1965 was not a declining rump like the LEL. By 1965, it contained a number of MPs and party grandees, which made it difficult for the party leadership and Central Office to deal with. If the party leadership appeased the Monday Club, it risked associating the whole party with the wider extreme right, but if it or Central Office antagonised the Monday Club, therefore, they risked dividing the party just before another General Election. As the Conservative leadership did mobilise the party machinery against the Monday Club, therefore it showed just how determined it was to act against the extreme right within the party's ranks. The leadership used its control of party conference to block Lord Salisbury's motion opposing sanctions in the event of the Unilateral Declaration of Independence (UDI).[59] The *Daily Telegraph* reported conference's overwhelming cry of 'No!' when asked if they should even debate Salisbury's motion.[60]

In a television broadcast on 30 October 1965, Prime Minister Wilson ruled out the use of force if Rhodesia declared independence, but threatened sanctions, particularly on oil. The following day, the Monday Club began preparations for 'a public campaign for support for Rhodesia'.[61] On 11 November, Ian Smith declared Rhodesia's independence. In parliament, the Conservative Party leadership reacted once more to contain the Monday Club and limit any split within the parliamentary party. On 13 November, Heath appeared before a meeting of the 1922 Committee of Conservative backbenchers and gained their assurance that they would not oppose the Government's bill enabling the application of sanctions.[62] The subsequent parliamentary debate on this enabling bill was notable for two incidents: the ejection of Colin Jordan for shouting slogans supporting National Socialism and Rhodesian independence;[63] and the failed attempt to force a division on the bill's second reading by the Monday Club's Edward Taylor, despite the 'black looks from his Front Bench'.[64] Jordan's intervention illustrated the danger of any Monday Club opposition to the agreed Conservative Party position, as the Monday Club's support for the Rhodesian regime would place Conservatives in the same camp as neo-Nazis like Jordan. Taylor's failure suggests that the leadership had headed off any Monday Club-inspired revolt. The result was the relatively easy passage of the Southern Rhodesia Bill on 15 November 1965.

However, the Monday Club quickly proved its resilience. It convened a 'Rhodesia Emergency Committee' in the House of Commons on 17 November, and planned a large-scale emergency public meeting.[65] This ability to react quickly and utilise the offices at Westminster put the Monday Club on a higher plane of credibility than all other extreme-right groups. Consequently, Conservatives viewed the Monday Club as a potential force in British politics, which contrasted with their usually dismissive attitude towards extreme-right wing groups. 'Peterborough' in the *Daily Telegraph* attributed the Monday Club's credibility to chairman Paul Williams: 'He has used his undoubted political acumen and experience of Westminster to shape a mixed assortment of Right-wingers into a more coherent force.'[66] 'Peterborough's' comments were dangerous for the Conservative leadership because they added to the Monday Club's growing credibility, which threatened to divide the Conservative Party. The *Daily Telegraph* recognised the possibility of division when it identified a Monday Club member as representative of the polarisation that beset the Conservative Party.[67]

When the Monday Club held its emergency meeting at the Caxton Hall on 22 November 1965, the *Daily Telegraph* reckoned that 500–600 people attended.[68] This was an impressive figure for a swiftly arranged meeting. The Monday Club distributed its pamphlet, *Rhodesia And You* at the meeting. The *Daily Telegraph* placed the platform's criticism of the new Conservative leader on its front page. The attendees passed a resolution deploring oil sanctions,[69] and ended the meeting with 'Three rousing cheers for Mr. Ian Smith.'[70] This was a potentially explosive situation. 'Peterborough' recognised that the Monday Club's meeting posed a danger to party unity, stating that it 'symbolised an incandescent element in the Conservative Party just now',[71] and tacitly acknowledged that the Conservative leadership had forced the Monday Club to operate in extreme-right political space. The Monday Club appeared to recognise the difficulty of operating in this space, and the difficulty of its position, when it released a press statement denying leading the approval of Smith.[72] Its awareness that association with the extreme right outside the party was risky came when Patrick Wall forwarded the resolution to party leader Edward Heath on 24 November stating that, 'we managed, I am glad to say, to eliminate Fascists or members of the League of Empire Loyalists, etc'.[73] It is doubtful that Wall's comments allayed Heath's suspicions and fears, especially as he admitted that the Monday Club's actions attracted fascists. Nor did the press statement condemn the ovation or say whether the platform joined in the audience's chorus of approval, and therefore it walked a very fine, obfuscating line. Wall did deny that the Monday Club platform had supported Smith when he wrote to a prominent Conservative, but showed his own partiality by warning that the Conservative Party had underestimated the extent of sympathy for Ian Smith and stating that this was dangerous.[74] Moreover, Wall also claimed that the Rhodesian Government's action was only 'technical treason' committed 'by some of Her Majesty's loyalist subjects'.[75] The Monday Club appeared to be engaging in double-speak, and the Conservative leadership did not accept its assurances. Evidence for the leadership's attitude came in barely-attributed comments on the *Daily Telegraph*'s front page on 30 November. It quoted former ministers who stated that they were 'quite happy for those MPs who were prepared to support an illegal regime to be smoked out', and stated that, 'The activities of the Right-wing Monday Club have incurred growing disfavour among members of the Shadow Cabinet.'[76]

On 21 December 1965, the Government placed an Order in Council to implement the embargo of all petroleum products to Rhodesia. The Opposition had accepted sanctions provided they were not punitive, but oil sanctions would be punitive because they would affect all sections of Rhodesian society. Wilson's action had placed the opposition leadership in a difficult position. Opposing the Order left the Opposition open to charges of racism for appearing to endorse a white regime's actions against its majority black citizens, but supporting the Order left the Opposition open to charges of weakness and desertion of Britain's 'kith and kin'. Heath used his predecessor, Home, to try to placate opponents of oil sanctions. Home was more amenable to the Monday Club, for under his leadership Central Office had been more positive towards it.[77] Home had attended the Monday Club's foundation dinner in 1964, and would later attend other prominent functions.[78] He called for a compromise that mirrored the Monday Club's position of accepting eventual majority rule in Rhodesia.[79] However, the Monday Club's response reinforced the idea that it engaged in double-speak. It did not accept the leadership's olive branch but saw it as a chance to end the Conservative leadership's bipartisan political approach on Rhodesia. On 16 December, ninety Conservative MPs signed a censure motion against Wilson's 'unconditional surrender', including many Monday Club members. The Conservative leadership responded by deciding that abstention was better than appearing to go back on its word. This political expedient backfired when 31 Conservative MPs voted with the Government and 50 voted against, and highlighted Conservative disunity. Nevertheless, the leadership's stance indicated that it was prepared to accept party disunity rather than the Monday Club's position.

Others opposed the Monday Club as well as the Conservative leadership. Some Conservative MPs were prepared to voice their opposition. Some saw themselves as a counter-balance to the Monday Club. They acted to meet the right's challenge. These Conservative MPs originally intended to abstain in the vote on sanctions, but eventually supported the Labour Government on 21 December because they became aware that Monday Club MPs were going to deny the leadership's instructions to abstain. Their motive was a belief that it was important to make the public aware of their more moderate views. However, these 'pro-sanctions' Conservatives suffered consequences. Local associations and officials subsequently exerted pressure on them to explain their actions, and one MP had to contend with the imposition of a hostile, sizeable, and clearly organised, meeting in his Worthing constituency. It is difficult to prove the Monday Club's role in these events. A failure to adhere to the party line was a sufficient reason for anger within local associations. Nevertheless, it is possible that the Monday Club was involved via its links with the Anglo-Rhodesian Society, which was active in these particular constituencies. However, the response of one MP showed that he was prepared to maintain his opposition to that of the Monday Club. Terence Higgins, the Conservative MP for Worthing, blocked the attempt of an 800-strong audience to pass a resolution in favour of Ian Smith by grabbing the microphone.[80] An Anglo-Rhodesian Society Council member complained that Higgins's views were 'indistinguishable from those of a Socialist', and compared them to the true Conservatism of Monday Club member Sir Patrick Wall.

On 14 January 1966, Monday Club Chairman Paul Williams responded to the events following the Order in Council. He issued a statement describing the Conservative Opposition as a 'meaningless irrelevance', and stated that, 'To some of us outside Parliament it appears to be neither Conservative nor an Opposition.'[81] These comments were the language of the extreme right, showing the extent of the Monday Club's alienation from the Conservative Party leadership. However, Williams's statement confirmed another reason for the Monday Club's alienation other than disagreement over Rhodesia. Williams argued that the Conservative Party was not in a position to attack the Labour Government thanks to Heath's reliance on 'a host of committees studying largely irrelevant details of policy'. This reflected the party leadership's exclusion of Monday Club members from its policy review groups. It also partly explains why the Monday Club's minutes frequently include discussion of bias against it by the party leadership. The leadership's perception of the Monday Club as a potentially dangerous group that attracted external extremists would explain its decision to exclude the Monday Club from policy review groups. Wall's letter to Heath after the Caxton Hall meeting showed that he understood that this was indeed the leadership's fear.[82] Otherwise, why would Wall mention them? Other commentators were linking the Monday Club with characteristics of fascism by this time. When Lord Salisbury claimed that the Monday Club stood for the 'traditional principles of Conservatism on which I was brought up long before fascism was thought of', the journalist Robert Kee asked him if these were the same principles of his grandfather, who thought home rule should be limited to 'people who are of Teutonic race'.[83] In the month before a General Election, Kee's comments were especially unwelcome. The Monday Club also acknowledged fears that it attracted external extremists when its Executive Council discussed the problems of infiltration and how to deter unwelcome members.[84] Williams would have understood this too, which may have explained him informing du Cann that Monday Club members were being encouraged to 'do whatever possible to help the Conservative Party during the Election'. However, when the electorate returned a Labour government with a much-increased majority at the end of March 1966, Williams reverted quickly to attacking the Conservative Party for its insufficient opposition to Labour, and to demanding fair treatment for the Monday Club.

On 4 April 1966, the Monday Club's Executive Council met at the Wig and Pen Club in Fleet Street. Foremost among the issues it discussed was the Conservative Party's post-election policies and attitudes. The Executive council agreed on a delegation to du Cann, and highlighted the need for aggressive opposition and a general philosophy that differed from Socialism.[85] This was a criticism of Heath's leadership, and his continuing study groups. The Executive Council also resolved to 'demand that Right-Wing Candidates receive fair consideration and the bias of the recent past be corrected'. Du Cann tacitly admitted that this bias existed when he explained that, 'the Right Wing has a dirty name', and later asked Williams to inform him if he 'ever came across any discrimination against the Monday Club'. This Williams did. Williams told du Cann that the Northern Area Young Conservatives had informed him that their National Officers implored them to cooperate 'with the universities and the Bow Group', and concluded, 'I hardly need say any more about discrimination'. The following day, Williams telephoned Central Office and complained that the CPC did not stock a particular Monday Club pamphlet, which he stated was contrary to du Cann's undertaking. Du Cann denied any 'conscious discrimination'. However, his personal assistant, Miss Benton, made enquiries by asking the Young Conservatives National Organising Secretary, Mr Durant, to comment on the information from its Northern Area. Layton-Henry argued in 1973 that in the 1960s the Young Conservatives' National Officers were firmly in the progressive mould of Butler, Macleod, Macmillan, and Boyle, and were to the left of its membership.[86] He described Durant as 'the embodiment' of the Young Conservatives' progressive leadership. Central Office files that were unavailable to Layton-Henry in 1973 proved that he was correct, as was the Monday Club's belief in bias. Mr Durant replied to Benton that, 'There is no doubt that the present National Officers have very little at all in sympathy with the aspirations of the Monday Club', claiming that it was therefore 'natural that they should tend to ignore them'. This proved the substance of the Monday Club's complaint. Durant denied that the Young Conservatives' National Officer's line was discrimination, describing it instead as 'their honest opinions as to the way the Party should go'. However, as this information came from an organisation that supposedly represented all Young Conservatives and not a policy-forming body, this was a specious argument that admitted to the omission of a sizeable and growing section of the party. Durant also tried to dismiss the Northern Area Young Conservatives by describing them as 'rather out on a limb politically, being rather extreme right wing', but all this did was reveal his belief that political respectability did not extend to those he considered extreme. When Durant added that this extremism made it 'natural' for Northern Area members to express their concerns to Williams, he made it clear that he did not consider the Monday Club respectable. Finally, when he suggested raising this matter when National Officers and the Party Chairman 'next had a meeting', Durant, whose office was within Central Office, revealed that the Young Conservatives' National Officers were indeed part of the party machine.[87]

Williams once more raised the Monday Club's suspicion of discrimination in July, when he complained again about the Young Conservatives. Williams advised du Cann that the last meeting of the Young Conservatives' National Advisory Committee had agreed to invite observers from outside bodies to its meetings, 'at the discretion of its National Officers'. Williams claimed that the Young Conservatives Committee did this 'to allow such people as the Bow Group's liaison officer to attend meetings without being made a formal member', and made a thinly veiled accusation of discrimination by expressing his 'trust that our liaison officer on these matters will also be welcomed to future meetings'. Williams had a strong case. There was no equitable reason for the Young Conservatives to treat a bone-fide Conservative organisation differently than any other. However, the Young Conservatives' response to Williams showed that they were prepared to continue doing exactly that. Inside Central Office, Mr Craig dismissed Williams as having a 'persecution complex both personally and on behalf of the Monday Club'. Sir Adrian FitzGerald, a founder member of the Monday Club, denied this description emphatically, describing it as indicative of someone with a 'bitter grudge' against Williams.[88] His comments are a reminder that personal animosities play a role in institutional relationships. Craig thought it necessary to acquire the advice of Richard Webster, who adopted the time-honoured Central Office tactic of disassociating itself from trouble. Webster stated that the Monday Club should put a proper request to the Young Conservatives, and that 'We should not be involved in this anyway.' However, Webster added in handwriting, 'I've warned Durant.' This added comment was not a disinterested action. Subsequent events proved that Central Office actually worked closely with the National Young Conservatives on Williams's accusation, despite Webster's formal response to Craig.

On 1 August 1966, Williams wrote to Alan Haselhurst, National Chairman of the Young Conservatives, and demanded fair treatment for the Monday Club. Haselhurst perfunctorily dismissed Williams's accusation of unfairness and criticised him for approaching the Party Chairman on a matter 'solely within the province of the Young Conservatives National Officers'. Williams replied that as a former Vice-Chairman of the Young Conservatives he understood that its responsibility was to reflect all opinions within the party, like all National Committees of the party. He also probably touched on Central Office's real concern when he argued that, 'many people have too easily accepted Harold Wilson's smear that we are semi-Fascist'. However, what Williams cannot have known is that, before Haselhurst responded to him he had forwarded a draft to Mr Craig at Central Office stating that, 'If the Chairman is happy about it, this is the reply I will send.' Central Office amended it, noted Haselhurst's agreement to their involvement, and added it to its growing Monday Club file.

These were not the only examples of bias against the Monday Club in the summer of 1966. On 26 May, Williams wrote to du Cann expressing his wish to submit names of suitable Monday Club members for Heath's study groups. This request does not seem to have borne fruit. Williams noted the following month that Heath had requested the Bow Group to examine capital taxation and asked du Cann whether 'there is any chance that the Monday Club will be consulted in a similar way'. Again, Williams's request appears to have been unsuccessful. In July, Williams enquired about the prospects of Monday Club member F. J. Abbott, who had applied to join the Conservative Research Department and had even secured an interview. Central Office officials concocted an excuse for

Abbott's failure, stating that no vacancies existed. These incidents seemed trivial taken in isolation, but collectively they suggest that the leadership and Central Office discriminated against a group that they considered extremist.

There were other reasons for the Conservative leadership's negative stance towards the Monday Club, including the nature of its publications and the company that it kept. In 1966, the Monday Club published *The Wreckers: Communist Disruption in British Trade Unions*. The author was Frederic Abbott, the unsuccessful applicant to the Conservative Research Department. The pamphlet identified widespread communist infiltration, citing the 1965 Devlin Report's judgement that communists and Trotskyites had caused the recent dock strikes. This confrontational document may have found approval in sections of the Conservative Party, but it is unlikely to have pleased Edward Heath, who had spoken during the 1966 General Election campaign of his belief in the need for 'partnership, not confrontation', in industrial relations. Moreover, the Monday Club again risked associating the Conservative Party with Edward Martell by choosing his Sapphire Press to print the pamphlet. Nor was Edward Martell the only problematic person with whom the Monday Club was associated. In October 1966, Sir Arthur Bryant was the Monday Club's Guest of Honour at its Hatfield House Conference. Andrew Roberts described Bryant as 'a Nazi sympathiser and fascist fellow-traveller, who only narrowly escaped internment as a potential traitor in 1940'.[89] Roberts exonerated those who gave Bryant an honorary lunch in 1979 because they did not have access to his private papers, and thus were ignorant of his past. This exoneration must also apply to the Monday Club in 1966. Yet, it is inconceivable that the Conservative Party bureaucracy or Monday Club was ignorant of Bryant's political sympathies. Before the Second World War, Bryant edited the party's Ashridge Journal, and was an educational adviser to Central Office with close connections to the Party Chairman. Bryant praised Hitler and Mussolini, kept company with members of Mosley's BUF, published anti-Semitic books authored by future internees, and justified Kristallnacht. One Conservative MP referred to Bryant's books when he visited Central Office to warn against the party's association with 'this kind of Fascism'. In June 1939, another MP proclaimed in the House of Commons that Bryant's fascist sympathies were well known. When war commenced, Bryant involved himself with 'pro-peace' extreme-right groups that were in reality pro-Nazi. Bryant backtracked furiously when the Government interned his fellow sympathisers and associates, and sought exculpation in producing patriotic histories lauding British fighting spirit. It is difficult to understand why the Government did not intern Bryant. His connections may have saved him. Bryant's associates included Conservatives with connections to the extreme right, such as Henry Drummond Wolff MP, and Sir Joseph Ball of the Conservative Research Department and *Truth*, as well as those at Central Office.[90] The Government did intern one Conservative MP who did not retract his views, Archibald Maule Ramsay MP.[91] Interning Bryant would have embarrassed the Conservative Party further. Yet, even though Bryant appeared to recant, his true feelings remained obvious even during the war. He joined

Kinship-in-Husbandry, a group Dan Stone identified as one of the 'organo-fascist' cultural representations of England's nativist fascist groups.[92] Bryant was the literary twin of A. K. Chesterton, and it is therefore unsurprising that in 1963 he too campaigned against black immigration.[93]

The Monday Club's desire to expand also disconcerted the Conservative leadership. Former Monday Club chairman Paul Bristol claimed that there was no intention of turning the early Monday Club into a mass organisation. However, from December 1966 to May 1967, the Monday Club debated in its monthly *Newsletter* whether it should remain a small, manageable organisation or seek growth throughout the country. The Monday Club chose growth and a higher profile. Central Office monitored events. On 2 January 1967, Central Office North West Area Agent, A. S. Garner, reported that individuals were meeting 'from all over Lancashire' to discuss forming a Monday Club branch. He stated that they 'all seemed to be very loyal to the Party', which revealed that the loyalty and intentions of Monday Club sympathisers was in question. The Monday Club was also to the fore in political demonstrations. In January 1967, it provided two speakers and eighty stewards for a 'Peace with Rhodesia' rally at Trafalgar Square that television stations broadcast. In a debate in the House of Commons, MPs denounced the rally as a nasty, racist, and squalid exercise, and referred to the 1962 ban on Fascist demonstrations at Trafalgar Square.[94] In June 1967, the Monday Club held a press conference launching an 'Action Fund' appealing for £100,000 to facilitate activity throughout the country. Chairman Paul Williams felt it necessary to state that the Monday Club 'considered itself realist rather than extremist',[95] which was a public admission that some perceived an association between the Monday Club and extremism. His statement failed to stop Central Office and the party leadership becoming extremely concerned about the Action Fund. The Party Chief Whip, William Whitelaw, reported to Heath that his investigations had revealed that the purpose of the Action Fund was 'to set up the Monday Club on a permanent basis with office, staff, etc'. Whitelaw identified G. K. Young as the Monday Club member behind the Action Fund, and highlighted his previous employment in the Foreign Office and Security Services. Also noted was the assistance of 'a "General Williams" formerly in our Central Office'. The realisation that General Williams was a Central Office pensioner provoked an investigation into the feasibility of using financial pressure to curtail his activities. No such sanction existed, but Lord Chelmer's advice that 'there surely should be in every future case', showed Central Office preparedness to harm individuals financially to counter the Monday Club.

Unsurprisingly, the party bureaucracy continued to obstruct the Monday Club. On 12 September, Monday Club member Dr Wyndham Davies visited Sir Michael Fraser at Central Office. The Monday Club had asked Davies to encourage its activities in the universities, and therefore he asked Fraser's permission 'to liaise with the Universities Department of the Central Office' and 'made a tentative suggestion about getting some central financial help for Monday Club conferences in the universities'. Fraser refused Davies' request. He stated that he wanted to 'maintain friendly relations with all the various Conservative groups – Bow Group, PEST, Monday Club – that have some membership in the universities and elsewhere', and that therefore the party 'could not favour any one of them more than the others'. However, Fraser's claims were disingenuous. Not only did Central Office look more favourably on Pressure for Economic and Social Toryism (PEST) than the Monday Club, it had also formed a close relationship with the Bow Group. At the same time that Central Office refused Davies' request, it was granting the Bow Group exactly the kind of assistance it denied to the Monday Club, and indeed much more.

In 1967, PEST was still a young organisation. Although formed in 1963, it 'emerged on the scene' only in 1965 according to the *Daily Telegraph*.[96] During 1965, PEST set out its progressive credentials. It desired easier entry for immigrants and their assimilation, an end to the Conservative Party's social isolation, greater social opportunity, an increase in economic planning, an increase in 'comprehensive' education, and it opposed Smith's regime in Rhodesia. PEST's views were diametrically opposite those of the Monday Club, a position it made clear by having R. A. Butler as its patron. Central Office exhibited no hostility towards PEST. Although Central Office was inclined to deny PEST's request for funds and offices in 1965, this was only until PEST had established itself and proved useful. Moreover, PEST was aware of Central Office's positive attitude towards it. Michael Spicer, PEST's chairman, wrote to Edward du Cann on 25 May 1965, and claimed to be 'well aware of how much you are in sympathy with our activities'. Du Cann's comments to Conservative MP Anthony Barber supported Spicer's claim. He advised Barber that Central Office had held a number of discussions about PEST, and decided that, 'we should try and give them limited encouragement'. Du Cann's involvement does not disprove the notion that Central Office was more sympathetic to the Monday Club under his chairmanship, merely that it consistently welcomed progressive views. By the end of 1965, PEST was solvent. It was an established progressive group when Sir Michael Fraser referred to it in 1967 to justify refusing Dr Davies' request. Two years later, Douglas Hurd, head of Heath's Private Office, wrote to Central Office noting that PEST had 'recently been doing good work, particularly in the universities'. This attitude contrasted with Central Office responses to Monday Club requests for assistance, but the contrast with the similarly progressive Bow Group was much starker.

On 12 June 1967, senior Central Office officials attended a Bow Group dinner. Beforehand, Mr Craig advised his Central Office colleagues of items that the Bow Group wished to discuss. These items included the Bow Group's activities and finances, the Conservative Party's reorganisation, policy-making and public meetings, all of which revealed the breadth of Central Office's connection with the Bow Group. On 13 June, the same colleagues received another memo from Craig noting the results of the dinner. Central Office had agreed with the Bow Group to coordinate relations with the press, liaise about the progress of Heath's study groups, allow the Bow Group to undertake a major policy study, form a diary to facilitate political statements reacting to events, and to use the Bow

Group to make statements deemed inappropriate for shadow ministers. Even more interesting, Craig's memo also revealed that the Bow Group received an annual subvention of £4,000 from a Colonel Hobbs, which for some reason was about to cease. Hobbs was the individual whom the Bow Group had contacted at Sir Toby Low's suggestion.[97] Passage of the Companies Act (1967) had made disclosure of political contributions obligatory, and that in turn threatened to reveal that the Bow Group's benefactor, British United Industrialists, existed for no other purpose than to channel funds to the Conservative Party and related organisations. The Bow Group sought Central Office assistance at the dinner meeting.

Du Cann wrote to the Bow Group Chairman Reginald Watts on the same day that Craig circulated the results of the Bow Group's dinner to his colleagues. He stated that he 'should be very pleased if we could have a discussion about finance in the immediate future'. Watts confirmed that the meeting they agreed for 30 June was to 'discuss finance', and asked du Cann if he was confident of reaching a solution to the Bow Group's difficulties before the end of the month. It is unclear whether the Bow Group found a solution in time. Nor is du Cann's role clear, for Heath replaced him with Anthony Barber in summer 1967. What is clear is that Central Office subsequently coordinated press releases with the Bow Group, and permitted the Bow Group to organise joint functions with the Federation of Conservative Students. Moreover, whereas Central Office frequently declined invitations to Monday Club functions, Party Chairman Barber actually proceeded to host a dinner for senior officers of the Bow Group. There is no record of a similar event in Central Office's Monday Club files. In contrast, a confidential Central Office memo of December 1967 from a Mr Drewe about the Bow Group stated that, 'Long ago it was decided that money should be provided to them from the British United Industrialists'. Drewe does not say who had decided this, but he was clearly aware of it. His comments supported the notion that Central Office was complicit in the initial help given to the Bow Group. Drewe also mentioned that Lord Chelmer had helped safeguard Bow Group funds by turning the British United Industrialists into an 'unincorporated association', and therefore not subject to the Companies Act (1967), and thus protect the Conservative Party's finances. Chelmer had advised Central Office over its earlier investigation into a former employee's pension.[98] It would seem, therefore, that Central Office had helped to resolve the Bow Group's financial concerns at the same time as it resolved the Conservative Party's wider concerns about its own revenue.

In September 1967, the Monday Club congratulated Barber on his appointment. Barber honoured du Cann's scheduled meeting with the Monday Club on 5 October. At the meeting, Paul Williams advised 'we are convinced that what is loosely called the Right Wing point of view has been under-represented in Party Councils in recent years', and promised to write to Barber about the specific example of the Commonwealth Council. On 16 October, Williams informed Barber that the Commonwealth Council had excluded his members, and that he believed that the Conservative Party funded and constituted this organisation.

Williams once more asked for fair treatment from an all-party organisation. A document in Central Office files that provided a comparison between the Commonwealth Council's current constitution and its previous one proved the accuracy of Williams's claim. The constitution of the Commonwealth Council showed that the party organisation appointed its president and chairman. The Conservative Overseas Bureau was the body nominally responsible for the Commonwealth Council, and its address was the same as that of Central Office. Williams's complaint failed. Mr Milne at Central Office reported to Mr Craig that, 'at no time has there been any discrimination against the Monday Club'. Unfortunately, Milne's list of those excluded contained prominent Monday Club members. Craig probably realised this, and asked Milne to 'draft a "safe" letter' to Paul Williams. A change of Party Chairman had not resulted in a more favourable attitude towards the Monday Club.

Yet, the Monday Club's attempt to influence youth opinion bore fruit with conferences of university students and Young Conservatives in November and December respectively, despite Central Office obstruction. Meanwhile, the Monday Club launched *The Monday World* in winter 1967, a magazine that provided a regular vehicle for its views. In the first edition, Chairman Williams protested that: 'Critics often assume that the Monday Club is composed of feudal Blimps wedded to an irrelevant past. In fact, as will be seen from this first issue of "The Monday World", the Club more nearly represents the attitudes, views and emotions of a modern Conservative.'[99] *The Monday World* frequently attacked the Conservative Opposition for its poor performance, re-inforcing the view that the Monday Club sought to either transform or replace the Conservative Party. In many respects, the Monday Club resembled Martell's Freedom Group, especially concerning domestic issues. On Rhodesia, it resembled the LEL. However, when it engaged in rallies, sought the creation of a mass movement including a youth wing, and highlighted fears about 'coloured' immigration, the Monday Club operated in a manner similar to extreme-right parties. The Monday Club's focus on black immigration was evident to all, as in its demand at a Caxton Hall meeting in October 1967 that the Government impose 'stringent limitations on immigration'. By the end of 1967, it had presented the Conservative Party with an altogether different level of concern.

However, the Conservative Party was experienced in neutralising right-wing extremists. In 1962, the Conservative Government had limited the extreme-right's appeal by reaching rightwards and passing the Immigration Act.[100] In 1967, the same year that the external extreme right coalesced into the National Front and the Monday Club determined on growth, the Conservative Party again reached rightwards. However, the Conservative leadership could not neutralise the extreme right by legislation as easily because it was in opposition. Instead, it moved its political stance, adopting a tougher stance on immigration and trade unions, and thus absorbing the resurgent right. A dramatic increase in the number of right-wing motions at party conference in the years 1967–69, the election of known right-wing MPs to parliamentary committees, and the selection of more

Monday Club members as parliamentary candidates are evidence of this change and absorption.

The National Front's emergence probably played a part in this rightwards move too. The Conservative Party always carefully distanced itself from it. In November 1969, the leader of Wandsworth Conservatives, Ernest Sorrie, claimed that there was little difference between Conservative Party and National Front policy.[101] This resulted in complaints from the Association of Jewish Ex-Servicemen and Women. Alderman Michael Fidler, the President of The Board of Deputies of British Jews, wrote to Central Office highlighting the National Front's Nazi connections, and argued that Sorrie's comments damaged the Conservative Party. Central Office had already realised the danger of Sorrie's comments. A Central Office Area Agent reported that Sorrie knew that he had 'dropped an almighty clanger', and suggested that Chairman Barber and Heath should coordinate repudiation of Sorrie's comments. Coordination duly occurred. Barber downplayed Sorrie's remarks as 'inadvertent' and 'not correct', and emphasised the Conservative Party's difference from the National Front when he replied to Jewish organisations. The absence of any further correspondence suggested that in this instance Central Office's action was effective. However, it is doubtful that the Conservative leadership knew much about the National Front at that time, other than it was dangerous to the party. Heath's Parliamentary Private Secretary reflected this when he advised in one 'co-ordinated' letter that, 'Mr. Heath has no precise knowledge of the policies of the National Front but they are in important ways different from those of the Conservative Party'. Nor, given its poor electoral performances to date, is it probable that the National Front unduly concerned the Conservative Party. Therefore, despite the Conservative Party's determination not to be associated with the National Front, if we are to identify any particular organisation as responsible for its rightward move it is the Monday Club. This showed that the Conservative leadership and Central Office also thought that the Monday Club was of a far higher calibre than other extreme-right groups, and that its location within the Conservative Party was more problematic. This situation made it difficult for the party leadership and bureaucracy to oppose the Monday Club. Any action against the Monday Club had to be more circumspect than that taken against other extreme-right groups. Therefore, when Heath moved the party in a rightwards direction it was both a response to the impact made by the Monday Club and a means of countering it. However, regardless of whether it was the National Front or the Monday Club that had the greater impact, there was one person who played the most visible role in the Conservative Party's rightwards change, Conservative MP, Enoch Powell.

Always right: the impact of Enoch Powell

On 20 April 1968, with the House of Commons about to debate the Race Relations Bill, Enoch Powell delivered arguably the most memorable post-war speech by a British politician. The speech contained incendiary language and apocalypti-cally warned that if black immigration continued it would result in 'rivers of blood'. Powell echoed the concerns of extreme-right parties and the Monday Club. However, his comments posed greater problems for the Conservative Party than any of these organisations. In 1937, Powell became the youngest professor in the Commonwealth. In the war, he rose from a private to become the youngest brigadier in the British Army. He was one of the high-calibre new Conservative MPs who entered parliament at the 1950 General Election. Thereafter, Powell gained a reputation as a powerful parliamentary performer, becoming Financial Secretary to the Treasury in 1957 and in 1960 Minister of Health. Moreover, Powell allied intellect and performance with principle. Denis Healey described Powell's criticism of the Hola Camp atrocities in 1957 as one of the greatest parliamentary speeches, delivered with moral passion and rhetorical force. In 1958, Powell resigned from the Treasury rather than accept spending compromises. Powell also refused to serve in Home's Government because he believed Macmillan had manipulated the succession. He came a poor third in the 1965 Conservative leadership election, but was an obvious option should Heath fall. Heath appointed Powell Shadow Defence Secretary. Powell's stature was far greater than his fellow anti-immigrant Conservative MPs. His 'rivers of blood' speech lent credibility to the extreme right.

Powell did not forward his speech to Central Office for prior approval, which breached accepted procedure, but indicated his awareness of Central Office's power. Former Conservative MP Humphrey Berkeley denounced Powell's speech as 'the most disgraceful public utterance since the days of Sir Oswald Mosley' and demanded his sacking. Heath believed that the speech was racist and sacked Powell on 21 April. Reaction to Powell's speech suggested that Heath was wise to do so. On 23 April, Midlands' workers staged token strikes in support of Powell,[102] and London's dockers and meat porters rose spontaneous-ly and marched on parliament with slogans proclaiming, 'We Want Enoch.'[103] Dan Harmston, a leading Union Movement member and lifelong Mosleyite, was prominent among the marchers. Harmston later contrasted this sponta-neity with his own inability to politicise Smithfield meat market for Union Movement. By 1968, Mosley's Union Movement was little more than the fan club of a discredited individual who was no longer even resident in Britain. The spontaneous marches showed that Powell's potential impact was greater than Mosley's was. The National Front was more prominent than Union Movement. On 24 April, A. K. Chesterton told *The Times* that, 'What Mr. Powell has said does not vary in any way from our view.' However, the editor of its regular pub-lication realised that Powell had encroached upon the National Front's politi-cal space, and reacted coolly by accusing Powell of political opportunism. Yet, the external extreme-right generally welcomed Powell's comments. If Powell's intervention resulted in his departure from the Conservative Party, he might provide the external extreme right with the calibre of leadership it had lacked since the 1930s. What, then, was Powell's impact on the recently coalesced extreme right?

Initially, Powell's intervention appeared to increase National Front membership. *The Times*' 'News Team' reported that Conservative officials claimed to be 'deluged with letters from Tories enraged because of Mr. Powell's dismissal from the Shadow Cabinet and expressing interest in the Front'.[104] Increased membership did allow the National Front to make organisational changes in autumn 1968, including the establishment of a training scheme for branch and group organisers, and appeared to give it a chance of joining the political mainstream. In December 1968, National Front members marched to Powell's home to register their approval of him. The National Front's organiser in Huddersfield claimed that, 'Before Powell spoke, we were getting only cranks and perverts. After his speeches we started to attract, in a secret sort of way, the right-wing members of the Tory organizations.' In 1969, the chairman of a Huddersfield local Conservative Association, councillor Colin Campion, formed the British People's Union, which acted as a platform for Powell's sympathisers and as a forum in which local Conservatives and the National Front could meet. Pro-Powell letters continued to pour into Central Office; many expressed a belief in the National Front's eventual success unless the Conservative Party adopted Powell's stance. Many National Front members and extreme-right voters saw Powell as their saviour.

However, the National Front also had to avoid losing its own members to the Powellite wing of the Conservatives. The National Front's emphasis of its differences with Powell is evidence that it was aware of this possibility. The National Front's regular publication, *Combat*, accused the 'so-called right-wing of the Tory Party' of jumping on the immigration issue simply because it was realised 'here is a vote-getter'.[105] Not all Powellite Conservative groups that emerged throughout the country were as attracted to the National Front as those in Huddersfield. Many stressed their Conservatism and independence, such as the Immigration Control Association of Mary Howarth and Joy Page. Even in Huddersfield, the local Conservative leadership exerted pressure to stop councillor Campion's British People's Union. However, the National Front felt that it was necessary to restore its connections with organisations such as the Racial Preservation Society, and bolstered its presence in areas traditionally sympathetic to the extreme right. The National front did this because although Powell's comments had highlighted its most obvious feature, an anti-immigration stance, this did not necessarily result in any sustained influx of new members. John Bean claimed that the initial spurt in membership after Powell's speech faded after twelve months.[106] Instead, Powell's comments simply reinforced the existing quandary posed to all extreme-right voters: whether to waste a vote by opting for a miniscule extreme-right party or vote Conservative. Dan Harmston reflected this quandary when he sought answers to the Smithfield workers' concerns over immigration in January 1970 not from the National Front, but from the Conservative Party Chairman. Powell's decision to remain within the Conservative Party made extreme-right voters' quandary even more acute, and thus increased the likelihood that they would vote Conservative.

Powell's speech had also affected the Monday Club by giving it impetus. The Monday Club had recently determined on growth. If Powell decided to join the Monday Club, he could probably become its leading figure. Former Monday Club Chairman Jonathan Guinness stated that he shared this view, and would not have resisted Powell's leadership.[107] Such an outcome would threaten the leadership and split the Conservative Party. Events after Powell's speech gave the party leadership further cause for concern. When the Monday Club publicly supported Powell, Edward Heath personally justified his sacking. Powell now accepted numerous invitations to speak at Monday Club events. In 1968, Powell was guest of honour at the Monday Club's annual dinner, telling his audience that people who might otherwise remain outside the Conservative Party had joined it because of the Monday Club. Nor were Powell's contributions to Monday Club events solely focused on immigration. In 1968, Powell gave his views on defence policy at a Monday Club meeting at Westminster, and on economics at Norcott Court, the home of a Monday Club member. Powell's contributions revealed that the Monday Club was not a single-issue entity, unlike many external right-wing parties. At the Monday Club's Annual General Meeting of April 1969, Chairman Williams announced that membership exceeded 1,500. This was a 90% increase on the figure in the month before Powell's 'rivers of blood speech'.

How could the Conservative Party combat Powell's alliance with the Monday Club? The answer lay not in the problem Powell posed to the Conservative Party, but in the reverse. Powell operated at the heart of a paradox. The Conservative Party needed, as a monolithic party within a liberal democracy, to secure enough votes to achieve power. That required the votes of progressive Conservatives for whom anything that resembled extremism was anathema. Yet, the Conservative Party also contained extremists. The result was a heterogeneous party that contained a wide range of views, and allowed the Conservative Party leadership room to manoeuvre between the centre and the right. The leader contained conflict by adjusting the composition of the front-bench. One example came in 1966 when Heath promoted prominent Monday Club member Geoffrey Rippon to the Shadow Cabinet. The Monday Club's divisions over Europe were well known. That Rippon favoured entry into Europe, unlike many Monday Club members, probably influenced the ardently pro-European Heath's decision. The leader's ability to act in this way also allowed for the exploitation of its members' disagreements. For example, Powell avoided supporting the National Front's call for compulsory repatriation, despite admitting at a One Nation Group dinner in 1968 that he favoured it. Powell admitted this to Geoffrey Rippon, whom Heath described as 'incandescent' on hearing it. Heath presumably would not have supported Powell's takeover of the Monday Club and possibly made his view known. This shows that the Conservative Party both absorbed and expunged its extremists, presenting those unwilling to accept its positions with the dilemma of staying within the party, striking out on their own, or joining an openly extremist party.

In 1968, the Conservative leadership used the opportunities afforded by this paradox to its advantage and marginalised Powell. In September 1968, Heath announced the end of bipartisan consensus, and stated that a future Conservative government would tighten immigration controls by removing Commonwealth citizens' right of entry as British passport holders and reducing their status to that of aliens. This announcement looked like a tougher line. Heath viewed it as a balanced approach to an intractable problem. However, the policy was not as tough as it sounded. Nowhere was there a promise to reduce the level of immigration, let alone the actual number of immigrants, or to impose a colour bar. Powell probably recognised this. However, Heath's move presented Powell with a choice: accept this as a step in the right direction, or remain outside the official party line and show his true feelings over black immigration. Heath probably suspected that Powell's real views on immigration were even extremer than his public pronouncements. Powell's support for Ulster's Loyalists and opposition to Britain's entry to the Common Market already mirrored the views of the National Front. Would he really identify himself further with an extreme-right party associated with neo-Nazism by advocating the same immigration policy? This was one option for Powell. The other was to hope that Heath lost the next election and, having proved his loyalty, challenge for the leadership. Powell decided to remain within the Conservative Party. That did not mean that he ceased to criticise the leadership. At the party conference in 1968, he argued that whatever steps any government took to limit immigration, the cost to Britain would still be unacceptable. The following month, Powell stated that a West Indian or an Indian did not become an Englishman simply by being born in England. This language was reminiscent of that of Hilton and True Tory.

In early January 1969, Heath responded to Powell by calling for legislation to stop further immigration. The Conservatives' opponents accused Heath of being, 'in effect Powell's Shadow Immigration Minister … The policy is basically the same. The aim is the same. Only the political accent is different.'[108] The details suggested that this accusation was not quite accurate. The Opposition demanded an end to the right of immigrants' dependants to settle in Britain, and annually renewable work permits that specified an immigrant's job and its duration. This was little more than administrative obfuscation on Heath's part. No limits were set, no means of enforcement suggested. In contrast, evidence exists suggesting that Central Office tried to marginalise Powell. A confidential Central Office letter to Douglas Hurd, Head of Heath's Private Office, written on the same day that Heath announced his apparently tougher stance, revealed what motivated Heath's immigration policy. It described it as one that, 'skillfully kept a balance between the liberal and the restrictionist opinions', and that Heath would presumably want to continue with it 'in any public statement in the West Midlands'. The West Midlands was the heartland of Powell's support, and contained the constituencies of many anti-immigration Conservative MPs. However, when Duncan Sandys quickly introduced a Bill that contained Heath's tougher line, Heath abstained, and only 126 Conservatives supported it. Perhaps Heath sought to avoid a damaging split. Maybe his abstention was a product of parliamentary procedure. Either way, Heath's abstention casts doubts as to how much he wanted to implement tougher immigration controls. Meanwhile, Powell remained a member of the Conservative Party, acting, as Samuel Brittan implied in *The Spectator*, as a safety valve that vented extreme-right views and retained its support.[109] Brittan was correct, but Heath had countered Powell's impact.

The comments from wider Conservatism also showed the workings of the Conservative Party's attitude towards the extreme right. In September 1968, a former Treasurer of the Seychelles advised the Gloucester Trades Council of his fears of 'a new onslaught' of fascism, and warned that, 'the extreme right wing of the Conservative party could be following in the footsteps of Sir Oswald Mosley'.[110] In November, the Liberal candidate in Worthing, where sanctions against Rhodesia were contentious,[111] pointed to tensions within the local Conservative Association and drew similarities between previous support for Mosley and current support for Powell.[112] He identified the Worthing Debating Society as the local Conservatives' front organisation for their rightwards move, and claimed that nearby Surbiton 'had become openly Powellite'. The response from some Conservative-supporting newspapers turned negative. The *Evening Standard* is London's regional newspaper and is from the same stable as the *Daily Mail*. In 1934, the *Daily Mail* had proclaimed 'Hurrah for the Blackshirts!'[113] Now, the *Evening Standard* proclaimed that, 'In Enoch Powell we always supposed we were dealing with a rational man with a background and assumptions common to our own. Now, with a growing sense of horror we realise we are not.'[114] The article used phrases such as 'cowardly' and 'illiterate demagogue', likening what was happening with Powell to Mosley in the 1930s. Conservatism itself was now raising the fear of association with the extreme right. The danger was obvious, and opponents quickly took advantage. Left-wing publications pointed to the similarity between Powell's views and the National Front and British Fascism.[115] However, in December 1968, *The Advertiser and Surrey County Reporter*, a regional newspaper from the Conservative stockbroker belt, succinctly summed up Powell's problem by stating that although many Conservatives agreed with Powell, loyalty to their leader resulted in them accepting policies they disagreed with.[116] The *Industrial Charter* was an earlier example of this. Furthermore, the article continued that although Powell was 'a man who might be prepared, in the last resort, to launch his own political organisation', he would never join the National Front out of despair at the Conservative Party because, as a historian, he understood that a similar motivation on Mosley's part had cost him his political life.

At the end of January 1969, the Conservative Party's fear of the public connecting it with the extreme right received satirical confirmation. *Private Eye* published an article headed 'League of Empire Powellists'. However, the article did more than simply reflect a perceived similarity between Powell's position and that of the League of Empire Loyalists. It also highlighted Conservative councillors' attempts to overturn a ban prohibiting Colin Jordan from using Birmingham Council property,[117] thus associating Conservatives with an individual who from 1968 had flaunted his Nazism in the British Movement. The article also referred to the emergence of other extreme-right anti-immigration groups. It identified a Peter Crozier as leading Action 69 and the United National Party, and Victor Norris as heading the 5000 Group. *Private Eye* tacitly associated the Conservative Party with the wilder shores of the extreme right by also mentioning Crozier's criminal record, Norris's prominence in the Anglo-Rhodesian Society, and their respective groups' use of violence and infiltration. Even more interesting is what the article said about how these groups viewed Powell. *Private Eye* claimed that they and other extreme-right groups held Powell 'in deep contempt' for remaining a Conservative Party member. *Private Eye* was a publication that usually saved its criticism for the political establishment and vested interests. Its article was a striking one revealing the Conservative Party's repulsion of extreme-right individuals, as well as Powell's unwitting role as its star attractant of them.

While Powell limited the National Front's chances, the Conservative Party bureaucracy continued to work against the Monday Club. In August 1968, Central Office South-Eastern Area Agent A. N. Banks forwarded a report on a meeting of the Monday Club's Surrey branch. Banks identified platform speakers, audience size, and its attitude towards the Conservative Party leadership. At the same time, Central Office North West Area Agent A. S. Garner watched the Monday Club's attempts to form a Liverpool branch. He reported the Monday Club's approach to a party contributor for funds, and asked Central Office to assist him in 'preventing their supporters collecting money in the Constituencies'. Mr Webster's response from Central Office showed exasperation at this inability to control the party's own extremists: 'I am afraid that we neither subsidise nor "control" the Monday Club in any way,' adding that, 'we cannot bring any pressure to bear on them with regard to their collecting funds'. Webster also revealed that Central Office monitoring of the Monday Club went further than just Liverpool by stating his awareness that 'they have been trying to raise [money] for some time'. Webster's request that Garner give him the 'name of the Monday Club collector in this case, just in case we have any contact with him in any other direction', suggests that he was prepared to find another means of limiting the Monday Club's efforts. Garner responded that the individual concerned was a 'hot-head' unsusceptible to Central Office pressure, and that therefore 'I think we will have to let the matter drop'. Webster's response is unknown, but Garner clearly knew that Central Office could exert pressure via other channels.

In September 1968, Paul Bristol resigned from the Monday Club. He was one of its founders. *The Times* explained that he had resigned 'because he believes it to be taking an "extreme attitude" on race relations'.[118] The catalyst for Bristol's resignation was a forthcoming Monday Club pamphlet on immigration, which, *The Times* explained, 'throws some light on the extent to which the club has attracted right-wing dissidents from Tory policy'. However, *The Times* revealed that Heath's actions had played an important role in Bristol's decision. Bristol, *The Times* reported, 'has declared himself to be in favour of the more moderate view urged 10 days ago by Mr. Heath'. This comment referred to Heath's plan to treat Commonwealth immigrants the same as non-EEC immigrants by removing their right of guaranteed entry as British passport holders,[119] and nothing more draconian. The conclusion reached by *The Times* over Bristol's resignation showed how Heath's position made the Monday Club appear even more right-wing. *The Times* used Bristol's support for Heath's stance as a yardstick, and concluded that, 'the pamphlet, which is now apparently being considered by the club executive for publication, must be considerably further right'. The article showed how a limited move rightwards by the leadership had driven a wedge between the party's extremists, pushing the Monday Club into a more open revelation of its extremism.

Central Office once again took an interest in the Monday Club's provincial activities one month after Bristol's resignation. Its East Midlands Area Agent Miss de Jonge reported that the Monday Club had hired Churchill House, home of Nottingham Conservative Association, for a meeting on 25 October where the guest speaker was to be Paul Biggs-Davison. The use of Churchill House appeared to give the Monday Club official Party backing. De Jonge's report that the individual who accepted the booking acted in good faith as the Monday Club 'was never mentioned', suggests that both she and the Monday Club understood that the use of Churchill House lent the Club party sanction. De Jonge's claim that there was 'a strong movement afoot to stop this meeting by telling the Monday Club that the hall will after all not be available', showed that animosity towards the Monday Club existed among the wider Conservative Party. After the event, another Central Office Agent, P. K. Livingston, confirmed that the Monday Club had used false credentials to book Churchill House. Livingston additionally claimed that one individual had resigned from the Young Conservatives because 'the Party was not enough to the right' and that the Monday Club had appealed for donations without prior approval in his area. One individual's resignation hardly mattered, but the Monday Club's request for donations was serious. Mr Webster at Central Office responded furiously, stating 'This is just the sort of ammunition I need when I receive the next visitation from the Director of the Monday Club.'

Concern about the Nottingham Monday Club continued into 1969. In April, Area Agent Livingston advised Central Office that the Monday Club had acquired offices in Nottingham, stating that 'It would seem that this club is setting up another political organisation in the city'. He added that the Monday Club intended holding a rally the same day that Enoch Powell visited the city, and reported the Chief Constable's incredulity at Nottingham Conservatives' inability to control the Monday Club. The Monday Club was again engaging in street politics that was typical of the extreme right, and the Chief Constable was holding the Conservative Party responsible. Was the Monday Club merely seeking to influence the Conservative Party, or was it forming a new party? Livingston believed that, 'before long, the Nottingham City Conservatives will publicly disown them'. However, he felt this would not stop the Monday Club and therefore asked Webster whether someone could exercise pressure on the two parliamentary candidates who appeared on the Monday Club's letterhead. Webster's response showed just how negatively Central Office viewed the Monday Club: 'It really does look as though they have gone too far this time and perhaps we may be able to solve the problem once and for all.'

Livingston's request for action bore fruit. On 1 May, one of the aforementioned parliamentary candidates, Geoffrey Stewart-Smith, reported the Chief Constable's concerns to a Monday Club official, and warned that if the Club was 'not above reproach', he would reconsider sponsoring the Nottingham branch. However, the Nottingham Monday Club did not accept this meekly. Instead, a Councillor Whitehead, having spoken to Stewart-Smith, sought clarification from the Chief Constable. The Chief Constable denied saying or implying that the Monday Club was involved in street demonstrations or violence, and therefore Whitehead wrote to Livingston with an alternative scenario. Whitehead claimed that there had been 'a number of attempts in recent months to maliciously misrepresent the Monday Club in this area', and that Livingston knew this. Whitehead named 'two individuals in particular' who were responsible for the misrepresentation, and, warning that the Monday Club's 'Executive Council has decided that any such future underhand activity shall be severely stamped upon', he challenged Livingston to tell him where he had received the information about the Chief Constable's views from. A number of interpretations of these events are possible, ranging from confusion to underhand activity on both sides. However, Central Office wanted to counter the Monday Club, while the Monday Club was prepared to name individuals and level accusations regarding Livingston's awareness. The Monday Club obviously suspected deliberate sabotage of its interests. There is no evidence that Central Office denied these accusations, so it is possible that it had engaged in a smear campaign similar to those it had implemented against the LEL and Martell's organisations.

Also in 1969, the Monday Club published G. K. Young's *Who Goes Home?* The pamphlet went to the heart of the issue raised by Powell's 'rivers of blood' speech. In 1968, Young had authored *Finance and World Power: A Political Commentary,* in which he stated, 'No subject has been so wrapped and trapped in esoteric semantic obscurantism as international banking finance.' This sounded like the usual euphemism for Jews that A. K. Chesterton adopted. Now, Young was proposing the repatriation of immigrants in his new pamphlet. Young was the chairman of the Monday Club's 'Action Fund' from 1967–69, and an increasingly prominent member. By 1969, he represented the section within the Club that accepted the logical consequences of Powell's views. In 1969 especially, Central Office monitored the Action Fund's money-raising activities closely, with its Agents forwarding many copies of a letter appealing for donations. These Agents noted that potential donors frequently asked whether this appeal meant that the Monday Club was 'forming another Party within the Party'. Central Office decided to use the Action Fund's activities against the Monday Club. It requested that Agents and Constituency Associations forward any original letters of complaint, which the Party Chairman was going to use 'in one of his regular series of meetings' with Paul Williams.

Another example of how the Conservative Party marginalised its extremists was the resignation on 15 October 1967 of the Monday Club's chairman, Paul Williams, albeit involving a different area of policy. Although Williams vaguely invoked business commitments for his resignation, he also stated a wish to be, 'completely free to criticise any possibility of Britain signing the Treaty of Rome'.[120] In this instance, the Conservative frontbench's desire to enter the European Economic Community deprived the Monday Club leadership of a valuable member as membership of the EEC divided the Monday Club's Executive and membership. The CPC reinforced the Monday Club's division in 1969 by publishing *Right Angle: A Philosophy for Conservatives*, written by pro-European Monday Club and Shadow Cabinet member Geoffrey Rippon. G. K. Young's work never received such an approving party imprimatur. These events also touched upon another way in which the Conservative Party limited the extreme-right's fortunes. The Conservative Party does not claim to be ideologically driven, preferring a pragmatic handling of social change, even if it is initially resistant to such changes. The *Industrial Charter* is one example of this, while organisations such as the One Nation Group, Bow Group, and PEST reflected this approach. Membership of the EEC was an example of social change, just as immigration was. The extreme-right's proscriptive, restraining attitude in these and other areas often clashed with the Conservative Party's pragmatism. Former Conservative MP Humphrey Berkeley reflected this when he rejoined the party in 1969 after Heath had effectively marginalised Powell. Berkeley identified the party's historical role as 'to accept the organic growth of society, and to bind people into one nation by mutual interdependence, while supporting freedom and the protection of minorities'.[121] The CPC's selection of which Monday Club works to publish is the party's pragmatism in action, and Williams's resignation is evidence of its effect.

A more obvious example of Conservative leadership opposition came after the Monday Club launched a 'Powell for Premier' campaign in October 1969. The Monday Club attempted to replace progressive Conservative MPs with Powellites. It had tried securing its candidates' selection for some time, but now its strategy was more organised. In November 1968, ex-Conservative MP turned journalist Julian Critchley, claimed that the Monday Club's recent growth allowed it to exert a disproportionate power, identifying candidate selection as 'the point at which pressure can best be applied'.[122] Critchley implied that the Monday Club's strategy was a response to Central Office's attempt to counter its influence by the 'gesture' of publishing a few of its publications. He added that the Monday Club had formed 'Constituency Liaison Committees' to encourage its members to 'join in the activities of the Conservative Party, and to advise them how to do so'. The Monday Club denied that it was a conspiracy aiming to subvert local Conservative Associations in a letter to the Editor of *The Times*, claiming instead to be an open and loyal group whose radical views Central Office and others heeded. However, when it claimed to present 'no challenge to the Conservative Party but only to the pseudo-intellectuals of the neo-Socialist fringe, who seek to move the Party away from Conservatism', the Monday Club made clear that it was willing to attack any party member that it felt fitted this description. Critchley thought that the Surrey branch of the Monday Club was the most interesting one outside London. He highlighted Surbiton where the sitting Conservative MP, Nigel Fisher, had to contend with a Monday Club 'cell' that considered him left-wing. Therefore, the Club's 'Powell for Premier' campaign of 1969 provided a credible figurehead to a campaign that was already running against Fisher. Critchley also stated that, 'What the Monday Club really cares about is colour', and this became evident when the local Monday Club attempted to remove Fisher in 1969.

Those attempting Fisher's removal demanded that the Conservative Association hold a secret referendum on his 'liberal views', and presented fifty signatures for an extraordinary general meeting if they refused.[123] The Conservative Party hierarchy responded by making their support for Fisher known. Shadow Cabinet members publicly supported Fisher, the 1922 Committee elected him to its National Executive for the first time, and the Party Chairman visited Surbiton. *The Times* covered events at Surbiton with 'A News Team Inquiry'. It described the campaign to remove Fisher as 'Sustained, skilfully directed, and totally unprecedented', stating that it threw 'a startling new light on the activities of certain members of the right-wing Monday Club', among whom many supported Powell.[124] The News Team claimed that Central Office and many Conservative MPs were, 'known to be disturbed by the implications of this attempt ... to oust a sitting M.P.' Such concern was understandable. The Conservative Party's opponents would have interpreted the adoption of a new candidate as a victory for racists. The comments of those attempting to remove Fisher reinforced the leadership's concern. Mr E. W. Chester was a Monday Club member who thought that, 'Integration could never work and the only solution was to offer coloured people the "necessary incentives" to leave.' Mr F. S. Legg was not a Monday Club member, but he supported it and thought he ought to be, stating that Fisher was 'all in favour of filling the country with niggers and browns'. Mrs Viola Roberts openly admitted her racism and thought a 'fifth column' of black immigrants had infiltrated Britain, which she wanted to keep white. Central Office maintained a file on events in Surbiton and especially noted any support for Powell. The leader of the campaign to remove Fisher realised the potential damage of the racist comments, but failed to deny or contradict them. The new Chairman of the Monday Club, George Pole, complained in a letter to the *The Times* that the News Team's article left the impression that the Monday Club and its Surrey branch was 'a group of sinister extremist conspirators', which he stated was 'most misleading'.[125] However, Pole did not condemn the racist views expressed by the Monday Club's supporters, but justified their actions instead, and stated disingenuously that he was surprised that the Monday Club was 'officially frowned on by the Conservative Central Office'.

As the 1970 General Election campaign began, the Monday Club released a statement denying accusations of disloyalty. However, the comments of the independent candidate who stood against Fisher in the election suggested that Central Office did not agree. He complained about pressures to stand down brought to bear upon not only him and Powell, but the Monday Club too.[126] Events in Surbiton had again showed the Conservative Party's willingness to act against the Monday Club.

Electively right

As the 1970 General Election approached, the extreme-right's position was different from any other time after the Second World War. Although small extreme-right parties still existed, many had coalesced into the National Front. Fears over immigration, the Common Market, the economy, and the permissive society, provided the extreme right with a propitious context. The National Front had grown and was increasingly well organised. It appeared capable of benefiting from dissident Conservative votes more than any other post-war extreme-right party had. The Monday Club also possessed more credibility and operated within the political mainstream. The danger that the Monday Club posed to Heath's chances of electoral success surfaced in a bizarre meeting in April 1970. The Market Bosworth Monday Club met and considered calls for the resignation from it of a Sir Wolstan and his wife Lady Dixie. The alleged offence was a briefing Sir Wolstan gave to a Derby news agency stating that, 'the Monday Club was run by a group of extremists' and that one senior figure 'was a henchman of Sir Oswald Mosley'.[127] The first part of the claim went to the heart of the Conservative Party's problem of how to deal with extremists within its ranks. The second part referred to prominent Monday Club member Jonathan Guinness. As Guinness was the son of Oswald Mosley's wife Diana Mitford, this was an easy accusation to make.

However, the problems that this growing and organised extreme right posed to Heath at the 1970 General Election were not as serious as they might seem. The Monday Club leadership made clear to Central Office that it supported 'all official party candidates to the full' and was ready to act against members who did not. Its support was essential to winning votes on the right, and could make Heath Prime Minister no matter how much he disliked the Monday Club. Although the National Front was growing, it was miniscule compared to the Conservative Party, and fielded only ten candidates. Their candidatures were in working-class constituencies, and arguably damaged the Labour Party more. Even if some Conservatives thought they might lose votes to the National Front, none other than Oswald Mosley provided them with reassurance on the eve of the 1970 General Election by claiming that even though the majority of the electorate agreed with his views on immigration, 'they nevertheless voted when it came to the point in the traditional party fashion'.[128]

From 1967 onwards, Heath had moved sufficiently rightwards to make Mosley's prediction more probable. The apparent climacteric of this rightward shift came in the so-called 'Selsdon Declaration' of January 1970. Asked in private if the party was moving to the right, Heath responded 'Just a bit'. This was quite an admission from a leader committed to One Nation Group principles. Heath subsequently complained that Harold Wilson used Selsdon to portray 'us all as right-wing extremists'. Heath had a point. The 'Selsdon Declaration' was a myth brought about by his mishandling of a press conference. Heath rejected Wilson's accusation, but the ability to level it confirmed the perception that the Conservative Party had moved rightwards, and that really was the point. For, although the change arguably went only so far, and certainly did not extend to the kind of policies desired by the National Front, people believed that the Conservative Party had become more right-wing. A desire to limit any damage to the Conservative Party's prospects by Enoch Powell's comments had motivated Heath's actions. Yet, the extreme right helped as much as hindered in that Powell attracted votes away from the likes of the National Front. On Election Day, 18 June 1970, a cartoon in *The Sun* graphically illustrated this by portraying Heath standing on a swing that reached 3%, but trailing Powell on a swing that had reached 4%.[129]

The Sun's message that a Conservative victory resulted from Powell's spectacular intervention of 1968 may have been an exaggeration. Many factors had pointed towards a Conservative victory. Heath's House of Commons performances had improved, while Labour's inability to stem rising industrial unrest, notably the failure of *In Place of Strife* (1969), made it more likely that the electorate would turn to the Conservatives. Labour's economic mismanagement had dissipated the goodwill it enjoyed in 1964. Devaluation had shattered Wilson's reputation, forever associating him with an oft-parodied and widely disbelieved claim that it 'would not affect the pound in the pocket'. The release of unexpectedly poor balance of payments figures in election week reminded the electorate of Labour's poor economic performance. Nonetheless, a 31-seat Conservative majority was a surprising result as virtually all polls had predicted a Labour victory. Powell received the credit for it. He received nearly six thousand letters during and immediately after the election. Diane Spearman, formerly of the Conservative Research Department, assessed them.[130] Only just over 1% of writers objected to Powell's views. Many revealed that they voted Conservative because of Powell's comments, or attributed the swing towards the Conservative Party to him. These letters came from across the country and included many social classes and occupations. From Colchester, one person wrote 'We are voting Tory just for you. Thank you.' From Cardiff: 'We feel you brought the campaign to life for the Conservative Party and set us all on the road to success.' From Dumbarton: 'You have helped the Conservative cause tremendously.' Letters from Conservative Party workers added weight to the centrality of Powell's role. Typical of this was the comment of one such individual in Essex who said that, 'Our Canvassing has proved overwhelming support for what you are saying.' Defeated Labour MPs attributed their loss to 'Powellism'. Perhaps most telling, only one letter disagreed with this interpretation, and that was from a defeated Conservative candidate. The sixteen substantial Central Office files that contain correspondence about Enoch Powell's race relations speeches support the breadth, depth, and opinion, of Spearman's findings. These letters alone did not prove that Powell secured Heath's 1970 victory. However, subsequent research argued confidently that Powell was responsible for attracting over 4 million votes to the Conservative Party.[131]

In summer 1970, a tough-minded individual took the reins of power having defeated a duplicitous leader. From outside the ruling establishment, this individual swept existing structures aside and contended with radicals' demands from within his own group. This was a brilliantly acted if factually flawed portrayal by Richard Harris in *Cromwell* (1970). Would Edward Heath, a lower-middle class grammar school boy, former Chief Whip, and pilot of the unpopular Resale Price Maintenance Bill, be able to deal with the demands of his radicals as effectively?

Notes

1 *Evening News*, 7 July 1960.

2 Philip Larkin, 'Annus Mirabilis', *High Windows*, Faber and Faber, London (1967).

3 G. Elton, *The Unarmed Invasion: A Survey of Afro-Asian Immigration*, Bles, London (1965), 7.

4 C. Booker, *The Neophiliacs: The Revolution in English Life in the Fifties and Sixties*, Pimlico, London (1969), 7.

5 *New Statesman*, 28 February 1964.

6 *The Times*, 10 October 1968.

7 N. Tebbit, *Upwardly Mobile: An Autobiography*, Weidenfeld and Nicolson, London (1988), 94.

8 A. K. Chesterton, *The New Unhappy Lords: An Exposure of Power Politics*, Candour, London (1965).

9 A. K. Chesterton, *Empire or Eclipse: Grim Realities of the Mid-Twentieth Century*, Candour, London (1965), passim.

10 'Freedom Group: M.P.s demand inquiry', *The Times*, 18 June 1965.

11 'Mr. Martell Replies To Challengers', *The Times*, 19 June 1965.

12 'Mr. Martell's Libel Action', *The Times*, 6 October 1965.

13 'Mr. Martell: Petitions Dismissed', *The Times*, 21 January 1966. 'Petitions Against Mr. E. Martell Adjourned', *The Times*, 11 February 1966.

14 'Martell Faces New Crisis', *The Times*, 20 September 1967.

15 'Mr. Martell's Debt Hopes', *The Times*, 6 October 1967.

16 '£179,000 debts of Mr. Martell', *The Times*, 16 March 1966.

17 See pp. 65, 107.

18 'Don Bennett's Election Address', 1967.

19 'Guarantee Error, Mr. Martell Says', *The Times*, 4 May 1968.

20 The following derives from D. Shipper, 'Trouble For The Tories', *Tribune*, 12 August 1966, unless stated.

21 See p. 121.

22 Bean, *Many Shades of Black*, 172.

23 See pp. 79, 92.

24 R. F. Beauclair to Major P. H. B. Wall, MC, MP (nd) 1964. Private papers of Sir Patrick Wall, University of Hull.
25 Wall to Beauclair, 23 November 1964, *ibid.*
26 Beauclair to Wall, 24 November 1964, *ibid.*
27 'Delegates Split On Immigrants', *Daily Telegraph*, 15 October 1965.
28 E. Heath, *The Course of My Life: My Autobiography*, Hodder & Stoughton, London (1998), 455.
29 See p. 129.
30 See p. 127.
31 Bean, *Many Shades of Black*, 173.
32 'The Political Priorities: What Is At Stake For Britain', *The Times*, 18 February 1965.
33 'Positions "East of Suez"', *The Times*, 25 March 1965.
34 'Four Steps', *The Times*, 19 July 1966.
35 *The New Daily* ceased publication in 1966.
36 See pp. 17–18.
37 'Slipping Tories', *West Wales Guardian*, 20 June 1969.
38 See p. 138.
39 D. Shipper, 'The Extreme Right Regroups', *Tribune*, 21 March 1969.
40 Copping, *Story of the Monday Club*, 8.
41 See pp. 117–118.
42 Tim Hardacre, 'The Monday Club', December 1964, 1. Private papers of Sir Patrick Wall, 40/2, November 1963–December 1964.
43 'Immigration Into the U.K.', 8. Private papers of Sir Patrick Wall, 40/3, December 1964–August 1965.
44 D. G. Stewart-Smith (ed.), *The Role of Subversion in Foreign Affairs*, Monday Club Foreign Affairs Study Group, London (1965), 4.
45 Minutes of the Executive Committee Meeting of the Monday Club, 6 April 1965, 1. Private papers of Sir Patrick Wall, 40/3.
46 Minutes of the Council Meeting, 5 July 1965, 'Bias Against the Monday Club', *ibid.*
47 Minutes of the Council Meeting, 14 July 1965, 'Bias Against the Monday Club within the Party Organization', 1, *ibid.*
48 Copping, *Story of the Monday Club*, 11.
49 Minutes of the Council Meeting, 2 August 1965. Private papers of Sir Patrick Wall, 40/3.
50 Minutes of the Council Meeting, 7 September 1965, *ibid.*
51 Minutes of the Council Meeting, 20 September 1965. Private papers of Sir Patrick Wall, 40/4, 1965.
52 See pp. 145–146.
53 'Tories Warn Rhodesia on Independence', *Daily Telegraph*, 6 October 1965.
54 'Dealings With Rhodesia', *Daily Telegraph*, 6 October 1965.
55 See p. 144.
56 'Chance For Rhodesia', *Daily Telegraph*, 6 October 1965.
57 'Resolution', 22 November 1965. Private papers of Sir Patrick Wall, 40/4.
58 See pp. 137–138.
59 'Tories Bar Motion By Salisbury', *Daily Telegraph* 13 October 1965.
60 'Salisbury Fails To Sway Tories', *Daily Telegraph*, 16 October 1965.
61 Minutes of the Council Meeting, 1 November 1965, 1. Private papers of Sir Patrick Wall, 40/4.
62 'Backbenchers Toe Tory "Shadow" Line', *Daily Telegraph*, 13 November 1965, 28.
63 'Colin Jordan in Commons Scene', *Daily Telegraph*, 16 November 1965.
64 'Sanctions Bill is Passed at 2 a.m. Lone Rebel M.P.: Lords Battle Collapses', *Daily*

Telegraph, 16 November 1965.

65 Minutes of the Meeting of the Monday Club Rhodesia Emergency Committee, 17 November 1965. Private papers of Sir Patrick Wall, 40/4.

66 'Peterborough', 'Coherent Force', *Daily Telegraph*, 22 November 1965.

67 'Peterborough', 'Gowns and Swords', *Daily Telegraph*, 22 November 1965.

68 'Tory Cheers For Ian Smith', *Daily Telegraph*, 23 November 1965.

69 'Resolution', 22 November 1965. Private papers of Sir Patrick Wall, 40/4.

70 'Tory Cheers For Ian Smith', *Daily Telegraph*, 23 November 1965.

71 'Peterborough', 'Monday Club Speak Out', *Daily Telegraph*, 23 November 1965.

72 'Press Statement', 22 November 1965. Private papers of Sir Patrick Wall, 40/4.

73 Sir Patrick Wall, MC, VRD, MP to the Rt. Hon. Edward Heath, MBE, MP, 24 November 1965, *ibid.*

74 Sir Patrick Wall, MC, VRD, MP to the Rt. Hon. Selwyn Lloyd, MP, 24 November 1965, *ibid.*

75 Copy Speech, 22 November 1965, *ibid.*

76 'Tory Row Over Zambia Troops', *Daily Telegraph*, 30 November 1965.

77 See pp. 118–119.

78 *Monday Club Newsletter*, 59 (December 1969).

79 Sir Alec Douglas-Home, 'The Need for a Fresh Start over Rhodesia', *Sunday Express*, 19 December 1965.

80 'Some Nerve!' *Sunday Express*, 20 November 1966.

81 Statement Issued by Mr. Paul Williams, Chairman of the Monday Club, on Behalf of the Monday Club on 14th January 1966 at 11.00 a.m. Private papers of Sir Patrick Wall, 40/5, February 1965–December 1966.

82 See p. 154.

83 Robert Kee, 'Monday Club', *The Times*, 9 February 1966.

84 Memorandum on Membership and 'Vetting' Problems for Discussion by Monday Club Executive Council, nd. Private papers of Sir Patrick Wall, 40/5.

85 Minutes of the Executive Council Meeting, 4 April 1966, 1–2. Private papers of Sir Patrick Wall, 40/5.

86 Z. Layton-Henry, 'The Young Conservatives 1945–70', *Journal of Contemporary History*, 8: 2 (1973), 143–156.

87 See p. 7.

88 Sir Adrian FitzGerald, author interview, 20 May 2008.

89 A. Roberts, *Eminent Churchillians*, Phoenix, London (1994), 288.

90 See p. 3.

91 See p. 3.

92 D. Stone, 'The Far Right Movement and the Back-to-the-Land Movement', in Julie V. Gottlieb and Thomas P. Linehan (eds), *The Culture of Fascism: Visions of the Far Right in Britain*, I. B. Tauris, London (2004), 182–198.

93 *Illustrated London News*, 27 March 1963.

94 'Squalid Exercise, in Trafalgar Square, *The Times*, 24 January 1964.

95 'Monday Club Appeal', *The Times*, 8 June 1966.

96 'PEST Attack "Feeble" Opposition', *Daily Telegraph*, 26 April 1965.

97 See pp. 71–72.

98 See p. 160.

99 'Message from Paul Williams, Chairman of the Monday Club', *The Monday World*, Winter 1967/68, 3.

100 See p. 93.

101 'We Won't resign – National Front Councillors', *Balham and Tooting News and Mercury*, 28 November 1969.

102 '50 Stop Work To Back Powell', *The Times*, 23 April.

103 'Dockers march for Powell', *The Times*, 24 April 1968.

104 'The Jordanites and Mosleyites are Rejoicing', *The Times*, 24 April 1968.

105 *Combat*, Spring 1968. Oswald Mosley Papers: Diana Mosley Deposit. University of Birmingham Information Services, Special Collections. XOMD/8/6.

106 Bean, *Many Shades of Black*, 209.

107 Author correspondence with Jonathan Guinness, 28 June 2008.

108 'Heath is Treading Powell's Path – MP', *Morning Star*, 10 February 1969.

109 Samuel Brittan, 'The Book of Enoch', *The Spectator*, 25 April 1969.

110 'City Group Warned on Dangers of the Tory Right Wing', *The Citizen*, 27 September 1968.

111 See pp. 155–156.

112 'Get Rid of This Middle Class Mafia: Liberals warned of a "Powellism centre"', *Worthing Gazette*, 12 November 1968.

113 *Daily Mail*, 15 January 1934.

114 'Enoch Powell', *Evening Standard*, 18 November 1968.

115 'Workers Must Unite Against Powellism', *Socialist Leader*, 23 November 1968. 'How Powell Lines up with the British Fascists', *Tribune*, 22 November 1968.

116 'On Choosing One's Friends', *The Advertiser and Surrey County Reporter*, 13 December 1968.

117 'League of Empire Powellists', *Private Eye*, 31 January 1969, 14.

118 'Monday Club founder quits on race policy', *The Times*, 30 September 1968.

119 See p. 168.

120 'Williams Quits As Monday Club Chairman', *The Daily Telegraph*, 15 October 1969.

121 Humphrey Berkeley, 'Why I Left and why I Rejoined the Tory Party', *Catholic Herald*, 9 September 1969.

122 Julian Critchley, 'The Monday Club's Idea of 'True Conservatism'', *The Times*, 23 November 1968.

123 'Secret Vote Demanded on Tory MP', *The Times*, 25 October 1969.

124 'Right-wing Move to Oust Tory', A News Team Inquiry, *The Times,* 25 October 1969.

125 'Move to Oust Tory: Position of the Monday Club', *The Times*, 28 October 1969.

126 'Candidate Officially Adopted: Independent's First Broadside', *Kingston Borough News*, 29 May 1970.

127 '"Resign" Call to Sir Wolstan after Row', *Leicester Mercury*, 21 April 1970.

128 Sam White, 'Surprise! What Mosley Thinks about Powell', *Evening Standard*, 18 June 1970.

129 *The Sun*, 18 June 1970.

130 D. Spearman, 'Enoch Powell's Election Letters', in J. Wood (ed.), *Powell and the 1970 Election*, Paperfront, Kingswood (1970), 19–49.

131 S. Heffer, *Like the Roman: The Life of Enoch Powell*, Weidenfeld and Nicolson, London (1998), 568.

5

'Heathco' meets the extreme-right's challenge, 1970–75

While historians often portrayed the 1940s and 1950s in Britain as decades of radical rebuilding, growth, and prosperity, and the 1960s as a cultural golden age, the 1970s have attracted a less flattering description. Christopher Booker judged that the 1970s were a 'sober, gloomy' decade, little more than 'a prolonged anti-climax to the manic excitements of the Sixties'.[1] Shrapnel stated that crises became a daily condition of life, and described the 1970s as a decade of increasing introversion when Britain developed a new insularity and withdrew into itself.[2] Whitehead accepted Shrapnel's judgement, concluding that, 'The Seventies will be remembered for their reactive pessimism as well as their sharper conflicts.'[3] This negative view of the 1970s has persisted. In 1998, Wheen argued that, 'If the Sixties were a wild weekend and the Eighties were a hectic day at the office, the Seventies were one long Sunday evening, heavy with gloom and torpor.'[4] In 2003, Weight described the Seventies as 'the most dreadful of the post-war era', in which a litany of racial conflict in England, nationalist discontent in Scotland and Wales, war in Ireland and perpetual strikes everywhere, led many to believe 'that their country was sliding into anarchy and even revolution'.[5] In 2008, Marquand stated that Heath became Prime Minister when the post-war golden age had begun 'petering out', capitalism had entered a 'turbulent new phase', and just after 'autumn had set in'.[6]

These descriptions have weaknesses. Ascribing a characteristic to a decade is arbitrary, and positive continuities existed. The 1970s were a decade containing social, political, economic, and cultural strengths and weaknesses in an overall post-war era of steadily improving conditions for many of its inhabitants. People who grew up in the decade do not necessarily recognise the picture of negativity either. Many fondly remember the popular culture that anaesthetised the gloom. The continued success of television programmes from the 1970s such as *Fawlty Towers*, *Dad's Army* and *The Two Ronnies* is evidence of this nostalgia, as is the popularity of the more recent *Life on Mars*, in which a twenty-first century policeman awakes in 1973 and experiences the type of policing made famous by the 1970s series *The Sweeney*. Nostalgia for the 1970s has even found expression in a proliferation of websites on the internet that hark back to the decade as a cultural golden age. Therefore, historians have re-appraised the 1970s. In 2004, the New Economics Foundation saw the mid-1970s as the time when Britain was at its happiest.[7] Sounes highlighted the quality and quantity of popular music, more socially liberal attitudes, radical humour, groundbreaking architecture, popular literature, and blockbuster films, as evidence that showed that the 1970s were a 'Brilliant Decade'.[8] Turner argued similarly that rather than being the decade 'that could scarcely be mentioned without condemnation, conjuring up images of social breakdown, power cuts, the three-day week, rampant bureaucracy and all powerful trade unions', the 1970s were 'a golden age of TV, popular fiction, low-tech toys and club football'.[9]

Yet, cultural manifestations cannot hide the serious problems of the 1970s. Glam Rock, Space-Hoppers, and *Monty Python's Flying Circus* were simply Elastoplast amnesia for Britain's most troubled post-war decade. Indeed, of all decades since the Second World War, the 1970s were the most propitious for political extremism. The 'golden age' of Britain's post-war economy ended. Inflation soared from an average of 4% from 1945–70 to a peak of 27% in mid-decade. A balance of payments surplus of over £400m in 1970 became a deficit exceeding £1500m by the end of 1974. When unemployment reached the totemic figure of one million in January 1972, anger in the House of Commons led to the suspension of Prime Minister's Question Time. Heath was unlucky in that he was Prime Minister at the time of the 1973 oil crisis, but there was a feeling that his government presided over an unfair economy in which unscrupulous capitalists enriched themselves while the hard-pressed masses paid the price for the Government's mistakes. In 1973, Pink Floyd parodied capitalism's acquisitiveness and effects of consumerism in the track 'Money' on their multi-award winning album *Dark Side of the Moon*. Heath seemed to agree, memorably denouncing the Lonrho Company, which was mired in a tax evasion scandal that benefited its chairman, as 'the unpleasant and unacceptable face of capitalism'. As Heath later admitted, the Lonrho affair was a considerable provocation at a time when the Government was urging workers to moderate wage demands for the sake of the country. Intriguingly, the chairman concerned was Monday Club member Duncan Sandys.

Opportunities for the exploitation of nationalist fears also increased in the 1970s. This possibility revolved around two issues: Britain's world role, and the state of the union of the United Kingdom. Rapid decolonisation had ended the British Empire. The imposition of decimal currency on 15 February 1971 ending Britain's peculiar millennium-old imperial weights and measures system monetarily symbolised the end of Empire. Meanwhile, the Commonwealth had evolved into a multi-racial entity of little political coherence in which Britain was little more than titular head. Britain's only viable avenue for continuing to play a role of world importance appeared to be membership of the European

Economic Community (EEC), an assessment that both Conservative and Labour frontbenches agreed with. The White Paper of July 1971 that supported Britain's entry into the EEC stated that there would be no diminution of essential national sovereignty, but admitted that Britain would lose some sovereignty. On 1 January 1973, Britain joined the EEC. Therefore, for those whose nationalism included imperialism, independent traditional currency, and national institutions, the political establishment had colluded and submerged Britain in internationalism. Worse still, the integrity of the United Kingdom itself appeared threatened. In the 1970 General Election, Plaid Cymru had failed to win a single constituency. However, Plaid Cymru possessed a solid base of support. It secured two and then three seats in the General Elections of February and October 1974 respectively and subsequently proved it was not simply a transient protest party. In Scotland, the Scottish National Party performed even better. It virtually trebled its vote, turning one seat in 1970 to eleven in 1974. Northern Ireland was even more worrying. In 1972, Heath's Government responded to the undeclared civil war between republicans and loyalists by suspending the Stormont Assembly. In July 1973, the Northern Ireland Constitution Act imposed a devolved assembly that forced loyalists to share power with republicans. Ulster's Loyalists viewed the Sunningdale Agreement of 1973 that resulted from this assembly as a sell-out that would lead to a united Ireland. Right-wing extremists on the mainland contacted Ulster's loyalists. Britain appeared endangered by separatist Celtic nationalism. Wilson had realised that this was a potential problem and had appointed a royal commission in 1969 to examine Britain's constitution and the governance of its constituent parts. On 31 October 1973, the Kilbrandon Commission reported. It accepted the need for Welsh and Scottish devolution. Devolution already existed in Northern Ireland. However, England was not to have its own Assembly. The commission suggested the division of England into eight regions. These events inflamed the passions of those whose nationalism entailed the maintenance of the United Kingdom, and those for whom nationalism meant 'England'.

Weak government made the growth of extremism even more likely in the 1970s. This was especially so during the Heath Government. The Conservative Party's 1970 manifesto promised an end to Macmillan's corporatism, thus signalling a softening of the leadership's attitude towards the neo-liberalism of the 'freedom groups' hitherto on the extreme right. When Heath came to power, he also promised a more businesslike approach in which, having carefully arrived at a policy, he and his colleagues would have the courage to stick to it. This manifesto was sufficient for many 'freedom groups' to lessen their activities. However, reality did not match promise as Heath abandoned neo-liberalism when difficulties arose. His government performed major policy U-turns not once, but five times. In industry, the promise to let so-called 'lame duck' industries fail ended when Heath's Government used public money to rescue Rolls Royce and the Upper Clyde Shipbuilders. In October 1970, the Budget removed the apparatus of state intervention in the economy, but in 1972 the creation of an Industrial Development Executive and the Industry Bill reintroduced state interventionism. Heath's Government passed legislation to solve industrial unrest, then undermined and eventually abandoned it when vigorously opposed by trade unions. The Government introduced a compulsory prices and incomes policy in an attempt to combat spiralling inflation, despite promises to the contrary. Finally, it ended the promise to reduce government spending when it massively increased public expenditure from late 1972. These U-turns resulted in the 'freedom right' returning to prominence.

Private Eye parodied Heath as the managing director of 'Heathco', an incompetent individual who was incapable of dealing with a useless company's problems. Heath was once the tough man of the Conservative Party, but as Prime Minister he seemed incapable of firm leadership, too easily forced to reverse policy when challenged. A growing genre of novels depicting the rise of a right-wing strong man emerged, which was an implicit response to Heath's weak leadership. They were also a reaction to a belief that Heath presided over an increasingly decadent society. On 17 November 1970, *The Sun*'s page 3 girl appeared topless for the first time. Increased incidence of abortion and divorce, and the widened gap between rich and poor, and young and old, juxtaposed in a society that remained largely conservative outside London. Britain in the 1970s presented an image of a society that had polarised morally and culturally as much as politically. At the cinema, *Get Carter* (1971) appeared to depict a world that was passing wherein there was an absolute demarcation between villain and citizen. Other films provided evidence of decadence for those who chose to interpret them thus. The release viewing of *Performance* (1971) shocked the wife of one film executive so much that she vomited. In the same year, *Straw Dogs* (1971) depicted rape in a violent British countryside, attracting from one film critic the description of 'a fascist work of art'. So intense was the reaction to *A Clockwork Orange* (1971), in which drug-taking youths engaged in rape and nihilistic destruction, that its producer withdrew it from viewing in 1974. These trends, and their cultural manifestations, continued throughout the decade, eventually finding a cathartic apogee in punk music. Whichever way you looked at it the 1970s were a decade that shocked the moralists.

Heath's Government seemed incapable of enacting any remedy for society's ills, or unwilling. Indeed, the passage of the Misuse of Drugs Act (1971), which separated the classification of cannabis from harder drugs like heroin, suggested that Heath's Government did not intend to roll back the permissive society at all. Mary Whitehouse, the once ridiculed former member of Moral Re-Armament and force behind the 'Clean-Up TV' campaign in the 1960s, became an influential figure. In 1971, she led the National Festival of Light that harked back to a supposedly less morally dubious time. Indeed 'harking back' to a mythical previous golden age was a feature of the 1970s. It is also a characteristic of fascist groups. Therefore, the 1970s clearly was a decade in which conditions for extremism existed, not least during Heath's Government. Two of the main battlegrounds for this extremism, industrial unrest and immigration, are particularly associated with Heath's Government.

Industrial unrest was the leitmotif of Heath's premiership. The official number of days lost to strikes during the Heath Government was never less than 10 million per year, exceeding any post-war decade. In 1970, the number of days lost were the most since the General Strike of 1926. In 1972, it more than doubled to give a figure ten times worse than when Harold Wilson became Prime Minister. Heath used the Emergency Powers Act (1920) five times to declare a State of Emergency in less than four years. Each declaration responded to a strike. Governments had only used this act twelve times in its eighty-four years on the statute book. However, it was not simply the number and extent of strikes, but their nature that particularly identified Heath's premiership with industrial unrest. During the 1972 miners' strike, television brought the police's inability to stop intimidatory flying pickets into people's homes. At Birmingham's Saltley Coke Depot in February 1972, the miners' legal use of sheer numbers defeated police efforts to block their attempt to close the depot. These events also brought National Union of Mineworkers' (NUM) leaders Arthur Scargill and Mick McGahey to prominence. Both men expressed objectives that went beyond improving their members' working conditions. Scargill thought Saltley proved the working class could bring the whole of Britain to a standstill. Late in 1973, at a meeting in Downing Street that attempted to secure an end to an NUM work-to-rule, McGahey told Heath that he sought the Government's downfall. Industrial relations now contained a clear political objective in which left-wing extremists apparently sought revolutionary ends. Many thought that Britain was perilously close to a pre-revolutionary situation. Monday Club members definitely held this opinion.

Heath's Government inflamed the situation and added to the impression of a pre-revolutionary Britain. In 1971, Heath's Government passed the Industrial Relations Act and implemented a National Industrial Relations Court (NIRC) as a mechanism to rule on industrial disputes. Heath subsequently claimed that the motivation for the Act was to redress the balance of power in industry and reduce the climate of confrontation, and not to weaken the trade unions. This explanation accorded with Heath's 'One Nation' Toryism. However, the minutes of the Selsdon Park Conference before the 1970 General Election showed that the Conservative frontbench did intend to lessen union power. As the Industrial Relations Act contained within it the means by which trade unions could lawfully avoid its provisions, it was seriously flawed. The Government's attempts to enforce it made it appear vindictive, bullying, and, worst of all for any government, impotent. In 1972, the Government capitulated to the miners and awarded them a pay rise three times greater than that initially offered. Later the same year, the Government failed to stand by the consequences of its own legislation and used its own Official Solicitor to overturn the NIRC's imprisonment of five dockers. This action signalled the end of the Industrial Relations Act's effective life.

Heath looked less like Cromwell and more like 'Brave Sir Robin' from *Monty Python and the Holy Grail*, inappropriately armed and unwilling to fight. This image of impotence extended to the rest of the government. When the Cabinet met in candlelight due to a power cut, it juxtaposed starkly with the image of vigorous mineworkers who had secured their objectives at Saltley by force. Popular culture reflected the contemporary situation. In 1971, *Carry On at Your Convenience* continued the parody of unions as seen in *I'm All Right Jack* (1959), and in 1973 The Strawbs criticised union power in *Part of the Union*. However, when Heath decided to take a stand against the miners he discovered that these representations did not reflect public sympathies. Heath responded to the miners' industrial action of late 1973 by imposing a three-day working week from January 1974. This action limited energy usage and imposed heavy penalties for non-compliance. Heath's action affected everybody negatively, but disproportionately hit those least able to cope. Those hurt the most included the elderly and disabled who had moved into the new tower blocks, and now relied on relatives to bring their shopping or hauled it up exhausting flights of stairs themselves. Heath showed no interest in popular culture, but he would have done better to observe the messages it sent before introducing the three-day week. Although Vic Spanner, the trade union official in *Carry On at Your Convenience*, was a comedic figure, he was also prepared to sanction violence. The film took five years to recoup its costs and was the *Carry On* team's first flop, which suggested that the film's target working-class audience disliked its negative portrayal of Spanner. As the February 1974 General Election loomed, the archetypal working-class Conservative voter Alf Garnett also turned his back on the Conservative Government and Prime Minister Heath. Many other working-class Conservatives probably did likewise. All that the three-day week achieved was to reinforce the existing image of governmental impotence. Therefore, when Heath called a General Election one month after imposing the three-day week and asked the electorate, who governed the country – the elected government or the unions?, the electorate responded with a resounding 'not you'.

Alf Garnett is associated in popular memory not with industrial unrest so much as immigration, another prominent issue of the 1970s. Enoch Powell's 1968 'rivers of blood' speech had placed immigration firmly at the centre of British politics, bedevilling Heath's leadership and Government. Before the 1970 General Election, Heath promised to assist those immigrants who wished to return to their country of origin, but he also added that, 'we are going to do everything to prevent a climate being created which will make them wish to leave against their own free will'.[10] Heath had made this stance explicit in the Conservatives' General Election manifesto, which also included the promise of no further large-scale immigration.[11] It was a position that contained obvious fault-lines. In 1972, two events tested these manifesto promises severely. In January, Bangladesh secured independence, which resulted in Pakistan seceding from the Commonwealth in protest. There were two consequences of these developments. Pakistani citizens who were resident in Britain were no longer British subjects. Bangladeshis who were resident in Britain became another ethnic minority for the extreme right to attack. Enoch Powell spotted the consequences and exploited them by pointing out that Pakistanis were now aliens and therefore lost the right to vote and bring their dependents to Britain, and called for the repatriation of both Pakistanis and Bangladeshis. Powell had created exactly the kind of negative climate that Heath and the party leadership wished to avoid. Idi Amin's decision to expel all Asians from Uganda in August caused even greater problems for Heath. The existence of approximately 57,000 stateless Ugandan Asians with British passports challenged Heath's promise that there would be no further large-scale immigration.

However, immigration posed greater problems for the Conservative Party than merely questioning the credibility of its election promises. Powell potentially provided the extreme right with charismatic leadership. His frequent comments on immigration, as well as other issues that troubled the Conservative Government, regularly reminded electors and elected that an alternative to Heath was available. Letters from people of all political persuasions supporting Powell continued to pour into Central Office, proving that the initial favourable response to him in 1968 was not a passing phenomenon. Opinion polls confirmed that many people supported Powell's views. The Government could not ignore this, but it had to be careful how it responded because Heath faced more than just a charismatic extreme-right individual. For a number of reasons, the extreme right was far more dangerous than at any time since 1945. Outside the Conservative Party, the extreme right experienced its longest period of unity in the shape of the National Front. From its creation in 1967, the National Front gained a reputation for street politics and violence against non-white immigrants. It dominated news coverage of extreme-right politics during Heath's premiership, and provided a potential repository for extreme-right voters. The National Front used events such as the Ugandan Asian crisis as an excuse for its activities, which increased its membership and gave it an electoral boost. In 1973, the National Front saved its first deposit when Martin Webster secured 16% of the vote at the West Bromwich by-election. Harold Wilson claimed there was a danger that Britain would 'lurch into fascism'. British Fascism seemed to be having more success during Heath's premiership than in the 1930s, only this time with blacks, not Jews as the scapegoats. Fears of a resurgent fascism were understandable, but its opponents were not prepared to allow the National Front to grow without a fight. Popular culture rejected the National Front. Youths took action against the National Front through 'Rock against Racism' concerts, counter-marches, and the Anti-Nazi League. From Powell's Wolverhampton constituency, Ambrose Slade adopted the 'skinhead' image of the late 1960s, but changed it when they realised its association with extreme-right violence, and subsequently became famous as simply Slade. In 1973, Pink Floyd lampooned the divisiveness at the heart of racism in the single from *Dark Side of the Moon*, 'Us and Them'. Therefore, if the Conservative leadership failed to act against the National Front it risked alienating a sizable section of the electorate.

Unfortunately for the Conservative leadership, the party's own extreme right contained supporters of the National Front's views. Connections between the Monday Club and National Front were public knowledge. This presented troubling possibilities. The number of dissident Conservatives who joined the National Front might increase. The Monday Club might exploit the immigration issue to capture control of the Conservative Party. Most dangerously, the National Front and Monday Club could amalgamate and present a far greater challenge to the Conservative Party. Immigration was the issue around which such possibilities revolved. However, the Conservative leadership could not easily dismiss the Monday Club because it was an integral part of the Conservative Party, and its growth suggested that it enjoyed significant support among party members. Yet the Conservative leadership was unable and unwilling to ignore the threat posed by the Monday Club and its association with the National Front. This threat revolved around attitudes towards race. The post-1945 Conservative leadership viewed any racist organisation as disreputable, identifying racism as a hallmark of fascism and Nazism. Its attitude was a long-standing consequence of the Second World War. The National Front was openly racist. The Monday Club tested the Conservative leadership's commitment to this post-1945 attitude severely by focusing on immigration and associating with the National Front. Yet, the Conservative leadership and Central Office adhered to their position, even though action against the Monday Club risked harming the party. The leadership once more reached rightwards and introduced a new Immigration Bill, while Central Office confronted the Monday Club and pressurised its leadership into removing the National Front from the Club's ranks.

Extreme-right reaction

The problems of the Heath Government provided veterans of the extreme right with an opportunity to grab the limelight from the beginning. Strikes seemed extensive and widespread soon after Heath became Prime Minister. They affected many and diverse concerns, such as beer production, rugby league, and even the *Daily Mail*. People considered the possibility that a General Strike was imminent three months after the General Election. Heath declared his readiness to meet such a challenge, and defended his government's non-intervention in industrial disputes. Council workers struck on 29 September, increasing public safety fears as raw sewage entered rivers and waste piled up. Arbitration resulted in an inflationary pay settlement. Heath criticised the settlement during a *Panorama* interview, but his later argument that this award led the Government to redouble efforts with employers that the Government could influence did not alter the view of some that he had not provided strong leadership. Newly elected MP Norman Tebbit acknowledged Heath's criticism of the settlement, but also noticed that he remained aloof from industrial disputes. In winter 1970, electricians began industrial action, which resulted in the first power cuts of Heath's premiership. Homes and businesses used candlelight, even the House of Commons. The extent and nature of strikes led some to believe that the extreme left was behind them. The unions' response to the impending Industrial Relations Bill added fuel to this belief. In November, British Leyland warned its workers of the dangers of a politically motivated action after they walked out in protest over the Bill. Heath announced at Prime Minister's Question Time that he would not tolerate any political strike. By 27 November, Britain had experienced its worst year for strikes since the General Strike of 1926.

When Heath appeared to promise a more free-market approach that included limiting trade union power at the Selsdon Park Conference, he altered the nature of 'freedom' groups. However, these groups misunderstood the reality of the 'Selsdon Declaration'. Heath later rejected any idea that Selsdon marked his conversion to new liberal economics, and ridiculed those who thought otherwise, but it probably encouraged the right wing's exaggerated view of its influence over the Conservative Party. Whatever the reality, Selsdon brought economic liberalism back into the political mainstream. Therefore, when Heath failed to deliver this 'programme', he forced these groups to return to operating in the political space outside the Conservative Party's right. It was during the electricians' dispute, for example, that Edward Martell resurfaced. He teamed up with former Freedom Group members and formed a company called Modern Organisers Ltd,[12] using his non-unionised printing company to publish a *News Special* on 8 December. Concerns about union activity dominated the *News Special*. It claimed that recent events had justified the Freedom Group's earlier warnings that failure to counter the unions would lead to politically motivated strikes, and particularly criticised the Heath Government for refusing to intervene in the electricians' dispute.[13] The *News Special* also argued that the Conservative Party's failure to promise trade union reform had lost it the 1964 General Election, whereas its commitment to it resulted in a return to power in 1970. The *News Special* did not accept that Heath's Government had fulfilled this commitment. Under the sub-heading 'Let's Have The Showdown', the *News Special* stated that, 'For all the bold faces they wear when they talk about the unions Mr. Heath and Mr. Carr are still treating them with velvet gloves. They gave way to the dockers. They gave way to the dustmen. It will be a grave mistake if they give way to the electricians.' Martell harboured concerns about the Government's approach, similar to Tebbit. However, unlike Tebbit, Martell had a drastic remedy. He called for the use of troops if necessary, implying that the Government was too cowardly to deal with strikers.

Martell's comments should have found a receptive audience. His 'extremism' had not usually amounted to more than advocating economic liberalism at a time when the Conservative Party pursued corporatist policies, apart from supporting Donald 'Pathfinder' Bennett at the Nuneaton by-election of 1967.[14] Heath had recently appeared to adopt economic liberalism and trade union reform. Industrial unrest continued. These factors should have increased Martell's credibility, and boosted him politically. Yet this was not the case. Instead, the *News Special* was merely a death spasm of Martell's political career. Martell's financial difficulties as the Freedom Group collapsed were the substantial reason,[15] but there were other explanations. The *News Special* was only four pages long, which compared unfavourably to *The New Daily*. This did not give an image of dynamic resurgence, or make Martell look capable of leading an offensive against the unions. Martell had also timed his attack badly. He may have been right to suspect the Government's resolve, but others who later shared Martell's view were not yet of the same opinion. New Conservative MPs like Tebbit at this stage simply wanted their government to adhere to what they thought the Selsdon programme was. Selsdon may have reduced the 'freedom groups' 'extremism', but only after the U-turns of 1972 proved that Heath was unable to deliver did these groups have the space to operate in outside the Conservative Party's right. These included the Selsdon Group (1973), a new Middle Class Alliance (1974), and the National Association for Freedom (1975). Heath's Government had been in power for less than four months when the *News Special* appeared, and could hardly have moved more swiftly against the unions. Martell had voluntarily placed himself outside the political mainstream by acting precipitately. People were hardly likely to act on Martell's demands when the Government had only four days previously published the Industrial Relations Bill with the aim of reducing industrial unrest. Martell's demands were risible, adding poor timing to his reputation as a financially discredited individual.

Meanwhile, concerns over immigration provided oxygen for those extreme-right individuals and groups who had not joined the National Front. In August 1970, the remnants of the Racial Preservation Society (RPS) produced a bulletin that revealed deep suspicions about the new Conservative Government. It levelled the extreme-right's usual accusation against a Conservative Government by stating 'The colour has changed from pale red to surreptitious pink … The song's the same; only the tempo is different.'[16] The bulletin claimed that the left dominated the Conservative Government, arguing that, 'For every new man of the Right elected there were at least three of the Tory left.' It also made personal attacks that combined anger over immigration with decadence, singling out 'the great pink creampuff Reggie Maudling'. The RPS levelled two charges at Maudling. He had failed to condemn his daughter for having children out of wedlock, thus indicating that he supported the permissive society, and he had allowed nearly one hundred Kenyan Asians to enter Britain on becoming Home Secretary, which showed his complicity in the hoodwinking of the vast majority of Conservative supporters. The bulletin blamed Heath for this state of affairs. It described his commitment to 'One Nation' principles as, 'quite simply, just a variation on the "melting pot" theme beloved of international collectivists of whom Heath is undoubtedly one'. The bulletin ended with a plea for Enoch Powell to provide the remedy: 'So speak up Enoch! Put country before party and earn the eternal gratitude of all honest patriots.'

However, the RPS's position was weak. It criticised the Government's tougher stance on immigration as unenforceable and demanded repatriation, but its attack was also premature as Heath's Government had been in power for barely two months. The RPS made their criticisms before U-turns and various crises had damaged Heath's reputation. As for Powell, what, exactly, did the Racial Preservation Society expect him to do? Attached to the bulletin was a 'Campaign for Democratic Conservatism' sticker that demanded 'Powell for Premier'. However, Powell had never revealed any desire to leave the Conservative Party and lead an extreme-right party like the National Front. Even Powell's political opponents knew this. Denis Barker in the *Guardian* considered whether Powell's popularity would lead him to front a new party. He decided that, 'As Mr Powell has never indicated nor even remotely implied that he would act other than through the normal machinery of the Conservative Party, such enthusiasm is not likely to provide the non-Conservative Right with a leader big enough and generally acceptable enough to bring unity.'[17] As there was no prospect in 1970 of the National Front forming a government, the only way that Powell could become premier was as leader of the Conservative Party. However, Conservative MPs elected the party leader, not extreme-right voters. Thus, if the RPS's claim that left-wing MPs dominated the Conservative parliamentary party is accurate, then the 'Powell for Premier' campaign was futile because of the Conservative Party's constitutional arrangements. The RPS subsequently declined and eventually merged into its Chairman's own organisation, the National Democratic Party, but neither successfully operated in the political space occupied by the Conservative Party and National Front.

However, extreme-right groups continued to proliferate despite limited political space. The situation in Worthing, where there had been tensions within the local Conservative Association over Rhodesian sanctions,[18] was of particular note. Nine far-right groups in Worthing formed a 'Patriotic Front' that included the National Front, Racial Preservation Society, Anglo-Rhodesian Society, and the Campaign for Democratic Conservatism, according to one reporter.[19] Major-General Richard Hilton, who by now was a veteran of the extreme-right's cause, was the President of the Worthing Debating Society, the Worthing Ex-Services Association, True Tory, and prominent in other groups that comprised this 'Patriotic Front'. The Worthing Debating Society shared the extreme-right's traditional concerns over immigration and decadence, viewing them as part of a Communist-led plan to bring Britain to the verge of a 1917-style revolution. Such views were common among ultra-Conservatives. However, when the Worthing Debating Society disseminated scurrilous poems depicting immigrants eating 'Good "PAL" to fill my tummy',[20] it expressed sentiments that were more in tune with Mosley's claims that immigrants consumed Kit-E-Kat. Fear of Communism led the Worthing Debating Society to become involved, from July 1972, in the outlandish attempts of Sir Walter Walker, the former Commander-in-Chief of NATO's forces in Northern Europe, to forge an organisation to resist the expected Communist invasion. The Worthing Debating Society, and the Patriotic Front, reflected an increased polarisation which some thought only a coup d'état could remedy.

Proliferation of extreme right-wing movements was evidence of the peculiarly propitious circumstances during the 1970s in general and Heath's Government in particular. However, Conservative Central Office's files do not to reflect any such proliferation. Indeed, Central Office activity provides an opposite image.

Whereas Central Office maintained files on an average of twenty-two outside organisations per year between 1941 and 1965, thereafter the figure drops to four. Of the fifty-five groups investigated after 1965, only four can be termed extreme-right, and one of these was Martell's defunct Freedom Group. In part, this reflected the extreme right's coalescence into the National Front in 1967, which made many groups appear even more miniscule. Yet, size had not previously stopped Central Office from investigating small extreme-right groups such as The Right Party, Clan Briton, or the Elizabethan Party. Most extreme-right groups prior to 1967 were, in fact, small. Nor does investigation of two of the remaining three files on extreme-right groups after 1965 show any concern within Central Office. The file on the Racial Preservation Society merely contains its bulletins, and no Central Office comment. The file on the National Front is similarly sparse. In 1971, a Central Office employee revealed his lack of concern by claiming that despite efforts to give an appearance of modernisation and respectability, 'In the event, of course, the National Front has degenerated into a fairly wild but right-wing organisation.' Abhorrence at the National Front's tactics, views, class base, and a belief it could never gain political power, probably fuelled the employee's disdain. Others who shared the Central Office employee's disdain for the National Front included high-ranking members of the Monday Club, even though many thought it shared the Front's objectives. Jonathan Guinness, Monday Club chairman 1972–74, described the National Front leadership as, 'very mediocre'.[21] Sir Adrian FitzGerald was even more dismissive. He recollected the National Front's neo-Nazi antecedents and the quality of people it attracted, and stated that the National Front had no chance of political representation and thus he always found it 'very hard to take seriously'.[22] More practically, the National Front's leadership was weak. Chesterton resigned in 1971 and retired to South Africa. *The Listener* magazine reported that Enoch Powell refused the chairmanship of the National Front when Chesterton resigned, despite being 'The one politician within the established parties who both fascinated the Front and constantly says the kind of things it wants to hear'.[23] Thereafter, the National Front indulged in a bitter leadership struggle that soon gave control of the party to the neo-Nazis initially barred from membership in 1967, at a time when it needed to consolidate its position by presenting a united image. These considerations explain the image of nonchalance garnered from Central Office's files on the National Front. However, this is deceptive. For, although Central Office was unconcerned with the National Front per se, it was nevertheless alarmed about its possible impact on the Conservative Party. What fed this alarm was the position of the Monday Club and its connections with the National Front.

Inside the inside right

The official history of the Monday Club described the 1970 General Election as 'The Break Through'. The number of Monday Club MPs increased from sixteen to twenty-nine, with six more joining subsequently, and there were thirty-three members in the House of Lords. These figures increased the likelihood that Monday Club members would gain government office, and Prime Minister Heath did appoint six Monday Club members. However, all but one was a junior position and none involved the sensitive issue of race and immigration. Only Geoffrey Rippon secured a high-profile position as Minister of Technology, despite some arguing that he was too right-wing. Rippon's opposition to Powell's position on immigration and his advocacy of Britain's entry into the EEC made him one Monday Club member whose credentials Heath appreciated. In July 1970, Heath made Rippon Chancellor of the Duchy of Lancaster to take charge of the negotiations for Britain's membership of the EEC. The Monday Club also grew outside Westminster. In November 1970, the Monday Club's University Group held its fifth Annual Conference at New College, Oxford, and claimed fifty-five branches by 1971. In March 1971, the Monday Club's provincial branches showed their growth and increased organisational capability by holding the first National Conference of Branches at Nottingham. The Monday Club now appeared to have overtaken the Bow Group in importance. It certainly reflected the views of many Conservatives.

However, the Monday Club was not necessarily in tune with a Central Office that continued to have a close relationship with the Bow Group and PEST. In December 1970, the Bow Group furnished the Party Chairman with details of its financial situation after he advised them that he would be meeting with the Party Treasurer. PEST's archive revealed a similarly positive relationship. Considering that Central Office's role reflected the leader's views, this means that the Monday Club presented Heath with a credible dissident organisation from the beginning of his premiership, one that Central Office had already described as extreme-right wing.[24]

The Monday Club did not precipitately condemn the Government's stance on industrial relations, unlike Martell. The Taunton & District Monday Club sent Heath their 'Congratulations on your firm stand' during the electricians' dispute, and advised him to 'Keep it up' and 'Don't submit to Communist inspired blackmail.' However, when it came to immigration the Monday Club was closer to the Racial Preservation Society, if not in tone, then in substance. Ranged against the Monday Club were those who pressurised the government to adopt a more permissive immigration policy. In July 1970, *The Times* reported the Bow Group's launch of its publication, *The Greatest Claim,* which demanded easier entry into Britain for Asians in Uganda and Kenya.[25] The following month, undisclosed *Times* sources reported that the Government's attitude to this issue had thawed, and individual ministers' private hints that they would not be embarrassed if anyone pressurised the Government to relax its stance on immigration in favour of the African Asians.[26] These comments reflected wider opinion. Attempts to enforce the Immigration Act (1968) received bad publicity. In October, those Asians holding British passports took their case to the European Commission on Human Rights. In Britain, opponents of the Government's official position began an 'Admit the British' national campaign. The Government's changing attitude became more obvious. Press reports suggested that the Government would make African Asians a special case in forthcoming immigration legislation, and that this would not result in all of the 170,000 passport holders coming to Britain. The Monday Club took this news as evidence that the Government did intend to allow up to 170,000 East African Asians into Britain. Its National Executive Council convened and released a press statement in November. The statement was a 'strong warning' that such a policy would raise racial tensions as it was contrary to the wishes of the people, and pointed out that it would also 'be to go back on an election pledge that there would be no further large scale immigration into Britain'.[27]

The Monday Club voted Enoch Powell their Politician of the Year at the end of 1970, for the second year in succession. Its choice indicated their opposition to the Government's stance on immigration, whether intentionally or not. The Monday Club appeared to be increasingly offering a viable alternative to Heath. In January 1971, the Monday Club reinforced differences between it and the party leadership when fifteen members, led by Chairman George Pole, re-established direct contacts with Ian Smith's renegade government during a trip to Rhodesia and South Africa. On 11 February, Enoch Powell attacked the official immigration figures. Four days later, he claimed that by 1985 black immigrants would total 4 million, and proposed massive, voluntary repatriation. On 16 February, the Monday Club issued a statement supporting Powell's warnings about the growing size of the coloured population and the ensuing problems it believed would result, and demanded that the Government accept Powell's argument and remedies. John Pilger noticed the Monday Club's activities. He outlined the Monday Club's growth and power in an article of 15 March billed as, 'Day one of an explosive series', which claimed that from 400 members in 1964, the Monday Club had grown to 2,100 in the national organisation and 6,000 in thirty and fifty-five regional and university branches respectively.[28] Pilger believed that the Monday Club could pressurise the existing leadership severely. He claimed that one-third of Conservative MPs supported the Monday Club, and quoted an anonymous Monday Club official's boast that, 'We are now able to bring pressure to bear in a number of constituencies where a member's ideas conflict with those of true conservatism.' What may have disconcerted the remaining two-thirds of Conservative MPs was the same official's claim that, 'Within ten years we, the party's tail, shall wag the dog.'

We could dismiss these comments as hyperbolic indiscretion happily reported by an opponent of the Conservative Party. However, Heath had not yet performed any policy U-turns, and Pilger's comment that the Monday Club's Director, Frederick Stockwell, had identified the Club with the Government's direction revealed that the Club was willing to work with Heath's Government. Far more worrying for the Conservative Party leadership was the changed composition of the Monday Club, which Pilger also noted. In doing so, Pilger touched on another way in which the Conservative Party used the issue of class in opposing the extreme right. Pilger described how five Chelsea Tories had founded the Monday Club in reaction to Macmillan's decolonisation policy, but argued that subsequent concentration on domestic issues had begun to change the Club's character. He stated that it was no longer heavily influenced by Lord Salisbury, and described how Monday Club members were 'now coming from the suburbs: municipal men who dream of garbage and glory and managerial men who see, at last, a chance of their elevation to a ruling class from which an absence of breeding has long excluded them'. Pilger thought that the Monday Club in 1971 was an 'alliance of upper class romanticism and middle class ambition'. However, the Monday Club was potentially even more dangerous than such an alliance suggested because Club members sympathised with the National Front, despite the views of leading members like Jonathan Guinness and Adrian FitzGerald who dismissed the National Front as politically irrelevant lower-class thugs.[29] Pilger intimated this by quoting Monday Club Chairman George Pole's qualified joke that the National Front were people who had not been given enough red meat that 'must not be turned aside as of no account; they have people who are motivated by the highest ideals'. Pole's comments showed that some members of the Monday Club shared the National Front's views. Pole was also disdainful, and did not seem to believe that the National Front was important. However, the Monday Club's provincial branches had no credible vetting system. This made them ripe for infiltration by the National Front. Pilger highlighted the possible dangers that the Monday Club leaders faced from its branches when he quoted John Ormowe, the twenty-five year old chairman of the Sussex Monday Club: 'The Monday Club you see in London is no more than a parliamentary debating group of rather socially exclusive people. We in the branches are what it's all about.' Ormowe also claimed to be a Hitler-admiring racialist.

A provincial Monday Club also made class-based comments later in 1971. On 27 May, Labour overturned a 10,874 Conservative majority at the Bromsgrove by-election. The Taunton & District Monday Club, once pleased by Heath's stance against the electricians,[30] blamed the Prime Minister. It claimed that Heath had shunned the limelight, left too much to his ministers, and enjoyed 'a rich man's sport in sailing'. The Conservative MP for Wells, Robert Boscawen, wrote to the Taunton & District branch and stated that such comments were 'adding to the reasons why I am at present seriously considering not renewing my subscription and withdrawing my support' from the Monday Club. Boscawen was the son of the eighth Viscount Falmouth and a member of the Cornish aristocracy. Boscawen sent a copy of his letter to Central Office. The correspondence between Boscawen, the Taunton & District Monday Club, and Central Office, indicated that class attitudes shaped views within the wider Conservative Party.

According to old-Etonian Jonathan Guinness, one common insult that National Monday Club members bandied about at this time was to describe someone as a National Front supporter.[31] This was not because of the political views that such an insult implied, but the class connotations. Actual proof of National Front membership would have led to automatic dismissal from the Monday Club. Sir Adrian FitzGerald, Monday Club founder member and old-

Harrovian, confirmed that National Monday Club members were disdainful of the National Front and that membership of it meant expulsion from the Club. When asked whether members he knew treated the National Front with disdain, FitzGerald replied, 'Oh Complete. I mean as soon as we knew somebody was in The National Front they were out.'[32] Harvey Proctor, a former Scarborough Boys High School pupil and York University student, was one Monday Club member who received the insult that Guinness revealed.[33] Proctor resigned as assistant to the Monday Club Director in November 1971 upon finding his personal mail opened at the club. Class may have played a role in Proctor's removal. Cedric Gunnery, the old-Etonian who was the Club's acting Director at the time, did not inform Proctor of Chairman Pole's instructions regarding the opening of private mail. Proctor offered to serve out his month's notice if he could open his own mail, but the Monday Club refused, which suggested that Proctor was the specific target of this measure. Jonathan Guinness re-called that, 'we all thought that Harvey Proctor was National Front'.[34] The fact that Proctor remained within the Monday Club indicated that factors other than class might have applied. However, the reaction to Proctor's dismissal did contain class-based comments. On 23 November 1971, *The Times* reported that Proctor's opponents within the Monday Club felt he was 'getting too big for his boots', whereas the activists who supported Proctor thought the Club had de-clined 'into a social clique' that did not live up to its reputation as 'a right-wing pressure group'.[35] Unfounded or un-provable suspicions over Proctor's affilia-tions may have determined Pole's actions. Alternatively, Pole may have doubted Proctor's loyalty. Proctor was a protégé of G. K. Young. On 24 November, *The Times Diary* described reaction to Proctor's resignation as a '*putsch* against George Pole, the chairman'.[36] It inferred that others wanted to lead the Monday Club, and stated that if Pole resigned it expected unidentified 'possible pretend-ers to come forward'. These events present an opaque picture, but they do reveal that class played a role within the Monday Club, and possibly that it limited the extreme-right's fortunes.

Jonathan Guinness admitted that class played a part in the Monday Club when he said that, 'One of the main things that got me into the Monday Club was a feeling that my own class, the toffs if you like, was letting down both the party and the country'.[37] The preponderance of individuals of similar class to Guinness resulted in accusations that a 'Chelsea Tea Set' dominated the National Monday Club.[38] Indeed, Guinness accepted that class determined some Monday Club members' attitude: 'the lower-middle people were more tolerant of the National Front … like it or not there was a certain correlation between class and the intensity of this pull'. The problem for Monday Club members sympathetic to the National Front was that the National Monday Club determined policy, not the provincial branches where the 'lower-middle people' predominantly were, and it was people of Guinness's ilk that dominated the National Monday Club. Guinness's perception of the Monday Club's relationship with the Conservative Party made it unlikely that the sympathies of the lower-middle class Monday Clubbers would ever be realised. He stated that, 'for me the whole point of the

Monday Club was that it was part of the Conservative Party and needed to have tolerable relations with the rest of the party. This meant that adhesion to any other party had to be out. This, to me, was a matter of definition. Members of the Monday Club had to be a subset of the Conservative Party, and that was that.' Consequently, if Chairman Pole resigned and 'pretenders' sympathetic to the National Front tried to gain control of the Monday Club, they would be thwarted if someone like Guinness, a friend of Pole who had brought Guinness into the Club, succeeded him.

Was Guinness good for them?

Suspicions of extreme-right infiltration provided the background to the Monday Club's 1972 leadership contest. Dennis Barker implied in his *Guardian* exposé that there were connections between the Monday Club and the Patriotic Front in Worthing. He identified the Society for Individual Freedom as part of the Patriotic Front and named Frederick Stockwell as its Secretary.[39] Stockwell was one of the Monday Club members Pilger had quoted. Barker identified a number of other extremists in the Patriotic Front. He named Alan Hancock, leader of the Racial Preservation Society, quoting his claim that, 'local Conservatives have used all our literature during the last general election'. Barker identified individual members of the National Front, including David Brown of the National Democratic Party, and Air Vice-Marshal Donald Bennett who now led an organisation called the Political Freedom Movement. Barker was associating the Conservative Party with racism, fascism, and neo-Nazism, via the Monday Club. Other evidence supported this connection. The Worthing Debating Society shared its meeting place with the local branch of the Monday Club, and invited prominent Monday Club and National Front members to address it. Barker thought that the Monday Club was 'the gauge of how far radical or Patriotic Right views are acceptable to those who wish and intend to stay firmly within the respectable ranks of the established Right'. Barker supported his opinion by quoting Michael Woolrych, the Monday Club's Director, who claimed that there was 'no danger of the Monday Club becoming a para-Fascist group', and that it had 'nothing to do with the National Front. We do not have any members in it. If we found them out, we would eject them. Generally speaking, we identify them before they get in.' Hence, Barker thought that the Monday Club determined respectability and ensured that less reputable elements could not join the Conservative Party through it. However, the proliferation of the Monday Club's branches had made Woolrych's views naive. The victor of the Monday Club's 1972 leadership contest would have to prove whether Woolrych's claims were accurate.

Jonathan Guinness, Richard Body, and Tim Stroud contested the Monday Club's 1972 leadership election. Guinness represented the pro-EEC element within the Monday Club while Body represented those who opposed it. Tim Stroud entered the contest late. He had little chance of success because he was aged only twenty-eight and little known in the Monday Club. Walker described Stroud as a pawn in G. K. Young's efforts to control the Monday Club.[40] Young had served as Chairman of the Action Fund and thus played a leading role in the Monday Club's expansion. He was the current chairman of the Monday Club's Economic Policy Group. Young's authorship of *Who Goes Home?* (1969), a hard-line pamphlet on immigration, placed him on the extreme right of the Monday Club. Walker claimed that Young funded Stroud's campaign in the hope that it would draw support away from Guinness and result in victory for Body, a member known to have little knowledge of the Club's administration, which would leave Young free to control the Monday Club. Conservative Central Office remained aloof from the contest, except for one event. Stroud wrote to Party Chairman Lord Carrington. He described the Monday Club's aims, and expressed his hope that Carrington would agree that they 'do not depart from acceptable Conservative thinking'. Ian Deslandes replied on behalf of Carrington, stating that, 'it would not be right for him to comment on them while the Monday Club's Election for a new Chairman was in progress'. Mr Webster at Central Office suggested this response because he believed that 'anything sent out above your name might be passed round the Monday Club in support of Mr. Stroud's candidature'. Deslandes' letter may have simply reflected Central Office's desire not to be involved in the Monday Club leadership election. However, the lack of documentation concerning other contestants leaves open the possibility that Central Office did not want to be associated with G. K. Young.

Guinness won the election comfortably. The Monday Club announced the results on 5 June. Newspapers portrayed it as a victory for the Right. For *The Times*, Guinness was 'unquestionably the candidate of the right' whose victory 'is seen by the more moderate members as a triumph for the "law and order fetishists"'.[41] The *Sunday Telegraph* headlined with 'Guinness is good for them', and revealed that Enoch Powell's rivers of blood speech had sparked Guinness's interest in politics, which meant that immigration would remain an important issue during his chairmanship, and reported Guinness stating that he intended to 'keep the Tory party on the "Right" road'.[42] He became chairman at a time when the Government was under attack for policy reversals and many in the Monday Club thought it had veered off the 'Right' road. The Monday Club had already participated in these attacks before Guinness became chairman. In February and March 1972, individual Monday Club members voiced their concerns about picketing miners and events in Northern Ireland. These attacks continued, becoming more concerted. Less than two weeks after Guinness's election, G. K. Young's Economic Policy Group issued a press statement criticising the Government's performance and recent U-turns. It stated that the Government had broken its election promises to oppose further nationalisation and reduce state involvement in nationalised industries. It added that the recent Industries Bill had reintroduced the mechanism of state intervention and the number of civil servants had actually grown, while remaining trade union power had resulted in public sector wage increases and inflation higher than during the previous Labour government. G. K. Young's group warned that the next election would not result from a past record, or a future programme of, neo-socialism. In July, John Biggs-Davison called for tougher action in Ulster. At the same time John de Vere Walker, chairman of the Monday Club's Ulster Group, wrote privately to Party Chairman Lord Carrington. He denounced the Government for appeasing terrorists and betraying loyalists, and warned Carrington that Heath's actions threatened 'an irrevocable split within the Conservative and Unionist Party'. When Walker received an anodyne and tardy reply that merely acknowledged his comments but did not address them, he reiterated charges of disloyalty tinged with cowardice, and described the use of British troops against Loyalists and working-class Conservative voters in Ulster thus: 'Doubtless this was done in the hope of appeasing the I.R.A. and Mr. Wilson.' There is no evidence in Central Office files that Carrington replied.

However, in 1972 the party leadership did respond openly to the Monday Club's criticism of its immigration policy. On 4 August, Idi Amin gave Asians in Uganda one month to leave. Heath recalled that the right wing placed intense pressure on the Government to renege on its political and moral obligations. Enoch Powell led the intense pressure, denying that there was any British obligation to the Ugandan Asians. Support for Powell had resulted in the formation of 'Powellight', a group devoted to his policies. Bee Carthew, Monday Club member and Honorary Secretary of 'Powellight', was one of many who attacked Powell's critics. In September, the Monday Club held a 'Halt Immigration Now' meeting at Central Hall, Westminster, and passed a resolution demanding an immediate halt to all immigration, repeal of the Race Relations Act, and the commencement of a full repatriation scheme. Guinness forwarded the resolution to Heath on 16 September. The response this time was neither anodyne nor tardy. Instead, Heath attacked the Monday Club's resolution by letter on 20 September, and immediately released it as a press statement. Heath's letter addressed the Monday Club's three demands. It stated that immigration had fallen, but the Government would not stop it altogether as Britain had a moral and legal responsibility to admit some immigrants, and needed those that possessed skills useful to Britain. Nor would the Government repeal the Race Relations Act, as this was not in the election manifesto. However, it was on the issue of repatriation that Heath questioned the Monday Club's respectability most. He pointed out that the Immigration Act (1971) contained provision for the voluntary repatriation of immigrants. When Heath asserted that the Government would not 'tolerate any attempt to harass or compel them to go against their will', he rejected the compulsory implication in the Monday Club's proposal. Moreover, when Heath witheringly stated that it had not been the Monday Club's earlier position 'that a future Conservative Government should attempt to find quibbles and excuses to enable it to run away from Britain's obligations', he made it clear that he was prepared to take on the Monday Club's challenge, if necessary in public.

It is unclear how far the Monday Club's resolution revealed that it had become unrespectable. It is possible that the resolution reflected the divisions within the Monday Club rather than any corporate move rightwards. Harold Soref maintained that G. K. Young had deliberately created the Halt Immigration Now Committee to bypass his opposition in the Monday Club's Immigration Committee. Jonathan Guinness believed that this claim 'sounds plausible' as 'Young and Soref loathed each other'.[43] It would seem that a personality clash played a role in the formation of the Halt Immigration Now Campaign. However, Soref did not base his opposition to Young solely on personality. Soref claimed to have opposed Young's control of the Monday Club's Action Fund from the beginning, and to have issued direct warnings to Guinness on becoming chairman about this and the dangers of takeover by extremists. Again, Guinness confirmed this. He described Soref as a 'moderating influence' on the Monday Club's Immigration Committee, and admitted that Soref 'never stopped warning me' about extremists within the Monday Club, and that, 'In many individual instances he was right.' How much credibility Guinness gave at the time to Soref's warning is unclear. It is possible that he ignored Soref's warnings simply because people disliked him. Yet, Soref possessed some personal credibility when it came to acquiring information as he was a former member of the Intelligence Corps, and he was the person who had previously informed Central Office of Martell's intentions.[44] Whatever the motivation, Soref ostentatiously refused to participate in a National Front march organised against the wishes of the Monday Club leadership, after a sizeable contingent of National Front members attended the Monday Club's Central Hall meeting in 1972. Therefore, Guinness was probably correct when he described the Halt Immigration Campaign as 'just a splitting tactic'. If so, Guinness was referring to G. K. Young, which meant that he was leading an organisation that was experiencing an extreme-right challenge.

If extremists unpalatable to the leadership were in the Monday Club, they would have entered predominantly via the branches. G. K. Young had played a leading role in creating provincial branches as head of the Monday Club's Action Fund. This was a dangerous development. The members of the National Monday Club voted for the Club's national officers. The National Monday Club vetted these members. However, as branch members did not vote for national officers, the National Monday Club allowed individual branches to act as they saw fit over membership. Jonathan Guinness subsequently admitted that this was rash. Sir Adrian FitzGerald, who had opposed the formation of branches, stated that he thought branches attracted 'undesirables' who 'brought the club into disrepute'.[45] For FitzGerald, this was an issue of control: 'There were branches everywhere, I mean there were branches at universities, there were branches in large towns, small cities, and I just don't accept that when you start building membership up on that basis there's any way that an organisation with two or three permanent members of staff can possibly vet membership.'

Central Office appeared to recognise the potential danger posed by the Monday Club's loose organisational control. In October 1972, the Oxford University Monday Club invited Lord Jellicoe to one of its functions. Known as a 'distinctly pink' Conservative, Jellicoe was also an honorary vice-president of PEST. He wrote to Party Chairman Lord Carrington and stated that he was unsure 'what attitude Ministers should take to invitations to speak at Monday Club functions'. His uncertainty suggests that no specific policy for ministers to take towards the Monday Club existed. However, it did not prove that Central Office did not have one, or had begun to form one. Jellicoe made his view known when he stated that, 'My natural inclination would be to turn down Monday Club invitations for a whole host of reasons of which I need not expand'. This suggested that Jellicoe expected that Carrington understood to what he referred. Jellicoe apparently also knew that different Monday Clubs possessed different characteristics. He stated that he had found the people within the Oxford University Monday Club to be pleasant, intelligent, and possibly not in agreement with Enoch Powell, and reasoned therefore that it might be 'foolish to adopt a stand-offish attitude' as they may wish to take themselves 'out of the fold'. This comment showed that Jellicoe realised that the Conservative Party worked on its own extremists' divisions. Jellicoe also stated that the Monday Club's opponents expected that Central Office opposed the Club, and that 'Central Office have probably worked out a policy line here'. Carrington denied that a firm policy towards the Monday Club existed, but added, 'I think there may come a time when we shall need one, but for the present I believe that one can only take such decisions in context'. No firm policy existed towards all the other extreme-right groups investigated by Central Office either, other than that it should investigate them, which is exactly what Central Office had done since the Monday Club's creation. Carrington also revealed why he thought a definite policy might become necessary. Carrington also stated that, 'Between ourselves, I would frankly not advise colleagues at this time to accept invitations from Monday Club branches', showing that he knew the national and provincial Monday Club were different, a difference that Carrington clearly did not believe extended to the universities, which, he added, were 'in a rather different situation'. Carrington was aware of the Monday Club's development, and its nature, making it unlikely that Central Office had no policy at all towards it. This might explain why Carrington qualified his denial of such a policy with the epithet 'firm'.

Carrington's caution may also have reflected a belief that the Monday Club, which once operated simply on the right of the Conservative Party, had become extreme. Admittedly, Central Office viewed the Monday Club as an extreme-right group from its beginning, but this may simply reflect its own contemporary political orientation. Central Office's opinion of the Monday Club did not surprise Sir Adrian FitzGerald. He explained it thus: 'I think you've got to remember that there were some pretty pink Tories at that stage both in the House of Commons party at large and in Central Office. And I would have said the pinkest were in Central Office. They had a number of members of staff who really fitted into that Butskellist category'.[46] Therefore, FitzGerald rejected the description 'extreme right' for the early Monday Club. However, he agreed that by 1972 the situation had changed: 'I do not deny that there were some people who I would regard as extreme right who infiltrated the club and not only in the branches. There were one or two who got onto the main committee.' The attempted removal of Geoffrey Rippon from the Monday Club suggested that FitzGerald was correct. Rippon's critics accused him of 'trying to face two ways on the question of immigration'.[47] The national committee comfortably defeated Rippon's critics. The official record of these events stated that by December 1972, signs of a revolt by extremists were apparent to all. It described the revolt as 'well financed and organised', stating that the rebels had acquired membership lists and began a campaign against the National Monday Club leadership. This was a more serious situation than mere infiltration of the branches. Suspicions about Monday Club collusion with extremists outside the party were already a matter of public record, but if extremists captured the National Monday Club it would present the Conservative leadership with an even greater problem. The activities of some Monday Club branches exacerbated these suspicions. However, they also showed that Central Office's policy towards the Monday Club, if not 'firm' beforehand, definitely became so.

On 7 December, the Conservative Government faced two by-elections, one at Sutton and Cheam, the other at Uxbridge. Both were Conservative seats. These by-elections would be difficult in normal circumstances as they occurred at the government's mid-term, but Heath's many U-turns had made them even more difficult. At Sutton and Cheam, the Conservatives enjoyed a comfortable 12,696 majority. The *Guardian* thought Sutton and Cheam a solidly Conservative seat in which the Liberal Party could only hope to come second.[48] The Conservative candidate also faced an anti-Common Market Candidate, and a National Independent Party Candidate described by the *Guardian* as 'a Powellite on the Market and immigration issues'. At Uxbridge, the Conservatives defended a less robust majority of 3,646. Four fringe candidates also stood. Dan Harmston, leader of the Powell-supporting Smithfield meat porters, represented Mosley's virtually defunct Union Movement. Clare Macdonald, a National Front treasurer who attended Patriotic Front meetings in Worthing, represented the National Independence Party. John Clifton was the National Front candidate. Reginald Simmerson, an opponent of the EEC, stood as a Democratic Conservative. The number of fringe candidates increased during the Heath Government, and for the first time since 1945 there were more fringe candidates than actual by-elections, with most fringe candidates being recognisably right-wing. Their chances of success were miniscule, but they could limit the Conservative candidates' chances if they attracted their potential voters. The Chairman's Office within Central Office monitored these by-elections, as was normal. However, reports from Central Office agents revealed that local Monday Club branches were supporting non-Conservative candidates.

At Sutton and Cheam, the secretary of the North Kent Monday Club stated that they supported the 'anti-Common Market' candidate Mr Frere-Smith because he disliked the EEC, and not because of anything to do with immigration.[49] Frere-Smith's position on the EEC was contrary to official Conservative policy. His statement that anyone who supported him thinking it would keep the blacks out 'will be voting under a misapprehension' backed-up the North

Kent Monday Club's claim. The West Middlesex Monday Club's position at the Uxbridge by-election was different. Its members supported the National Front candidate, and some even worked for him. This was more dangerous. Moreover, other branches seemed willing to follow North Kent Monday Club's example. Len Lambert, chairman of the Essex Monday Club, which at some 300 members was one of the largest branches, threatened that, 'There is a strong possibility that this branch would support the National Front or any other right-wing candidate if, in an Essex election, the Conservative candidate was not following what we believe was Conservative policy. This feeling is general throughout the Monday Club branches, especially in the Midlands.' Typically, Lambert wanted the Conservative Party to stand for 'true-Conservatism'. The action of the two Monday Club branches was disloyal to the Conservative Party and confirmed the fears of those like FitzGerald who had opposed the creation of a branch system.

At this stage, Guinness and the National Executive of the Monday Club proved their loyalty to the Conservative Party. Guinness suspended the West Middlesex Monday Club and recommended its disaffiliation and the expulsion of all those found to have worked for the National Front. On 4 December, the Monday Club's National Executive met to consider events. *The Times* quoted a spokesman who claimed that the Monday Club, 'had always expelled people who did not support officially adopted Conservative candidates'.[50] The National Executive duly disbanded the West Middlesex branch unanimously and insisted that its secretary, Mrs Gillian Goold, resign.[51] The *Daily Telegraph* quoted Guinness's insistence that the Monday Club condemned any support for non-Conservatives.[52] Guinness followed up this action with an explicit and unequivocal circular to all Monday Club branches stating that any support for non-Conservative candidates was 'incompatible with membership of the club, just as it would be incompatible with membership of a Conservative association or branch'.[53] Guinness declared that the case for expelling anyone who contravened this rule was 'irrefutable'. He added that the Monday Club, as a part of the Conservative Party, had no special rights to choose party officers, candidates, ministers or leader, and owed any position of influence it enjoyed to 'a total loyalty to the organization'. Guinness and the Monday Club's National Executive had acted as the Conservative Party's barrier against the extreme-right's activities in the West Middlesex Monday Club.

However, the treatment meted out to the other branches was different. The Monday Club's National Executive did not take any immediate action against the North Kent Monday Club. Instead, it preferred to seek clarification after the North Kent Monday Club's chairman, Mr Deverell Stone, claimed that the individuals concerned had acted privately.[54] The Essex Monday Club also appeared to escape any punishment. Their respective offences probably explained this difference. The West Middlesex Monday Club had openly supported the National Front candidate, an offence that Guinness described as 'an open and shut one'.[55] Guinness cannot explain why the National Executive did not treat the North Kent Monday Club immediately in the same manner. However, Frere-Smith was not a National Front candidate, and therefore his candidature brought no obvious link to fascism or neo-Nazism. Len Lambert had threatened to support National Front candidates on behalf of the Essex Monday Club, but he was only one individual and there was no actual evidence that he carried out his threat. Therefore, it was proof of a National Front connection, and consequently with Nazism, which put Uxbridge beyond the pale. Guinness's comments supported the idea that the Monday Club took a harder line with the West Middlesex Monday Club when he warned them that, 'They can appeal but we are not going to forgive them. Working for a National Front candidate is unacceptable.'[56]

Mrs Goold of the West Middlesex Monday Club swiftly joined the National Front. Guinness's action had forced Goold to leave the comfort of a successful political monolith for the cold reality of the National Front's miniscule chances. Nevertheless, the equivocal treatment of the different Monday Club branches did leave room for Central Office to doubt the National Executive's desire to purge extremists within the Club. Moreover, disbandment of the West Middlesex Monday Club had not stopped the media from reporting the Monday Club's connections with extremists. For example, later in December *The Listener* carried an article based on a recent BBC *Midweek* documentary. It quoted a West Middlesex Monday Club member who said that they only disagreed with the National Front over whether to send Asians 'back by boat or in boxes'.[57] This type of report kept recent events at Uxbridge fresh in the public's mind. The article also prominently noted that former Conservatives were in the National Front, such as John O'Brien. *The Listener* mentioned O' Brien's support for Enoch Powell, and described him as, 'for 20 years a pillar of the Shrewsbury Conservative Association'. It also noted that O' Brien had left the Conservative Party and eventually succeeded A. K. Chesterton as chairman of the National Front. *The Listener* also identified Monday Club member Oliver Gilbert as the Patriotic Front's liaison officer in Worthing and as the National Front's local organiser. It also noted that Gilbert was a member of the Worthing Conservative Association, where he had tried to oust the Conservative MP Terrence Higgins for 'not being right-wing enough'. Gilbert reinforced the notion that the Conservative Party and the fascist, neo-Nazi extreme right were linked. The article reminded its readers of the type of person with whom the Conservative Party associated with via the Monday Club by resurrecting the Nazi past and paramilitary proclivities of the National Front's John Tyndall. It also quoted Chesterton's comments when he retired that: 'Two percent of the members of the National Front are really evil men – so evil that I placed intelligence agents to work exploring their backgrounds, with results so appalling that I felt obliged to entrust the documents to the vaults of a bank. Some of these men are at present placed close to the centre of things.' The article set out Guinness's challenge: could he maintain the Monday Club's position as a barrier to the National Front, or would it increasingly become the gateway for further infiltration of the Conservative Party? Its portrayal of Guinness as a political naif who admitted that he was 'not experienced in fringe-type politics', probably did not inspire confidence within Central Office. This feeling would explain why Central Office proceeded to construct a 'firm policy' towards the Monday Club in the wake of the by elections at Uxbridge, and Sutton and Cheam.

A by-election at Lincoln expected early in 1973 provided Central Office with the opportunity to implement its firmer policy against the Monday Club. Lincoln's pro-EEC Labour MP had resigned his seat to fight against his own party's anti-EEC stance. Labour defended its majority of 4,750 with an official candidate, which meant that the Conservative Government had an unexpected chance of a rare by-election gain. *The Times* described the Conservative Party as seeing these developments as 'an excellent chance of gaining from the Labour split', and reported that Central Office had made 'urgent calls' to the local Conservative leaders, who had not even picked a candidate, and told them to 'get on with it'.[58] Within Central Office, Chris Patten informed chairman Lord Carrington on 20 November that he was concerned that Jonathan Guinness was one of the two candidates short-listed by the Lincoln Conservative Association. Patten stated that, 'The disadvantages of the selection of Guinness (quite apart from the fact that it would not be very easy to win the seat with him) are numerous and obvious.' What, exactly, did Patten mean? Guinness made comments that embarrassed the Conservative leadership. He stated a preference for gassing over hanging, and advocated leaving razor blades in convicted murderers' cells so they could do the decent thing.[59] Guinness's comments earned him the nickname 'Old Razor Blades'. They also highlighted the Conservative Party's divisions over capital punishment. However, as they occurred four months later than Patten's letter to Carrington, Guinness's comments cannot explain Patten's concerns. Patten may have suspected that Guinness was likely to make gaffes like this, but he did not mention it if he did. Another possibility for Patten's comments was Guinness's connection with pre-war fascism. Guinness was Oswald Mosley's stepson, so a connection with pre-war fascism was easy to make. However, this was a barely credible accusation as Guinness was not Mosley's blood relative, and had played no part in active politics until the late 1960s when Mosley's political career was long over. This leaves Guinness's connection with the Monday Club as the likely explanation for Patten's comments. Guinness's victory at Lincoln would add electoral credibility to an organisation operating within the Conservative Party that contained extremists according to recent events and reports.

Unfortunately for Central Office, the Lincoln Conservatives selected Guinness as their official candidate on 23 November. Central Office files prove that it was indeed concerned at such an outcome. Political opponents also were in no doubt about the root cause of the Conservative leadership's concern. The *Manchester Evening News* pointed to the power of the Monday Club as responsible for Guinness's selection, and stated that, 'It was the organisational ability of this "party within a party" – plus the undoubted talents of Mr Guinness himself – that gave the Tory leadership and Mr Heath the shock of having Mr Guinness as their standard-bearer.'[60] Central Office responded to Guinness's selection by concocting a plan to limit the harm that his candidature could do to the Conservative Party.

Guinness provided Central Office with the opportunity to implement its policy on 30 November. The Conservative Party's 1972 Conference Handbook listed the Chairman of the Bow Group as the Vice President of the National Advisory Committee of the Federation of Conservative Students (FCS). Guinness expressed to Lord Carrington his delight at seeing 'another group within the Conservative party' gain official party recognition, and requested that the FCS afford the Monday Club similar treatment as, 'we feel we are entitled to it, having more members than the Bow Group, and with 140 full members who are students, almost certainly more students'. This was the Monday Club's persistent complaint that the Conservative Party organisation barred its members from offices within the party. If Monday Club members had been aware of Central Office's reaction to Guinness's complaint, their suspicions would have increased. The FCS was under progressive leadership at this stage, and had joined with the Young Conservatives to defeat Enoch Powell's resolution at the 1972 Party Conference attacking the Government's decision to admit the Ugandan Asians. So incensed was one Young Conservative, Anthony Reed-Herbert, that he resigned after the conference and joined the National Front. Like the Young Conservatives, the FCS was effectively part of the Conservative Party's approved organisation. Chris Patten sought advice from the FCS on how to respond to Guinness's complaint. The National Secretary of the FCS, John Bowis, replied that Guinness would not welcome it if Carrington interfered in Monday Club elections and suggested that Patten tell Guinness to approach the FCS directly if the Monday Club wanted representation on it. However, Bowis also intimated strongly that any such approach would fail because the Monday Club had never shown any interest in the FCS, and had not even provided them with a copy of their recent publication on Higher Education. Carrington responded to Guinness using Bowis's comments on 18 December, but also invited him to arrange a mutually convenient time to discuss the Lincoln by-election. This invite was really a command because Carrington was the Party Chairman and Guinness was the party's candidate.

Patten wrote an eight-point plan for Carrington to adopt before his meeting with Guinness on 10 January. He wrote another note after the meeting recording Carrington's conversation with Guinness. Comparing these documents reveals that Carrington implemented Patten's plan closely. Both documents claimed that the loss of Sutton and Cheam had resulted in Carrington wishing to take a closer look at all by-elections before any campaign started, and was the reason why Carrington had asked Guinness to meet him. The lack of similar meetings in the Chairman's by-election files for other contests questions this reasoning, although it does not disprove it. Both documents expressed concern that extremists might take over Guinness's campaign, and result in voters deserting the Conservative Party. Yet who were these extremists? Patten noted that Guinness reassured Carrington in their meeting that he would not invite Powell to speak, and that 'A number of extreme Monday Club supporters would have some difficulty in getting up to Lincolnshire and others like Harvey Proctor he hoped to exclude.' These comments showed that Central Office viewed Powell as an extremist and that Guinness was aware of its view. It also showed that Guinness thought that there were extremists within the Monday Club, including Proctor. Guinness believed that Central Office's main concern at this meeting was Powell's possible involvement in the by-election.[61] Guinness may be correct. However, although Patten mentioned Powell in his earlier document, he limited his suggestion to Carrington doing nothing more than ascertaining what Guinness had to say about this possibility. Patten did not mention what response Carrington should make to any information Guinness imparted about Powell's involvement. Nor did he mention Harvey Proctor. However, when Patten commented in the first document about the Monday Club's role in general, he revealed the real objects of Central Office concerns. Patten advised Carrington to say that although he personally had never been a member of any pressure group or lobby within the Conservative Party, there was room for such organisations provided that any disagreements 'were subordinated to the general objectives of supporting the Party and furthering its interests'. Patten was urging Carrington to imply that the Monday Club was disloyal to the Conservative Party, which is exactly what Carrington did. His comments made it plain that Carrington could take this approach because of the Monday Club's connections with the National Front and other extreme-right organisations. He suggested that Carrington should claim to be 'disturbed by some indications that the Monday Club has been increasingly concerned with attacking Government and the official Party line rather than supporting it', and advised Carrington to use the Uxbridge by-election as the 'most notorious example' of it. Furthermore, Patten stated that Carrington should say to Guinness that he was 'not convinced that this is the only example where this sort of thing has happened', and provided an example for Carrington to use. Carrington duly told Guinness that he was concerned at 'reports of Monday Club support for National Front candidates at by-elections and of prominent Monday Club supporters speaking at meetings organised by bodies like the British Campaign to Stop Immigration which had fought against the Conservative Party in Parliamentary and local elections'.

Therefore, the loss of Sutton and Cheam was really an excuse that Central Office used to confront Guinness about the Monday Club's connections with the National Front. The National Front had not even contested Sutton and Cheam. It had contested Uxbridge, which was the by-election that Patten advised Carrington to use against the Monday Club. However, Carrington delivered much more than Central Office concerns to Guinness. Both documents explicitly stated that Central Office believed that the National Front had infiltrated the Monday Club. Carrington stated this belief to Guinness by saying that, 'He wondered to what extent the Monday Club had been infiltrated from the extreme right.' Any such infiltration was an intolerable situation for the Conservative Party leadership. Patten advised Carrington to inform Guinness of his intention to take 'a very firm line from now on, especially as we get closer to the next Election, with those who seem more interested in pursuing political vendettas than in helping widen support for the Conservative Government and Conservative policies'. Carrington did so, to which Guinness replied that he was willing to pass on to Central Office the names of anyone suspected of infiltration, but refused to participate in 'hounding' members of the Monday Club. Carrington then told Guinness that 'if anybody was to take responsibility for removing extremists from the Monday Club then it had to be Mr. Guinness'. Guinness recalled that his main desire at the meeting was to be the party's candidate at Lincoln and thought Carrington addressed him cordially,[62] but Carrington had made it clear that it was Guinness's duty to remove extremists from the Monday Club, no matter how cordially he did so.

However, one other feature of the meeting between Carrington and Guinness was definitely not cordial. Patten advised Carrington to warn Guinness that the involvement of extremists made it difficult for the 'Party Organisation and for your colleagues to give their whole-hearted and committed support to Guinness in Lincoln both during the Election campaign and in the longer term'. This was an astonishing threat for Central Office to make to a candidate selected by the local Conservative Associations. It was completely contrary to the principle of local Conservative Association autonomy. Nevertheless, Carrington delivered it unequivocally. Carrington's threat contrasted sharply with Guinness's circular to Monday Club members stressing the requirement of its members' loyalty to the Conservative Party.[63] When Carrington threatened not to support an officially adopted candidate in a contest in which a Labour Party division had presented the Conservative Party with an opportunity for victory, he revealed that Central Office was even prepared to accept electoral defeat rather than countenance infiltration by the extreme right.

The day after Patten recorded the meeting with Guinness, an article in *The Times* reported Conservative Party managers' fears about extremist infiltration. The tone and content indicated strongly that these 'managers' were the source of the report. The article identified the Monday Club as one of two sources of trouble, and stated that party managers had asked, 'whether something drastic needs to be done to check the mischief that is feared'.[64] One possible remedy suggested in the article was 'that before long the Conservative candidates' list will be purged of a few members of the Monday Club whose loyalties to the Conservative Party and Mr Heath come under question'. This threat targeted aspiring candidates, especially as it was Central Office and the party leadership who would do any questioning. The reporter also seemed to know that it was the Monday Club leadership's responsibility for purging its extremists, and was aware that 'Senior Conservatives' believed 'that the Monday Club is dangerously vulnerable to infiltration from the undemocratic right-wing extreme of politics'. There were also comments that reflected Carrington's views on membership of groups within the Conservative Party. The article admitted that the Monday Club's organisation and promotion in no way 'differed from the methods of the Bow Group and PEST', although interestingly it described PEST as having more backbenchers and Ministers. However, the article stated that doubts about the Monday Club's loyalty after recent by-elections set it apart from these groups. It claimed that, 'Party managers are therefore watching the Monday Club anxiously', and while the loyalty of most members was undoubted, these managers 'still feel it necessary to ask whether the club may not be at risk of being used by extremists to do Mr Heath and the Government serious harm'. There was even a threat of 'circumstances in which ministers and backbenchers might come under persuasion to end their association with the club'. There was some support for Guinness's claim that Powell was Central Office's main concern at their meeting. However, the article limited its comments on Powell to his criticisms of the Government and mention of his power-base in the crucial West Midlands constituencies, and described the similarities and differences between him and the Monday Club. In contrast, the Monday Club was the subject of approximately three-quarters of the article. The article mirrored the record of Carrington's meeting with Jonathan Guinness closely, indicating that Central Office were the 'party managers' either directly or indirectly behind it. If so, Central Office had ensured that Carrington's message to Guinness reached a much wider audience.

Guinness may recall the cordiality of his meeting with Carrington, but his reaction to the article in *The Times* was scathing. He was bewildered as to how the reporter 'gets the idea those he describes as "Conservative party managers" think Mr Heath's Government is damaged by the Monday Club'.[65] He added that the Monday Club was able to voice concerns that the leadership was sometimes unable to, and, arguing that it was sometimes necessary to criticise government policy, he warned that any witch-hunt against the Monday Club would question the party leadership's 'credentials as Conservatives'. Guinness was not the only senior Monday Club member who responded to the article in *The Times*. Sam Swerling, the author of two Monday Club publications, retorted: 'If there is any mischief in the Conservative Party which needs to eradicated, as is suggested, it lies in the small but growing coterie of self-effacing liberals who have infiltrated the party at all levels, particularly in the Young Conservative movement. That is where the real danger to Conservatism lies.'[66] Nor did the wider Monday Club cease its criticism of the Conservative Party, or the Government. On 2 February 1973, the Essex Monday Club Chairman Len Lambert requested as Honorary Secretary of the Provincial Council of Monday Club Branches, that Central Office included the Monday Club in future party diaries 'as a Conservative political organisation'. This was once more the complaint that the party organisation denied the Monday Club official recognition while granting it to others like the Bow Group. Central Office replied that it had 'no intention, or reason' to change current practice. On 24 March 1973, the Monday Club passed a resolution criticising the Government's White Paper on Ulster. Carrington rejected it by telling Guinness witheringly that, 'There is a responsibility on everyone of good-will to try and make these proposals work rather than to stir up old fears and antagonisms.'

Carrington's meeting with Guinness had not stopped the Monday Club's attacks on the Government. In the event, Guinness failed to win the Lincoln by-election on 1 March and finished a poor third and nearly three times further behind the victor than the previous Conservative candidate. The following day Chris Patten wrote confidentially to Carrington outlining what the party's position about this outcome should be. He cited the presence of three Cabinet Ministers and other junior ministers in the Lincoln campaign, and claimed that therefore, Guinness's chairmanship of the Monday Club 'made no difference to the support we gave him'. Patten's claim is justifiable in that Central Office could hardly have refused to support Guinness after he had provided the assurances they wanted. Yet, if Patten meant to convey Central Office's constant and total support for Guinness, this position was disingenuous as its support for Guinness was conditional, as the meeting of 10 January shows.

One month after the Lincoln by-election, evidence appeared of a campaign against the Monday Club by the 'self-effacing liberals' that Swerling stated had infiltrated the Conservative Party. Late in March, the Monday Club's Halt Immigration Now Campaign (HINC), led by G. K. Young, launched a national petition seeking one million signatures in support of 'an end to all "tropical immigration" and the institution of an effective repatriation policy'. On 2 April, the Bow Group attacked the petition, arguing that it would harm race relations, and that the HINC could only achieve its objectives 'if accompanied by intimidation'. Here, the Bow Group pinpointed the violent element inherent in all repatriation schemes, regardless of claims to the contrary. PEST joined this criticism in the press on the following day. It described the Monday Club's position on immigration and repatriation as 'rabid extremism' and 'emotional bigotry', in which the word 'effective' was synonymous with 'compulsory', and called on ministers Rippon, Amery, and Goodhew to resign from the Club.[67] PEST also sent a letter on the same day to its university branches urging them to start a letter-writing campaign against the Monday Club's HINC. PEST and the Bow Group's actions look orchestrated. However, what probably disconcerted the Monday Club leadership more was an attack upon it by opponents within the Club. The leadership proceeded to prove that by resisting this attack the Monday Club remained subordinate to the Conservative Party, and its gatekeeper against the extreme right.

The revolt within the Monday Club became public knowledge in the same month that PEST and the Bow Group attacked the HINC's immigration policy. The leadership had known of an internal campaign against it since December 1972. Now that the campaign was in the open, three Club members who were also MPs wrote to papers in April stating that a political mafia within certain branches, and in the Executive itself, were orchestrating a disloyal and disruptive propaganda attack. If their claims were correct, extremist infiltration of the Monday Club went further than the provincial branches. Sir Adrian FitzGerald corroborated that by this time one or two right-wing extremists had indeed managed to join the Monday Club's National Executive.[68] G. K. Young led the challenge to Guinness, and was the one extremist that FitzGerald explicitly identified. Young was largely responsible for the Monday Club's growth as chairman of its Action Fund, especially the formation of branches. Young was also prominent in the Monday Club's stance on immigration, first as chairman of the Immigration Committee and then as leader of HINC. Thus, Young was at the forefront of the populist issue that his supporters argued was responsible for the Monday Club's huge increase in publicity. This made Young a formidable opponent.

The campaign was acrimonious, with accusations of underhand activity. All Monday Club members received anonymous broadsheets that used a fictitious address, and a letter with Guinness's signature forged on it. This activity revealed that someone had illegally acquired the Monday Club's membership list, which resulted in the Club's National Executive asking Scotland Yard to investigate. The Monday Club leadership vaguely put the blame on right-wing extremists. However, the *Guardian* reported that the Monday Club had called in the police because it believed that 'its offices have been infiltrated by a supporter of the extreme Right who has used its membership list in an effort to discredit the chairman, Mr Jonathan Guinness, in his campaign for re-election'.[69] An anonymous document stating that 'shadowy figures' controlled the Monday Club appeared, claiming that connections between individual members and extreme-right groups continued, with fascists and neo-Nazis still 'very close to the heart of the Club and its leaders', despite recent expulsions. This may have been an attack on Young, whom the document described as the 'single most powerful political figure in the Monday Club'. However, whether the purpose was to smear Young is unclear. Guinness explicitly rejected any involvement by the Monday Club leadership, and stated that, 'I don't think we ever discovered who was responsible for that pamphlet.'[70] Powell's involvement is extremely unlikely. He showed no interest in the contest probably because by 1973, as Guinness believed, it had become 'increasingly clear that his agenda was simply to dish Heath'. This was not the behaviour of a putative leader of a new, credible extreme-right political force.

In the poll in April, Guinness defeated Young comfortably by 625 votes to 455. *The Times* announced the result, and thought that Guinness's success meant 'that the "moderates" have won the first stage of their campaign against more extreme right wingers'.[71] In one year, Guinness had gone from being the champion of the right to leader of the moderates! Nevertheless, *The Times*'s comment confirmed that Guinness had indeed blocked the extreme right. However, *The Times* was only partly accurate when it described Guinness's victory as the first stage of a campaign against the extreme right. Guinness had already commenced this campaign when he expelled the West Middlesex Monday Club in December 1972. Carrington had then added impetus to the campaign by threatening Guinness in January 1973, which 'party managers' then reinforced in the press. However, what ensured the success of this 'campaign' was the actions of the Monday Club's own MPs and many of its members. For, as *The Times* also reported, many Monday Club MPs had 'let it be known privately that they would resign if Mr Young and his faction came out on top', while many members had supported Guinness 'because they believed he would be firmly against reported infiltration by National Front members'. Therefore, Guinness's victory was also the culmination of pressure applied by Monday Club members who opposed the extreme right, and voted accordingly. The final stage of the campaign came when Guinness finished what he started. In June, Guinness expelled Young supporter Len Lambert from the National Monday Club because he had invited the National Front's John Tyndall to address the Essex Monday Club. When Lambert tried to use his membership of the Essex Monday Club to counter the expulsion, Guinness disaffiliated the whole branch. Guinness also oversaw the expulsion of fifty extremists from the National Monday Club in July, dismissing them by saying that the 'old, solid members of the club have finally lost patience with this disruptive minority'. The expelled rebels retorted that Guinness was a weak chairman who had acted under orders from Lord Carrington. They claimed that, 'Lord Carrington is known to have told Mr Guinness when he was adopted as the Conservative candidate at Lincoln that under no circumstances were the "wild men on the right of the club" to go to Lincoln to canvas for their chairman.' The rebels were correct, but all this proved was Guinness's agreement with the Conservative Party chairman of the need to remove extremists from the Monday Club, and Carrington's role of course. Guinness maintained this position, defeating two further attempts to remove him in 1973.

Guinness's chairmanship severely damaged the ambitions of those who saw the Monday Club as a vehicle for the extreme right. Young swiftly resigned. In 1974, Young formed Tory Action, and subsequently wrote for the anti-Semitic *Liverpool Newsletter*. Others also left, many joining the National Front. However, recent events had also damaged the Monday Club. Expulsions and infighting undermined its credibility. In August, *The Journal of Commerce* described the Monday Club as having disintegrated, leaving a need for 'an effective right-wing pressure group within the Conservative Party'.[72] Several correspondents at the *Daily Telegraph* turned on the Monday Club, claiming that they no longer understood what its role was. Fewer MPs retained their Monday Club membership, while the national membership figure more than halved. This contrasted markedly with the Monday Club's confidence in 1970. Some members closest to events thought that all of the Monday Club's troubles were the result of a conspiracy by someone who had infiltrated it to wreck it. Jonathan Guinness appeared to accept this view in 1973 when he stated his certainty in the systematic nature of the disruption. Yet, to whom did this refer? The National Front denied any involvement, claiming that such activity was in any case unnecessary as Monday Club defections were inevitable. The lack of any similar accusation in any official Monday Club material supports the idea of National Front innocence. However, the Monday Club's historian implied the guilt of 'a main instigator of the troubles' who soon 'gave indications of Communist sympathies' and campaigned against the Conservatives in the February 1974 General Election.[73] He did not name the individual, but the only person ever identified at the forefront of the Monday Club rebellion was G. K. Young. This fact led Monday Club members to wonder who exactly G. K. Young was.

Some investigators have portrayed G. K. Young as a sinister extreme-right figure. However, these accounts often attempt merely to prove the nastiness of the right wing rather than consider other issues, and therefore sometimes rely on questionable evidence and conspiracy theory. For example, a focus on proving that Young engineered the extreme right's takeover of the Conservative

Party with Thatcher's leadership fails to consider what impact the Conservative Party had on the extreme right, and consequently relies on 'guilt by association'. Highlighting Guinness's connection to fascism because his mother had married Oswald Mosley, and implying that Margaret Thatcher was an extremist because her 'close personal associate' Nicholas Ridley 'lived in the same block of flats' as two fascist activists, is an unrevealing method. A better approach is to examine the known facts about Young, the impact this had on events he was involved in, and the opinion of contemporaries. Young was a merchant banker with Kleinwort Benson. Therefore, he probably had the personal wealth to fund campaigns, as in Stroud's 1972 leadership challenge and the HINC, and the financial resources to challenge Guinness. Also verifiable is Young's previous membership of the Labour Party, his employment on the left-wing *Glasgow Herald*, and his subsequent diplomatic career. Additionally, Young possessed, as a former deputy head of MI6 involved in intelligence activities for a substantial period, the experience and knowledge to run the type of dirty tricks campaign witnessed in the 1973 Monday Club leadership challenge. This knowledge made the Monday Club's decision to call in the police over the forged letter that purported to come from Guinness more interesting. The person responsible for the forgery used a letterhead closely resembling that of the Market Bosworth Monday Club, of which Guinness was a member. Young was also adept at the subtle response, as seen in his reply to Guinness's accusation that Young's supporters were behind the forgery. When Young stated that, 'I thought it was vintage Guinness, an exact account of Jonathan's views. I was surprised to learn it was a forgery',[74] he gave the impression of ignorance yet still smeared Guinness.

These details and actions resulted in some contemporaries wondering about Young's motives. The most remarkable accusation came from John Gouriet, who was a new recruit to the Monday Club in 1973. Gouriet identified Young as one of the dubious characters 'hanging around' a British political establishment that he believed communists had deeply penetrated.[75] Gouriet recalled that he was not alone in thinking that Young 'might be a member of the Cambridge Group, along with Philby and Burgess, Maclean and Blunt', and that there was 'certainly circumstantial evidence to suggest he could have been the fifth man'. He also included Conservative Central Office in his theory of a communist conspiracy, describing it as 'deeply penetrated, deeply infiltrated'. Therefore, Gouriet implied that Young had attempted to destroy the Monday Club as some minor part in a wider communist plot, and that Central Office accepted or directed his activity. If Gouriet is correct, then Central Office definitely blocked the extreme right, although clearly not to protect the Conservative Party. However, the absence of any evidence corroborating Gouriet's opinion leaves it stuck in the realms of conspiracy. This is not to deny the possibility that Young was a communist agent. Guinness inferred this possibility after his 1973 victory when he said of the leadership challenge that, 'He had a sneaking suspicion that the minority was Communist-run.'[76] There is no doubt that Young ran the 1973 challenge to Guinness. Recently, Guinness described Young as

'Sinister',[77] but remained unsure about his role and motives. Asked if he thought Young was trying to wreck the Monday Club, Guinness answered: 'Wreck it or control it? If he was going to control it, what did he want to control it for? God knows, there were those who said he was trying to wreck it. That was said, but all sorts of things were said … So he might have just been out to wreck it, but from what point of view, Communist? I don't know.' However, although Guinness considered the possibility that Central Office supported Young in the Monday Club leadership election, he believed they would have preferred him to Young. Sir Adrian FitzGerald's recollections chimed with Guinness's comments. He also wondered which part of the political spectrum Young was in, but opted for the extreme right rather than extreme left by stating, 'I think he was extreme right.'[78] FitzGerald believed Young was 'a racialist with a capital R', adding that if Young had secured the chairmanship, 'I would have walked straight out as would others.' Here, FitzGerald confirmed the unwillingness of many Conservatives to allow the extreme right to succeed. However, when it comes to Young's motives, FitzGerald too remains perplexed: 'I wish I knew. I really don't know. He must have known what he wanted to do. But I just don't know.' As for Central Office's opinion of Young, FitzGerald too is unsure, but believed that, 'In purely political terms everything should indicate that they'd be very concerned about him,' and that therefore they would have supported Guinness.

On balance, and saving contradictory evidence, the most feasible interpretation is that Young operated on the extreme right and probably intended to use the Monday Club to form a larger political bloc that included the National Front. With this larger bloc, Young could challenge the Conservative Party. There were rumours of a specific meeting between Young and the National Front's John Tyndall, but the Front's Martin Webster denied that this took place. Yet, Webster only denied that a specific meeting occurred, not that any meeting at all took place, and Guinness believed that Young probably was in contact with the National Front.[79] Therefore, in this scenario Central Office probably viewed Guinness as the lesser of two evils, and, having ensured that Guinness understood its position, refrained from involvement in the leadership contest and happily watched the Monday Club tear itself apart. The lack of any comment at all about the Monday Club's 1973 leadership contest within Central Office's files supports this theory, but there is also more tangible evidence. Carrington said to Guinness after bringing the Monday Club under control, 'Well done that, getting it under control.' Guinness confirmed this account and pithily paraphrased Carrington's view of the Monday Club as, 'if the bloody thing must exist let it be under respectable leadership'.

Therefore, Heath's Government by 1974 had effectively marginalised the Monday Club. It had done this by moving closer to the Monday Club on issues such as immigration, but also by threatening its leadership. This assured that any associations with the National Front would not be a significant issue in the February 1974 General Election, but it is difficult to assess what impact this action had on that contest. The electorate was probably more concerned about increased inflation and unemployment. Five states of emergency and five major policy U-turns probably weighed heavier on voters minds than the Conservative Party's shadowy connections. Nor did the Conservative Party benefit from Powell's electoral appeal in 1974. Powell resigned from the Conservative Party just before the General Election, electing to stand for the Ulster Unionists instead. Until the Sunningdale Agreement, the Ulster Unionists were the political associates of the Conservative 'and Unionist Party'. Thus, Powell continued proving his commitment to his personal perception of Conservatism. There is no evidence that Powell seriously contemplated taking over the National Front. Nor did Powell ever advocate a vote for the extreme right on the mainland. Instead, Powell announced his postal vote for the Labour Party in 1974, based on what he saw as their opposition to membership of the EEC, and called on the electorate to do likewise. For Powell, the principle and logic of an argument overrode any desire to be leader of a political party other than the Conservative Party: that and the desire to harm Heath of course.

There is some evidence that Central Office minimised the prospects of Powellites before the 1974 General Election. The neo-Conservative American Institute for Public Policy Research published A. Ranney's analysis of the 1974 General Election.[80] Ranney's article identified Central Office's increased control of candidate selection via changed bureaucratic procedures, which allowed it to veto selection of Powellite candidates. If correct, Ranney's analysis supported Guinness's perception that Central Office was more concerned about Powell's impact than the Monday Club. However, the evidence is not strong. Ranney based his article on a single *Sunday Times* article, and lacked any corroboration. For example, Ranney stated that the vice-chairman at Central Office passed a 'word' to local Conservative Associations on the unsuitability of specific Powellite candidates. This does sound similar to the claims of Donald Johnson MP,[81] and it is feasible that Central Office officials operated this way, but this claim remains unproven without supporting evidence. The examples Ranney cited also weakened his claim. The three Powellites that Ranney identified as vetoed by Central Office aimed to contest Labour-controlled constituencies. As Powell attracted voters who had never previously voted Conservative, it is possible that these candidates would secure unexpected victories. However, the wider context of economic crises and industrial unrest weakened this argument. So, too, does Ranney's admittance that Central Office approved twenty-four other Powellites. As Ranney does not identify any of these approved Powellites, it is impossible to conclude whether these individuals had already secured nomination, or were even MPs already. The lack of any Powellight membership exacerbates this difficulty. Ranney also quoted Sir Richard Webster's claim in the *Sunday Times* that Central Office had, 'no policy to exclude Right-Wing candidates, Powellites, or Monday Clubbers'. A number of facts suggest that Webster was not being wholly accurate. These were the long-standing general policy of investigating the extreme right, the exclusion of Monday Club members from the party's organisations, and written evidence of a policy to counter the danger posed by the Monday Club composed before Carrington summoned Guinness to Central

Office. These considerations question Webster's claim severely. However, if Webster's claim reflected Central Office's belief that it had already contained the threat posed by the Monday Club, Enoch Powell, and the extreme right, it was accurate apart from the fact that the remit empowering Central Office to investigate the extreme right remained in force.

The results of the February 1974 General Election indicated that the extreme right was indeed contained. The electorate did not turn to it. The most successful of the extreme-right parties was the National Front, which polled a miserly 0.2% of the vote. This result justified the opinion of those Conservatives who dismissed the National Front's electoral prospects, and indicated that the saved deposit at the West Bromwich by-election of 1973 would probably be the National Front's political apogee. Other extreme-right parties fared even worse. The National Independence Party, which by 1974 included the former National Front chairman John O'Brien alongside Donald 'Pathfinder' Bennet, lost its deposit at Tottenham. The National Democratic Party, the political manifestation of the Racial Preservation Society, fared even worse at Ipswich. The British Movement of former League of Empire Loyalist Colin Jordan, which was the most overt neo-Nazi Party, attracted less than one thousand votes. In contrast, the Conservative Party retained nearly 38% of the vote, and won the popular vote in a contest that provided no party with an overall majority. This proved that the extreme right was unable to capitalise on the most propitious circumstances since the Second World War. Heath had fewer seats than the Labour Party and resigned after failing to forge a coalition with the Liberals. Harold Wilson formed a minority Labour Government. Commentators expected Wilson to seek another General Election soon, to provide a majority government. When Wilson went to the country in October 1974, the extreme right fared little better. At 0.4% of the vote, the National Front's performance proved Adrian FitzGerald's view that they were 'a pretty good joke'.[82] Former 'Independent Conservatives', many opposed to entry into the EEC, banded together as the United Democratic Party, but its fourteen candidates attracted an average of less than 400 votes. The October 1974 General Election was also a personal disaster for Edward Heath, with twenty fewer seats and a drop of nearly one-and-a-half million votes. The Conservative Party was not prepared to accept the continuing leadership of an individual beaten at three of the previous four General Elections. It removed Heath and on 11 February 1975 installed Margaret Thatcher as leader.

Notes

1   C. Booker, *The Seventies: Portrait of a Decade*, Allen Lane, London (1980), 3.
2   N. Shrapnel, *The Seventies: Britain's Inward March*, Constable, London (1980), 13.
3   P. Whitehead, *The Writing on the Wall: Britain in the Seventies*, Michael Joseph, London (1985), xv.
4   F. Wheen, 'The Stagnant Years', *The Modern Review*, March 1998, 25.
5   R. Weight, *Patriots: National Identity in Britain 1940–2000*, Pan, London (2003), 475 &

519.

6   D. Marquand, *Britain Since 1918: The Strange Career of British Democracy*, Weidenfeld & Nicolson, London (2008), 235.

7   'Social Progress Stagnant as GDP Soars', www.neweconomics.org/gen/news_mdp.aspx, 16 March 2004.

8   H. Sounes, *Seventies: The Sights, Sounds and Ideas of a Brilliant Decade*, Simon & Schuster, London (2006), passim

9   Alwyn W. Turner, *Crisis? What Crisis? Britain in the 1970s*, Aurum, London (2008), ix–xx.

10 *The Campaign Guide 1970* (Conservative and Unionist Central Office, 1970), 469.

11 *A Better Tomorrow: The Conservative Programme for the Next 5 Years* (Conservative Central Office, 1970), 23–24.

12 See p. 135.

13 *News Special*, 8 December 1970, 1.

14 See pp. 134–135.

15 See pp. 133–134.

16 'R.P.S. News Bulletin', July/August 1970, 1.

17 D. Barker, 'On the Patriotic Frontier', *Guardian*, 2 June 1972.

18 See pp. 155–156.

19 M. Cockerell, 'Inside the National Front', *The Listener*, 28 December 1972, 879.

20 *England My England*', in British Library, Mic. F. 19 (5) 1975.

21 Author interview with Jonathan Guinness, 23 May 2008.

22 Author interview with Sir Adrian FitzGerald, 20 May 2008.

23 Cockerell, 'Inside the National Front', 880.

24 See pp. 110, 157.

25 'Tory Call to Ease Entry for Asians, *The Times*, 27 July 1970.

26 'Asians Get New Hope of Entry', *The Times*, 13 August 1970.

27 'Monday Club Opposed to More Asian Admissions', *The Times*, 14 November 1970.

28 J. Pilger, 'What The Monday Club Men Have in Store for You', *Daily Mirror*, 15 March 1971.

29 Author interviews with Jonathan Guinness (Lord Moyne), 23 May 2008, and Sir Adrian FitzGerald, 20 May 2008.

30 See p. 193.

31 Author interview with Jonathan Guinness, 23 May 2008.

32 Author interview with Sir Adrian FitzGerald, 20 May 2008.

33 Author interview with Jonathan Guinness, 23 May 2008.

34 *Ibid.*

35 'How Proctor was Pole-axed', *The Times,* 23 November 1971.

36 'The Times Diary: More Ado at the Monday Club', *The Times,* 24 November 1971.

37 Author correspondence with Jonathan Guinness, 24 May 2008.

38 Author correspondence with Jonathan Guinness, 28 June 2008.

39 D. Barker, 'On the Patriotic Front', *Guardian*, 2 June 1972.

40 M. Walker, *The National Front*, Fontana/Collins, Glasgow (1977), 127.

41 'Right Wing Victory in Monday Club poll', *The Times*, 6 June 1972.

42 'Guinness is Good for Them', *Sunday Telegraph*, 11 June 1972.

43 Author correspondence with Jonathan Guinness, 28 June 2008.

44 See p. 85.

45 Author interview with Sir Adrian FitzGerald, 20 May 2008.

46 *Ibid.*

47 'Monday Club Move to Oust Mr Rippon Fails', *The Times*, 18 October 1972.

48 M. Lake, 'Hard Core of Conservatism', *Guardian*, 29 November 1972.

49 L. Marks and D. Keys, 'Monday Club Clash over Anti-Tory Candidates', *Observer*, 3 December 1972.

50 'Monday Club Will Expel By-Election "Rebels"', *The Times*, 4 December 1972.

51 'Monday Club Branch to be Disbanded', *The Times*, 5 December 1972.

52 R. Summerscales, 'Monday Club Ban Branch', *Daily Telegraph*, 5 December 1972.

53 'Back Tories Warning by Monday Club', *The Times*, 13 December 1972.

54 'Monday Club Branch to be Disbanded', *The Times*, 5 December 1972. R. Summerscales, 'Monday Club Ban Branch', *Daily Telegraph*, 5 December 1972.

55 Author correspondence with Jonathan Guinness, 28 June 2008.

56 R. Summerscales, 'Monday Club Ban Branch', *Daily Telegraph*, 5 December 1972.

57 Cockerell, 'Inside the National Front', 877.

58 'Lincoln Tories are Hoping to Break Labour's Hold', *The Times*, 9 November 1972.

59 'Lincoln Urged to Reject Extremes', *The Times*, 22 February 1973. J. Ramsden and R. Jay, 'Lincoln: The Background to Taverne's Triumph', in C. Cook and J. Ramsden (eds), *By-Elections in British Politics*, Macmillan, London (1973), 304–305.

60 A. Roth, 'No Outsider in the Lincoln Handicap', *Manchester Evening News*, 27 December 1972.

61 Author interview with Jonathan Guinness, 23 May 2008.

62 *Ibid.*

63 See p. 203.

64 'Curbing critics on the Tory Right Wing', *The Times*, 15 January 1973.

65 'Monday Club: Jonathan Guinness', *The Times*, 20 January 1973.

66 'Monday Club: S. M. Swerling', *The Times*, 27 January 1973.

67 'Ministers Urged to Quit Monday Club', *The Times*, 3 April 1973.

68 Author interview with Sir Adrian FitzGerald, 20 May 2008.

69 M. Stuart, 'Monday Club Suspects Spy', *Guardian*, 10 April 1974.

70 Author correspondence with Jonathan Guinness, 28 June 2008.

71 'Mr Guinness is Re-elected Chairman of the Monday Club', *The Times*, 30 April 1973.

72 J. Szemerey, 'What's in the Wind at Westminster', *The Journal of Commerce*, 2 August 1973, Oswald Mosley Papers, Diana Mosley Deposit, University of Birmingham Information Services, Special Collections, XOMD/8/6.

73 R. Copping, *The Monday Club – Crisis and After*, Monday Club, London (1975), 9.

74 M. Stuart, 'Monday Club Suspects Spy', *Guardian*, 10 April 1974.

75 Author interview with John Gouriet, 19 June 2007.

76 '50 expelled as Move to Oust Monday Club Chairman Fails', *The Times*, 25 July 1973.

77 Author interview with Jonathan Guinness, 23 May 2008.

78 Author interview with Sir Adrian FitzGerald, 20 May 2008.

79 Author correspondence with Jonathan Guinness, 28 June 2008.

80 A. Ranney, 'Selecting the Candidates', in Howard R. Penniman (ed.), *Britain At The Polls: The Parliamentary Elections of 1974*, American Enterprise Institute for Public Policy Research, Washington DC (1975).

81 See pp. 119–120.

82 Author interview with Sir Adrian FitzGerald, 20 May 2008.

Conclusion: keeping it right

The Conservative Party had a sanguine attitude towards indigenous fascism and extreme-right movements before the Second World War. However, the war made association with right-wing extremism unacceptable as it associated it with the horrors of Fascism and Nazism. A title that included labels such as 'Fascist', 'Nazi' and 'National Socialist' was no longer acceptable for political movements. Very few groups or individuals identified themselves with these pariah terms and ideologies. No organisation with such a title appeared in the Conservative Party Archive as one of the outside organisations that Central Office investigated. The same is true of groups tainted by internment as possible collaborators with Nazi Germany. There is no file on Mosley's Union Movement or the British People's Party in the Conservative Party Archive, although in these cases the rudimentary nature of Central Office's intelligence-gathering may also play a role. There is one reference to an open National Socialist, Colin Jordan, but it is superficial and reveals that Central Office was eager to avoid any association with him. The Conservative Party may have shredded its files on these groups and individuals, if they existed at all, but what is certain is that the party leadership and bureaucracy adopted a different attitude towards the extreme right after 1945. No longer was the Conservative Party sanguine about its connections with the extreme right. However, avoiding connections with right-wing extremism was not easy.

Many extreme-right groups undoubtedly eschewed their inter-war positions or conveniently forgot them, particularly those that had sympathised with Nazi Germany and Fascist Italy. Admittedly, not all pre-war extreme-right groups were fascist or Nazi. Some were ultra-Conservatives who wanted nothing to do with mass politics and groups containing lower-middle and working-class people, but these were fine distinctions. Ultra-Conservatives in Europe had allied with fascism and Nazism, and it was therefore unlikely that the British electorate would distinguish between various strands of the extreme right. Moreover, Britain's pre-war extreme-right groups had unarguably contained Conservatives. This was a matter of public record. It was also a source of embarrassment for the Conservative Party after the Second World War. The Conservative Party did not want the public reminded of these associations, and it could not afford any recurrence of them. Consequently, the Conservative Party decided to investigate the extreme right.

The Conservative Party's main response was bureaucratic. Initially, it used what remained intact of the party bureaucracy after the Second World War to gather intelligence, but soon reinvigorated the party machine. This reinvigoration included increasing the number of Central Office Agents, which had a significant impact on intelligence-gathering. Additionally, Central Office used an existing ad hoc committee to formalise intelligence-gathering within its Voluntary Organisations Section in 1948. This department's terms of reference mandated the monitoring of extreme-right groups and the taking of action against them. Central Office and its Area Agents played a prominent role in these activities. A substantial part of the files in the Conservative Party Archive's 'Outside Organisations' section consists of information sent by Area Agents, or their requests for information on certain groups or individuals. However, Central Office's intelligence-gathering went beyond passively receiving extreme-right groups' literature. At times, Central Office was proactive. Its representatives posed as disinterested members of the public to ascertain the nature of extreme-right groups, and on at least one occasion infiltrated an extreme-right group. However, not all information emanated from the party bureaucracy. Wider Conservatism played a role too. Conservative MPs forwarded extreme-right literature, or advised Central Office of events and rumours in their constituencies. Party members and contacts in business provided information. Sometimes, the information and intelligence was superficial and short-lived, which usually reflected the small size of the group concerned. This was the case with the Right Party. At other times the forwarding of information resulted in correspondence that lasted years. Central Office commissioned reports on some extreme-right groups. These, too, varied in size. Reports on The New Crusade and New Reform Party consisted of a few pages, while those on the People's League for the Defence of Freedom, Middle Class Alliance, League of Empire Loyalists, Elizabethan Party and Freedom Group were more extensive. However, regardless of the nature and extent of its investigation into these groups, Central Office obstructed or blocked them all.

The degree of Central Office's response varied, usually reflecting its opinion of an organisation's nature. Central Office's minimally hostile response was to suggest that an organisation's members would have more chance of success if they pursued their objectives with the Conservative Party and not an outside organisation. Another similar response was to warn individuals not to fund a group because that would reduce contributions to the Conservative Party. Central Office adopted this stance towards organisations that it identified as predominantly mainstream Conservative and therefore posing little threat to the party, as in the examples of the Middle Class Union and Middle Class Alliance. Central Office adopted a slightly different minimally obstructive response to those groups with which it had an unofficial relationship, but wished to avoid becoming public knowledge. These groups operated outside the political mainstream, yet possessed views or objectives with which many Conservatives agreed, or methods that the Conservative Party found difficult to employ at that time. For example, AIMS and Drake's Drum advocated policies that many Conservatives agreed with, but were inexpedient in the contemporary climate. The Conservative Party may have signalled acceptance of Labour's political programme by producing the *Industrial Charter*, but there was no large-scale rejection of this programme when the Conservatives regained office in 1951. Too close a connection with the likes of AIMS and Drake's Drum would lay the Conservative Party open to charges of hypocrisy. However, both of these groups attempted to convey their argument in areas that seemed beyond the Conservative Party's reach. If AIMS and Drake's Drum were successful, it would make it possible for the Conservative Party leadership to put forward policies that its membership favoured without angering an electorate that had so overwhelmingly welcomed Labour's policies in 1945. Consequently, Central Office only minimally obstructed them, if at all. Obstruction often amounted to little more than Central Office instructing Area Agents to deny any connection with these groups, and ensuring that these groups denied any connection with the Conservative Party. Denial of association with these groups might also include ensuring that Conservatives ceased involvement with them, as occurred with the Workers' Forum. Thus, groups whose 'extremism' amounted to no more than a Conservative reaction to a new paradigm usually attracted only these limited counter-measures.

However, Central Office's view of these 'Conservative' groups sometimes hardened. Initially, Conservatives shared platforms with the British Housewives' League. However, when Central Office considered that the British Housewives' League's response to the Labour Government was too extreme, it explicitly denied any connection with it, and thereafter consistently refused to assist it. Likewise, Central Office came to view the Society for Individual Freedom as an extreme-right organisation, and consequently discouraged Conservatives from joining it. The same applied to Common Cause. Central Office was initially unconcerned about Common Cause. It therefore merely discouraged Conservative officials from joining it, but saw no reason why individual Conservatives should not. However, as Central Office became increasingly aware that Common Cause contained an extreme potential, it dispatched officials to attend its meetings and warned Conservatives not to join it.

It is also possible that Central Office based its identification of a group as 'extreme' on the harm that it could do to the Conservative Party. For example, Central Office was wary of the Fighting Fund for Freedom from the beginning, probably due to its involvement in 'anti-alien' campaigns, but it only explicitly identified it as an extreme-right organisation after a right-wing Conservative MP had resigned from it. Nevertheless, the common thread that applied to

Central Office's increased blocking activity was its perception that a group was 'extreme-right wing'. This perception also applied when Central Office's attitude was apparent from the beginning without it necessarily identifying the group explicitly as an extreme-right one. The New Reform Party is one example. Central Office advised its Area Agents to warn Conservatives against any connection with the New Reform Party because it perceived it as a bigoted, sectarian movement. The New Reform Party's ultra-Protestantism placed it beyond the non-confessional Conservative Party, as did its anti-trade union rhetoric. Even though there was no obvious connection between the New Reform Party and fascism, Central Office viewed its opinions as ones that divided society in extreme-right terms and consequently wanted nothing to do with it.

Central Office could also appear to modify its attitude towards an extreme-right movement, as seen in its relationship with Edward Martell's groups. Central Office was particularly active against Martell's People's League for the Defence of Freedom. It formed a Committee of Investigation, and advised that the Conservative Party as a whole should not have any connection with the PLDF. This was not the limit of Central Office's action against Martell and the PLDF. It refused Martell's offer of a joint candidature to defeat Labour at the East Ham by-election in 1957. Central Office also observed the PLDF's meetings during the East Ham by-election campaign, ensured that Cabinet Ministers were present during it, recruited an individual for 'intelligence duties' in the constituency, and was prepared to smear Martell with accusations of fascism to limit his chances. Central Office continued to try to harm Martell's chances six years later in a by-election that the Conservatives were not even contesting. The Conservative Party did not contest the 1963 Bristol South East by-election because it did not believe that Tony Benn should have to forfeit his seat on becoming a peer, and advised its members to abstain. This advice also limited Martell's chances of success as he was standing as a 'National Fellowship Conservative' in an attempt to attract Conservative votes. The negative comments of local Conservative officials during the by-election showed that Central Office wanted to stop Martell from taking advantage of the Conservative Party's absence. Nevertheless, Central Office did later enter into a relationship with Martell's Freedom Group during the 1964 General Election by accepting his offer of assistance, especially his attempt to unseat Labour leader Harold Wilson. However, this relationship was short-lived. After the 1964 General Election, Central Office reverted to its negative stance towards Martell. It denied any association with Martell and monitored his involvement with the National Party closely.

These changes of attitude merely reflected different contexts. The PLDF's fierce anti-unionism placed it firmly to the right of the Macmillan Government, making it attractive to Conservatives who believed that the Conservative leadership had accepted Labour's programme without a fight. Hostility to the party leadership explained Central Office's action at East Ham and Bristol. Home's acquisition of the Conservative Party leadership in 1963 changed Central Office's stance. Home was a recognised right-winger. This made Martell's Freedom

Group appear to be less outside the political mainstream, and explained why Central Office had a more positive relationship with Martell at the 1964 General Election. Central Office's desire to avoid association with Martell's financial difficulties ostensibly explained its reversion to a more negative stance after the 1964 General Election, but it is probably not coincidental that this occurred after the more progressive Heath replaced Home. Neither is it surprising that Central Office monitored Martell's involvement with the National Party. Martell had continued his rightwards journey in supporting the National Party, leaving 'freedom right' organisations for an overtly anti-immigrant extreme-right one at a time when immigration was an increasingly difficult political phenomenon. However, regardless of changes, at no time was Central Office's collaboration with Martell unconditional. It heavily qualified its cooperation with Martell during the 1964 General Election, which suggested that this was a temporary situation reflecting Home's leadership. In reality, Central Office consistently countered Martell's groups.

There is no ambiguity when it came to groups or individuals capable of being associated with the wilder forms of right-wing extremism, especially Fascism or Nazism. Central Office's attitude towards these groups never deviated. It was always careful to identify anti-Semitism or Nazism in groups that it investigated, such as in The Guild of Good Neighbours and The New Crusade. When Central Office discovered that the anti-Semitic L. N. Tomlinson of Clan Briton was a Conservative Party member, it abruptly stopped corresponding with him. Andrew Fountaine's anti-Semitism resulted in Central Office withdrawing official party support from him. Central Office's discovery of BUF antecedents led it to take further action against the founder of the Right Party, and its knowledge that John Charnley was a former BUF member was probably the factor in its decision to block his attempts to become a Conservative MP or local councillor. Additionally, Central Office explicitly identified the miniscule Elizabethan Party as fascist when it warned all Conservative MPs, candidates, constituency and area agents, to have nothing to do with it

The most obvious example of Central Office's perception of fascism involved the League of Empire Loyalists, a 1950s reaction to decolonisation. Here, Central Office did not act alone, as wider Conservatism contributed to thwarting this greater threat from the extreme right. Central Office was aware that some LEL members had BUF antecedents, and commissioned a report that concluded that the LEL was fascist and anti-Semitic. It advised Conservative MPs, candidates, and party officials, of this conclusion, some of whom repeated this accusation in the press. Central Office introduced more vigorous vetting of party membership applications to block LEL supporters from joining the Conservative Party. It also sought the identities of party members already within the LEL, some of whom subsequently left the Conservative Party. It was made clear that membership of the LEL was incompatible with Conservative Party membership. The LEL leader complained of a wider campaign to ostracise its members, and it is likely that ordinary Conservatives were hostile to it. Many Conservatives probably simply disliked the fact that fellow party members had joined an organisation that opposed the Conservative Government. However, many were probably angry at the way the LEL acted, and saw it as a re-emergence of fascism. The LEL's actions allowed Central Office to infer that it was fascist and orchestrate denigration of it by using the Conservative-supporting *Daily Telegraph*. The LEL's disruption of Conservative Party events met increasingly stiff resistance from local Conservative Association officials, culminating in their violent removal from the Party Conference at Blackpool in 1958. The Conservative Party leadership then cut the ground away from the LEL's anti-immigrant stance by introducing the Immigration Bill in 1961. This action applied also to the neo-Nazi or racial nationalist groups that had splintered from the LEL from 1958, including True Tory of Richard Hilton and those variously associated with John Bean, Colin Jordan, John Tyndall, and Andrew Fountaine. The LEL declined from its peak in 1958, and its splinter groups made no impact. The Conservative Party's actions played a significant role in their failure.

Decolonisation also provided the impetus for the emergence of the Monday Club in 1961. This development was more troubling for the Conservative Party than the LEL as the Monday Club's members were unarguably Conservative Party members. Central Office was initially unsure of the Monday Club's nature and dismissed it as an example of youthful exuberance. However, when Central Office concluded that the Monday Club was an extreme-right organisation it attempted to hinder the Club's growth. Central Office ordered Young Conservatives to cease all contacts with the Monday Club, to which it denied financial or any other assistance. Its attitude towards the Monday Club temporarily thawed during Home's leadership, but became even more negative after Home's departure in July 1965, similar to Martell's case. An unattributed *Daily Telegraph* report of Shadow Cabinet criticism in November 1965 indicated that the new leadership disapproved of the Monday Club. Monday Club complaints of prejudice by the party bureaucracy increased from 1965 onwards. Over the following two years, the Monday Club identified discrimination from Conservative organisations and in their omission from the party's policy study groups. Central Office correspondence confirms the Monday Club's accusation.

Central Office's counter-measures against the Monday Club continued in the pivotal years of 1967 and 1968. In early 1967, the external extreme right coalesced into the National Front. At this stage, Central Office exhibited no concerns over the National Front, dismissing it as an irrelevant amalgamation of discredited fascists like Chesterton and former members of the LEL. However, the Monday Club's decision to become a mass movement in June 1967 was a different matter. The Conservative Party could not tolerate a potential threat to take it over from within, or the possibility of a credible party forming to its right. The activity engendered by the Monday Club's decision reflects the Conservative Party's concern. The party's Chief Whip became involved in investigating the Monday Club's activities. Central Office denied the Monday Club fair access to the Universities Department within Central Office, and dismissed the Club's claim that other 'all-party' groups discriminated against it. Central Office even considered the extraordinary possibility of harming a former employee's pension and restricting the activities of its future pensioners.

Enoch Powell's 'rivers of blood' speech in April 1968 transformed the situation. The Monday Club or the National Front now had a potential leader. The Conservative Party leadership opposed the extreme right even more determinedly from this moment onwards. Heath's immediate sacking of Powell was an obvious attempt to limit any damage to the Conservative Party, but also to blunt Powell's appeal. More effective in limiting Powell's appeal was a rightwards move in the Conservative Party's political programme, which had commenced in 1967, and continued with legislative measures and policy statements that attracted Powell's potential supporters without ever acceding to all of his demands. At the same time, Central Office continued thwarting the Monday Club. Area Agents monitored the Monday Club's fundraising activities and requested help from Central Office to counter it. Central Office organised the collation of complaints to counter the Monday Club chairman's frequent allegations of bias. Senior Conservatives supported an incumbent MP when faced with a local Monday Club campaign to deselect him. Meanwhile, the Conservative Party denied any connection with the National Front.

Such was the success in constraining Powell and his supporters within Conservatism, that the Conservative Party scored an unexpected victory at the 1970 General Election. However, although Powell's threat never materialised, a growing realisation of an increasing connection between the extreme right outside and within the party became a source of serious concern. The 'freedom right' still existed in the likes of the Society for Individual Freedom and AIMS, but these groups remained peripheral. Nor did the freedom right possess any charismatic figures. Martell had long since left the freedom right behind, and no organisation had yet appeared that was capable of uniting the freedom right. This situation left the field clear for the National Front, a nationalist-racist organisation possessing antecedents, policies and behaviour that marked it in many eyes as a fascist or neo-Nazi party. This situation was as intolerable to the Conservative leadership as any connection with the LEL. Indeed, it was more so. Most of the openly neo-Nazis who left the LEL were by now in the National Front, which was increasingly connected with the Monday Club. The Monday Club was no longer a rudimentary organisation but a developed and growing entity capable of challenging the Conservative Party. This was a dangerous situation, and the most serious test of the Conservative Party's determination to block the extreme right after the Second World War. The Conservative bureaucracy did not deviate from the mandate given to the Voluntary Organisations Department in 1948. Nor did the party leadership remain idle. Heath's Government neutralised the Monday Club's appeal by moving towards it in areas such as the economy, trade unions, and immigration, while in public it attacked the Monday Club's objectives. In January 1973, Central Office formulated a policy threatening not to support the Monday Club chairman's by-election campaign unless he removed extremists from the Club. The Monday Club chairman complied, effectively making the Monday Club Central Office's agent in blocking the extreme right.

From 1945–75, the Conservative Party leadership, and Central Office especially, consistently blocked the extreme right. They did so by implementing counter-measures against the extreme right, and sometimes by adopting some of its themes. This was an institutionalised policy with the objective of avoiding embarrassing or inexpedient associations. The level of blocking correlated to the perceived degree of extremism and the threat posed. The Conservative Party bureaucracy implemented this policy not only to external extremists, but also to its own extreme right, the Conservative Monday Club. In contrast, Central Office acted favourably towards progressive groups such as the One Nation Group, Bow Group, and PEST. This policy limited the extreme-right's political space and attracted its potential voters. At the same time, the Conservative Party's policies made some party members into extremists, forcing them to either operate without the comforts provided by a monolithic, powerful and successful mainstream party, or shut up. Extreme-right voters constantly faced the dilemma of whether it was worth voting for any party other than the Conservative Party, while extreme-right parties persistently faced the dilemma of whether they could make any electoral impact. From 1945–75, the extreme right failed abjectly to win political representation, its highlight being one saved deposit at a 1973 by-election. Its failure indicates that the Conservative Party's attempts to limit it were successful.

After 1975, the Conservative Party continued its policy towards the extreme right. The Conservative Party met the challenge of a resurgent 'freedom right', particularly in the shape of the National Association for Freedom, by adopting many of its policies in its 1979 General Election manifesto. It marginalised the National Front further. In January 1978, Conservative leader Margaret Thatcher commented on Granada TV's *World in Action* that 'people are really rather afraid that this country might be rather swamped by people with a different culture'.[1] Thatcher's statement was premeditated. Her subsequent comments in the interview make clear this was an appeal to the National Front's potential voters. The National Front interpreted Thatcher's comments this way. It accused her of simply uttering 'cunning phrases which SOUND anti-immigration at first hearing but which on closer study do not commit a future Conservative government to take ANY action to halt immigration', and warned the electorate that the Conservative Party had pulled off this 'trick' before.[2] The National Front was correct. It recognised that the Conservative Party was again reaching rightwards, and consequently attacked its immigration policy as a fraud right up to the General Election.[3] However, there was little that the National Front could do to counter the Conservative Party's election manifesto promise of a British Nationality Act that offered a tougher stance on immigration. At the 1979 General Election, all 303 National Front candidates lost their deposits, gaining only 0.61% of the total vote.[4] The National Front blamed the Conservative Party, accusing it of stealing National Front policies and supporters.[5] The Conservative Government subsequently implemented the

British Nationality Act (1981), providing stricter immigration criteria without fully acceding to the National Front's demands. This Act probably helped the Conservative Party retain extreme-right voters and contributed to the National Front's demise in the early 1980s.

The purged Monday Club welcomed Thatcher's leadership as promising 'a return to Conservatism'.[6] While in opposition, Thatcher appointed Lord Thorneycroft Party Chairman at Central Office. Thorneycroft was the Chancellor who resigned in 1958 when Macmillan's Cabinet refused to cut government spending sufficiently, and was thus more in tune with Monday Club thinking. Thorneycroft headed a much-changed party machine, reflected in Sir Victor Raikes's February 1977 comment to him that the Monday Club 'has deep loyalty to our leader and our relations with you as Chairman of the Party are very happy'. In government, Thatcher absorbed much of the Monday Club's objectives. Economic policy, anti-trade union legislation, and a tough anti-Soviet Union stance, were but some of the areas agreeable to the Monday Club, while the British Nationality Act (1981) went as far as moderate Monday Clubbers ever went. Thatcher's three governments were economically liberal yet socially authoritarian, and therefore amenable to many in the Monday Club. After Thatcher's removal, the Conservative Party entered into a prolonged internecine struggle revolving ostensibly around whether to maintain 'Thatcherism', or present a more progressive, tolerant image. A bitterly divided Conservative Party lost the 1997 General Election by a landslide to a reformed 'New Labour' that accepted much of Thatcherism while promising to heal the social divisions it had caused. New Labour's position appealed to an electorate still coming to terms with the economic restructuring that had damaged communities in the 1980s, and with a younger generation more amenable to an increasingly cosmopolitan society and the European Union.

Therefore, the Conservative Party at the end of the twentieth century faced a new paradigm, as it had in 1945. Unable to resolve its divisions, the Conservative Party lost the next two elections in 2001 and 2005. In quick succession, William Hague, Iain Duncan Smith, and Michael Howard, joined Austen Chamberlain as the only Conservative leaders since 1900 who failed to become Prime Minister. The Conservative Party, realising as always the pragmatic need to adapt to society's changes, found itself increasingly at odds with the Monday Club's intolerant positions on race and immigration. The Monday Club's call for voluntary repatriation, which once more placed it firmly on the extreme right, was unacceptable. In October 2001, the Conservative leader instructed three MPs to leave the Monday Club, and the Shadow Chancellor declared that, 'There is no room for extremist views in the Conservative Party'.[7] Two weeks later, the leader suspended the Monday Club from the Conservative Party.[8] In May 2002, the Monday Club expressed its desire to re-establish links with the Conservative Party,[9] and a belief in a quick return to the Tory fold.[10] However, the Monday Club remains estranged from the Conservative Party. When this research commenced, Central Office's guardian of the Conservative Party Archive advised that 'The modern day Monday Club is not an organisation that we wish to be affiliated or associated with' and that he considered it an 'unpleasant organisa-tion'.[11] Together with the party's actions after 1975, these comments show that the Conservative leadership and bureaucracy today continues and maintains the negative attitude that blocked the extreme right in the period 1945–75.

Notes

1 TV Interview for Granada *World in Action* ('rather swamped'), 27 January 1978, www.margaretthatcher.org, accessed 15 January 2008.

2 'Immigration: Tories Re-issue 1970 Vote-Catch Swindle', *National Front News*, March 1978, 1.

3 For example, 'Unveiled: The Great Tory Damp Squib'; '"Tories? We Don't Hate Them – We *Despise* Them"'; 'Labour-Tories Agree: "Black Immigration Must Continue"', *National Front News*, May 1978, 1.

4 www.psr.keele.ac.uk/area/uk.htm, accessed 1 October 2005.

5 'Thatcher The Betrayer', *National Front News*, October 1979, 1; 'Tory Betrayals Are N.F. Opportunities', *National Front News*, October 1979, 2.

6 Copping, *Monday Club Crisis*, 22.

7 'Tory MPs Resign from Far-Right Club', *BBC News*, 7 October 2001.

8 'Tories Cut Monday Club Link over Race Policies', *Guardian*, 19 October 2001.

9 'Right-Wing Club Appeals for Tory Return', *BBC News*, 10 May 2002.

10 'Monday Club Predicts a Quick Return to Tory Fold', *The Independent*, 11 May 2002.

11 Personal communication with author, 12 December 2005.

Bibliography

Archives

British Library Newspapers, Colindale.
Conservative Party Archive: CCO 1 Series; CCO 2 Series; CCO 3 Series; CCO 4 Series; CCO 20 Series; CCO 60 Series; CCO 120 Series; CCO 170 Series; CCO 500 Series; CPA CRD; CPA NUA; CPA NUEC; CPA PUB.
Hansard.
John Beckett Collection, University of Sheffield, Special Collections.
LSE Pamphlet Collection.
National Front Archive, Modern Records Centre, University of Warwick.
Oswald and Diana Mosley Papers, University of Birmingham Information Services, Special Collections.
Papers of the Radical Right in Britain, British Library.
Private Papers of Sir Patrick Wall, University of Hull Modern Political Papers Archive.
Tory Reform Group, LSE Archives.

Books and pamphlets

Abbott, F. *The Wreckers: Communist Disruption in British Trade Unions*, Monday Club, London (1966).
Addison, P. *Churchill on the Home Front, 1900–1955*, Pimlico, London (1993).
Aldgate, A. *Censorship and the Permissive Society: British Cinema and Theatre 1955–1965*, Clarendon Press, Oxford (1995).
Aughey, A. 'Philosophy and Faction', in , P. Norton (ed.), *The Conservative Party*, Prentice Hall/Harvester Wheatsheaf, London (1996).
Baker, D. *Ideology of Obsession: A. K. Chesterton and British Fascism*, Tauris, London (1996).
Ball, S. 'The National and Regional Party Structure', in A. Seldon and S. Ball (eds), *Conservative Century: The Conservative Party since 1900*, Oxford University Press, Oxford (1994), 169–220.
Ball, S. and Holliday, I. *Mass Conservatism: An Introduction*, Frank Cass, London (2002).
Ball, S. and Seldon, A. *The Heath Government: A Reappraisal*, Longman, London (1986).
Barnett, C. *The Verdict of Peace: Britain Between Her Yesterday and the Future*, Pan, London (2002).
Barr, J. *The Bow Group: A History*, Politicos, London (2001).
Bean, J. *Many Shades of Black: Inside Britain's Far-Right*, New Millenium, London (1999).
Beckett, F. *The Rebel Who Lost His Cause: The Tragedy of John Beckett, MP*, London House, London (1999).
Bedford, Duke of *The Financiers Little Game: or, the Shape of Things to Come*, Strickland Press, Glasgow (1945).
Benewick, R. *The Fascist Movement in Britain*, Allen Lane, London (1972).
Bernstein, G. L. *The Myth of Decline: The Rise of Britain Since 1945*, Pimlico, London (2004).

Blake, R. *The Conservative Party: From Peel to Major*, Heinemann, London (1997).

Blinkhorn, M. (ed), *Fascists and Conservatives: The Radical Right and the Establishment in Twentieth-Century Europe*, Unwin Hyman, London (1990).

Booker, C. *The Neophiliacs: The Revolution in English Life in the Fifties and Sixties*, Pimlico, London (1969).

Booker, C. *The Seventies: Portrait of a Decade*, Allen Lane, London (1980).

Braine, J. *A Personal Record*, Monday Club, London (1968).

Burton-Hyde, C., Commander R.N. (retd.), FCA, *The Great Betrayal: An Indictment of the Conservative Governments' Departure from Conservative Principles, 1951–1963*, Johnson London (1963).

Campbell, J. *Edward Heath*, Jonathan Cape, London (1993).

Carpenter, H. *That was the Satire that was: The Story of the Satirical Sixties*, Victor Gollancz, London (2000).

Catterall, A. and Wells, S. *Your Face Here: British Cult Movies Since the Sixties*, Fourth Estate, London (2001).

Catterall. P. (ed.), *The Macmillan Diaries: The Cabinet Years, 1950–1957*, Macmillan, London (2003).

Charmley, J. *Descent to Suez: Diaries 1951–1956*, Weidenfeld and Nicolson, London (1986).

Charmley, J. *A History of Conservative Politics*, Macmillan, London (1996).

Charnley, J. *Blackshirts and Roses: An Autobiography by John Charnley*, Brockingday, London (1990).

Chesterton, A. K. *Beware the Money Power: A Warning To The British Nations*, Candour Publishing Company, Croydon (1954).

Chesterton, A. K. *Sound The Alarm! A Warning To The British Nations*, Candour Publishing Company, Croydon (1954).

Chesterton, A. K. *Stand by the Empire: A Warning To The British Nations*, Candour Publishing Company, Croydon (1954).

Chesterton, A. K. *Empire or Eclipse: Grim Realities of the Mid-Twentieth Century*, Candour, London (1965).

Chesterton, A. K. *The New Unhappy Lords: An exposure of power politics*, Candour, London (1965).

Clark, A. *The Tories: Conservatives and the Nation State 1922–1997*, Phoenix, London (1999).

Clark, A. *Diaries I: Into Politics 1972–1982*, Phoenix, London (2001).

Clarke, P. *Hope and Glory: Britain 1900–2000*, Penguin, London (2004).

Cockett, R. *Thinking the Unthinkable: Think-Tanks and the Economic Counter-Revolution 1931–1983*, Harper Collins, London (1994).

Colwell, M. *The Radical Right and Patriotic Movements in Britain during 1975: A Bibliographical Guide*, Harvester, Hassocks (1978).

Copping, R. *The Story of the Monday Club*, Monday Club, London (1972).

Copping, R. *The Monday Club – Crisis and After*, Monday Club, London (1975).

Coxall, W. N. *Parties and Pressure Groups*, Longman, London (1986).

Craig, F. W. S. *Minor Parties at British Parliamentary Elections 1885–1974*, Macmillan, London (1975).

Cronin, M. (ed.) *The Failure of British Fascism: A Failure of Imagination?* Macmillan, London (1996).

Daniel, M. *Cranks and Gadflies: The Story of UKIP*, Timewell, London (2005).

Davies, A. J. *We, The Nation: The Conservative Party and the Pursuit of Power*, Abacus, London (1995).

Donnelly, D. *Gadarene '68: The Crimes, Follies and Misfortunes of the Wilson Government*, Kimber, London (1968).

Dorril, S. *Blackshirt: Sir Oswald Mosley and British Fascism*, Viking, London (2006).

Dorril, S. and Ramsay, R. *Smear! Wilson and the Secret State*, Fourth Estate, London (1991).

Durham, M. 'The Conservative Party, the British Extreme Right and the Problem of Political Space', in M. Cronin (ed.), *The Failure of British Fascism: The Far Right and the Fight for Political Recognition*, Macmillan, London (1996), 81–98.

Eatwell, R. *Fascism: A History*, Pimlico, London (2003).

Eisenberg, D. *The Re-emergence of Fascism*, MacGibbon & Kee, London (1967).

Elton, G. *The Unarmed Invasion: A Survey of Afro-Asian Immigration*, G. Bles, London (1965).

Evans, H. *Downing Street Diary: The Macmillan Years 1957–1963*, Hodder and Stoughton, London (1981).

Ferguson, N. *Empire: How Britain Made the Modern World*, Penguin, London (2004).

Fielding, N. *The National Front*, Routledge & Kegan Paul, London (1981).

Fisher, N. *Iain Macleod*, Deutsch, London (1973).

Foot, P. *Immigration and Race in British Politics*, Penguin, Baltimore (1965).

Gamble, A. *The Conservative Nation*, Routledge & Kegan Paul, London (1974).

Gilmour, I. and Garnett, M. *Whatever Happened to the Tories: The Conservatives Since 1945*, Fourth Estate, London (1998).

Gottlieb, J. V. and Linehan, T. P. The *Culture of Fascism: Visions of the Far Right in Britain*, I. B. Tauris, London (2004).

Gracchus, Tiberius (pseud.) *Your M.P.*, Victor Gollancz, London (1944).

Green, E. H. H. *Ideologies of Conservatism: Conservative Political Ideas in the Twentieth Century*, OUP, Oxford (2002).

Griffin, R. *The Nature of Fascism*, Routledge, London (1991).

Griffin, R. 'British Fascism: The Ugly Duckling', in M. Cronin (ed.), *The Failure of British Fascism*, Macmillan, London (1996), 141–165.

Griffin, R. '"No Racism, Thanks, we're British": How Right-Wing Populism Manifests Itself in Contemporary Britain', in W. Eisman (ed.), *Rechtspopulismus in Europa: Analysen und Handlungsperspektiven*, Czernin-Verlages, Graz, Austria (2002), 1–16.

Griffin, R. 'The palingenetic core of generic fascist ideology', in A. Campi (ed.), *Che Cos'e il fascismo? Interpretazioni e prospective*, Ideazione editrice, Roma (2003), 97–122.

Griffiths, R. *Patriotism Perverted: Captain Ramsay, The Right Club and British Anti-Semitism*, Constable, London (1998).

Grundy, T. *Memoir of a Fascist Childhood: A Boy in Mosley's Britain*, Heinemann, London (1998).

Hamm, J. *Action Replay: An Autobiography*, Howard Baker Press, London (1983).

Harper, S. and Porter, V. *British Cinema of the 1950s: The Decline of Deference*, Oxford University Press, Oxford (2003).

Heath, E. *The Course of My Life: My Autobiography*, Hodder & Stoughton, London (1998).

Heffer, S. *Like the Roman: The Life of Enoch Powell*, Weidenfield & Nicholson, London (1998).

Hennessey, P. *Having It So Good: Britain in the Fifties*, Penguin, London (2006).

Hennessey, P. *Never Again: Britain 1945–51*, Penguin, London (2006).

Hoffman, J. D. *The Conservative Party in Opposition, 1945–51*, MacGibbon & Kee Ltd., London (1964).

Holder, N. *Noddy Holder – Who's Crazee Now? My Autobiography*, Ebury Press, London (2000).

Hollis, C. 'The Conservative Opportunity', *New English Review*, XI (June, 1945), 109, quoted in J. D. Hoffman, *The Conservative Party in Opposition, 1945-51*, MacGibbon & Kee Ltd., London (1964), 21.

Ingrams, R. *The Life and Times of Private Eye 1961–1971*, Harmondsworth, London (1971).

Jarvis, M. *Conservative Governments, Morality and Social Change in Affluent Britain*, Manchester University Press, Manchester (2005).

Johnson, D. McIntosh *On Becoming an Independent MP*, Johnson, London (1964).

Johnson, D. McIntosh *A Cassandra at Westminster*, Johnson, London (1967).

Jones, N. *Mosley*, Haus, London (2004).

Kavanagh, D. and Morris, P. *Consensus Politics from Attlee to Major*, Blackwell, Oxford (1994).

Keegan, W. *Mrs Thatcher's Economic Experiment*, Penguin, Harmondsworth (1985).

King, R. 'The Middle Class in revolt', in R. King and N. Nugent (eds), *Respectable Rebels: Middle Class Campaigns in Britain in the 1970s*, Hodder & Stoughton, London (1979).

King, R. and Nugent, N. (eds), *Respectable Rebels: Middle Class Campaigns in Britain in the 1970s*, Hodder and Stoughton, London (1979).

Kitschelt, H. 'Racism, Right-Wing Populism, and the Failure of the Extreme Right in Britain', in H. Kitschelt and J. McGann, *The Radical Right in Western Europe: a Comparative Analysis*, University of Michigan Press, Ann Arbor (1995), 241–256.

Kynaston, D. *Austerity Britain 1945–51*, Bloomsbury, London (2007).

Layton-Henry, Z. 'Immigration and the Heath Government', in S. Ball and A. Seldon (eds), *The Heath Government 1970–1974: A Reappraisal*, Longman, London (1996), 215–234.

Levin, B. *The Pendulum Years: Britain in the Sixties*, Icon, Cambridge (2003).

Lewis, D. S. *Illusions of Grandeur: Mosley, Fascism and British Society 1931–81*, Manchester University Press, Manchester (1987).

Lindsay, T. F. and Harrington, M. *The Conservative Party, 1918–1979*, Macmillan, London (1979).

Linehan, T. *British Fascism 1919–39: Parties, Ideology and Culture*, Manchester University Press, Manchester (2000).

Macklin, G. *Very Deeply Dyed in Black: Sir Oswald Mosley and the Resurrection of British Fascism after 1945*, I. B. Tauris, London (2007).

Macmillan, H. *The Middle Way*, Macmillan, London (1938).

Macmillan, H. *Autobiography: Riding the Storm, 1956–1959*, Macmillan, London (1971).

Macmillan, H. *At the End of the Day, 1961–1963*, Macmillan, London (1973).

Maguire, G. E. *Conservative Women: A History of Women and the Conservative Party*, Macmillan, London (1998).

Maoláin, C. Ó. *The Radical Right: A World Directory*, Longman, Essex (1987).

Marquand, D. *Britain Since 1918: The Strange Career of British Democracy*, Weidenfeld and Nicolson, London (2008).

Martin, P. 'Echoes in the Wilderness: British Popular Conservatism, 1945–51', in S. Ball and I. Holliday, *Mass Conservatism: The Conservatives and the Public Since the 1880s*, Frank Cass, London (2002).

Mills, A. C. *Mosley in Motley*, nd, np (c.1937).

Monday Club, *Policy and Aims of the Monday Club*, Monday Club, London (1961).

Monday Club, *Wind of Change or Whirlwind?* Monday Club, London (1961).

Monday Club, *Conservatism Lost, Conservatism Regained*, Monday Club, London (1963).

Morgan, K. O. *Britain Since 1945: The People's Peace*, Oxford University Press, Oxford (2001).

Mosley, N. *Beyond the Pale: Sir Oswald Mosley and Family 1933–1980*, Martin Secker and Warburg, London (1983).

Mosley, O. *My Life*, Nelson, London (1968).

Murphy, P. *Party Politics and Decolonisation: The Conservative Party and British Policy in Tropical Africa, 1951–1964*, Oxford University Press, Oxford (1995).

Norton, P. *Conservative Dissidents: Dissent within the Parliamentary Conservative Party, 1970–74*, Maurice Temple Smith, London (1978).

Norton, P. 'The Party in Parliament', *The Conservative Party*, Prentice Hall/Harvester Wheatcroft, London (1996).

Nugent, N. 'The Political Parties of the Extreme Right', in R. King and N. Nugent (eds), *The British Right: Conservative and Right Wing Politics in Britain*, Saxon House, Farnborough (1977).

Nugent, N. 'The National Association for Freedom', in R. King and N. Nugent (eds), *Respectable Rebels: Middle Class Campaigns in Britain in the 1970s*, Hodder and Stoughton, London (1979), 76–100.

Nugent, N. 'Post-war Fascism?', in K. Lunn and R. C. Thurlow (eds), *British Fascism: Essays on the Radical Right in Inter-War Britain*, Croom Helm, London (1980), 205–225.

Passmore, K. *Fascism: A Very Short Introduction*, Oxford University Press, Oxford (2002).

Petrie, C. *Chapters of Life*, Eyre and Spotiswoode, London (1950).

Pimlott, B. *Harold Wilson*, Harper Collins, London (1992).

Poole, A. 'Oswald Mosley and the Union Movement: Success or Failure?' in M. Cronin (ed.), *The Failure of British Fascism: The Far Right and the Fight for Political Recognition*, Macmillan, London (1996).

Pugh, M. *'Hurrah for the Blackshirts!' Fascists and Fascism in Britain Between the Wars*, Pimlico, London (2006).

Ramsden, J. *The Making of Conservative Party Policy: The Conservative Research Department since 1929*, Longman, London (1980).

Ramsden, J. *The Age of Churchill and Eden, 1940–1957*, Longman, London (1995).

Ramsden, J. *The Winds of Change: Macmillan to Heath, 1957–1975*, Longman, London (1996).

Ramsden, J. *An Appetite for Power: A History of the Conservative Party Since 1930*, Harper Collins, London (1998).

Ramsden, J. 'The Prime Minister and the Making of Policy', in S. Ball and A. Seldon (eds), *The Heath Government 1970–1974: A Reappraisal*, Longman, London (1996), 21–46.

Ramsden, J. and Jay, R. 'Lincoln: The Background to Taverne's Triumph', in C. Cook and J. Ramsden (eds), *By-Elections in British Politics*, Macmillan, London (1973).

Ranney, A. 'Selecting the Candidates', in Howard R. Penniman (ed.), *Britain At The Polls: The Parliamentary Elections of 1974*, American Enterprise Institute for Public Policy Research, Washington DC (1975).

Rees, P. 'Changing Interpretations of British Fascism: A Bibliographical Survey', in K. Lunn and R. C. Thurlow (eds), *British Fascism: Essays on the Radical Right in Inter-War Britain*, Croom Helm, London (1980), 187–204.

Renton, D. *Fascism, Anti-Fascism and Britain in the 1940s*, Macmillan, Basingstoke (2000).

Roberts, A. *Eminent Churchillians*, Phoenix, London (1994).

Robinson, J. A. T. *Honest to God*, SCM Press, London (1963).

Rose, L. S. *Fascism in Britain: Factual Survey No. 1*, London (1948).

Rose, L. S. *Fascism in Britain: Factual Survey No. 2*, London (1948).

Roth, A. *Heath and the Heathmen*, Routledge & Kegan Paul, London (1972).

Sampson, A. *Anatomy of Britain*, Hodder & Stoughton, London (1962).

Sandbrook, D. *Never Had it so Good: A History of Britain from Suez to the Beatles*, Abacus, London (2006).

Sandbrook, D. *White Heat: A History of Britain in the Swinging Sixties*, Little, Brown, London (2006).

Seldon, A. *Churchill's Indian Summer: The Conservative Government, 1951–1955*, Hodder & Stoughton, London (1981).

Seldon, A. and Ball, S. *Conservative Century: The Conservative Party since 1900*, Oxford University Press, Oxford (1994).

Seyd, P. 'Factionalism in the 1970s', in Z. Layton-Henry (ed.), *Conservative Party Politics*,

Macmillan, London (1980), 231–243.

Shaw, A. *British Cinema and the Cold War: The State, Propaganda and Consensus*, I. B. Tauris, London (2006).

Shepherd, R. *Iain Macleod*, Hutchinson, London (1994).

Shrapnel, N. *The Seventies: Britain's Inward March*, Constable, London (1980).

Skidelsky, R. *Oswald Mosley*, Macmillan, London (1990).

Sounes, H. *Seventies: The Sights, Sounds and Ideas of a Brilliant Decade*, Simon & Schuster, London (2006).

Spearman, D. 'Enoch Powell's Election Letters', in J. Wood (ed.), *Powell and the 1970 Election*, Paperfront, Kingswood (1970).

Stewart-Smith, D. G. (ed.), *The Handmaidens of Diplomacy*, Monday Club, London (1964).

Stewart-Smith, D. G. (ed.), *The Role of Subversion in Foreign Affairs*, Monday Club Foreign Affairs Study Group, London (1965).

Stone, D. 'The Far Right Movement and the Back-to-the land Movement', in J. V. Gottlieb and T. P. Linehan (eds), *The Culture of Fascism: Visions of the Far Right in Britain*, I. B. Tauris, London (2004), 182–198.

Swerling, S. *Who's Getting at Our Kids?* Monday Club, London (1972).

Sykes, A. *The Radical Right in Britain: Social Imperialism to the BNP*, Palgrave Macmillan, Basingstoke (2005).

Taylor, R. 'The Heath Government and Industrial Relations: Myth and Reality', in S. Ball and A. Seldon (eds), *The Heath Government 1970–1974: A Reappraisal*, Longman, London (1996), 161–190.

Taylor, S. *The National Front in English Politics*, Macmillan, London (1982).

Tebbit, N. *Upwardly Mobile: An Autobiography*, Weidenfield and Nicolson, London (1988).

Thayer, G. *The British Political Fringe: A Profile*, Arthur Blond, London (1965).

Thurlow, R. C. 'The Developing British Fascist Interpretation of Race, Culture and Evolution', in J. V. Gottlieb and T. P. Linehan (eds), *The Culture of Fascism: Visions of the Far Right in Britain*, I. B. Tauris, London (2004), 66–82.

Thurlow, R. C. *Fascism in Britain: From Oswald Mosley's Blackshirts to the National Front*, I. B. Tauris, London (2006).

Toczek, N. *The Bigger Tory Vote: The Covert Sequestration of the Bigotry Vote*, AK Press, Stirling (1992).

Trythall, A. J. *'Boney' Fuller: The Intellectual General, 1878–1966*, Cassell, London (1977).

Turner, A. W. *Crisis? What Crisis? Britain in the 1970s*, Aurum, London (2008).

Walker, M. *The National Front*, Fontana/Collins, Glasgow (1977).

Wallop, G., Earl of Portsmouth, *A Knot of Roots: An Autobiography by the Earl of Portsmouth*, Geoffrey Bles, London (1965).

Webber, G. C. *The Ideology of the British Right*, Croom Helm, London (1986).

Webster, R. *When Britain Waived the Rules and Sampled Anarchy*, Roger Webster, Burwash (2000).

Weight, R. *Patriots: National Identity in Britain 1940–2000*, Pan, London (2003).

Wheatcroft, G. *The Strange Death of Tory England*, Penguin, London (2005).

Whitehead, P. *The Writing on the Wall: Britain in the Seventies*, Michael Joseph, London (1985).

Wood, J. *Powell and the 1970 General Election*, Paperfront, Kingswood (1970).

Woodbridge, S. 'Purifying the Nation: Critiques of Cultural Decadence and Decline in British Neo-Fascist Ideology', in J. V. Gottlieb and T. P. Linehan (eds), *The Culture of Fascism: Visions of the Far Right in Britain*, Tauris, London (2004), 129–146.

Articles and theses

Aldrich, R. J. 'The Secret State: British Internal Security in the Twentieth Century', *Contemporary British History*, 11:1 (1997), 171–173.

Allardyce, G. 'What Fascism Is Not: Thoughts on the Deflation of a Concept', *American Historical Review*, 84:2 (1979), 367–388.

Baker, D. 'The "Political Economy of Fascism": Myth or Reality: or Myth *and* Reality?' *Political Economic Research Centre Seminar Paper Series*, University of Sheffield, 10 March 2005.

Ball, S. J. 'Banquo's Ghost: Lord Salisbury, Harold Macmillan, and the High Politics of Decolonization, 1957–1963', *Twentieth Century British History*, 16:1 (2005), 77–81.

Beer, S. 'The Conservative Party of Great Britain', *The Journal of Politics*, 14:1 (1952), 41–71.

Beichman, A. 'The Conservative Research Department: The Care and Feeding of Future British Political Elites', *The Journal of British Studies*, 13:2 (1974), 92–113.

Brand, J. 'Faction as its Own Reward: Groups in the British Parliament 1945 to 1986', *Parliamentary Affairs*, 42:2 (1989), 148–164.

Canovan, M. 'Trust the People! Populism and the Two Faces of Democracy', *Political Studies*, 47 (1999), 2–16.

Cockerell, M. 'Inside the National Front', *The Listener*, 28 December 1972.

Cockett, R. B. 'Ball, Chamberlain and Truth', *The Historical Journal*, 33:1 (1990), 131–142.

Critchley, J. 'Stresses and Strains in the Conservative Party', *Political Quarterly*, 44:1 (1973), 401–9.

Dean, D. W. 'Conservative Governments and the Restriction of Commonwealth Immigration in the 1950s: The Problem of Constraint', *The Historical Journal*, 35:1 (1972), 171–194.

Deedes, W. 'Conflicts Within the Conservative Party', *Political Quarterly*, 44 (1973), 391–400.

Dorril, S. and Ramsay, R. 'In a Common Cause: The Anti-Communist Crusade in Britain 1945–60, *Lobster*, 19.

Durham, M. 'The Home and the Homeland: Gender and the British Extreme Right', *Contemporary British History*, 17:1 (2003), 67–80.

Eatwell, R. 'Towards a New Model of Generic Fascism', *Journal of Theoretical Politics*, 4:2 (1992), 161–194.

Epstein, Leon D. 'Politics of British Conservatism', *The American Political Science Review*, 48:1 (1954), 27–48.

Fair, J. D. and Hutcheson, Jr. J. A. 'British Conservatism in the Twentieth Century: An Emerging Ideological Tradition', *Albion: A Quarterly Political Journal Concerned with British Studies*, 19:4 (1987), 549–578.

Findley, R. 'The Conservative Party and Defeat: The Significance of Resale Price Maintenance for the General Election of 1964', *Twentieth Century British History*, 12:3 (2001), 327–353.

Griffin, R. 'Interregnum or Endgame? Radical Right Thought in the 'Post-fascist' Era', *Journal of Political Ideologies*, 5:2 (2000), 163–178.

Griffin, R. 'The Reclamation of Fascist Culture', *European History Quarterly*, 31:4 (2001), 609–620.

Griffin, R. 'The Primacy of Culture: The Current Growth (or Manufacture) of Consensus within Fascist Studies, *Journal of Contemporary History*, 37:1 (2002), 21–43.

Griffin, R. 'The Concept that Came Out of the Cold: The Progressive Historicization of Generic Fascism and its New Relevance to Teaching Twentieth Century History', *History Compass*, 1:1 (2003), 1–41.

Harman, N. 'Minor Political parties in Britain', *Political Quarterly*, 33:3 (1962), 268–281.

Hillman, N. '"Tell me Chum, in Case I got it Wrong. Wrong. What was it we were Fighting

During the War?", The Re-emergence of British Fascism, 1948–1958', *Contemporary British History*, 15:4 (2001), 1–34.

Holmes, C. 'Beckett: John [William] Warburton (1894–1954), *The Dictionary of Labour Biography*, 6 (1982), 24–29.

Hornby, C. MP, 'Conservative Principles', *Political Quarterly*, 32 (1961), 229–237.

Kavanagh, D. 'The Postwar Consensus', *Twentieth Century British History*, 3:2 (1992), 175–190.

Layton-Henry, Z. 'The Young Conservatives 1945–70', *Journal of Contemporary History*, 8:2 (1973), 143–156.

Lewis, G. K. 'The Present Condition of British Political Parties', *The Western Political Quarterly*, 5:2 (1952), 231–257.

McKee, V. 'Conservative Factions', *Contemporary Record*, 3:1 (1989), 30–32.

Mosse, G. L. 'The Genesis of Fascism', *Journal of Contemporary History*, 1:1 (1966), 14–26.

Newton, S. 'The Two Sterling Crises of 1964 and the Decision not to Devalue', *Cardiff Historical Papers*, 1 (2007), 1–45.

Ovendale, R. 'Macmillan and the Wind of Change in Africa, 1957–1960', *The Historical Journal*, 38:2 (1995), 455–477.

Passmore, K. 'History, Political Science and Fascism', *History Compass*, London, www. history-compass.com, accessed 27 September 2005.

Paxton, R. O. 'The Five Stages of Fascism', *The Journal of Modern History*, 70:1 (1998), 1–23.

Payne, S. G. 'Review Article', *Journal of Contemporary History*, 35:1, Special Issue: Shell-Shock (2000), 109–118.

Phillips, J. 'The Postwar Political Consensus and Industrial Unrest in the Docks, 1944–55', *Twentieth Century British History*, 6:3 (1995), 302–319.

Pitchford, M. 'The Conservative Party and the Extreme Right 1945–75', unpublished Ph.D. thesis, Cardiff University, 2009.

Pugh, M. 'Popular Conservatism in Britain: Continuity and Change 1880–1987', *The Journal of British Studies*, 27:3 (1988), 254–282.

Ramsay, R. 'The British Right – Scratching the Surface', *Lobster*, 12, 50–74.

Renton, D. 'Was Fascism an Ideology? British Fascism Reconsidered', *Race and Class*, 41:3 (2000), 72–84.

Roberts, D. D., De Grand, A., Antliff, M. and Linehan, T. 'Comments on Roger Griffin, 'The Primacy of Culture: The Current Growth (or Manufacture) of Consensus within Fascist Studies', *Journal of Contemporary History*, 37:2 (2002), 259–274.

Rollings, N. 'Poor Mr Butskell: A Short Life, Wrecked by Schizophrenia'?, *Twentieth Century British History*, 5:2 (1994), 183–205.

Rose, R. 'The Bow Group's Role in British Politics', *The Western Political Quarterly*, 14:4 (1961), 865–878.

Rose, R. 'Parties, Factions and Tendencies in Britain', *Political Studies*, 12:1 (1962), 33–46.

Ruotsila, M. 'The Antisemitism of the Eighth Duke of Northumberland's the *Patriot*', *Journal of Contemporary History*, 39:1 (2004), 71–92.

Seldon, A. and Ramsden, J. 'The Influence of Ideas on the Modern Conservative Party', *Contemporary British History*, 10:1 (1966), 168–185.

Seton-Watson, H. 'Fascism, Right and Left', *Journal of Contemporary History*, 1:1 (1966), 183–197.

Seyd, P. 'Factionalism within the Conservative Party: The Monday Club', *Government and Opposition*, 7:4 (1972), 464–487.

Shipley, P. 'The National Front: Racialism and neo-Fascism in Britain', *Conflict Studies*, 97 (1978), 1–16.

Shipper, D. 'Trouble for the Tories', *Tribune*, 12 August 1966.

Shipper, D. 'The Extreme Right Regroups', *Tribune*, 21 March 1969.

Shipper, D. 'The Extreme Right and the Conservatives', *Tribune*, 28 March 1969.

Stone, D. 'The Place of Race Theory in British Fascism and Conservatism', *Fascism Disguised? Conservatism and the Extreme Right in Interwar Britain*, Conference paper at Université de Paris VII, Institut Charles V, 2 June 2006.

Stuart, M. 'A Party in Three Pieces: The Conservative Split over Rhodesian Oil Sanctions, 1965', *Contemporary British History*, 16:1 (2002), 51–88.

Szemerey, J. 'What's in the Wind at Westminster', *The Journal of Commerce*, 2 August 1973.

Taylor, S. 'The Incidence of Coloured Populations and Support for the National Front', *British Journal of Political Science*, 9:2 (1979), 250–255.

Thurlow, R. C. 'The Guardian of the "Sacred Flame": The Failed Political Resurrection of Sir Oswald Mosley after 1945', *Journal of Contemporary History*, 33:2 (1998) 241–254.

van Hartesveldt, F. R. 'Race and Political Parties in Britain, 1954–1965', *Phylon*, 44:2 (1983), 126–134.

Walsha, R. 'The One Nation Group: A Tory Approach to Backbench Politics and Organization, 1950–55', *Twentieth Century British History*, 11:2 (2000), 182–214.

Ward, P. 'Witness Seminar: Anti-Fascism in 1970s Huddersfield', *Contemporary British History*, 20:1 (2006), 119–133.

Wheen, F. 'The Stagnant Years', *The Modern Review*, March 1998.

Wickham-Jones, M. 'Right Turn: A Revisionist Account of the 1975 Conservative Party Leadership Election', *Twentieth Century British History*, 8:1 (1997), 74–89.

Fiction

Amis, K. *Lucky Jim*, Penguin, London (1954).

Barstow, S. *A Kind of Loving*, Michael Joseph, London (1960).

Bennett, A. *Forty Years On*, Faber and Faber, London (1969).

Braine, J. *Room at the Top*, Eyre and Spottiswoode, London (1957).

Braine, J. *Life at the Top*, Eyre and Spottiswoode, London (1962).

McInnes, C. *Absolute Beginners*, Allison and Busby, London (1959).

Osborne, J. *Look Back in Anger*, Faber, London (1957).

Sillitoe, A. *Saturday Night and Sunday Morning*, Flamingo, London (1958).

Films

The Proud Valley (1940).

The Life and Death of Colonel Blimp (1943).

High Treason (1951).

Hindle Wakes (1951).

Lucky Jim (1957).

Look Back in Anger (1958).

No Trees in the Street (1958).

Violent Playground (1958).

Carlton-Browne of the FO (1959).

I'm All Right Jack (1959).

Sapphire (1959).

Room at the Top (1959).

The Mouse That Roared (1959).

And Women Shall Weep (1960).

Saturday Night and Sunday Morning (1960).

The Angry Silence (1960).
The Entertainer (1960).
Flames in the Streets (1961)
Winds of Change (1961).
A Kind of Loving (1962).
Some People (1962).
It Happened Here (1964).
Darling (1965).
Stand Up Nigel Barton (1965)
Up the Junction (1965).
Vote, Vote, Vote for Nigel Barton (1965).
Blowup (1966).
Cathy Come Home (1966).
Poor Cow (1967).
If … (1968).
Kes (1969).
The Italian Job (1969).
Carry On at Your Convenience (1971).
A Clockwork Orange (1971).
Cromwell (1970).
Get Carter (1971).
Performance (1971).
Straw Dogs (1971).

Websites

www.margaretthatcher.org.
www.psr.keele.ac.uk/area/uk.htm

Index